Palgrave Studies in Economic History

Series Editor
Kent Deng, London School of Economics, London, UK

Palgrave Studies in Economic History is designed to illuminate and enrich our understanding of economies and economic phenomena of the past. The series covers a vast range of topics including financial history, labour history, development economics, commercialisation, urbanisation, industrialisation, modernisation, globalisation, and changes in world economic orders.

More information about this series at
http://www.palgrave.com/gp/series/14632

Patricia Marsh

The Spanish Flu in Ireland

A Socio-Economic Shock to Ireland, 1918–1919

palgrave
macmillan

Patricia Marsh
Bangor, Co Down, UK

ISSN 2662-6497 ISSN 2662-6500 (electronic)
Palgrave Studies in Economic History
ISBN 978-3-030-79499-6 ISBN 978-3-030-79500-9 (eBook)
https://doi.org/10.1007/978-3-030-79500-9

Cover credit: Mackie's Munitions Factory in Belfast showing the women munitions workers during the period in question PRONI Ref: D3964/H/12A

This Palgrave Macmillan imprint is published by the registered company Springer Nature Switzerland AG
The registered company address is: Gewerbestrasse 11, 6330 Cham, Switzerland

This book is dedicated to the memory of my mother Mary McKavanagh and my father Thomas McKavanagh

Acknowledgements

This book is the culmination of many years work that started in 2005 when my interest in the 'Spanish Flu' was first aroused. Starting with my M.A. and Ph.D. research in Queen's University, Belfast, where my first faltering steps were encouraged by Professor Peter Gray, who recognised that the topic would be a worthwhile one to follow. I would like to thank him and my excellent supervisor in the Department of History and Anthropology for both of these theses, Professor Marie Coleman, who along with Professor Liam Kennedy, provided continued help, patience and guidance through to completion of my Ph.D. I am also grateful to the Department of Education and Learning (DEL) NI for the award that supported my Ph.D. research.

Special thanks goes to Ida Milne who has been both a supportive colleague as well as an encouraging friend as we took our separate paths through our Ph.Ds. and our subsequent joint projects on 'Spanish Flu' in Ireland. Also thanks to Guy Beiner who has been a generous and supportive collaborator on the topic.

Thanks also to the staff of the Public Records Office of Northern Ireland, especially Graham Jackson, Lorraine Bourke, Grace Gordon, Joy Carey and Stephen Scarth. Also thanks to Niamh Brennan, archivist at the Donegal County Council, Bernadette Walsh, archivist at Derry City Council Archive, Londonderry, Mary T. McVeigh from the Irish and Local Studies Library, Armagh, the staff from the Office of the Registrar General in Roscommon, the staff from the Public Record Office, The

National Archive in Kew and the staff from the Belfast Newspaper Library for their help with my research.

Finally I would also like to thank my husband, Francis Marsh who supported my decision to go back to university in 2004 to complete my M.A. and Ph.D. He has always shown continued patience and encouragement when completing my Ph.D. and more recently during lockdown when he has encouraged me through to completion of this book.

Chronology of the 1918 Influenza Pandemic

First Wave

- 5 March 1918: first case, Albert Gitchell, reported at Camp Funston, Kansas.[1]
- March, April and May 1918: the US population was infected.[2]
- Early April 1918: influenza reached France via American troop ships.
- May 1918: spread to Portugal, Greece, Macedonia and neutral Spain.
- May 1918: spread to Bombay via sea and elsewhere in India via rail network.
- Early June 1918: influenza was in Germany, Scandinavia, Britain and Ireland.
- July and August: the first wave of influenza began to wane in Europe.[3]
- September 1918: Australia, New Zealand were infected.[4]

Second Wave

- End of August 1918: an extremely virulent mutation to the influenza virus caused epidemics to break out in three port cities, thousands of miles apart; Brest, Boston, Massachusetts and Freetown, Sierra Leone.[5]
- 15 August 1918: first cases appear in Sierra Leone after the arrival of British ship HMS *Mantua* from England.

- From England the virus spread north to Scotland and to neutral Scandinavia.
- In France, influenza spread south, down through Italy to Sicily and then onto the Greek islands.
- Spain was infected both from Portugal and across the Pyrenees in the north.
- September 1918: Russia became infected initially by allied troops, then via the rail system by its own soldiers and refugees.
- October 1918: Influenza engulfed Europe within a few weeks which, resulted in most cities in western and central Europe succumbing to influenza.
- Mid-October: Iceland was infected by ships from America and Europe.
- October 1918: New Zealand was infected by ships from the US.
- January 1919: influenza spread to Australia after their stringent quarantine was lifted.
- End of January 1919: influenza had reached virtually every inhabited place in the world.[6]

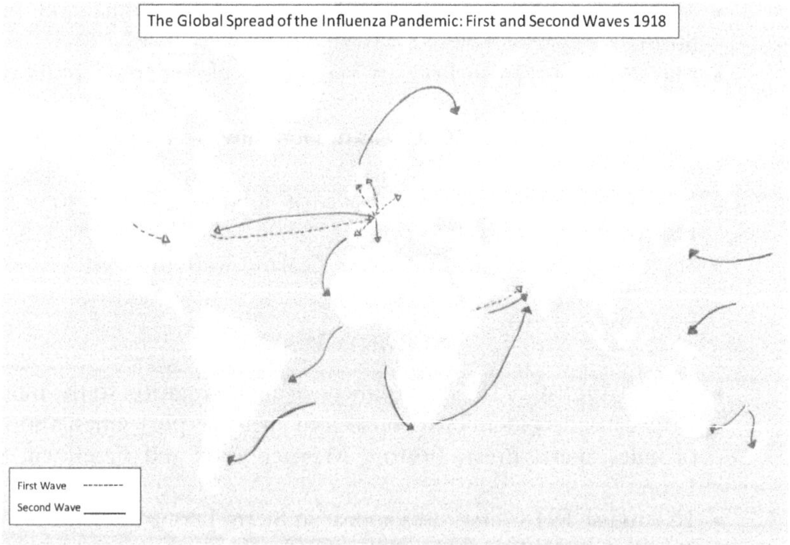

Notes

1. Patterson and Pyle (1991, p. 5).
2. Langford (2002, p. 4).
3. Patterson and Pyle (1991, pp. 7–8).
4. Rice (2020, p. 422).
5. Crosby (2003, p. 37).
6. Patterson and Pyle (1991, pp. 8–11).

References

Crosby, Alfred W. *America's Forgotten Pandemic: The Influenza of 1918*. Cambridge, Cambridge University Press, 2003.

Langford, Christopher, 'The Age Pattern of Mortality in the 1918–19 Influenza Pandemic: An Attempted Explanation Based on Data for England and Wales', *Medical History*, 46:1 (2002): 1–20.

Patterson, David, and Gerald F. Pyle, 'The Geography and Mortality of the 1918 Influenza Pandemic', *Bulletin of the History of Medicine*, 65 (1991): 4–21.

Rice, Geoffrey, W. 'How Reminders of the 1918–19 Pandemic Helped Australia and New Zealand Respond to COVID-19', *Journal of Global History*, 15:5 (2020): 421–433.

Contents

Abbreviations

AMA	American Medical Association
BOG	Board of Guardians
DORA	Defence of the Realm Act
EL	Encephalitis Lethargica
GAA	Gaelic Athletic Association
HC	House of Commons
IPP	Irish Parliamentary Party
JP	Justice of the Peace
LGB	Local Government Board
LGBI	Local Government Board for Ireland
MO	Medical Officer
MOH	Medical Officer of Health
MSOH	Medical Superintendent Officer of Health
NHS	National Health Service
PRONI	Public Records Office of Northern Ireland
RAMC	Royal Army Medical Corps
RGI	Registrar-General for Ireland
SARS	Severe Acute Respiratory Syndrome
TNA	The National Archive, Kew
UDC	Urban District Council
UK	United Kingdom
US	United States of America

List of Figures

List of Tables

CHAPTER 1

Introduction

Towards the end of World War I a devastating disease spread across the world. Dubbed 'Flanders' grippe' by the English soldiers; *Blitzkatarrh'* by the Germans; 'the Japanese referred to it as wrestler's fever'; in Persia it was termed 'the disease of the wind': and later when it entered the worst phase, people called it 'the purple death'. However, the name it became commonly known as was the 'Spanish Influenza'.[1] There is no doubt that it was the single worst natural demographic disaster of the twentieth century. The exact mortality figures are unknown and may never be known, but this pandemic was responsible for the deaths of more people than World War I.[2] Gina Kolata has argued that this pandemic killed more Americans in a single year than died in battle in both World Wars, the Korean and Vietnam Wars combined.[3] This disease was a global tragedy, affecting most countries in the world, so influenza in Ireland cannot be investigated in isolation. This chapter places the Irish experience of the 1918–1919 pandemic in context. Starting with an explanation of the history of previous epidemics leading up to 1918. It then moves on to influenza in Great Britain and thereafter explores the historical work on the pandemic in Ireland.

P. Marsh, *The Spanish Flu in Ireland*, Palgrave Studies in Economic History, https://doi.org/10.1007/978-3-030-79500-9_1

History of the Influenza Virus

The term influenza derives from the Italian/Latin *influentia* which means influence.[4] The word 'influence' was used in the fourteenth and fifteenth-century accounts of a Florentine family to suggest that an unusual conjunction of planets at times of these epidemics was responsible for them[5] and William Beveridge noted that in the past, influenza had been attributed to volcanic eruptions, earthquakes and the weather. He suggested that many outbreaks of influenza attracted attention mainly because of their explosive character and their power to spread either within a country or from one country to another.[6] As influenza had such a dramatic effect on many people of different ages within a short space of time, the superstitious looked to outside influences to explain what was happening.[7]

According to Charles Graves there have been outbreaks of influenza every few decades since at least 415 B.C. when it decimated the Athenian army in Sicily. He noted that in 827, Charlemagne's army returning from Italy was greatly affected by the disease, while in 976 there was an outbreak of influenza throughout Spain and France.[8] In 1894, Charles Creighton noted there were four influenza epidemics in London between the years 1557 and 1680.[9] While, contemporary written evidence shows that Mary Queen of Scots suffered from a mild form of influenza in Edinburgh in 1562.[10] Beveridge argued that there were eight major influenza epidemics that occurred between 1700 and 1900 which could be judged as probable pandemics.[11]

The epidemic in 1847–1848 was widespread in Europe, North America, the West Indies and Brazil. In Paris between a quarter and half of the population developed influenza. In Britain it was referred to as the 'Great Influenza of 1847' and there were at least 25,000 cases in London, which resulted in considerable mortality.[12] Although this epidemic reached Ireland, it was just one of a plethora of diseases that killed people during the Great Famine that was raging through the country. Apart from starvation, diseases such as cholera, typhoid, dysentery and fever swept over Ireland during the Famine years taking many lives.[13] In 1894, Charles Creighton noted that the 1847–1848 influenza epidemic was the first great epidemic that came under the new system of registration in the United Kingdom. Over 5,000 deaths occurred during its six weeks, a quarter of these were attributed to influenza and the rest to pneumonia, bronchitis asthma, etc. It spread over England in a short time, reaching peak mortality in December 1847, with a death toll greater than the 1832 cholera epidemic.[14]

The next major influenza pandemic to impact on the United Kingdom was the 1889–1894 pandemic known in Europe as the 'Russian Influenza' or the 'Asiatic Influenza'.[15] This particular pandemic was said to have occurred in the following waves during January 1890, March 1891, January 1892 and December 1893, but Beveridge suggested that these so-called waves would now be referred to as separate epidemics rather than waves of the same pandemic.[16] In January and February 1890, the first of four epidemics spread all over England, Scotland and Ireland, yet Great Britain and Ireland appeared to escape the high mortalities of many Continental European countries. It was less severe than the second and third outbreaks that returned in the spring of 1892 and in the winter of 1893–1894.[17] Influenza continued through the decade, with major outbreaks in 1895 and again in 1899–1900,[18] which leads us to the next major outbreak of the disease, the Influenza pandemic of 1918–1919, commonly known as 'Spanish Influenza'.

The 1918–1919 Pandemic in Great Britain

The major contemporary study of influenza in Great Britain was the Ministry of Health Report published in 1920. This report proposed the pandemic in Great Britain consisted of three waves, of which the second was the most severe. It stated that the first wave began at the end of May 1918 and peaked in the first half of July 1918: it lasted approximately six weeks. The second lasted approximately 12 weeks, started in October 1918 and reached its height in early November 1918 where it remained high for two to three weeks and slowly decreased to the end of December 1918. The third commenced at the beginning of February 1919, rose to its height in the third week of the same month and fell slowly to the end of March 1919. This third wave lasted eight weeks and had a higher mortality than the first, but was not as high as the second. The Registrar-General attributed 151,446 deaths in England and Wales—of which 141,989 were civilians—to the disease during the 46 weeks from 23 June 1918 to 10 May 1919 and approximately three quarters of these deaths occurred in the second wave.[19]

The Registrar-General for England and Wales as well as the Registrar-General for Scotland published supplementary reports on the mortality from influenza during the pandemic of 1918–1919.[20] The Registrar-General for England and Wales recognised that previously published mortality figures were an underestimation[21] and—to remedy this—he re-estimated the mortality figures for England and Wales by using three different methods to ascertain the total mortality, attributable either directly or indirectly to influenza. Using these methods, he recalculated a mortality figure for England and Wales of approximately 200,000.[22] These methods will be explained in more detail in Chapter 2. More recently in 2003, Niall Johnson estimated that the total mortality for the pandemic in England, Wales and Scotland was more likely to be around 225,000.[23]

Despite the high influenza death toll in Great Britain, it was not until the late 1980s that this subject was addressed with academic rigour. In research following her PhD thesis, which investigated the influenza pandemic regarding Britain and its colonies, Sandra Tomkins explored official responses to the pandemic. In British Africa, she found the Colonial Office's response to be passive, which contrasted to the other colonial governments in Africa that responded promptly and practically to the outbreak, but were still quickly overwhelmed by the disease.[24] Examining local authority responses to the pandemic by the London boroughs, Tomkins argued in 1992 that although Britain had one of the most sophisticated public health systems of that time, it still launched one of the least effective responses to the pandemic.[25] In 2000, Amy Norrington addressed the British medical response to influenza. Although she agreed with Tomkins about the official response, Norrington believed that Tomkins' assessment of them was flawed and suggested that Tomkins expected more from medicine than could be delivered at the time.[26]

In 2002, Andrea Tanner investigated the official response to the pandemic in London. She proposed that the central government in Britain did not use its powers to put in place the same stringent restrictions that were present in other countries in case it hindered the war effort. Instead, the response to the pandemic was mainly left to the local public health departments, which lacked the appropriate authority to impose restrictions.[27] The case studies in Chapters 6–10 will show that the Irish response to influenza suffered from similar problems. In 2005, Alice Reid focussed on the overlooked area of infant and child health in Derbyshire. Although the pandemic was renowned for targeting young adults, the mortality of the young infants was still remarkably high. Reid concluded that influenza in pregnant women could provoke premature delivery, while older children also suffered indirectly as their mothers were unable to care adequately for them.[28] Chapters 2 and 3 will address mortality and trends in Ireland for age, gender and occupation of those who died in the country.

Geographer Niall Johnson has one of the most prolific outputs on influenza in Great Britain. His contribution to the edited volume *Spanish influenza pandemic of 1918–1919: New perspectives* addressed the reasons for public amnesia of the disease.[29] Along with Juergan Mueller, he recalculated the global mortality of the pandemic in 2002.[30] In 2004, he also made a study of the pandemic in Scotland.[31] In 2006 he published the book *Britain and the 1918–19 influenza pandemic: A dark epilogue*. This book used an inter-disciplinary approach to examine the British experiences of the pandemic and was the first comprehensive study of the pandemic for Britain. However, even this work has excluded Ireland from the narrative.[32] To coincide with the ninetieth anniversary of the disease in November 2008, Mark Honigsbaum's book *Living with enza: The forgotten story of Britain and the Great Flu pandemic of 1918*, takes a journalistic look at the influenza outbreaks in Great Britain. This book drew on the Richard Collier collection, which had little Irish information, so again Ireland is ignored. [33] As the centenary of the pandemic approached, interest in the disease heightened and books by Laura Spinney and Catherine Arnold were published.[34] Again, even though Ireland was part of the United Kingdom during both 1918 and 1919, a study of influenza in the country has been excluded from these studies. The next section will examine what work has been completed in Ireland in relation to the pandemic.

Influenza and Ireland

Speaking in November 1919, the Registrar-General for Ireland, Sir William Thompson, stated in the President's address to the Statistical and Social Inquiry Society of Ireland that: 'Since the period of the Great Famine, with its awful attendant horrors of fever and cholera, no disease of any epidemic nature created so much havoc in any one year in Ireland as influenza'.[35] Nevertheless, apart from the statistics for 1918 that were contained in his address, the pandemic was largely ignored in contemporary reports and subsequent medical history works. In 2004, Diarmaid Ferriter noted that Ireland appeared to ignore influenza at the time as, there was no supplementary report on the disease summited to Parliament like those produced by the Registrar-General for England and Wales and his counterpart in Scotland. This was hardly surprising due to the political unrest and upheaval in the country during that period and subsequently.[36] This was the period of the Irish War of Independence (Anglo-Irish War) which was fought from 1919 (the end of the pandemic) and 1921 and the subsequent, partition of the country and the Irish Civil War. Needless to say record keeping during this period would have been the least of the concerns.

Although Sir George Newman, Chief Medical Officer, said of the 1920 Ministry of Health report on influenza that: 'There can be no doubt that as a historical survey it will prove invaluable for future reference in the event of subsequent epidemics',[37] this report—of approximately 600 pages—only allocated four pages to the discussion of the pandemic in Ireland.[38] There were contemporary articles by physicians such as William Crofton, MD, lecturer in Special Pathology, University College Dublin, discussing the subject of vaccines and further investigation of the disease in major cities.[39] There were a number of articles in the *Dublin Journal of Medical Science* during the height of the pandemic in December 1918, but there was no mention of influenza after this period.[40]

Biographies of Countess Markievicz, Arthur Griffith, Kathleen Clarke, Michael Collins and Eamon de Valera[41] refer to influenza in passing, while that of Kathleen Lynn devoted five pages to her outstanding medical role treating the sick in Dublin during that period.[42] Other books such as Darrell Figgis's *Recollection of the Irish War* mentions how influenza impacted on the interned prisoners in Usk and Durham, while Frank Gallagher's *The Four Glorious Years* briefly recounts the devastation that influenza caused in Ireland during the 1918 election campaign.[43] Sean McConville's *Irish Political Prisoners* touched on it in relation to the political prisoners interned in the British jails.[44] Fionán Lynch recollected the medical treatment of influenza sufferers interned in Belfast Jail in *Sworn to be Free*,[45] while Shouldice and Geraghty's recollections of the escape from Usk Jail in the same collection also made reference to influenza in the prison.[46] The use of influenza as a tool for Sinn Féin propaganda purposes during the pandemic will be addressed further in Chapter 4.

Given that influenza was also largely ignored in contemporary reports such as that of the Ministry of Health, it is hardly surprising that medical histories also ignore the disease. Ruth Barrington's *Health, medicine and politics in Ireland 1900–1970* only allocated a few lines to the pandemic.[47]

Considering the high death toll in Belfast from influenza, Richard Clarke's history of the Royal Victoria Hospital does not refer to the disease in the hospital,[48] nor does John O'Sullivan's pictorial history of the Belfast City Hospital.[49] D.H. Craig's history of the City Hospital in Belfast does include a paragraph about influenza at the Belfast Union Hospital but has dated it incorrectly to 1920 rather than 1918–1919.[50]

In the early years of the new millennium interest in the influenza pandemic in Ireland awakened and research began on the subject. The first academic study of the pandemic in Ireland was completed in 2005, by Ida Milne. This MA thesis explored the pandemic in Ireland to 'help to rescue the Irish experience of the Spanish flu from the scrap heap of history, to move it from the realm of myth and family lore into the sphere of social, economic and political history'.[51] In doing so Milne gave a chronological history of influenza and examined Irish statistics and cures attributed for the disease. The current author's MA dissertation was completed in 2006. Although it recalculated the influenza mortality for the Ireland as a whole, it concentrated on the medical and local authority response to the disease in Belfast.[52] As the ninetieth anniversary of the influenza outbreak approached, the subject of the pandemic in Ireland was addressed by documentary makers for the first time in *Aicid: The Great Flu in Ireland* which was broadcast in November 2008. This Irish language documentary discussed the impact of influenza throughout the island of Ireland.[53]

After a delayed start, work on influenza in an Irish context began to snowball. Catriona Foley's PhD entitled '"The last Irish Plague": the Great Flu in Ireland, 1918–19' was completed in 2009. This thesis 'focuses on themes rather than chronology in order to portray the varied and diffuse nature of the Great Flu's effects on Irish Society'.[54] In 2011, this thesis was published as a monograph of the same title.[55] Although Foley explores influenza in Ireland as a whole, her geographic cover of the country is patchy, for example her main Ulster references are in relation to County Donegal. County Donegal was not typical of the counties in Ulster, as the province was in a unique position as it was the industrial centre of Ireland, meaning the north-east of Ulster especially bore closer comparison to industrial regions in Britain than it did with other parts of Ireland.

More recently, in 2018 on the one-hundredth anniversary of the pandemic, Ida Milne published *Stacking the Coffins: Influenza, War and revolution in Ireland, 1918–1919*. Based on her 2011 PhD thesis, Milne's book examines the impact of the 1918–1919 influenza pandemic on Irish society and politics. It examines contemporary medical understanding of the disease, and the patient experience influenza, through a series of oral history interviews. Milne unlike Foley examines the mortality of the pandemic, producing graphs, maps and statistics.[56] Again, although Milne refers to Donegal and Belfast in the province of Ulster, the Ulster experience of the disease is not examined at length.

While these works have their own research strengths and geographic focus, they do not address the unique features which mark the Ulster experience of the pandemic. Tied closely into Ulster's more unionist politics, and the fact that it was then the most industrialised region in Ireland. Allied to the fact that the pattern of flu in Donegal is particularly intriguing. Ulster is quite special and worth a separate study, more than any other Irish province.

This book examines the Irish experience of the influenza pandemic through a detailed study of the disease in the province of Ulster. By exploring the different themes of: dispersion of the disease; mortality; morbidity; gender; medical response and politics—and through case studies of different towns in the province of in Ulster—it builds up a picture of the social, economic and political impact of influenza in Ireland. The Ulster experience of this pandemic is examined by constructing micro-histories of industrial cities and towns, along with provincial market towns and a naval port, to provide a basis for comparison of the differing approaches taken to combat the influenza outbreaks.

This book aims to: re-examine and recalculate Irish mortality rates; explain the origin and diffusion of the three waves of the disease in Ireland; and explore official responses to the disease, to ultimately piece together a picture of life in Ireland during the 1918–1919 pandemic but with particular focus on the province of Ulster. It uses a combination of official local authority and boards of guardians' minutes in Ulster, as well as national and local contemporary newspaper reports, to gauge the extent and severity of the influenza pandemic in Ireland.

This book examines issues concerning the influenza pandemic in the island of Ireland and may—on some occasions—overlap on the work of both Foley and Milne. However, it includes a wider study on how the disease impacted on the province of Ulster. The 1920 Ministry of Health report suggested that 'the reaction of the war upon the Irish population was less prejudicial than in other divisions of the United Kingdom, and both the age and sex constitution and housing aggregation were not forced so far from the normal equilibrium'.[57] However, this book will show that the war did have a significant impact on how the influenza pandemic in Ireland impacted on the Irish population from an economic, social and medical point of view.

Chapter 2 identifies the origins and dispersal of the three influenza outbreaks in Ireland, by using both the annual and weekly reports of the Registrar-General for Ireland, local authority and boards of guardians' minutes, along with national and local newspapers, The theory that the war played a major part in the introduction and spread of influenza in Ireland is discussed, along with other possible explanations on how the disease entered and dispersed throughout the country. It enlarges on Milne's work in relation to the Irish mortality figures by applying similar calculations to that of the Registrar-General of England and Wales to the Irish figures for years 1918 and 1919. The resulting re-estimated data is discussed in detail. The mortality statistics are reviewed to establish if any patterns regarding age groups, location, social class or gender have emerged in Ireland.

Chapter 3 considers the question: did gender played a part in one's susceptibility to the disease? The vulnerability of Irish pregnant women to influenza is examined. Women were the main care givers in the home and this role along with other areas of female activity, such as nursing both professionally and as volunteers as well as factory work are discussed to ascertain if gender factored in exposure and susceptibility to the disease.

Chapter 4 explores media coverage of influenza in both national and local newspapers. It has been argued that it was difficult to find traces of the pandemic from official sources in British archives[58] and this too was the case in Ireland. Therefore, it has been essential to use newspaper reports to research the day-to-day effects of the pandemic in the country. This chapter illustrates—through the newspaper coverage—that the war impacted on the way in which influenza was reported in certain Irish newspapers, especially during the first wave. It shows how other contemporary political concerns were considered more newsworthy than the influenza outbreaks. Reasons for the pandemic's subsequent exclusion from Irish history are presented along with consideration to the theory that the lack of contemporary newspaper coverage of the disease was a factor on why influenza has been forgotten in Irish history.

Chapter 5 focuses on the medical response to the disease in Ireland. Starting with causes and symptoms of the 1918–1919 pandemic. It moves on to a brief description of public health in Ireland. Issues around the lack of medical personnel to treat the disease are discussed. The lack of sound medical knowledge on how to treat influenza is illustrated through the examination of suggested cures and advertisements—promising alleviation of the disease—published in the newspapers during this period.

Chapters 6–10 investigate the response of central authorities such as the Local Government Board for Ireland (LGBI) and the dual responses at a local level of local authorities and the poor law medical system through case studies of individual towns. Although these will concentrate on the province of Ulster, the experiences would be typical of many Irish towns during this period. Case studies of industrial towns such as Belfast, Londonderry, Lurgan and Portadown, as well as the naval port of Larne, the market towns of Ballyclare, Strabane, Newry, Clones and Cookstown are constructed to demonstrate the lack of a cohesive response to this medical crisis. These case studies show commonalities and differences in approach to dealing with the pandemic in different towns. They illustrate that war impacted on local responses to the pandemic through discussion of issues such as: the lack of central government guidance from the LGBI on the disease; and shortages of hospital accommodation.

Chapter 11 focuses on the aftermath of the pandemic. It examines what if any differences the pandemic made in Ireland in the short term. The reaction of the LGBI to the next influenza scare that occurred in 1920, is examined. It also considers the response to the viral disease *Encephalitis Lethargica*, which was prevalent for ten years after the pandemic, and was considered by some to be a health complication of influenza. Finally, comparisons are made between the responses of local authorities and central government to the influenza pandemic in 1918–1919 and those from the central UK government; and the Irish government in Dublin to Covid-19, (arguably the most severe pandemic since 1918–1919). It discusses, what if, any lessons were learnt from 1918 and if they have been applied to the outbreak of Covid-19.

Notes

1. Collier (1974, pp. 10–11) and Davies (1999, p. 58).
2. Phillips and Killingray (2003, pp. 3–4).
3. Kolata (1999, p. x).
4. Graves (1969, p. 14).
5. Stuart-Harris and Schild (1976, p. 112).
6. Beveridge (1977, p. 1).

7. Stuart-Harris and Schild (1976, p. 112).
8. Graves (1969, p. 14).
9. Creighton (1894, pp. 397–398).
10. Graves (1969, p.14).
11. Beveridge (1991, pp. 225–227).
12. Beveridge (1977, p. 29) and Beveridge (1991, p. 227).
13. Geary (1996, p. 27).
14. Creighton (1894, pp. 389–390), Beveridge (1991, p. 227).
15. Graves (1969, p. 14) and Creighton (1894, p. 392).
16. Beveridge (1977, p. 21).
17. Creighton (1894, p. 393).
18. Smith (1995, p. 59).
19. Ministry of Health, *Report on the Pandemic of Influenza, 1918–19* (London: 1920), p. xiii.
20. *Supplement to the Eighty-First Annual Report of the Registrar-General of Births, Deaths and Marriages in England and Wales: Report on the Mortality from Influenza in England and Wales During the Epidemic of 1918–19* [Cmd 700], H. C. 1920, x, 791; *Report on the Mortality from Influenza in Scotland During the Epidemic of 1918–19: A Supplement to the Annual Reports of the Registrar-General for Scotland* [Cmd 282], H. C. 1919, x, 1223.
21. *Report on the Mortality from Influenza in England and Wales During the Epidemic of 1918–19*, p. 3.
22. Ibid., pp. 3–7.
23. Johnson (2003, pp. 3–4).
24. Sandra Tomkins, 'Britain and the Influenza Epidemic 1918–1919' (Ph.D. thesis, University of Cambridge, 1989); Tomkins (1994, pp. 60–83).
25. Tomkins (1992, pp. 435–454).
26. Amy C. Norrington, '"The Greatest Disease Holocaust in History": The British Medical Response to the Influenza Pandemic of 1918–19' (B.Sc. thesis, Wellcome Institute for the History of Medicine, 2000), 53.
27. Tanner (2002, pp. 51–76).
28. Reid (2005, pp. 29–54).
29. Johnston (2003, p. 149).
30. Johnson and Mueller (2002, pp. 105–115).
31. Johnson (2004, pp. 216–226).
32. Johnson (2006)
33. Honigsbaum (2008).
34. Spinney (2017) and Arnold (2018)
35. Thompson (1920, p. 1).
36. Ferriter (2004, p. 185).
37. Newman (1920, p. iv).

38. 'A General Account of Influenza in the United Kingdom During 1918–19', *Ministry of Health, Report on the Pandemic of Influenza*, pp. 51–54.
39. Crofton (1918, pp. 659–665).
40. *The Dublin Journal of Medical Science* (3rd Series), 146 (1918) pp. 249–258 and pp. 284–288.
41. Haverty (1988, p.189), Van Voris (1967, pp. 256–257), Colum (1959, pp. 187–188, 191), Clarke (1997, p. 165), Coogan (1990, p. 103; 1993, p. 130).
42. Ó hÓgartaigh (2006, pp. 40–45).
43. Figgis (1927, p. 47 and p. 53).
44. McConville (2003, p. 646).
45. Lynch (1973, p. 69).
46. Shouldice and Geraghty (1973, pp. 25–31).
47. Barrington (1987, p. 74.).
48. Clarke (1997).
49. O'Sullivan (2003).
50. Craig (1985, p. 57).
51. Ida Milne, 'Epidemic or Myth: The 1918 Flu in Ireland' (M.A. thesis, National University of Ireland, Maynooth, 2005).
52. Patricia Marsh, 'The Effect of the 1918–19 Influenza Pandemic on Belfast' (M.A. thesis, Queen's University Belfast, 2006).
53. *Aicid: The Great Flu in Ireland*, produced by Mary Jones, ArkHive Productions, Dublin and broadcast on 5 November 2008 on TG4 and 9 November 2008 on BBC2.
54. Catriona Foley, '"The last Irish plague": The Great Flu in Ireland, 1918–19' (Ph.D. thesis, University College, Dublin, 2009).
55. Foley (2011).
56. Milne (2018, pp. 56–84).
57. 'A General Account of Influenza in the United Kingdom During 1918–19', p. 54.
58. Johnson (2003, p. 154).

References

Arnold, Catherine. *Pandemic 1918: The Story of the Deadliest Influenza in History*. London: Michael O'Mara Books Limited, 2018.

Barrington, Ruth. *Health, Medicine and Politics in Ireland 1900–1970*. Dublin: Institute of Public Administration, 1987.

Beveridge, W. I. B. 'The Chronicle of Influenza Epidemics', *History and Philosophy of the Life Sciences*, 13:2 (1991): 223–224.

Beveridge, W. I. B. *Influenza: The Last Great Plague: An Unfinished Story of Discovery*. London: Heinemann, 1977.

Clarke, Kathleen. *Revolutionary Woman: My Fight for Ireland's Freedom*. Dublin: The O'Brien Press, 1997.
Clarke, Richard S. J. *The Royal Victoria Hospital, Belfast: A History, 1797–1997*. Belfast: Blackstaff, 1997.
Collier, Richard. *The Plague of the Spanish Lady: The Influenza Pandemic of 1918–1919*. London: Macmillan, 1974.
Colum, Padraic. *Arthur Griffith*. Dublin: Browne and Nolan, 1959.
Coogan, Tim Pat. *Michael Collins: A Biography*. London: Hutchinson, 1990
Coogan, Tim Pat. *De Valera: Long Fellow, Long Shadow*. London: Hutchinson, 1993.
Craig, D. H. *Belfast and Its Infirmary: The Growth of a Hospital*. Belfast: Brough, Cox & Dunn, 1985.
Creighton, Charles. *A History of Epidemics in Britain Vol 2: From the Extinction of the Plague to the Present Time*. Cambridge: Cambridge University Press, 1894.
Crofton, William. 'The Influenza Epidemic', *Studies: An Irish Quarterly Review*, 7:28 (December 1918): 659–665.
Davies, Pete. *Catching Cold: 1918's Forgotten Tragedy and the Scientific Hunt for the Virus That Caused it*. London: Michael Joseph, 1999.
Figgis, Darrell. *Recollections of the Irish War*. London: Ernest Benn Ltd, 1927.
Ferriter, Diarmaid. *The Transformation of Ireland 1900–2000*. London: Profile Books Limited, 2004.
Foley, Catriona. *The Last Irish Plague: The Great Flu in Ireland, 1918–19*. Dublin, Irish Academic Press, 2011.
Geary, Laurence. Epidemic diseases of the Great Famine. *History Ireland*, 4:1 (Spring 1996): 27–32.
Graves, Charles. *Invasion by Virus: Can It Happen Again?* London: Icon Books Limited, 1969.
Haverty, Anne. *Constance Markievicz: An Independent Life*. London: Pandora Press, 1988.
Hogan, David [Frank Gallagher]. *The Four Glorious Years*. Dublin: Irish Press, 1953.
Honigsbaum, Mark. *Living with enza: The Forgotten Story of Britain and the Great Flu Pandemic of 1918*. New York: Macmillan, 2008.
Johnson, Niall P. A. S. 'The Overshadowed Killer: Influenza in Britain' in *Spanish Influenza Pandemic of 1918–1919: New Perspectives*, edited by Howard Phillips and David Killingray, 132–156. London: Routledge, 2003.
Johnson Niall P. A. S. 'Scottish 'Flu: The Scottish Experience of "Spanish Flu"', *The Scottish Historical Review*, 83:2 (2004): 216–226.
Johnson, Niall P. A. S. *Britain and the 1918–19 Influenza Pandemic: A Dark Epilogue*. London: Routledge, 2006.

Johnson Niall P. A. S. and Juergan Mueller. 'Updating the Accounts: Global Mortality of the 1918–1920 "Spanish" Influenza Pandemic', in *Bulletin of the History of Medicine*, 76:1 (2002): 105–115.

Kolata, Gina. Flu: The Story of the Great Influenza Pandemic of 1918 and the Search for the Virus That Caused It. New York: Simon & Schuster, 1999.

Lynch, Fionán. 'Recollections of Jail Riots and Hunger Strikes: Grim Times in Mountjoy, Dundalk and Belfast Jails', in *Sworn to Be Free: The Complete Book of IRA Jailbreaks 1918–1921*, edited by Florence O'Donoghue, 63–76.Tralee: Anvil Books Ltd, 1973.

McConville, Sean. *Irish Political Prisoners, 1848–1922: Theatres of War*. London: Routledge, 2003.

Milne, Ida. *Stacking the Coffins: Influenza, War and Revolution in Ireland, 1918–19*. Manchester: Manchester University Press, 2018.

Newman, Sir George. 'Chief Medical Officer's Introduction', *Ministry of Health, Report on the Pandemic of Influenza, 1918-19*, iv-xxiii. London: HMSO, 1920.

Ó hÓgartaigh, Margaret. *Kathleen Lynn: Irishwoman, Patriot, Doctor*. Dublin: Irish Academic Press, 2006.

O'Sullivan, John F. *Belfast City Hospital: A Photographic History*. Donaghadee: Ballyhay Books, 2003.

Phillips, Howard and David Killingray. 'Introduction', in *Spanish Influenza Pandemic of 1918–1919: New Perspectives* edited by Howard Phillips and David Killingray, 1–26. London: Routledge, 2003.

Quinn, Tom. *Flu: A Social History of Influenza*. London: New Holland, 2008.

Reid, Alice. 'The Effects of the 1918–19 Influenza Pandemic on Infant and Child Health in Derbyshire', *Medical History*, 49 (2005): 29–54.

Shouldice, Frank and George Geraghty, 'The Break-Out from Usk Jail in Wales by Four 'German Plot' Prisoners', in *Sworn to Be Free: The Complete Book of IRA Jailbreaks 1918–1921*, edited by Florence O'Donoghue, 25–34.Tralee: Anvil Books Ltd, 1973.

Smith, F. B. 'The Russian Influenza in the United Kingdom, 1889–1894', *Social History of Medicine*, 8:1(1995): 55–73.

Spinney, Laura. *Pale Rider: The Spanish flu of 1918 and How It Changed the World*. London: Vintage, 2017.

Stuart-Harris, Charles H. and Geoffrey C. Schild, *Influenza: The Viruses and the Disease*. London: Edward Arnold, 1976.

Tanner, Andrea, 'The Spanish Lady Comes to London: The Influenza Pandemic 1918–1919', *London Journal*, 27:2 (2002): 51–76.

Thompson, William J. 'Mortality from Influenza in Ireland', in *Journal of the Statistical and Social Inquiry Society of Ireland*, 14:1 (1920): 1–14.

Tomkins, Sandra M. 'The Failure of Expertise: Public Health Policy in Britain During the 1918–1919 Influenza Epidemic,' *Social History of Medicine*, 5:3 (1992): 435–454.

Tomkins, Sandra, 'Colonial Administration in British Africa During the Influenza Epidemic of 1918–19', *Canadian Journal of African Studies*, 28:1 (1994): 60–83.

Van Voris, Jacqueline *Constance de Markievicz: In the Cause of Ireland*. Amherst: University of Massachusetts Press, 1967.

CHAPTER 2

'Ravages of Influenza': The Human Cost of Influenza in Ireland

Introduction

This chapter examines two distinct aspects of the pandemic in Ireland, how and where did influenza enter Ireland? What was the human cost to the country? Starting with the exploration of theories about the origin of the pandemic, it moves on to consider how and where influenza entered Ireland. Using a combination of newspaper reports, local authority and boards of guardians' (BOG) minutes, as well as official reports from the Registrar-General for Ireland's (RGI) for 1918 and 1919, the origin of each of the three influenza outbreaks in Ireland is identified and theories on factors contributing to its dispersal throughout the country are discussed.

There is a need to re-examine the Irish mortality figures to look at why it is so difficult to be definitive about the number of fatalities that occurred during this influenza pandemic, and particularly so in the context of an Ireland at war. The global mortality figures are reviewed as well as the existing Irish figures. Unlike the rest of the United Kingdom (UK), no supplementary report on influenza or re-assessment of the Irish figures was produced. Problems associated with establishing accurate Irish mortality figures are discussed. Using the RGI's annual reports for 1918 and 1919 as well as the same methods as those of the Registrar-General for England and Wales, the Irish mortality figures are re-estimated. Both

P. Marsh, *The Spanish Flu in Ireland*, Palgrave Studies in Economic History, https://doi.org/10.1007/978-3-030-79500-9_2

the methods and results are discussed, along with any trends relating to age, location or occupation.

Origin of the 1918–1919 Pandemic

There were three waves of Influenza in the northern hemisphere during 1918–19 which occurred in less than twelve months. The first took place in spring/summer 1918, the second in autumn/winter 1918 and the third in early 1919.[1] In Scandinavia, however, there was a fourth wave that took place during February 1920.[2] During the first wave, influenza was thought to have originated in Spain, leading to the misnomer 'Spanish Influenza'. Spain's neutrality during World War I meant that there was no newspaper censorship in that country and consequently reports about the disease were published not only in Spanish newspapers, but also in the worldwide press. During May and June 1918, the Madrid newspapers reported the disease and its effects on Spain.[3] By early June 1918 news of the disease in Spain had become an international story. On 3 June 1918, *The Times* reported there were 100,000 victims in Madrid of an unknown disease, which at first appeared benign but was now responsible for 700 deaths in ten days. It advised that public services, offices and factories had been disrupted. King Alfonso XIII of Spain and other leading politicians were among those afflicted.[4] This gave the erroneous impression that influenza had originated in Spain, leading to the pandemic being dubbed Spanish influenza. However, the Spanish believed that it had been blown over from the battlefields of France.[5]

The Spanish were correct in that the pandemic did not originate in Spain. In 1969, Charles Graves proposed that influenza first appeared in certain Chinese villages, followed by an outbreak in Canton in late February 1918. Agreeing with Graves, Christopher Langford has suggested that influenza could have originated in China and that the movement of a very large number of workers from China to France during World War I might have played a part in the pandemic's development.[6] Another theory is that of John Oxford and others, which suggested that the pandemic had its origins as early as the winter of 1916 on the Western Front at the British Army camp at Étaples. An article published in 1917 by J. A. R. Hammond, W. Rolland and T.H.G. Shore described an outbreak of purulent bronchitis—a respiratory infection—in the winter of 1916. The outbreak occurred at a large British Army base in Étaples, which housed 100,000 soldiers on any one day. This outbreak was characterised by extremely high mortality as well as acute respiratory infection, high temperature, cough and heliotrope cyanosis—a condition where the face became lavender, heliotrope or violet in colour—which was a prominent feature of the 1918 outbreak. The disease was diagnosed as acute purulent bronchitis. However, on reviewing this paper, Oxford suggested that instead of purulent bronchitis, this disease could be described as classic influenza as it was essentially similar to the influenza deaths in 1918–19.[7] Although the outbreaks at Étaples were diagnosed at the time as purulent bronchitis, Dr Herbert French—in his contribution to the Ministry of Health report of 1920—was strongly of the opinion that these fatal cases were likely to be the same as the 1918–19 influenza.[8] Oxford was so confident of his theory that in an article in 2005, he renamed the pandemic as Anglo-Gallic influenza.[9]

Nevertheless, the most popular theory was that influenza originated in the United States (US) and—Patterson and Pyle suggested—the earliest recorded outbreak of the disease was on 5 March 1918 among army recruits at Camp Funston, Kansas from where—by end of March—it had spread to military training installations in several mid-western and south eastern states.[10] John Barry argued that the first influenza victims could have been as early as late January/early February 1918 in Haskell County, Kansas and that it was from here that influenza travelled to Camp Funston.[11] Subsequently, influenza spread around the world, reaching France via American troop ships in early April 1918. These troop ships were a breeding ground for infection, so if the influenza virus was present it would have spread like wildfire through the ship.

Origin and Spread of Influenza in Ireland

One of the initial outbreaks of influenza in mainland Britain was in the grand fleet, at its Scottish naval stations of Scapa and Rosyth, which was attacked by the disease in May 1918 and reached its height on 10 May 1918.[12] Similarly in Ireland, the first reported influenza outbreak was at a naval base in Queenstown (now Cobh) in County Cork in May 1918. The Annual Report of the Secretary to the United States of America Navy for 1919 advised that there was an outbreak of influenza on United States Ship *Dixie* that was stationed at Queenstown in May 1918. Eleven per cent of the crew had the disease, 77 cases in total.[13] It is uncertain if this outbreak of influenza spread to Queenstown as there are no reports of the disease in the town in the national press. Presumably, these influenza cases were confined to the crew members on the ship at this early stage.

Influenza mortality figures were not included in the weekly returns for the eighteen major towns in Ireland for 1918 and 1919, but pneumonia mortality was. Pneumonia was the most serious complication associated with influenza, so theoretically the peaks from deaths from this disease should be coincident with the reports of influenza in the various towns and could act as an indicator for peaks of influenza. These along with newspaper reports and other official records, might suggest how each of the waves of influenza spread through Ireland.[14]

The First Wave—Summer 1918

The Local Government Board for Ireland (LGBI) report for 1918 suggested that the first wave of the pandemic was principally in Belfast and other districts of the north of Ireland.[15] Pneumonia deaths in Belfast peaked on 29 June 1918. Lisburn peaked on 6 July 1918 and then Lurgan, Portadown, Londonderry and Ballymena all peaked on 13 July 1918. There was small pneumonia peak in Newry around 20 July 1918, but on further examination there was no evidence that these deaths were influenza-related.

Newspaper evidence confirms that influenza was in Belfast as early as 11 June 1918 with the appearance of a notice in Belfast newspapers regarding the reopening, after influenza, of a department in James Mackie & Sons munition factory.[16] However, one of the first reported victims died on 7 June after suffering from influenza for five days, which indicates that the disease was in Belfast from the beginning of June. From Belfast it spread eastwards to Holywood by 15 June 1918 and to Newtownards and Bangor by the end of June.[17] It also spread south-west from Belfast to Lisburn, Lurgan and Portadown by mid-June 1918.[18] There were outbreaks in Ballymena, Ballymoney and Larne in the north of Ulster. Influenza and pneumonia deaths were recorded the naval port of Larne from the end of June and in Ballymena by mid-June 1918.[19] Londonderry, Enniskillen and Strabane in the north-west also had outbreaks during this period. The first recorded victim in Londonderry died on 24 June after suffering from influenza for 10 days, indicating the disease was in the town as early as 14 June 1918. It should be noted that Londonderry had its own port and shipyards that could have acted as an independent point of entry to the province.

There were other sporadic influenza outbreaks elsewhere in Ireland: in Dublin on 25 June 1918 and the Portabello military hospital in Dublin reported 190 influenza cases with 16 deaths during July 1918.[20] In Wexford, at the US Naval Air Station, an influenza outbreak lasted for two weeks during June 1918, attacking 65 people.[21] Other outbreaks were reported in Ballinasloe on 20 June 1918, Tipperary town and Athlone on 24 June 1918, and in Waterford by 3 July 1918 where it was said to be in a large city factory.[22] By 6 July 1918 a number of military and civilians in Sligo were victims of the disease.[23] Influenza returned to Queenstown but this time to the military medical hospital, where 87 patients contracted the disease between 26 June and 27 July 1918. There was also a total of 243 influenza cases at the US Naval Air Station based in Queenstown, between July and 1 November 1918.[24] Influenza was in Cork by 6 July 1918 and there were 119 cases with 6 fatalities in the military hospital during June and July 1918.[25]

Interestingly most of these outbreaks were in army hospitals or in towns near an army or naval base. A contemporary medical report stated there was a very severe outbreak of influenza in Ulster especially in June and July 1918, when there were approximately 5,000 cases. All the military hospitals in the district were proportionately affected. These hospitals were in Belfast, Armagh, Enniskillen, Holywood, Londonderry, Omagh, Newry, Donegal, Dundalk and Drogheda.[26] There was a consensus during the first wave in contemporary Irish nationalist newspapers that influenza was spread by the return of troops from the western front. The evidence shows there was more than a grain of truth in these allegations that the war and returning soldiers were linked to influenza.[27]

The exceptions in Ulster were the towns of Lisburn, Lurgan and Portadown, which were all major linen towns with many linen factories and workshops.[28] All lay on the Belfast to Dublin railway line. Coal to run the power looms and in turn completed linen goods were transported from towns such as Lurgan to Belfast via the railway. It could be argued that as influenza entered Ireland via Belfast in early June 1918, it then spread to mid-Ulster via the rail system. Once the virus entered these towns it would have spread quickly due to the close working and living conditions of factory workers. Influenza and the danger to factory workers, particularly the linen industry, will be discussed in more detail in Chapter 3. The evidence indicates that most outbreaks during this wave were in Ulster towns.

The Second Wave—Autumn 1918

The second wave originated in Leinster in the Howth district of Dublin on the east coast where influenza was first reported on 1 October 1918.[29] Pneumonia deaths in Dublin started to increase around 12 October 1918, peaking between 2 and 9 November 1918. The Portabello military hospital in Dublin reported 453 influenza cases with 34 deaths during October 1918 and 315 cases with 44 deaths during November 1918.[30] In County Lough, Dundalk and Drogheda both reported influenza on 16 October and 25 October 1918, respectively.[31] It may have spread to Dundalk from Dublin or via the military due to the military hospital based here. In County Kildare influenza was rife in Naas and it was in Carlow by 18 October 1918. In County Wexford, it was in New Ross by 18 October and Wexford town by 25 October 1918[32] and in Kilkenny by 22 October 1918.[33] Pneumonia mortality peaked here on 9 November and Kilkenny had the highest pneumonia mortality in Leinster. The 2nd King Edward's Horse was based in Kilkenny during 1918 so the proximity of this regiment might have been a factor in its virulence here.

Influenza was in Munster by mid-October. In County Tipperary, the disease was in Thurles by 18 October 1918, in Tipperary and Bansha districts by 21 October and Nenagh by 23 October 1918.[34] By 28 October influenza was serious in Clonmel, which had one of the highest death rates from pneumonia in the province of Munster of 0.78 per thousand of population. The town was the home of Victoria barracks which during the war was a training depot to the Royal Irish Regiment and the South Irish Horse regiments. However, there were outbreaks of influenza among workers at both the Clonmel Condensed milk factory and Messrs Thomas Murphy & Sons Ltd brewery, which may also account for the high pneumonia figures.[35]

In County Cork, there were 19 influenza admissions to the Queenstown military hospital between 23 October 1918 and 23 November 1918.[36] The disease was in Carrigaline by 23 October 1918, Cork city by 25 October and Youghal by 4 November.[37] There were 142 influenza cases with 22 fatalities during November and December 1918 in the Cork military hospital and 191 influenza cases at Buttevant military hospital with 17 fatalities between the end of October and the end of December 1918. While in Fermoy military hospital between October and December 1918 there were 209 influenza cases with eight fatalities.[38] Fifteen influenza deaths were reported in Limerick on 24 October

1918.[39] However, there is no record of any influenza patients in the military hospital in Limerick. There was an outbreak in Waterford reported on 29 October 1918 and pneumonia deaths peaked here between 9 and 16 November 1918. In Tralee, County Kerry, pneumonia deaths peaked initially between 9 and 16 November and subsequently on 7 December 1918.

Influenza in Connaught was first reported in County Galway on 18 October 1918 in Ballinasloe and by 21 October 1918 it had reached Tuam.[40] It was in Galway town by 28 October 1918[41] with pneumonia deaths first peaking in the town on 9 November and again on 7 December 1918. On 19 October 1918 severe influenza attacks were reported in Mohill, County Leitrim and district.[42] It reached Swinford and Charlestown in County Mayo by 23 October 1918 and the Knockmore district of Ballina by 16 November 1918.[43] By 9 November it had spread to Roscommon and Strokestown, and Sligo by 13 November 1918.[44] Pneumonia deaths in Sligo peaked initially on 30 November and again on 21 December 1918. However, the most notable aspect of the pandemic in Connaught was that influenza bypassed many rural parts of the province completely during this wave.

In Ulster there were early reports of influenza in towns as far apart as Larne, Newry, Dungannon and Londonderry. In Ulster, influenza was first reported in County Antrim in Larne on 9 October 1918, where it probably entered independently via the port and Royal Naval base that was situated there.[45] From Larne it spread to Ballymena by the end of October 1918. Another early outbreak was in Country Tyrone at Dungannon on 11 October 1918.[46] Interestingly, Dungannon was served by four different rail networks which spread out to Londonderry, Donegal, Omagh and southern Ireland. From Dungannon it may have spread to Omagh and Fintona by 25 October 1918 and Cookstown by 31 October 1918.[47]

In County Down, influenza in Newry was first reported on 21 October 1918, but initial deaths from the disease occurred in the district on 10 October 1918.[48] This was a particularly virulent outbreak as, Newry had the highest pneumonia death rate among the principal towns in Ireland during this wave. Influenza was in Cavan town by 27 October 1918 and in Clones, County Monaghan by 2 November 1918.[49]

Although there were press reports that influenza was in Londonderry on 21 October 1918, first deaths from the disease were recorded as early as 9 October 1918.[50] Influenza might have entered here independently at Londonderry's port and then spread towards Strabane and Enniskillen by 25 October 1918[51] via the rail system. However, there were army barracks in the vicinity of these towns. Influenza was in County Donegal by 1 November in Ballyshannon,[52] where one of the first deaths was of a soldier at the Finner military camp, who died on 6 November 1918 after 16 days suffering from influenza and pneumonia, indicating that influenza was in the camp in late October 1918. It was in Inishowen by 4 November 1918 and by 6 November 1918 it had spread to Letterkenny.[53] The Londonderry and Lough Swilly Railway extended throughout the county of Donegal and originated in Londonderry which may have been a factor in the spread of influenza to County Donegal.

In County Down influenza was in Holywood from the third week of October 1918.[54] The presence of an army barracks in the vicinity of the town may account for its appearance there before it was reported in Belfast. It may have spread from Holywood to the Newtownards district in by 29 October 1918.[55] Elsewhere in County Down it appeared in the Ballykinlar army camp by 16 November where it may have spread to areas such as Downpatrick, Castlewellan and Newcastle by 30 November 1918.[56] First reports in Belfast were at the end of October 1918.[57] Nevertheless, influenza deaths were recorded on 21 October 1918 in the union infirmary, indicating that the disease had taken hold in Belfast earlier in the month. It is unclear how influenza spread to Belfast during this wave: it may have entered independently or spread from either Holywood or Larne. Alternatively, it may have come from Dublin with injured troops as all sick and wounded soldiers from overseas were landed from France or England from the hospital ships in Dublin, where they were brought to Belfast by ambulance train.[58] First reports in Lurgan, County Armagh were on 26 October 1918, but the first death took place on 19 October 1918 after three days of illness.[59] The first victim in nearby Portadown died on 28 October 1918 after suffering from influenza and pneumonia for nine days, thus dating influenza in the town to the third week of October 1918.[60]

The second wave of influenza seemed to originate in either a naval port or army barracks, supporting the theory that the disease in Ireland was due to returning soldiers. Married to this was the extensive rail network present in much of Ireland at that time which helped to disseminate the disease throughout the country. The absence of influenza in the rural parts of Connaught—where the rail network was less prominent—would substantiate this theory. Once in industrial towns or villages, influenza could spread rapidly through factories and if the workers brought it home it would then spread quickly among families. However, it is highly probable that both the movement of troops and the railway network played a significant part in the spread of the disease throughout Irish towns during this wave (Fig. 2.1).

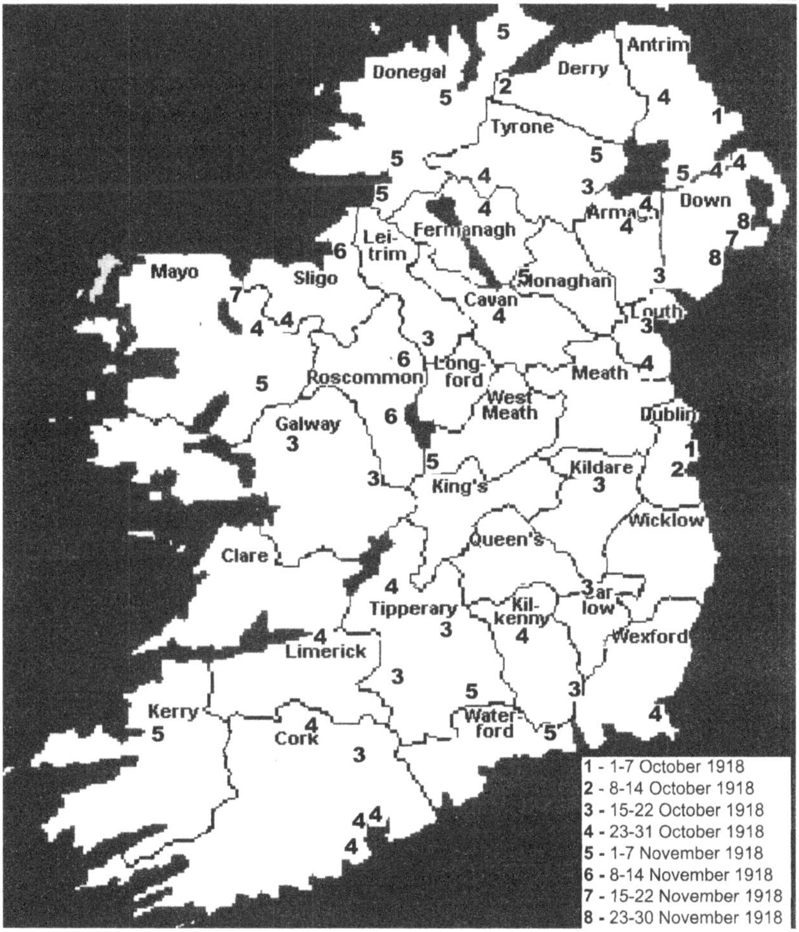

Fig. 2.1 Dispersal of Second Wave of Influenza in Ireland

The Third Wave—Spring 1919

The first influenza outbreaks were again in Leinster, when it was reported in the Celbridge district, County Kildare on 5 February 1919 and in Kildare town on 17 February.[61] By 8 February it was in County Wexford in Enniscorthy and Dublin on 7 February.[62] During February and March 1919 there were 411 influenza cases admitted to Portabello military hospital in Dublin, with 44 fatalities.[63] Elsewhere in Leinster influenza was in Queens County (now Laois) districts bordering on Carlow and Athy by 5 February 1919[64] and in Wexford town by 22 February 1919.[65] In County Lough, pneumonia deaths in Dundalk peaked on 22 February 1919 while in Drogheda they began to rise on 22 March 1919, peaking on 5 April 1919.

First reports of the disease in Munster were again in County Cork at the Queenstown military hospital where between 3 February and 3 March 1919, there were 18 influenza admissions with two deaths. On 17 February 1919 influenza was widespread in Cork city and pneumonia deaths peaked here on 8 March 1919. Also in County Cork, 101 influenza cases were admitted to Buttevant military hospital between the beginning of January and the end of February 1919, two proved fatal. In Fermoy military hospital there were 185 influenza cases admitted between February and May 1919, with two fatalities.[66] Influenza was present in parts of East Limerick on 17 February 1919 and pneumonia deaths peaked in Limerick town on 22 February 1919. In County Kerry, influenza recurred in Listowel on 17 February 1919[67] while Tralee had the highest pneumonia death rate per thousand of population in Munster, with deaths peaking here on 1 March 1919.

In Connaught the first reported outbreak was in County Mayo in Castlebar on 14 February 1919.[68] By 22 February 1919 it was in County Galway where there were 25 influenza cases in the Ballinasloe military barracks,[69] which suggests that this outbreak was spread by soldiers. It had reached Galway town by 26 February 1919[70] where pneumonia deaths peaked on 8 March 1919. Renmore army barracks in Galway was home to the Connaught Rangers, therefore influenza could have entered the barracks independently with returning soldiers. This outbreak of influenza appeared to spread further into Connaught than the previous waves. It was reported on 22 March 1919 that influenza had spread to the Aran Islands and this virulent outbreak spread to the islands of Gorumna and Lettermullen off Connemara.[71] The mortality rate in Connaught was noticeably higher in 1919 than during 1918, no doubt affected by the more widespread infection in Connaught during this wave.

In Ulster, there was a recurrence of influenza in Holywood on 6 February 1919'.[72] Again the disease appeared in Holywood before Belfast, where it was first reported on 12 February 1919.[73] Belfast had the lowest influenza death rate not only in Ulster but in the whole of Ireland during this wave. In Lurgan, County Armagh, the first influenza death was recorded on 9 February.[74] and in nearby Portadown the first influenza death was recorded on 5 February 1919.[75] Influenza was first reported in Newry on 10 February 1919, although this was not thought to be a new wave as the second outbreak never died out in the town.[76] By 11 March 1919, there were several cases in Warrenpoint probably spread there from Newry.[77] Elsewhere in County Down influenza was in the Newcastle district by 12 March 1919 and there were several deaths near Ballykinlar military camp,[78] suggesting that the disease was spread by army personnel.

In County Donegal influenza reappeared in Ballyshannon and Pettigo by 17 February 1919 while there was a severe outbreak of disease along the north-east seaboard of the county, especially in Falcarragh, attributed to a large number of demobilised soldiers returning home.[79] By 8 March 1919 there were over 150 patients in the Pettigo dispensary district.[80] Influenza was not in Pettigo during the second wave, but there were two deaths on 18 February both victims had suffered from influenza for seven days, indicating the disease was there in early February. Influenza spread throughout county Donegal and on 1 March 1919 a high death toll in Dunfanaghy and Glenties Union was reported and the disease had reached Letterkenny and Milford unions.[81]

On 15 January 1919 numerous influenza cases were reported in Coleraine since the beginning of the month[82] and on 20 February there were 175 extra cases in the Coleraine district.[83] The 1920 Ministry of Health Report referred to a dance held near Coleraine that was attended by a soldier convalescing from influenza, which resulted in an outbreak of the disease among the 60 guests present, several of whom died.[84] Similarly in County Antrim hundreds of Ballymena inhabitants had influenza by 13 March, mainly due to a large attendance at a local entertainment event.[85] These examples not only support the opinion that influenza could be spread by the military but also by attendance at large public indoor gatherings.

On 20 February 1919, influenza was reported in County Tyrone in Omagh[86]; from where it may have spread via the rail network to the village of Trillick by 27 February 1919. On the same date, influenza was reported to be in County Fermanagh in the district of Brookeborough.[87] By 1 March 1919 there was a recurrence in Londonderry.[88] Influenza and pneumonia deaths in Londonderry peaked on 22 March 1919, suggesting that influenza spread to the town later than other major Ulster towns. Elsewhere in County Londonderry, influenza was in the Limavady area by 26 February 1919.[89] As March progressed the disease spread to the rural areas that had avoided previous waves.

The way influenza spread throughout Ireland during all waves of the pandemic suggests that it entered different parts of the country via naval bases, army hospitals or barracks, with military personnel returning to Ireland on leave, or to convalesce in the various military hospitals. It then probably spread via the railway network across the country. In Fig. 2.2 the shaded counties in the map of Ireland show those counties that suffered a higher mortality during 1919 than they did in 1918. Most of these counties are in the west of Ireland and Connaught was especially affected. The absence of influenza in the rural parts of Connaught and the west of Ireland during the first and second waves may be due to the absence of rail networks in that part of the country. However, by the third outbreak in February 1919, influenza spread to all parts of the country. This could be due to military movements, or as in Newry, a continuation of the previous wave. However, once influenza was in an industrial town or village, it spread rapidly through factory workshops and infected the workers' families who lived in close quarters together. Attendance at crowded entertainments such as dances, cinemas or church services and meetings would also help disseminate the disease through a community.

Global Mortality of 1918–1919 Pandemic

The global death toll from influenza was enormous and will probably never be accurately estimated, despite being constantly updated over the years. In the 1920s Edwin Oakes Jordan calculated it to have been around 21.5 million. However, this figure seemed to be unreasonably low, as the Indian mortality alone was estimated at 18 million in 1986 by Ian Mills.[91] In 1977, Beveridge advised that the total worldwide mortality had been estimated as being between 15 and 25 million.[92] In 1991 David Patterson and Gerald Pyle estimated a conservative global total of 30

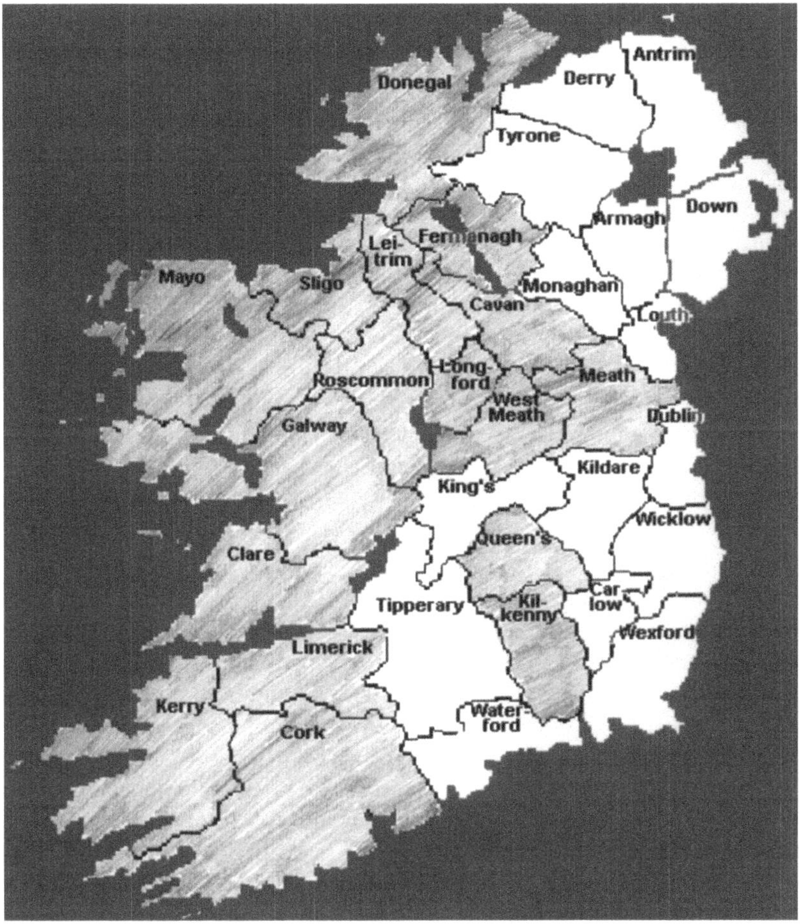

Fig. 2.2 Irish counties that suffered higher mortality in 1919 than 1918[90]

million deaths.[93] In 2002, Niall Johnson and Juergen Mueller estimated the global mortality to have been approximately 50 million, but believed that even this figure might be significantly lower than the actual death toll, suggesting that the mortality may have been as high as 100 million.[94]

There are many reasons why the true mortality figures may never be accurately calculated. There were vast areas of the world for which there was little or no information; moreover, what information there was can be of doubtful quality and contradictory. In some countries the data only covered certain cities or populations, and in certain cases ignored the deaths of the indigenous populations.[95]

Accurate diagnosis of influenza was problematic as there were difficulties in assigning the correct cause of death. Some deaths were recorded as influenza while others were recorded as influenza accompanied by pneumonia. Deaths attributed to pneumonia, cardiovascular disease, diabetes, or renal disease sometimes had influenza as a contributory cause but were not recorded as death from influenza. Additionally, in many European countries the official registration systems were disrupted due to the war, and influenza mortality figures were often estimates or guesses by overworked doctors.[96] Therefore, under these combined circumstances, it is unlikely that a completely accurate mortality figure for the pandemic can ever be calculated.

Problems Associated with Irish Mortality Figures for 1918 and 1919

Sir William Thompson, (RGI), noted in November 1919 that the influenza pandemic of 1918 was by far the most serious epidemic in the country since the Great Famine and had the highest mortality of any epidemic in Ireland since 1864.[97] In 1864 compulsory registration of births, deaths and marriages was introduced to Ireland and the dispensary doctor was made the local registrar of births and deaths.[98] This means that accurate death tolls only started to be calculated from that date. Nevertheless, the recorded influenza mortality for Ireland, like that for the rest of the world, is almost certainly inaccurate. In Ireland, deaths were sometimes uncertified, misdiagnosed and in some cases not reported at all, meaning the official mortality figures for the country are probably an underestimation.

The official recorded influenza mortality for Ireland in 1918 was 10,651 and in 1919 was 9,406. However, in his 1919 report, the RGI assigned only 2,571 deaths in Ireland with influenza as the only cause, but he produced a list of deaths, from influenza associated with other diseases, for that year. Diseases included pulmonary tuberculosis; other forms of tuberculosis; meningitis; insanity; convulsions; heart diseases; bronchitis; bronchopneumonia; lobar pneumonia; septic pneumonia; pneumonia (type not stated); other diseases of the respiratory system; bright's disease (acute and chronic); and disease of pregnancy and childbirth. Similar data was not produced for the RGI's 1918 report, suggesting that many deaths from similar causes as those listed in 1919 were not associated with influenza in 1918 and thus not included in the official influenza figures for that year. Therefore, the actual death toll from influenza in Ireland during 1918 may have been considerably higher than the official reported figures.[99]

Furthermore, the Registrar-General for England and Wales and the Registrar-General for Scotland published supplementary reports on the influenza mortality during the pandemic of 1918–1919 in which they re-assessed the mortality figures in those countries due to influenza.[100] No similar supplementary report on influenza was produced for Ireland. However, the RGI delivered a presentation on 14 November 1919 to the *Society of the Statistical and Social Inquiry Society of Ireland* meeting in which he addressed influenza in Ireland during 1918; but information or figures from 1919 were not included.[101] Weekly reports from the Medical Officers of Health (MOH) of all the dispensary districts throughout Ireland had been sent to the RGI, presumably including influenza deaths. However, despite his awareness of the gravity of the pandemic, Thompson does not appear to have analysed these figures in an in-depth a manner as his counterparts in Scotland, England and Wales.

Another problem with the official figures was that influenza was not a notifiable disease during the pandemic. In 1918, notifiable diseases included scarlet fever, measles, typhus, cholera and tuberculosis. This meant that those who had such a disease, had to notify the doctor who in turn advised the local authority. They then had the power to isolate those people who were suffering from the disease, trace it to the source and stop the spread by various methods such as isolation of the patient and their contacts.[102] The RGI used the weekly MOH returns to compile an official return of weekly death figures produced in both 1918 and 1919 of the births and deaths in Dublin and eighteen of the principal urban districts in Ireland.[103] These reports contained weekly breakdowns of the deaths from various notifiable diseases in the following large Irish towns and cities—Dublin, Belfast, Cork, Londonderry, Limerick, Waterford, Galway, Dundalk, Lurgan, Drogheda, Lisburn, Newry, Portadown, Wexford, Ballymena, Sligo, Kilkenny, Tralee and Clonmel—but unfortunately, with the exception of Dublin, weekly figures for influenza were not included as it was not a notifiable disease.

In 2002, Johnson and Mueller recalculated global mortality for the pandemic using figures that were derived in various ways by many researchers. They advised that the methods employed included revisiting official records and recompiling the recorded numbers and calculating 'excess' deaths from recorded mortality for influenza, respiratory causes, or all causes. This was the method by which they calculated the British figures for Scotland England and Wales.[104] Their report quoted re-estimated figures for all the countries affected by the pandemic. There were re-estimated mortality figures for England and Wales, Scotland and 'Éire'. Éire presumably refers to the 26 counties of Ireland meaning the figures for the six counties of Northern Ireland—Armagh, Antrim, Down, Fermanagh, Londonderry and Tyrone—were not considered in this re-estimation. Johnson and Mueller's re-estimated mortality for 'Éire' was 18,367; while the contemporary RGI's official figures were 20,057 for the 32 counties of Ireland for the duration of the pandemic.[105] Ida Milne suggested that this figure, which was originally offered by Edwin Oakes Jordan was based on one from William Thompson that included all influenza deaths for 1918 as well as the first quarter in 1919 and this may explain the discrepancy.[106]

Johnson and Mueller acknowledged that there were 'many problems' with their figures as some data covered only certain populations or certain areas in a country.[107] It would appear that the Irish figures fall into this category. The following section will attempt to recalculate the mortality figures for the 32 counties of Ireland during the pandemic. However, it should be noted that the accurate influenza mortality for Ireland will probably never be known.

Influenza Mortality in Ireland

The official Irish influenza mortality for 1918 was 10,651 compared to an annual average of 1,234 for the preceding ten years and the mortality from pneumonia was 6,120 as opposed to an annual average of 4,067 for the same period. The 1919 official mortality figures were 9,406 for influenza and 5,245 for pneumonia. In 1919 Thompson stated 'it may, I think, be fairly assumed that an appreciable number of deaths in 1918 classified to pneumonia were in reality cases of influenza, although not so stated in the medical certificates'. In his 1919 annual report he advised that, although deaths from pneumonia in 1919 were not as numerous as those for 1918 that they were still well above the average of the previous ten years. He proposed in 1919 that there were 1,178 more pneumonia deaths above the previous ten years annual average of 4,067 and that these were attributable to influenza. He concluded that if these excess pneumonia figures were added to the number of deaths from influenza, the total for 1919 would be nearer 10,584.[108] Applying the same logic to 1918, the excess pneumonia deaths for that year would be 2,053, which when added to the official influenza figures gives a total of 12,704 deaths from the disease for 1918. This resulted in an influenza mortality figure of 23,288 for 1918 and 1919. Ida Milne came to the same conclusion in 2018. However, she only re-estimated the mortality based on the excess pneumonia figures and did not proceed with a statistical analysis for other diseases such as bronchitis, 'organic heart disease' and pulmonary tuberculosis as the Registrar-General for England and Wales did in his supplementary report.[109]

The Registrar-General for England and Wales re-estimated the influenza mortality for those countries, in his supplementary report on influenza published in 1920. He recognised that previously published figures were an underestimation and stated:

> It is well known that during influenza epidemics the mortality attributed to the disease does not represent the whole of that caused by it. The entries under other headings especially those of respiratory diseases, are always found to increase during an epidemic, and though this has not occurred during 1918 to the same extent as other recent outbreaks it is still necessary to make allowances for these increases in mortality, allocated to other causes but really attributable to influenza, in endeavouring to measure the loss of life caused by the epidemic.[110]

He advised that there were several possible ways of making such an estimate, but that none of them were 'wholly satisfactory in themselves' but were still 'capable to pointing to the approximate truth'.[111] The first 'excess' death method he used involved comparing the deaths for each quarter of the pandemic against deaths in the previous five years (1913–1917) for specific causes of death. Deaths from all forms of pneumonia, bronchitis, 'organic heart disease' and pulmonary tuberculosis (phthisis) were examined for 'excess' deaths based on annualised deaths rates and then these deaths were re-allocated as influenza caused deaths.[112]

The second 'excess' death method he employed was to assess the comparative healthiness of 1918 to the average for the previous five years (1913–1917) for the 'other causes'—excluding influenza, pneumonia, bronchitis, 'organic heart disease' and pulmonary tuberculosis (phthisis)—and then to assume that in the absence of the influenza pandemic, the mortality from all causes would have been in the same ratio as the average of the previous five years (1913–1917). The excess mortality between that recorded for 1918 and that estimated for the non-epidemic average could thus be regarded as influenza-related.[113]

The third 'excess' death method he employed depended on the assumption that, in the absence of the influenza pandemic, mortality during the third and fourth quarters would have been comparable to that during the first and second quarters of 1918. From there it is possible to calculate expected mortality and compare it with actual mortality.[114] Again the excess could be claimed to be influenza related.

The Registrar-General for England and Wales first calculated these excess mortality estimates for the female population only due to wartime changes in the male population and the available male population data being for civilians only. Furthermore, this civilian population had undergone major structural change during 1913–1917 due to the war. Because of this he made estimates for male deaths for the civilian population only and just used 1917 data for comparison rather than the five-year period used for the female calculations.[115] The results of these three methods were averaged and the average excess deaths were added to the existing influenza deaths for England and Wales of 151,446, thus increasing the estimated death toll in England and Wales to approximately 198,000.[116]

In this chapter the above methods are applied to the Irish statistics to recalculate the mortality in the country. In Ireland, although the male population was disrupted due to the war it was not disrupted to the extent of England and Wales. David Fitzpatrick has suggested that 'Ireland's aggregate male contribution to wartime forces was about 210,000',[117] but conscription was never introduced to Ireland, unlike in Great Britain. Therefore, for the purposes of this recalculation, these methods were applied to the Irish population, using the data from the RGI's annual reports for 1913–1917, rather than just to the female population. Again, problems arise when trying to apply these methods to the available Irish figures contained in the annual and weekly reports. The first 'excess' death method requires access to quarterly figures of all forms of pneumonia, bronchitis, 'organic heart disease' and pulmonary tuberculosis (phthisis) to determine 'excess' deaths based on annualised death rates. Unfortunately, although there are annual death rates for these diseases in the annual reports, the quarterly breakdowns were not available in the annual reports, so this method was not applied to the Irish figures.

However, the Registrar-General for England and Wales' second and third 'excess' death methods were applied to the Irish mortality figures to re-estimate the deaths from influenza in Ireland during 1918. These methods were only applied to 1918 as in 1919 the RGI accounted for deaths that were from influenza associated with other diseases, indicating the influenza mortality for that year was probably reasonably accurate. The fact that the official influenza death toll for 1919—when only the third wave took place—was 9,406, compared to 10,651 for 1918, when both the first and extremely virulent second waves of the pandemic occurred, implies there was an underestimation of the influenza death toll for 1918.

The second 'excess' death method of the Registrar-General for England and Wales, as previously described, implied that if there had not been an influenza pandemic, the mortality from the 'other causes' would have been in the same ratio as the average of the previous five years.[118] The mortality from 'other causes' (all diseases except influenza, all forms of pneumonia, bronchitis, 'organic heart disease' and pulmonary tuberculosis) in 1918 was 89.86% of the mortality of their average for the previous five years (1913–1917).[119] This method would give an excess mortality for this year of 12,860 (See Table 2.1 for breakdown of calculation). This figure could be claimed to be excess influenza deaths for 1918 and could be added to the recorded influenza figure for that year of 10,651, giving an estimated influenza total for 1918 of 23,511. Adding

Table 2.1 Calculation of second 'excess' death method—'other causes' applied to the Irish mortality figures

		Calculation	*New total*
Average Mortality (1913–1917)	73,261		
Expected Mortality		(89.86%) × (73,261)	65,835
Official Mortality (1918)	78,695		
Excess deaths other causes		78,695—65,835	12,860
Recorded influenza mortality (1918–19)	20,057		
Estimated total pandemic mortality (1918–1919)		20,057 + 12,860	32,917

this figure to the existing figure for 1919 of 9,406 would give a new estimated total of 32,917 influenza deaths in Ireland.[120]

The third 'excess' death method of the Registrar-General for England and Wales, as previously described, implied that if there had been no pandemic then the mortality for the whole year (1918) would have been similar to the first two quarters of the year. The total mortality for the first quarter of 1918 was 81.50% of the average from the first quarter (1913–1917), and the mortality for the second quarter for the same year was 94.43% of the average of the same quarter (1913–1917); which gave an average for the first two quarters of 87.96%. This gives an excess mortality for this year of 14,253 (See Table 2.2 for breakdown of calculation). Again, this figure could be claimed to be excess influenza deaths and, if added to the recorded influenza figure for 1918 of 10,651, would give an estimated influenza total for 1918 of 24,904. Adding this figure to the existing figure for 1919 of 9,406 would give a new estimated total of 34,310 influenza deaths in Ireland during 1918 and 1919.[121] The recalculated influenza mortality figures suggest that the recorded influenza mortality figures were not a true indication of the virulence of the pandemic. The re-estimations imply that influenza mortality in Ireland for years 1918 and 1919 could fall within a lower band of 20,057 and an upper band of 34,310.

These re-estimated influenza mortality figures pose an interesting question. Were the Irish influenza deaths for 1918 as high as these recalculated figures would suggest? These recalculated figures suggest that approximately 30% of all deaths in 1918 were influenza-related as compared to

Table 2.2 Calculation of third 'excess' death method—'1918 improvement method' applied to the Irish mortality figures

		Calculation	*New total*
Average Mortality (1913–1917)	73,261		
Expected Mortality		(87.96%) × (73,261)	64,442
Official Mortality (1918)	78,695		
Excess deaths other causes		78,695—64,442	14,253
Recorded influenza mortality (1918–19)	20,057		
Estimated total pandemic mortality (1918–1919)		20,057 + 14,253	34,310

Table 2.3 Deaths from respiratory diseases—comparison of average 1913–17 and 1918, 1919, 1920 and 1921[211]

Cause of Death	*Death Toll (Average 1913–1917)*	*Death Toll (1918)*	*Death Toll (1919)*	*Death Toll (1920)*	*Death Toll (1921)*
Pneumonia	4,987	6,120	5,254	4,134	3,502
Bronchitis	6,424	5,794	6,593	5,241	4,415
Heart Disease	8,072	7,065	7,565	7,010	6,954
Pulmonary TB (Phthisis)	7,407	7,556	6,687	5,911	5,557

the official estimation of 13.5%. This implies that there were twice as many influenza deaths in 1918 as originally recorded. Why would this be? The Registrar-General for England and Wales found that the deaths from respiratory diseases always increased during influenza epidemics. He stated that pneumonia, bronchitis, 'organic heart disease' and pulmonary tuberculosis (phthisis)—along with influenza itself '—are generally found to yield increased rates during influenza epidemics'.[122] Was this the case in Ireland?

Pneumonia

Table 2.3 shows that the pneumonia death toll rose significantly during both 1918 and 1919 in Ireland. Not surprisingly as pneumonia was recognised as the most serious complication associated with influenza. Therefore, the higher pneumonia mortality during 1918 and 1919 was mostly due to influenza. Therefore the influenza mortality during 1918–19 would at least be 23,288.

Bronchitis

The RGI recorded 5,794 bronchitis deaths for 1918 a decrease of 632 over the five-year average (1913–1917) of 6,424.[123] In 1919, there were 6,593 bronchitis deaths, an increase of 167 on the five-year average (1913–1917) of 6,426.[124] In Ireland—like that of England and Wales—there was a decrease in bronchitis deaths during 1918 but a slight increase during 1919. Niall Johnson argued that deaths attributed to bronchitis in England and Wales may not have been particularly influenced by the influenza pandemic, although he does not elaborate as to his reasoning.[125] Conversely, Charles Stuart-Harris noted in 1976 that some forms of chronic pulmonary or cardiac disorder among elderly persons assisted in the development of bronchitis during influenza and doubtless contributed to the mortality from influenza in the aged.[126] In Ireland the decrease in the bronchitis mortality in 1918 could possibly be attributed to people who would normally have died from bronchitis, who instead died of influenza during that year. The continued decrease of bronchitis deaths in 1920 and 1921 may indicate that those suffering from the disease had already succumbed in 1918 and 1919 due to the influenza pandemic.

Heart Disease

The RGI recorded 7,065 deaths under the heading of heart disease for 1918, a decrease of 1,007 over the five-year average (1913–1917) of 8,072.[127] In 1919, there were 7,565 deaths from heart disease, a decrease of 507 on the five-year average (1913–1917) of 7,565.[128] Similarly, in England and Wales heart disease showed a decrease during the pandemic. Niall Johnson suggested that deaths attributed to heart disease may not have been particularly influenced by the influenza pandemic. Again, as with bronchitis, he does not elaborate as to why this is the case.[129] The decrease in deaths from heart disease in Ireland during both 1918 and 1919, especially the decrease in 1918, could be attributed to susceptible people who would have instead died of influenza. This is a persuasive argument as in 1976 Stuart-Harris noted that those people with hypertensive or ischaemic heart disease were probably more at risk from influenza than persons of similar age with a healthy cardiovascular system.[130] More recently in 2012 it has been suggested that influenza epidemics are associated with a rise in coronary deaths especially acute myocardial infection (AMI).[131] As with bronchitis, the continued decrease of deaths from heart disease in 1920 and 1921 may be an indication that those suffering from the disease had already succumbed to influenza in 1918 and 1919.

Pulmonary Tuberculosis

Sandra Tomkins suggested that although influenza was often associated with a rise in tuberculosis mortality and an increase of new cases of pulmonary tuberculosis, there was little solid evidence of this effect during the 1918–19 pandemic in the United Kingdom.[132] In 1919, Raymond Pearl posed the following question in the US: 'Were actively tuberculous persons more or less likely to contract influenza during the epidemic than non-tuberculous members of the general population?'[133] Although this was a preliminary report, he found that having tuberculosis did not significantly increase your chances of contracting influenza during the pandemic.[134]

Niall Johnson queried in the United Kingdom: 'were those who would normally have died of tuberculosis being claimed by influenza or were their deaths being attributed to influenza?' He found in England and Wales that deaths from pulmonary tuberculosis decreased during the pandemic and summed up his findings with the somewhat unsatisfactory conclusion that 'a link between phthisis deaths and the influenza seems more problematic'.[135] A similar question could be asked with respect to Ireland. The RGI recorded 7,556 pulmonary tuberculosis deaths for 1918.[136] The average mortality from pulmonary tuberculosis in the preceding five years was 7,407, indicating a slight increase in deaths from this disease during 1918. In 1919 the deaths from pulmonary tuberculosis were 6,687—a decrease of 720 on the preceding five years.[137]

The increase in pulmonary tuberculosis deaths in Ireland in 1918 compared to the five-year average (1913–1917) was negligible (less than two percent of the total mortality for the year). However, there was a 10% decrease in deaths in 1919. This may signal that pulmonary tuberculosis sufferers died from influenza in 1918, thus causing a decrease in mortality from the disease in 1919. Deaths from pulmonary tuberculosis decreased again in 1920 to 5,911[138]—a decrease of 1,496 on the five-year average (1913–1917) and was the lowest mortality figure from the disease since 1908. In the US Noymer and Garrene found the steepest decline of tuberculosis death rates in the twentieth century was experienced in the years following the 1918 pandemic. They suggested that influenza and tuberculosis were likely to have interacted during 1918 and that tuberculosis infection was a significant risk factor to contracting influenza.[139] They concluded that the huge losses of life which occurred because of the 1918 pandemic were 'borrowed against future deaths from tuberculosis'.[140] Therefore, the decrease of pulmonary tuberculosis deaths in 1919, 1920 and 1921 in Ireland may also have been due to this.

Deaths from bronchitis and heart disease both decreased during 1918, while those from pulmonary tuberculosis increased only slightly on the average of the previous five years (1913–1917), but the pneumonia mortality increased considerably. This indicates that the influenza mortality during the pandemic should at least have included the excess pneumonia deaths and would be 23,288. The influenza mortality could be somewhere between the lower band of 23,288 and the higher band of 34,310. However, as the deaths from other respiratory diseases did not increase, it is unlikely that the deaths that can be allocated to the disease were as high as the estimated upper band of 34,310 might suggest. Consequently, it is very doubtful that accurate influenza mortality figures for Ireland will ever be known.

Comparison of Irish Mortality Figures for 1918 and 1919 with the Average of the Preceding Ten years (1908–1917)

The mortality in Ireland from all causes in the first and second quarters of 1918 was 18,286 and 18,272 as compared to 22,088 and 19,427, respectively, for the ten-year average for years 1908–1917—a decrease of 3,802 and 1,155 for those quarters. In the third quarter of 1918 the mortality from all causes was 15,426 compared to the average for years 1908–1917 of 15,223—an increase of 204 for that quarter. However, during the final quarter of 1918 the mortality from all causes was 26,711 compared to 17,035 for the average for years 1908–1917- an increase of 9,676 for that quarter. These figures show that there was a dramatic decrease in the mortality from all causes in the first quarter of 1918, which preceded the pandemic. This suggests that 1918 in Ireland began as a particularly healthy and the RGI confirmed in 1919:

> It may be considered worthy of note that if the mortality from influenza in 1918 had only reached the normal, the number of deaths from other causes being the same as is shown in my Annual Report, a record for low mortality in Ireland would have been the result.[141]

The second quarter coincided with the first wave of the pandemic and the mortality figures showed a decrease in the ten-year average for years 1908–1917. These figures along with those for the third quarter which were marginally higher in 1918 compared to the average annual mortality for 1908–1917 support the theory that the first wave of influenza in Ireland, as elsewhere, was milder, with high morbidity but not high mortality. It is not until the final quarter of 1918, which coincided with the second wave, that there is a remarkable increase in the mortality compared to the same period over years 1908–1917—an increase of 9,676. Again, this reinforces the view that the second wave was more virulent than the first.

In the first and second quarters of 1919 the mortality from all causes for Ireland was 28,106 and 20,854 as compared to 22,088 and 19,427, respectively, for the average annual mortality of 1908–1917—an increase of 6,018 and 1,427 for those quarters. In the third and fourth quarters of 1919 the mortality from all causes was 13,759 and 15,893 as compared to 15,223 and 17,035, respectively, for the average annual mortality for 1908–1917—a decrease of 1,464 and 1,142 for those quarters.

It is noteworthy that there was an increase in deaths from all causes in both the first and second quarters of 1919. The first quarter coincides with both the end of the second and the beginning of the third wave of influenza in Ireland. The increase in mortality from all causes of 6,018 further illustrates that influenza was still rife in the country during this period. Again, during the second quarter of 1919 the increase in mortality from all causes, of 1,427 on the ten-year average for years 1908–1917, indicates that influenza was still prevalent in Ireland during this period of 1919. Although there was an increased mortality, the extent of the increase suggests that this final wave was not as virulent as the second. These figures also imply that the third wave of influenza in Ireland was more virulent than the first, in the summer of 1918, because during the equivalent quarter in 1918, there was a decrease in mortality from all causes compared to the ten-year average for years 1908–1917.

Age Distribution of the 1918–1919 Pandemic

The first wave of influenza was thought to be mild as it did not have unusually high mortality. The attack rate from the virus varied with age. It infected 30–40% of people between 0–30 years, 20% of those aged 50 and 10% of 70 years old. As was usual with influenza, most of the mortality in this wave was old people, but there were also usually a significant number of deaths in the age group of 20–40 years. The second and most virulent wave commenced in the autumn of 1918 with a unique global peculiarity that about half the associated deaths were in the 20–40 age group. The third wave, which occurred early in 1919, was more virulent than the first but less severe than the second and this wave had a similar age distribution of the deaths to that of the second wave.[142]

Normally the very young or the very old are more likely to die during an influenza outbreak, but the 1918–19 pandemic showed an unusual age distribution of deaths. In the United States the death rates from influenza and pneumonia during 1918 showed that not only was there a high mortality for the very young and very old, but there was also an extreme departure from the norm for the age group between 15 and 44, which also had a spike of deaths during 1918.[143] This situation was not unique to the US, as the Spanish experience was also that young adults aged between 20 and 44 recorded the highest influenza mortality rates and in Sydney, Australia, the 25–39 age group was hit most severely by the disease.[144] The same situation was true in Britain where mortality seemed to be concentrated among those aged 20–40 and especially those 25–35.[145] Niall Johnson suggested that this peculiarity contributed to Britain's 'lost generation' caused not only through the high mortality of young men who fought on the Western Front, but also from those who succumbed to influenza on the home front, where deaths of young men and women who were not involved in the armed forces were common among this age group.[146] Tragically many service men returned home from the war to Ireland safely only to contract influenza and die from the disease soon after.

Age Distribution in Ireland

The RGI produced breakdowns of the influenza mortality by age, gender and location in Ireland in his 1918 and 1919 reports. As previously discussed, these figures may be under-estimated, but it would be difficult to determine where any refinements could be made to the age and gender figures with any degree of accuracy. Although the RGI acknowledged in 1919 that a large proportion of the excess pneumonia figures in 1918 should be considered as influenza cases, he still used the official influenza statistics (which excluded the excess pneumonia deaths) to identify trends in age and gender mortality from the disease.[147] Even though the RGI's influenza figures for 1918 and 1919 may be inaccurate, they are the only ones available for analysis.

The 1911 census was used to identify population numbers to calculate age- specific mortality trends. Again, these figures are not accurate but even though the RGI produced amended population figures for 1918, these were not further broken down by either gender or age.[148] In the absence of more up-to-date population estimations, the 1911 figures are the only ones available that can be used to make the calculation. However, it should be taken into consideration that the population (especially of males between 20 and 40) may have declined to some extent since 1911 because of the war. Therefore, any estimations or graphs produced using both the RGI's mortality figures and the 1911 census, are the best approximation that can be made with available data.

The RGI noted in 1918 that 55.5% of all influenza deaths in Ireland were of people aged between 15 and 45.[149] In 1919 he reported that, although the disease appeared to have caused death at all periods of life, that more than 58% of the total influenza mortality were of those people between the ages 20 and 65.[150] During 1918, 22.73% of all influenza deaths were of people between 25 and 35 years, and in 1919 is was 18.95%, suggesting that this age group was particularly susceptible to influenza.[151] Dr Donough Macnamara, recounted that during 1918 all the deaths that he encountered in the Mater hospital in Dublin were of people aged 28.[152]

Using 1911 census figures, the age specific death rate for influenza was estimated for both 1918 and 1919. This is the ratio of the number of deaths of individuals in a particular age group in a year to the actual number of individuals in that age group[153] (see Table 2.4). Figure 2.3 is a graphical representation of this Table and compares age specific deaths rates for 1918 and 1919. It forms a W-graph for both years. In 1918,

Table 2.4 Age-specific death rates from influenza per thousand of the age group population (1911 census) in Ireland for the years 1918 and 1919[212]

Age group	*1918*	*1919*
Under 1 Year	3.51	4.95
1–5 Years	2.70	2.45
5–10 Years	1.20	0.87
10–15 years	1.03	0.76
15–20 Years	2.28	1.80
20–25 Years	3.29	2.48
25–35 Years	3.81	2.80
35–45 Years	2.39	2.13
45–55 Years	2.22	2.26
55–65 Years	2.26	2.63
65–75 Years	2.21	2.53
75 Years plus	2.57	2.94

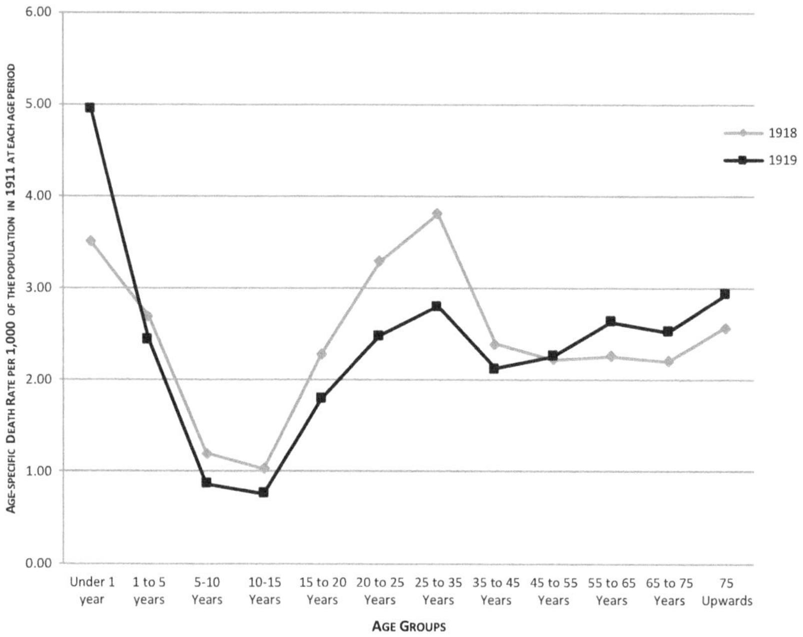

Fig. 2.3 Age-specific influenza death rates for Ireland for 1918 and 1919

the 25–35 years age group had the highest age-specific death rate from influenza of 3.81, closely followed by those aged under one year (3.51). In 1919, however, it was those that were aged under one year that had far and away the highest influenza age-specific death rate of 4.95 followed by the 25–35 age group with 2.80.

It is no great surprise that those aged less than one year suffered to such a great extent during the pandemic. Ruth Barrington stated that the national statistics for Irish infant mortality in 1915 suggested that Ireland fared better than both England and Wales with a rate of 92 per thousand live births (out of 95,583 babies born, 8,753 died before they reached their first birthday) as compared to rates of 110 and 120 for England and Scotland, respectively. However, the Irish rate was declining more slowly than that of England and Scotland. The average rate masked the great differences that existed in the country between urban and rural areas as indicated by the high rate of 160.3 per thousand live births in Dublin during 1915. Infant mortality in the urban areas of Ireland was always high, mainly due to infection and poor diet,[154] so it was hardly surprising that this particular group would suffer during the influenza pandemic. The Carnegie Trust, a philanthropic organisation, commissioned research on maternal and child health in the United Kingdom and Dr Edward Coey Biggar prepared the Irish report which was published in 1917. In this he pointed out that the infant mortality rate of 90 per thousand births was higher than the mortality for soldiers at the front, implying that a baby had a greater chance of dying in Ireland than its father serving in the war.[155]

Many theories have been suggested as to why the 1918–19 pandemic was so detrimental to the 25–35 age group. Ann Reid, Jeffrey Taubenberger and Thomas Fanning believed that the lower death rates among the elderly in 1918 could indicate that an H1 subtype virus, similar to that of the 1918 virus, was circulating before 1850, giving elderly people an immunity that people between 15 and 45 years of age would not have as they had not been exposed to this virus.[156] A behavioural explanation is that young adults were more likely to attempt to work through illness, which would thus maximise their risk of succumbing to influenza.[157] However, this would seem to be a very simplistic explanation as this a common behavioural trait which implies that all pandemics would have similar age mortality. Another theory was that many of the age group 20–45 had been soldiers living in miserable conditions on the western front. There is no doubt that young men living and fighting in the trenches, would have been particularly vulnerable to infection but it does not explain why men and women in this age group who had remained and worked at home had suffered the same infection and death rates.[158]

Professor Michael Worboys has suggested that the young people in their late twenties were exposed to a H3 virus that was thought to have been circulating in the community between 1880 and 1900. This virus had surface proteins that were quite different from those of the H1N1 pandemic strain of 1918. Therefore, the immune system of young adults would have made antibodies to combat this H3 virus, but these would have been ineffective against the 1918 virus. Consequently, this 'mismatch between antibodies trained to H3 virus protein and the H1 protein of the 1918 virus may have resulted in the heightened mortality in the age group—that happened to be in their late 20s during the pandemic'.[159] This plausible reasoning could give some explanation as to why people between 25 and 35 were most at risk.

In 2001 Reid, Taubenberger and Fanning rejected the explanation that it was the strong immune system of young adults which overreacted to the virus.[160] However, a scientific study in 2005, on macaque monkeys showed that those infected with the isolated 1918 virus experienced a rapid spread of the influenza throughout the respiratory system causing them to die within days, damage that mirrored reports of human patients in 1918. The results showed that the 1918 virus caused the immune system of the monkeys to go into overdrive, causing immune proteins to be expressed at abnormally high levels and attack the body.[161] Therefore, the strong immune systems of young adults may have overreacted to the virus causing this age group to be at most risk during the pandemic. All these theories have validity and perhaps it was one or a combination of them that caused the spike in deaths of this age group. However, 'the jury is still out' as to an explanation of this phenomenon.

Influenza Mortality in Different Parts of Ireland

In his 1918 report, the RGI noted that in Leinster, the County Borough of Dublin had the highest influenza mortality rate in Ireland of 4.1 per thousand of population, followed by Kildare County with 3.95, while in Ulster the Belfast County Borough had the third-highest rate of 3.85 per thousand of population. Although the military have been blamed for the transmission of influenza, this may not have been the case in Kildare. Although the county was the home of the Curragh army camp, influenza was less widespread among the military in the camp than the civilian population of the neighbouring area.[162] Ida Milne linked the high death rate in County Kildare to hardship caused by water and power shortages in Naas, which accounted for over half of the deaths in the county.[163] County Clare had the lowest influenza death rate in Ireland of 0.46 per thousand.[164] As Ida Milne suggests, this may be due to the lack of a rail connection in that part of the country.[165] In his 1919 report, the RGI advised that influenza reappeared 'with virulence during the March quarter of the year'. He noted that the deaths were not as numerous as in 1918 but that the figures were still 'far in excess of the number in any of the preceding years'.[166]

Figure 2.4 compares the influenza death rate for all the counties in Ireland for years 1918 and 1919. This graph illustrates that during 1918 the provinces of Leinster and Ulster had the highest mortality from influenza while the province of Connaught was mostly

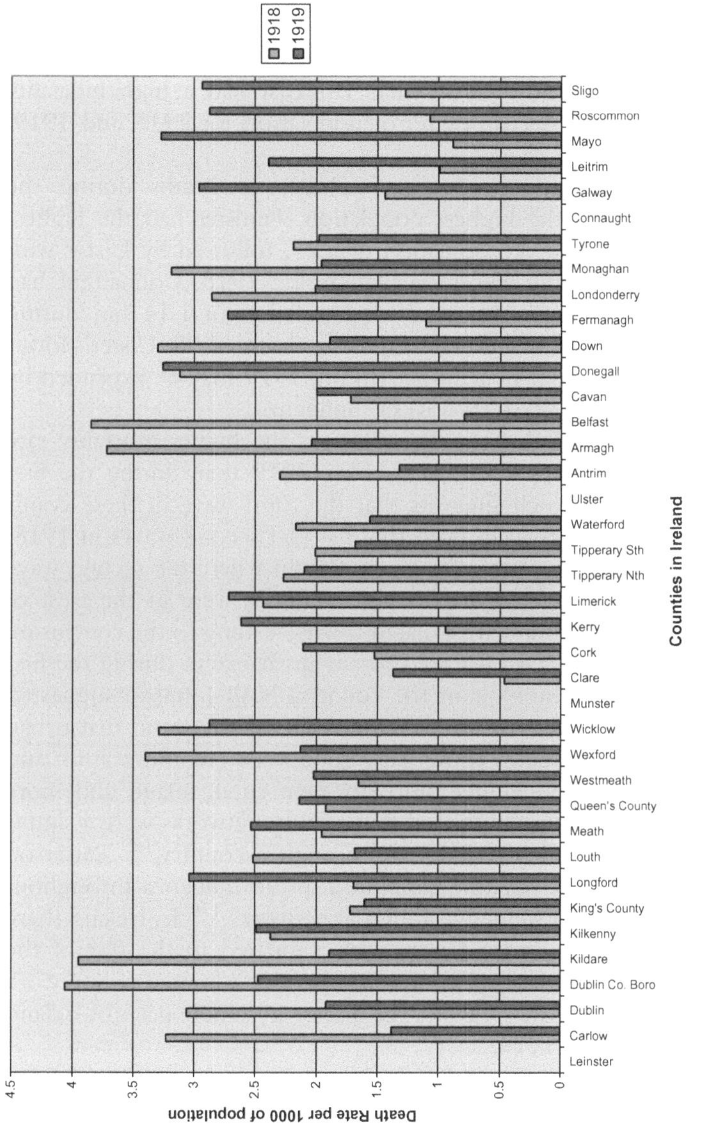

Fig. 2.4 Comparison of death rate from influenza in all the counties of Ireland in 1918 and 1919[167]

unscathed. However, in 1919, although Leinster and Ulster again have a high mortality, the mortality rate in Connaught was noticeably higher than during the first and second waves in 1918. In Ulster, Counties Fermanagh, Cavan and Donegal had a higher mortality rate during 1919 than 1918. It is also noteworthy that Donegal had a high mortality rate of 3.12 and 3.26 per thousand of population for 1918 and 1919, respectively.

Although Ulster had the highest number of deaths during the pandemic it also had the highest population. Leinster had the highest death rate per thousand of population of 5.27, followed by Ulster with 4.79. Another interesting feature is that during 1918, Connaught had the lowest death rate per thousand of population of 1.14 but during 1919, it had the highest of all the four provinces with 2.98. Ulster's lower death rate, as well as that of Leinster, during 1919 may be explained by immunity gained from previous waves of influenza.

Another trend highlighted in Fig. 2.4 was the higher mortality rate in over half the counties in Ireland during 1919 than during the first two waves in 1918, which suggests that the third wave in these counties was more virulent than in both the first and second waves in 1918. This does not follow the trend for Great Britain where the second wave was the most virulent.[168] Most of these counties were in the west of Ireland, typically very rural with isolated towns, leading to the conclusion that influenza may not have featured to any great extent during the first and second waves in the west of the country. Niall Johnson suggested that the patterns of influenza in Scotland reflected the trend that urban and coastal areas—as well as those with good mass communication and transport links—suffered higher mortality than rural, inland and more isolated areas. He further contended that railway networks were a significant method of spreading the disease through a country.[169] Patterson and Pyle suggested that wartime disruption spread influenza throughout Europe via the troop movements along rail networks.[170] In Ireland there was a limited rail network in Connaught compared to the rest of the country. Therefore, the lack of troop movement and limited rail network may have slowed down the spread of the disease in remote parts of Ireland until the third wave in 1919.

At this juncture it is important to highlight that many deaths recorded as influenza deaths in 1919 did in fact occur in 1918. In the Clones poor law district in County Monaghan it was reported that there were 39 influenza deaths in 1918 and 42 influenza in 1919.[171] However, an investigation of the number of influenza deaths showed a figure nearer 65 in 1918 and 16 in 1919.[172] This discrepancy raises some questions as to the accuracy of the influenza death figures for 1919, and thus the third wave in Ireland. More work in this area is required to establish a truly accurate picture of mortality during the third wave in Ireland.

Explaining the Donegal Figures

Maybe one of the most surprising occurrences in Ireland during the influenza pandemic was the high death rate in County Donegal during 1918 and 1919. In 1918, Inishowen poor law district had highest influenza death rate in Ulster of 5.15 per thousand of population, while other Donegal districts such as Letterkenny, Donegal and Stranorlar also had high death rates during 1918. Again, during the 1919 outbreak, County Donegal was severely affected. The Donegal poor law district had the highest influenza death rate per thousand of population in Ulster and the districts of Dunfanaghy, Stranorlar, Glenties, Ballyshannon and Letterkenny also had high death rates. This begs the question 'why did this mainly rural county have such a high death rate during the pandemic?'.

The high death rate in Inishowen, Letterkenny, Donegal and Stranorlar was even more surprising as in 1918, Londonderry city and county Borough, which had the second-highest population after Belfast, had a death rate of 3.11, yet still lower than nearby poor law districts of Inishowen, Letterkenny, Stranorlar and Donegal. County Donegal suffered higher mortality during the third wave in 1919 than the combined mortality of the first two waves in 1918 (See Fig. 2.4). Using the *Irishgeneology.ie* website, some basic statistics were produced of influenza and pneumonia deaths during 1918 and 1919 in the Donegal districts. These figures, although not totally accurate, were used to examine trends in the county and they do provide a good indication as to ages, gender and occupation of those who died from influenza and pneumonia during the pandemic years in these poor law unions.

Why was the death rate in the Inishowen poor law union so high in 1918? The following registration districts of Buncrana, Malin, Clonmany, Moville and Carndonagh- where the workhouse and infirmary were situated—were part of the Inishowen poor law union. It is notable in Inishowen that 23 influenza deaths were recorded during the early months of 1918 in Carndonagh, Malin and Moville. Most of these deaths occurred before the end of May 1918—the official start of the influenza pandemic in Ireland. This beggars the question: 'were these influenza deaths in Moville, Malin and Carndonagh—that occurred between January and the end of May 1918—the earliest outbreak of influenza in Ireland?' If so, it would suggest that the first outbreak may have started in Ireland on the Inishowen peninsula.

The first influenza victims in the United States could have been as early as late January/early February 1918. Ture near Moville was home to American naval airmen during 1918,[173] so was there an early outbreak in Donegal due to infected sailors coming to Ireland, landing at Moville and bringing the virus with them from America? The answer is probably no. This is an unlikely scenario as none of the fatalities in the Inishowen poor law district during any of the three waves were of sailors. In fact the majority of influenza victims in Moville, Malin and Carndonagh between January and May 1918 were members of the farming community.

A more likely scenario is that the influenza deaths that occurred during the early months of 1918 were unrelated to the pandemic. The majority of the victims did not have a medical attendant present when they died so, although recorded as influenza, they may not have died from the disease at all. These deaths, which were probably unrelated to the pandemic, were included in the RGI's influenza figures for 1918. In all probability they have skewed the influenza mortality figures for the Inishowen district. This area had a population of just over 27,500 based on the 1911 census and 142 influenza deaths were reported for the year 1918. If 23 of these deaths were not from the pandemic then that would reduce the influenza death rate for 1918 from 5.51 to around 4.31 per thousand of population. Nevertheless, this is still a high death rate, higher than the industrial areas of Belfast, Londonderry and Lurgan poor law districts for 1918.

This poses a further question 'is there anything distinct about the Inishowen poor law district that may have triggered this death rate?' The Lough Swilly Defences were situated there and, during the war years between 4,000 and 6,000 troops were associated with Lenan Fort, Dunree Fort and Malin Head barracks. Ida Milne has suggested that the presence of naval vessels in Lough Swilly may have played a factor in Donegal's high level of infection during all three waves of the pandemic.[174] The presence of so many soldiers and sailors in the area may have had a bearing on how influenza entered this rural area, which may have eventually resulted in a high death rate during 1918.

A contemporary report stated that the 'epidemic of influenza was severe in this area in 1918'. The same report stated there were non-Dieted Hospitals established at Dunree, Lenan, Clonmany, and Luddan Camps, however, all cases of sickness that required more than a few days of treatment were transferred to the military hospital in Londonderry. Lough Swilly was also the home of the Grand Fleet of the Royal Navy with its main bases in Rathmullan situated in the Milford union district and in Buncrana situated in the Inishowen poor law district. The Royal Navy had no hospital accommodation in Lough Swilly, so their casualties were sent either to the military hospital or county infirmary in Londonderry. Soldiers and sailors would have socialised in Buncrana and coincidently 43 influenza deaths were registered there in 1918. Around 60% of these deaths were from the farming community. Forty-six per cent were of people between 15 and 45, which corresponds with the age distribution of this pandemic. Military patients stationed in Buncrana were normally treated in the Inishowen workhouse infirmary based in Carndonagh.[175]

Interestingly there are no deaths of soldiers registered in 1918 in any of the Inishowen registration districts including Carndonagh. The transfer of both military or naval casualties and presumably influenza sufferers to the Londonderry military hospital or infirmary for treatment may explain this. During the second wave in November 1918, influenza was rampant in the military barracks in Londonderry where 12 military deaths were reported (See Chapter 7).[176] It is a reasonable assumption that the military and naval presence in the Inishowen district may have been the source of the infection in the area and could have been responsible for its spread especially in Buncrana.

During the second wave the first deaths in Inishowen were recorded in Malin and Moville in October. The areas of Cardonagh, Clonmany and Buncrana had fatalities in early November. The Londonderry and Lough Swilly Railway came from Londonderry and travelled through Buncrana, Clonmany and Carndonagh. There were deaths recorded in Londonderry in late October, so this wave may have spread from Londonderry via the rail network as far as Carndonagh. The Lough Swilly line also connected Londonderry to Glenties via Donegal, Stranorlar and Cloghan, as well as to Dungloe via Letterkenny, Churchill, Falcarragh and, Gweedore. There were high death tolls in the Donegal poor law district particularly in Donegal town, Mount Charles and Laghey with most of the victims were again from the farming community as were those that died and were registered in the Churchill district during 1918. However, in 1919, 50%

of the influenza and pneumonia victims in Letterkenny came from the asylum. If influenza entered an institution like an asylum it could spread like wildfire through the inmates. Between January and May 1918, there were 13 influenza deaths in Cloghan, which was situated in Stranorlar poor law union district. Again, as in Carndonagh, Malin and Moville in the Inishowen poor law union, these deaths were probably unrelated to the pandemic as most did not have a medical attendant present when they died. Notably, 77% of these deaths were of people aged over 70, which indicates that they died of a seasonal influenza. Many of the victims were from the farming community. The third wave in Cloghan was also quite severe, with 29 influenza deaths, again 79% of these were from the farming community.

Seasonal Migration

Seasonal migration of Donegal inhabitants to Scotland was a strategy that helped to bolster the income in the poorer parts of the county. However, due to the industries of fishing and sewing for shirt factories in nearby Londonderry, there was little need for this seasonal labour in Inishowen.[177] While this custom can be disregarded as a reason for the high death rate in Inishowen district, other parts of Donegal continued this practice and Catriona Clear suggested that the Congested District Boards encouraged people to continue their seasonal migration to Britain to free up the British male labour for the war effort.[178]

Seasonal migration could be a factor in the high death rates in the Dunfanaghy and Glenties districts. It may not be surprising that migratory workers were vulnerable to infection. A report in the *Irish Independent* in July 1918 advised that the potato harvesters working in Ayrshire in Scotland were housed in unsanitary accommodation. One of the better accommodations was that of a large building used as a stable during the winter that had been divided into two apartments by a wall. The door of each apartment did not close properly, letting the wind in from outside. Externally there was an immense manure heap with the liquid trickling towards the building where the workers had to lie on straw bedding on the floor.[179] Donegal clergy were also concerned not only from a sanitary but also a moral point of view. In Dundee, there was no partition in the accommodation between males and females and it was unsanitary. In Kinnochtry, seven miles from Dundee, the sanitary arrangements were worse as the workers were accommodated on the first floor of a long barn above stables for horses or cattle.[180]

'Waking the Dead'

So it is hardly surprising that in March 1919, the *Belfast Newsletter* reported that over 50 natives of Donegal employed in Scotland had died from influenza.[181] There were reports that those people who had died from influenza in Scotland were returned home to Donegal to be waked and buried. The *Ulster Herald* reported on 21 December 1918 that the remains of two brothers, 'young men of the labouring class', had passed through Letterkenny, to Gweedore, for burial. They had travelled to Glasgow for work 10 days previously and died from influenza. Another young man from Letterkenny who was working in Scotland for two weeks also died of influenza and his remains were brought home for interment.[182] On 1 March 1919, the *Ulster Herald* was concerned about 'a reprehensible custom' in the westerly portion of Donegal of:

> Bringing home for burial of persons dying of the epidemic in Scotland. It is undoubtedly true that the coffins containing remains of victims of the disease, three or perhaps four days ahead, are for a night 'waked' in the home, the coffin lid being taken off. The gravity and far-reaching effect of this dangerous procedure can be understood when it is stated that on Saturday there passed through Letterkenny on motorcars six coffined dead from Scotland. This danger should at once be dealt with.'[183]

Richard Collier may have been referring to this incident in his book *Plague of the Spanish Lady*. He stated that 'following one disastrous weekend, the disease struck Letterkenny, Ireland, like a cyclone, in six cottages; mourners had held a two-day wake around the open coffin of a flu victim'.[184]

It was not only in Donegal that the custom of 'waking the dead' was frowned upon. It was a controversial practice that came in for much criticism. In Dublin, during the second wave, an *Irish Times* editorial complained that attending wakes of people who had died from influenza was an objectionable practice that was believed to be a significant cause of the spread of infection and that this custom more than anything else frustrated the efforts of the public health authorities to eradicate influenza. Sir Charles Cameron, Medical Superintendent Officer of Health for Dublin, disapproved of the practice and thought 'that persons who disregarded the injunctions and advice, which had been publicly circulated in the interests of the health of the citizens wilfully made themselves disseminators of infection, and risked their own lives'.[185] He believed that the bodies of persons who died from an infectious disease should be isolated and 'not waked'. He drew attention to the fact that 'almost all of the individuals, who had attended a wake of an influenza victim, had caught the infection and most of them were far advanced before the following day'.[186] There were also objections to the practice of bringing corpses of influenza victims to the church before burial. A correspondent to the *Freeman's Journal* could not 'imagine any more fruitful method of spreading disease', adding that it was 'very wrong to expose healthy persons to the danger of contagion in this manner'.[187]

Dr Graves, MOH for Cookstown, recommended that interments should take place as soon as possible after death to protect the living and that 'wakes' should be abolished as they were a certain method of spreading the infection.[188] At the annual meeting of the Armagh District Nursing Association, the Church of Ireland Archdeacon of Armagh stated that 'crowded houses at the solemn time of death were a contradiction of everything that was desired in a time of sorrow. It was a most undesirable custom and a most fruitful source of spreading the disease'.[189] The Archdeacon was not alone in his opinion as a correspondent to the *Belfast News-Letter* pointed out 'the habit of overcrowding houses at funerals' was 'a fruitful cause of the spread of infection during an epidemic like the present'. He believed that mothers and children who crowded into a small house at a funeral were running an unnecessary risk and that 'the crowding of children round the coffin on the street is an old custom against which the clergy have frequently protested'. The custom was particularly noticeable at that time as the children were not at school.[190]

An editorial in the *Portadown Express* on 29 November 1918, stated that it 'would like to utter a word of warning against the practice of overcrowding at wakes'. It considered that the sanitary authorities in one or two neighbouring towns had taken appropriate action by steadfastly opposing wakes during the outbreak as it was one of the greatest causes of the spread of the disease. It was hoped that 'public opinion will show its condemnation of wakes in the public interest'.[191] In December, the Dungannon rural council, were of the opinion that 'waking' victims of influenza should not be permitted and that their bodies should be buried immediately. However, although they disapproved of the custom, the council did not take any official action to stop it. The clerk stated 'the doctors should see to that'.[192]

At an emergency meeting of the Belfast public health committee on 7 December 1918, Councillor English stated: 'What he wanted to impress on the citizens was that they should avoid visiting persons suffering from septic pneumonia, and they should also keep away from wakes of those who had died from the disease'.[193] Again the council did not act on this suggestion with any official recommendation.

Under the Public Health Act (Ireland) 1878 there was provision for the LGBI to enforce 'the speedy interment of the dead' if Ireland appeared to be threatened by any formidable endemic, endemic or infectious disease. However, the LGBI did not take any action.[194] In Larne, the town clerk asked the LGBI whether any order had been made regarding persons attending wakes, however, he was given no guidance in the matter.[195] The custom of 'waking the dead' was largely associated with the Roman Catholic faith and its critics argued that the wake was little more than an excuse for excessive drinking of alcohol and general revelry in the presence of the corpse.[196] Although there were many objections to the custom during the pandemic, it seems there was no official central government sanction to forbid the holding of and attendance at wakes; it remained a recommendation of individual local authorities.

Regardless of the moral objections to wakes, the practice was one that would have facilitated the spread of the disease. At the time, infection was thought to remain in the corpse and therefore could be spread to the living. However, there is no evidence that this was the case with the influenza virus.[197] Waking the body in an open coffin would not have spread the disease through the corpse, but, wakes involved the congregation of many people in a confined space. If an attendee at the wake had influenza it could spread very quickly within a community. Problems arose due to the large number of deaths of young people that occurred in Scotland, where the disease was rife. Their bodies were subsequently waked back in Donegal and anyone who had contracted influenza could bring the infection to a wake. Traditionally an attendee at a wake would shake the hands of all the bereaved in the house and pass on their sympathies and it was this action that would have facilitated the spread of the virus throughout that household and others within the area. Thus these wakes would be instrumental in disseminating the disease in these rural districts.

Therefore, seasonal migration and the return for the burial of those infected in Scotland, along with the tradition of 'waking' the dead, could account for the high death rates in Dunfanaghy and Glenties especially during 1919. There is evidence of multiple deaths within families living in close quarters in the Dunfanaghy union district such as the Gallagher family who were farmers in Meenaboy. Sheila Gallagher, (32) and her daughter Mary (7) died from influenza on 19th February 1919. Her husband Joseph, (30), son Denis, (5) and a labourer, who lodged with them, Patrick Shovelin (21) all died four days later on 23 February 1919. On 8 March 1919, Sheila's son, John died from influenza and boronchopneumonia and the surviving children all had contracted the disease.[198]

The figures show that majority of deaths in the poor law union districts of Inishowen, Glenties, Dunfanaghy and Stranrolar and elsewhere in Donegal were people from the farming community like the Gallaghers. This implies that members of these communities were congregating in places where infection would spread quickly, maybe at church for Sunday services or funerals or more likely small, confined cottages at wakes. A more recent event that may support this theory comes from Hara in Northern Spain. Here in March 2020 more than 60 people were believed to have caught Covid-19 that was traced back to attendance at a funeral that took place in the Basque country at Vitoria-gastreiz.[199] This illustrates the danger of infection from attending crowded events such as funerals or wakes.

Although the pandemic was particularly lethal to those of the age group 20–40. In County Donegal, it was those over 65 that suffered the highest influenza mortality of any age group in both 1918 and 1919. The 1911 census shows that 19.22% of males and 21.13% of females in County Donegal were over 60 years of age as compared to 12.17% males and 13.55% females in the province of Ulster.[200] Seasonal migration in some cases could lead to permanent settlement overseas of young men and women, which resulted in a high percentage of older people living in this part of the country.[201] Older people were more vulnerable to any influenza pandemic including this one. Furthermore the deaths of those young men and women who died from influenza in Scotland were registered in Scotland before their bodies were returned to Donegal to be buried. This gives the impression that those between the ages of 15–45 did not suffer to the same extent as the older age group in

Donegal. However, this age group was as susceptible in County Donegal as elsewhere.

The high death rates in Donegal were due to several local factors peculiar to that county at the time. First, the presence of the military and naval bases on the Inishowen peninsula acted as a point of entry for the virus from soldiers within the district. Once in Inishowen, the virus could spread via the rail networks to other parts of the district. The practice of seasonal migration meant that young people from rural Donegal travelled to areas in Scotland where influenza was rife. They lived in unsanitary, crowded conditions making them vulnerable to infection and inevitably many died of influenza. The return of their bodies to Donegal for burial, meant that a wake would take place in confined crowded cottages. If anybody attending had the virus, it could spread very quickly within a community. Wakes would have been commonplace in this part of the country so this may explain why so many people from the rural farming community in Donegal succumbed to influenza.

Influenza Morbidity

Unfortunately calculating accurate morbidity figures for influenza is problematic as it was not a notifiable disease. Therefore, instances of influenza did not have to be reported to doctors and were not counted.[202] Influenza morbidity data was rarely collected and, even if it was, it was generally inaccurate as the disease was often self-diagnosed and self-treated and only a small proportion of cases visited a doctor.[203] Difficulties in calculating exact numbers of Irish people infected by the disease were illustrated in Lurgan when the MOH, Dr Samuel Agnew disputed reports that between 500 and 600 people in the town had contracted influenza, during one week in November. He admitted that he did not know exact numbers of influenza sufferers, but acknowledged the difficultly in calculating an accurate figure as many sufferers had not visited a doctor.[204]

It has been suggested by Jeffery K. Taubenberger and David M. Morens that the mortality rate of the 1918–19 virus was 2.5% of those infected compared to around 0.1% during other influenza pandemics.[205] Using this calculation, an approximate morbidity figure for Ireland can be calculated. Table 2.5 shows the estimated morbidity figures for the four provinces of Ireland using the official mortality figures. It shows that

Table 2.5 Recorded Influenza mortality and estimated morbidity in the four provinces of Ireland

Province	*Total population*	*Influenza deaths*			*Estimated morbidity*
		1918	*1919*	*Total 1918 and 1919*	
Leinster	1,162,044	3,535	2,588	6,123	245,000
Ulster	1,581,696	4,773	2,809	7,582	303,000
Munster	1,035,495	1,646	2,187	3,833	153,000
Connaught	610,984	697	1,822	2,519	101,000
Total	4,390,219	10,651	9,406	20,057	802,000

as many as 802,000 people or 18% of the Irish population contracted influenza during 1918 and 1919.

These figures are of course only estimates but still indicate how infectious the disease was, and the likely extent of absenteeism and disruption to local industries that would have resulted. While the disruption to everyday life will be discussed in-depth in Chapters 6–10 some examples are worthy of note here. Generally, there were factory closures and staff shortages in businesses throughout Ireland. Gaelic Athletic Association (GAA) matches were postponed throughout the country. Culminating in the postponement of the All Ireland Hurling Final in November 1918 because of influenza, but it was eventually played on 26 January 1919.[206] Meetings and dances throughout the country were postponed. Schools and technical colleges throughout Ireland were closed as were and public libraries.[207] Despite the disruption caused by the disease, everyday life had to go on. The following recollection from Jack Pole, from Nenagh, County Tipperary perhaps sums up best how some people dealt with the situation. He advised that one of his earliest childhood memories concerned the influenza pandemic. He recollected:

> Our entire house was stricken with flu. I was the youngest, but I think I must have got some sort of immunity because I was always running around with hot drinks. We had no antibiotics. Nothing to treat the symptoms. My father carried on anyway, the farm had to go on. Cows had to be milked'[208]

Who Died from Influenza?

Ida Milne suggests that the collated weekly death statistics for Dublin indicate that high death rates from influenza 'were not so much class-dependent as job- dependent'. She states that people who worked with the public such as shop workers, police, medical personnel, bank officials and clergy were more likely to be infected by influenza and subsequently die from the disease.[209] The death toll in the Royal Irish Constabulary (RIC) throughout Ireland was high especially during the second wave. Three members of the RIC died in July 1918 from influenza or pneumonia, but during the second more virulent wave 63 members of the force died between 1 October 1918 and the end of January 1919 while in the third wave, between the 1 February 1919 and the end of May 1919, there were 27 fatalities from influenza and pneumonia.[210]

In Ulster towns, people dealing with the public were also at greater risk with many deaths reported of policemen, nurses and doctors. Also, not surprisingly, there were many fatalities among the military and in the naval port of Larne, sailors. Added to this were those people who worked in crowded conditions in factories, especially linen and textile factories in large industrial towns such as Belfast, Lurgan, Londonderry and Newry. However, factory workers in many smaller Ulster towns such as Bessbrook outside Newry and Upperlands in Maghera were also at risk. While it's often understood or assumed that it's the cramped living conditions of urban areas that contribute to high death rates, disease spreading uncontrollably in crowded rural housing is also a major factor. Take, for example, Donegal where all members of the Gallagher family contracted influenza and five family members and a lodger died, indicating that families in rural areas who lived in very close quarters were at particular risk.

There are many questions still to be answered about Influenza morbidity and mortality during both 1918 and 1919 and, as previously stated, it is unlikely that completely accurate Irish influenza mortality figures can ever be calculated. Nevertheless, with the information that we do have, between 23,288 and 34,310 people could have died from influenza or pneumonia during 1918 and 1919 and at least 802,000 people could have contracted the disease. As in other countries, those between the ages of 25 and 35 had an unusually high death rate in both 1918 and 1919. However, in Ireland it was those that were under one year of age that had the highest death rate in 1919 and the second-highest death rate in 1918, highlighting again the high infant mortality in cities such as Dublin and Belfast where poverty and working practices could leave children vulnerable to disease and especially this influenza pandemic. In the following Chapter these issues along with influenza and factory workers will be discussed in more detail.

Notes

1. Beveridge (1977, p. 31).
2. Engberg (2009, p 434).
3. Echeverri (2003, p. 173).
4. *The Times*, 3 June 1918.
5. Echeverri (2003, p. 173) and Crosby (2003, p. 26).
6. Graves (1969, p. 18) and Langford (2005, p. 492).
7. Oxford (2001, pp. 1857–1859) and Oxford et al. (2002, pp. 111–115); Oxford et al. (2005, pp. 940–945).
8. French (1920, p. 66).
9. Oxford and Lambkin (2005, p. 211).
10. Patterson and Pyle (1991, p. 5).
11. Barry (2004, pp. 92–93).
12. *The Times*, 15 January 1920.
13. United States Navy Department, *Annual Report of the Secretary of the Navy, Miscellaneous Reports* (Washington, 1919), pp. 2423–2425.
14. *Weekly Returns of Births and Deaths in the Dublin Registration Area and in Eighteen of the Principal Towns in Ireland 1918*, (Dublin, 1919) and *Weekly Returns of Births and Deaths in the Dublin Registration Area and in Eighteen of the Principal Towns in Ireland 1919*, (Dublin, 1920)—pneumonia peaks in the major Irish towns were calculated using these reports.
15. *Forty-Seventh Annual Report of the Local Government Board for Ireland for Year Ended 31 March 1919* (1920) xxi, CMD 578, p. xxxvii.
16. *Belfast Evening Telegraph*, 11 June 1918; *Belfast News-Letter*, 12 June 1918.
17. The Public Records Office Northern Ireland [Hereafter PRONI], LA/20/9/AA/5, Bangor Public Health Committee meeting, 2 July 1918; PRONI, LA/38/9/AA/3, Holywood Public Health Committee Minutes, 4 July 1919.
18. PRONI, LA/51/9/D/6, Lurgan Medical Officer of Health Report, 1 July 1918; PRONI, LA/48/9/AB/6, Lisburn Medical Officer of Health Report, 1 July 1918.
19. PRONI, BG/4/A/69, Ballymena Board of Guardians Minutes, 22 June 1918.

20. The National Archive [Hereafter TNA], WO 35/179/4, Returns: Historical Review of medical and sanitary work in the Irish Command during the war, Report on King George V Hospital during the period 1914–1919. *Irish Independent*, 25 June 1918,
21. *Annual Report of the Secretary of the Navy*, pp. 2423–2425.
22. *Irish Independent*, 20 June 1918; *Irish Independent*, 24 June 1918; *Waterford Standard*, 3 July 1918.
23. *Sligo Independent*, 6 July 1918.
24. *Annual Report of the Secretary of the Navy*, pp. 2423–2425.
25. TNA, WO 35/179/4, Returns: historical review of medical and sanitary work in the Irish Command during the war, Historical review of the medical and sanitary work of the Cork District; *Nenagh Guardian*, 6 July 1918.
26. TNA, WO 35/179/4, Returns: historical review of medical and sanitary work in the Irish Command during the war, Report of the medical and sanitary work of the Ulster Brigade, p. 4.
27. Reports about the returning soldiers bringing the disease to Ireland appeared in the following newspapers and this will be discussed in more detail in Chapter 4; *Irish News*, 12 July 1918; *Irish Independent*, 24 June 1918; *Derry Journal*, 26 June 1918.
28. Patricia Marsh, 'The Impact of the Linen Industry on Lurgan' (M.A. thesis, Queen's University Belfast, 2004), p. 75.
29. *Irish Times*, 1 October 1918; *Irish Independent*, 1 October 1918.
30. *Irish Independent*, 25 June 1918, TNA WO 35/179/4, Returns: historical review of medical and sanitary work in the Irish Command during the war, Report on King George V Hospital, p. 5.
31. *Irish Times*, 16 October 1918; *Irish Independent*, 25 October 1918.
32. *Irish Independent*, 18 October 1918, *New Ross Standard*, 18 October1918; *Irish Independent*, 25 October 1918.
33. *Kilkenny Moderator*, 26 October 1918.
34. *Irish Independent*, 18 October 1918; Ibid., 21 October 1918; Ibid., 23 October 1918.
35. *Irish Times*, 28 October 1918.
36. TNA, WO 35/179/4, Returns: historical review of medical and sanitary work in the Irish Command during the war, Historical review of the Cork District.
37. Ibid., *Irish Independent*, 25 October 1918; *Irish Independent*, 4 November 1918.
38. TNA, WO 35/179/4), Returns: historical review of medical and sanitary work in the Irish Command during the war, Historical review of the Cork District 4–5; *Nenagh Guardian*, 6 July 1918.
39. *Irish Times*, 24 October 1918.
40. *Irish Independent*, 18 October 1918 and 21 October 1918.

41. *Irish Times*, 28 October 1918.
42. *Leitrim Observer*, 19 October 1918 and 26 October 1918.
43. *Irish Independent*, 23 October 1918; *Sligo Champion*, 16 November 1918.
44. *Leitrim Observer*, 9 November 1918, *Sligo Champion*, 16 November 1918.
45. PRONI, BG/17/A/132; Larne Board of Guardians Minutes, 9 October 1918.
46. *Irish News*, 11 October 1918.
47. *Irish Independent*, 25 October 1918; *Mid-Ulster Mail*, 31 October 1918.
48. *Belfast News-Letter*, 22 October 1918.
49. *Anglo-Celt*, 2 November 1918.
50. *Irish Independent*, 21 October 1918.
51. *Irish Independent*, 25 October 1918.
52. *Belfast Evening Telegraph*, 1 November 1918; Donegal County Archives Collection, Lifford, BG/38/1/83, Ballyshannon Board of Guardians Minutes, 16 November 1918.
53. Donegal County Archives Collection, Lifford, BG/97/1/58, Inishowen Board of Guardians meeting, 4 November 1918; *Freeman's Journal*, 6 November 1918.
54. PRONI, LA/38/9/AA/3, Holywood Public Health Committee Minutes, 7 November. 1918.
55. PRONI, LA/60/2/CA/5, Newtownards Urban District Council Minutes, 4 November 1918.
56. *Down Recorder*, 16 November 1918; *Down Recorder*, 30 November 1918.
57. *Belfast News-Letter*, 30 October 1918.
58. TNA, WO 35/179/4, Returns: historical review of medical and sanitary work in the Irish Command during the war: Report of the Ulster Brigade, p. 3.
59. *Lurgan Mail*, 26 October 1918.
60. PRONI, LA/64/2/CA/8, Portadown Borough Council Minutes, 4 November 1918.
61. *Irish Independent*, 5 February1919; *Irish Times*, 17 February 1919.
62. *Dublin Evening Telegraph*, 7 February 1919.
63. TNA, WO 35/179/4, Returns: historical review of medical and sanitary work in the Irish Command during the war, Report on King George V Hospital, p. 5.
64. *Kilkenny Moderator*, 5 February 1919.
65. *Irish Times*, 22 February 1919.
66. TNA, WO 35/179/4, Returns: historical review of medical and sanitary work in the Irish Command during the war, Historical review of the Cork District, p. 4; *Irish Independent*, 17 February 1919.

67. *Irish Times*, 17 February 1919.
68. *Irish Independent*, 14 February 1919.
69. *Connaught Tribune*, 22 February 1919.
70. *Irish Times*, 26 February 1919.
71. *Connaught Tribune*, 22 March 1919; *Connaught Tribune*, 12 April 1919.
72. PRONI, LA/38/9/AA/3, Holywood Public Health Committee Minutes, 6 February 1919.
73. *Irish Independent*, 12 February 1919.
74. PRONI LA/51/9/D/6, Lurgan Medical Officer of Health Report, 1 March 1919.
75. *Portadown Express*, 28 February 1919; 14 March 1919.
76. *Irish Independent*, 10 February 1919; *Frontier Sentinel*, 22 February 1919.
77. *Newry Reporter*, 11 March 1919.
78. *Belfast News-Letter*, 12 March 1919.
79. *Irish Independent*, 17 February 1919.
80. *Derry Journal*, 12 March 1919.
81. *Derry People*, 1 March 1919.
82. *Irish News*, 15 January 1919.
83. *Irish News*, 20 February 1919.
84. 'A General Account of Influenza in the United Kingdom During 1918–19', pp. 53–54.
85. *Belfast News-Letter*, 13 March 1919.
86. *Irish News*, 20 February 1919.
87. *Fermanagh Times*, 27 February 1919.
88. *Irish Times*, 1 March 1919.
89. *Belfast News-Letter*, 26 February 1919.
90. Shaded areas represent those counties that suffered higher mortality in the third wave than in the first two waves.
91. Johnson and Mueller (2002, p. 108).
92. Beveridge (1977, p. 32).
93. Patterson and Pyle (1991, p. 19).
94. Johnson and Mueller (2002, p. 115).
95. Ibid.
96. Patterson and Pyle (1991, p. 13).
97. Thompson (1920, p. 1).
98. Burke (1987, p. 278).
99. *Fifty-Fifth Detailed Annual Report of the Registrar-General (Ireland) (1918) (Births, Deaths and Marriages)*, SP 1919 [Cmd.450], x, 849, p. v; *Fifty-Sixth Detailed Annual Report of the Registrar-General (Ireland) (1919) (Births, Deaths and Marriages)*, SP 1920 [Cmd.997], xi, 629, pp. v and xxv.

100. *Supplement to the Eighty-First Annual Report of the Registrar-General of Births, Deaths and Marriages in England and Wales: Report on the Mortality from Influenza in England and Wales During the Epidemic of 1918–19* [Cmd 700], H. C. 1920, x, 791; *Report on the Mortality from Influenza in ScotlandDuring the Epidemic of 1918–19: A Supplement to the Annual Reports of the Registrar-General for Scotland* [Cmd 282], H. C. 1919, x, 1223.
101. Thompson (1920, pp. 1–14).
102. Barrington (1987, p. 12).
103. *Weekly Returns of Births and Deaths in the Dublin Registration Area and in Eighteen of the Principal Towns in Ireland 1918* and *Weekly Returns of Births and Deaths in the Dublin Registration Area and in Eighteen of the Principal Towns in Ireland 1919.*
104. Johnson and Mueller (2002, pp. 108–109).
105. Johnson and Mueller (2002, p. 113); *Fifty-Fifth Detailed Annual Report of the Registrar-General (Ireland)*, p. v and *Fifty-Sixth Detailed Annual Report of the Registrar-General (Ireland)*, pp. v and xxv.
106. Milne (2018, p. 59).
107. Johnson and Mueller (2002, p. 109).
108. *Fifty-Fifth Detailed Annual Report of the Registrar-General (Ireland)*, p. v; *Fifty-Sixth Detailed Annual Report of the Registrar-General (Ireland)*, pp. v and xxv; Thompson (1920, pp. 1–2).
109. Patricia Marsh, 'The Effect of the 1918–19 Influenza Pandemic on Belfast' (M.A. thesis, Queen's University Belfast, 2006), 42; See also Milne (2018, pp. 58–59).
110. *Report on the Mortality from Influenza in England and Wales During the Epidemic of 1918–19*, p. 3.
111. Ibid.
112. Ibid.
113. Ibid., pp. 3–4.
114. Ibid., p. 4.
115. Johnson (2006, pp. 71–72).
116. Johnson (2003, pp. 134–136).
117. Fitzpatrick (1996, p. 388).
118. *Report on the Mortality from Influenza in England and Wales During the Epidemic of 1918–19*, p. 3.
119. The averages of the previous five years was used in line with the Registrar-General for England and Wales' recommendations as this was deemed to represent the average normal experience at that time.
120. Average figures calculated by using figures from *Annual Reports of the Registrar-General (Ireland)* for years 1913–1917.
121. Average figures calculated by using figures from the *Annual Reports of the Registrar-General (Ireland)* for years 1913–1917.

122. *Report on the Mortality from Influenza in England and Wales During the Epidemic of 1918–19*, p. 3.
123. *Fifty-Fifth Detailed Annual Report of the Registrar-General (Ireland)*, p. xxiii.
124. *Fifty-Sixth detailed Annual Report of the Registrar-General (Ireland)*, p. xxiv.
125. Johnson (2006, pp. 73).
126. Stuart-Harris and Schild (1976, p. 103).
127. *Fifty-Fifth Detailed Annual Report of the Registrar-General (Ireland)*, p. xxiii.
128. *Fifty-Sixth Detailed Annual Report of the Registrar-General (Ireland)*, p. xxiv.
129. Johnson (2003, p. 138), Johnson (2006, p. 73).
130. Stuart-Harris and Schild (1976, p. 106).
131. Siriwardena (2012, pp. 1636–1637).
132. Sandra Tomkins 'Britain and the Influenza Epidemic 1918–1919' (Ph.D. thesis, University of Cambridge, 1989), p. 29.
133. Pearl (1919, p. 536).
134. Ibid., p. 537.
135. Johnson (2006, p. 73).
136. *Fifty-Fifth Detailed Annual Report of the Registrar-General (Ireland)*, xvii.
137. *Fifty-Sixth Detailed Annual Report of the Registrar-General (Ireland)*, xxi.
138. *Fifty-Seventh Detailed Annual Report of the Registrar-General (Ireland) (1920) (Births, Deaths and Marriages)*, SP 1921 [Cmd.1532], ix, 47, 17.
139. Noymer and Garenne (2000, pp. 570–573).
140. Noymer and Garenne (2000, p. 578).
141. Thompson (1920, p. 14.).
142. Beveridge (1977, p. 31).
143. Noymer and Garenne (2000, pp. 566–567).
144. Echeverri (2003, p. 183) and McCracken and Curson (2003, p. 121).
145. French (1920, pp. 90–91).
146. Johnson (2006, p. 84).
147. Thompson (1920, p. 8).
148. *Fifty-Fifth Detailed Annual Report of the Registrar-General (Ireland)*, p. 58.
149. Thompson (1920, p. 183).
150. *Fifty-Sixth Detailed Annual Report of the Registrar-General (Ireland)*, xvi.
151. Figures calculated from *Fifty-Fifth Detailed Annual Report of the Registrar-General (Ireland)*, xvi and *Fifty-Sixth Detailed Annual Report of the Registrar-General (Ireland)*, xvii.

152. Macnamara (1954, p. 308).
153. Langford (2002, p. 2).
154. Barrington (1987, p. 75).
155. Coey Biggar (1917, p. 2).
156. Reid et al. (2001, p. 83).
157. Johnson (2006, p. 88).
158. Reid et al. (2001, p. 83).
159. Catherine. Paddock, 'Why Was 1918 Flu Pandemic so Deadly? Research Offers New Clue.' *Medical News Today*, (written on 29 Apr. 2014) https://www.medicalnewstoday.com/articles/276060, Accessed 21 January 2021.
160. Reid et al. (2001, p. 83).
161. Smith (2007, p. 23).
162. TNA, WO 35/179/4Returns: historical review of medical and sanitary work in the Irish Command during the war, Report of the medical and sanitary work of the Dublin and Curragh Brigade, sanitary work during the war, 2.
163. Milne (2018, p. 63).
164. *Fifty-Fifth Detailed Annual Report of the Registrar-General (Ireland)*, xvi–xvii.
165. Milne (2018, p. 63).
166. *Fifty-Sixth Detailed Annual Report of the Registrar-General (Ireland)*, xiii.
167. Information for graph taken from *Fifty-Fifth Detailed Annual Report of the Registrar-General (Ireland)*, xvii and *Fifty-Sixth Detailed Annual Report of the Registrar-General (Ireland)*, xvii.
168. Newman (1920, pp. xii–xiii).
169. Johnson (2004, p. 220).
170. Patterson and Pyle (1991, p. 10).
171. *Fifty-Fifth Detailed Annual Report of the Registrar-General (Ireland)*, pp. 50–51 and *Fifty-Sixth Detailed Annual Report of the Registrar-General (Ireland)*, pp. 50–51.
172. These figures were calculated using the information on IrishGeneology.ie from the indexes to the Civil Records of Irish Deaths in 1918 and 1919 for Clones poor law union found on https://civilrecords.irishgenealogy.ie/churchrecords/civil-search.jsp.
173. *Derry Journal*, 4 December 1918,
174. Milne (2018, pp. 63–44 and 102).
175. TNA, WO 35/179/4, Returns: historical review of medical and sanitary work in the Irish Command during the war, Report of the Ulster Brigade, Appendix D; BBC Radio Ulster: Lough Swilly, County Donegal: The Grand Fleet takes shelter.
176. *Derry People*, 9 November 1918.

177. Freeman (1940–1941, p. 40).
178. Clear (2008, p. 166).
179. *Irish Independent*, 19 July 1918.
180. MacFhionnghaile (1987, p. 127).
181. *Belfast News-Letter*, 13 March 1919.
182. *Ulster Herald*, 21 December 1918.
183. *Ulster Herald*, 1 March 1919, *Down Recorder*, 8 March 1919.
184. Collier (1974, p. 76).
185. *Irish Times*, 4 November 1918.
186. *Freeman's Journal*, 2 November 1918; *Irish Independent*, 2 November 1918, *Irish Times*, 4 November 1918.
187. *Freeman's Journal*, 20 November 1918.
188. *Mid-Ulster Mail*, 30 November 1918.
189. *Armagh Guardian*, 6 December 1918.
190. *Belfast News-Letter*, 26 November 1918.
191. *Portadown Express*, 29 November 1918.
192. *Tyrone Courier*, 19 December 1918.
193. *Belfast News-Letter*, 9 December 1918; *Irish News*, 9 December 1918.
194. Elliott and Elliott (1907, p. 40).
195. PRONI LA/43/2/7A/4, Proceedings of the Larne Urban Sanitary Authority and Urban District Council, 11 November 1918.
196. Strange (2005, p. 87).
197. Bakhshi (2001, p. 284).
198. *Derry People*, 12 March 1919.
199. *The Guardian*, 7 March 2020.
200. Figures calculated from the 1911 census of Ulster, age of population tables.
201. Freeman (1943, p. 3).
202. Tomkins (1992, p. 441).
203. Johnson (2003, p. 144).
204. *Irish Independent*, 4 November 1918; *Lurgan Mail*, 9 November 1918.
205. Taubenberger and Morens (2006, p. 15).
206. *Irish Independent*, 25 January1919.
207. *Irish News*, 9, 16, 23 November 1918, *Newry Reporter*, 10 November 1918.
208. Fennell and Banbury (2006, p. 99).
209. Milne (2018, p. 71).
210. Raw data supplied by Peter McGoldrick in association with his article 'Police Deaths in Ireland as a Result of the Spanish Flu Epidemic, 1918' (January 2021).
211. Figures taken from the *Annual Reports of the Registrar-General (Ireland)* for years 1913 to 1921.

212. Figures from the 1911 census of Ulster, age of population tables and *Fifty-Fifth Detailed Annual Report of the Registrar-General (Ireland) (1918)*, p. xxiii and *Fifty-Sixth Detailed Annual Report of the Registrar-General (Ireland) (1919)*, p. xvi.

References

Bakhshi, S. S. 'Code of Practice for Funeral Workers: Managing Infection Risk and Body Bagging', *Communicable Disease and Public Health*, 4:4 (2001): 283–287.

Barrington, Ruth. *Health, Medicine and Politics in Ireland 1900–1970*. Dublin: Institute of Public Administration, 1987.

Barry, John M. *The Great Influenza: The Epic Story of the Deadliest Plague in History*. New York: Viking Books, 2004.

Beveridge W. I. B. *Influenza: The Last Great Plague: An Unfinished Story of Discovery*. London: Heinemann, 1977.

Burke, Helen. *The People and the Poor Law in Nineteenth Century Ireland*. Dublin: Arlen House,1987.

Clear, Caitriona. 'Fewer Ladies, More Women', in *Our War: Ireland and the Great War*, edited by John Horne, 157–170. Dublin: Royal Irish Academy, 2008.

Coey Biggar, E. *Report on the Physical Welfare of Mothers and Children*. The Carnegie United Kingdom Trust, Vol. 4 (Ireland). Dublin, 1917.

Collier, Richard. *The Plague of the Spanish Lady: The Influenza Pandemic of 1918–1919*. London: Macmillan, 1974.

Crosby, Alfred W. *America's Forgotten Pandemic: The Influenza of 1918*. Cambridge: Cambridge University Press, 2003.

Echeverri, Beatriz. 'Spanish Influenza Seen from Spain', in *Spanish Influenza Pandemic of 1918–1919: New Perspectives*, edited by Howard Phillips and David Killingray, 173–189. London: Routledge, 2003.

Elliott, Martin and Gilbert Elliott. *The Public Health Acts and Other Sanitary Laws and Regulations*. London: H. K Lewis, 1907.

Engberg, Elizabeth. 'Invisible Flu: Community Response to the 1918–1920 Flu Pandemic in the Rural Areas of North Sweden', *Varia História*, 25:42 (December 2009): 429–456.

Fennell, James and Turtle Banbury. *Vanishing Ireland*. Dublin: Hodder Headline Ireland, 2006.

Fitzpatrick, David. 'Militarism in Ireland 1900–1922', in *A Military History of Ireland*, edited by Thomas Bartlett and Keith Jeffery, 379–406. Cambridge: Cambridge University Press, 1996.

Freeman, T. W. 'The Changing Distribution of Population in Donegal, with Special Reference to the Congested Areas', *Journal of Statistical and Social Inquiry Society of Ireland*, 16:4 (1940/1941): 31–46.

Freeman, T. W. 'The Congested Districts of Western Ireland', *The Geographical Review*, 33:1 (January 1943): 1–14.

French, Herbert C. B. E. 'The Clinical Features of the Influenza Epidemic of 1918–19', in *Ministry of Health, Report on the Pandemic of Influenza, 1918–19*, 66–109. London: HMSO, 1920.

Graves, Charles. *Invasion by Virus: Can It Happen Again?* London: Icon Books Limited, 1969.

Johnson, Niall P. A. S. and Juergan Mueller. 'Updating the Accounts: Global Mortality of the 1918–1920 "Spanish" Influenza Pandemic', *Bulletin of the History of Medicine*, 76:1 (2002): 105–115.

Johnson, Niall P. A. S. 'The Overshadowed Killer: Influenza in Britain', in *Spanish Influenza Pandemic of 1918–1919: New Perspectives*, edited by Howard Phillips and David Killingray, 132–156. London: Routledge, 2003.

Johnson, Niall P. A. S. 'Scottish 'Flu: The Scottish Experience of "Spanish Flu"', *The Scottish Historical Review*, 83:2 (2004): 216–226.

Johnson, Niall. *Britain and the 1918–19 Influenza Pandemic: A Dark Epilogue*. London: Routledge, 2006.

Langford, Christopher. 'Did the 1918–19 Influenza Pandemic Originate in China?', *Population and Development Review*, 31:3 (2005): 473–505.

Langford, Christopher. 'The Age Pattern of Mortality in the 1918–19 Influenza Pandemic: An Attempted Explanation Based on Data for England and Wales', *Medical History*, 46:1 (2002): 1–20.

MacFhionnghaile, Niall. *Donegal, Ireland and the First World War*. Donegal: An Crann, 1987.

Macnamara, D. W. Dr. 'Memories of 1918 and "The 'Flu"', *Journal of the Irish Medical Association*, 35:208 (1954): 304–309.

McCracken, Kevin and Peter Curson. 'Flu Downunder: A Demographic and Geographic Analysis of the 1919 Epidemic in Sydney, Australia', in *Spanish Influenza Pandemic of 1918–1919: New Perspectives*, edited by Howard Phillips and David Killingray, 110–131. London: Routledge, 2003.

Milne, Ida. *Stacking the Coffins: Influenza, War and Revolution in Ireland, 1918–19*. Manchester: Manchester University Press, 2018.

Newman, Sir George. 'Chief Medical Officer's Introduction', in *Ministry of Health, Report on the Pandemic of Influenza, 1918–19*, iv–xxiii. London: HMSO, 1920.

Noymer, Andrew and Michel Garenne. 'The 1918 Influenza Epidemic's Effects on Sex Differentials in Mortality in the United States', *Population and Development Review*, 26:3 (2000): 565–581.

Oxford, J. S. 'The So-called Spanish Influenza Pandemic of 1918 May Have Originated in France in 1916', *Philosophical Transactions of the Royal Society*, 356 (2001): 1857–1859.

Oxford, John S. and Robert Lambkin. 'Mother Nature and the Great Influenza Pandemic', *Biologist*, 52:4 (August 2005): 211–212.

Oxford, J. S., et al. 'A Hypothesis: The Conjunction of Soldiers, Gas, Pigs, Ducks, Geese and Horses in Northern France During the Great War Provided the Conditions for the Emergence of the "Spanish" Influenza Pandemic of 1918–1919', *Vaccine*, 23:7 (2005): 940–945.

Oxford, J. S., et al. 'World War I May Have Allowed the Emergence of "Spanish Influenza"', *The Lancet Infectious Diseases*, 2:2 (2002): 111–114.

Patterson, David and Gerald F. Pyle. 'The Geography and Mortality of the 1918 Influenza Pandemic', *Bulletin of the History of Medicine*, 76:1 (1991): 4–21.

Pearl, Raymond. 'Note on the Incidence of Epidemic Influenza Among the Actively Tuberculous', *American Statistical Association*, 16:128 (December 1919): 536–540.

Reid, Ann H., et al. 'The 1918 Spanish influenza: Integrating history and biology', *Microbes and Infection*, 3:1 (2001): 81–87.

Siriwardena, A. Niroshan. 'Increasing Evidence That Influenza Is a Trigger for Cardiovascular Disease', *The Journal of Infectious Diseases*, 206:11 (2012): 1636–1638.

Smith, Kerri. 'Concern as Revived 1918 Flu Virus Kills Monkeys', *Nature*, 445 (18 January 2007): 237.

Strange, Julie-Marie. *Death, Grief and Poverty in Britain, 1870–1914.* Cambridge: Cambridge University Press, 2005.

Stuart-Harris, Charles H. and Geoffrey C. Schild. *Influenza: The Viruses and the Disease*. London: Edward Arnold, 1976.

Taubenberger, Jeffery K. and David M. Morens. '1918 Influenza: Mother of All Pandemics', *Emerging Infectious Diseases*, 12:1 (2006): 15–22.

Thompson, William J. 'Mortality from Influenza in Ireland', *Journal of the Statistical and Social Inquiry Society of Ireland*, 14:1 (1920): 1–14.

Tomkins, Sandra M. 'The Failure of Expertise: Public Health Policy Britain During the 1918–1919 Influenza Epidemic', *Social History of Medicine*, 5:3 (1992): 435–454.

CHAPTER 3

'Woe unto Them That Are with Child': Gender and Influenza

Introduction

The influenza pandemic of 1918 appeared to be an indiscriminate killer, attacking and killing children, old people, young adults, rich and poor alike. However, as discussed in Chapter 2, there were certain patterns that were specific to this pandemic such as the global peculiarity of how it targeted young adults. Niall Johnson noted that different locations showed a slight difference in mortality between genders, which did not appear to be significant or consistent. Yet the United States (US), Australia, New Zealand, Norway and South Africa reported noticeably more male deaths than female.[1] The question of gender in Ireland is interesting as official figures for the island of Ireland show that male mortality was higher than female, but in the province of Ulster more women than men died.

The role of women during the pandemic, as in many other areas, has gone unnoticed, but women played an important part in combating influenza. They were the main care givers within the home, looking after family members who contracted influenza and many worked in both a voluntary and professional level as nurses. They also stepped up to the mark by working in munitions and other factories during the war. This chapter explores gender in relation to influenza, particularly in the province of Ulster. Gender-related mortality is examined and compared with Scotland, England and Wales. As the title suggests, pregnant women

P. Marsh, *The Spanish Flu in Ireland*, Palgrave Studies in Economic History, https://doi.org/10.1007/978-3-030-79500-9_3

were deemed to be at particular risk from influenza. Their susceptibility to the disease and subsequent mortality is explored. Female activity such as nursing family members along with volunteer and professional nursing is discussed along with one of the main areas of female employment in Ulster, factory work. Posing the question: was gender a deciding factor in susceptibility to the disease.

Ulster had the highest influenza mortality of any province in Ireland, but it was Leinster that had the highest death rate. In 1918 the Registrar-General for Ireland (RGI), Sir William Thompson, estimated that 5,591 males and 5,060 females died from influenza in Ireland in that year,[2] while in 1919 there were 4,921 male and 4,485 female deaths.[3] This equates to 4.79 per thousand of the male population and 4.34 per thousand of the female population dying of influenza in Ireland during the pandemic.

In Scotland, England and Wales more female deaths were recorded than male. The Registrar-General for England and Wales re-calculated the female deaths in those countries at approximately 100,000 and the male deaths at 84,000.[4] In Scotland, 8,403 or 47.8% of the male population, and 9,172 or 52.2% of the female population, died from influenza between July 1918 and April 1919. However, the Registrar-General for Scotland stated that this did not indicate that the pandemic was more fatal to females than males in that country as the rates depended on estimated populations which were unreliable due to the war.[5] Interestingly, although more male than female influenza deaths were recorded in Ireland, in the province of Ulster the official figures indicate there were slightly more female than male deaths. There were 3,773 male and 3,809 female influenza deaths recorded in the nine counties for 1918 and 1919, equating to 4.89 per thousand of the male population and 4.69 per thousand of female population. This is hardly surprising as there was a higher female than male population in the province. However, calculations show, slightly more females than males died from influenza in counties Armagh, Donegal, Londonderry and Belfast County Borough (see Table 3.1). This chapter will discuss the reasons why the female death rate might be higher in these counties.

Pregnant Women and Influenza

Sandra Tomkins suggested that pregnant women within the young adult age group were particularly vulnerable to attack from influenza.[7] Niall

Table 3.1 Gender-specific death rates from influenza per thousand of the male/female population (1911 census) in Ulster for years 1918 and 1919[6]

Counties in Ulster	*Influenza mortality*		*Influenza mortality per thousand of population*	
	Male	*Female*	*Male*	*Female*
Belfast County Borough	848	982	4.68	4.77
Antrim	369	335	3.94	3.34
Armagh	327	365	5.58	5.91
Cavan	194	145	4.06	3.34
Donegal	523	551	6.18	6.57
Down	533	529	5.44	4.97
Fermanagh	127	109	4.01	3.62
Londonderry County and County Borough	319	364	4.71	4.99
Monaghan	202	166	5.62	4.68
Tyrone	331	263	4.61	3.71

Johnson argued that an important component of female mortality—the death of pregnant women—was masked by the Scottish Registrar-General's remarks that the higher incidence of female deaths in Scotland did not indicate that it was more fatal to females than males.[8] In Scotland there were 266 deaths from 'diseases and accidents of pregnancy and childbirth associated with influenza, 2.9% of the total recorded female deaths from the disease.[9] Aleck Bourne stated that in England and Wales the influenza mortality of all women aged between 15 and 49 during the pandemic was 4.9 per thousand of female population, but that of pregnant women was between 5.3 and 5.7 per thousand of pregnant women.[10] Alice Reid advised that studies performed in the US found that, compared to women not recorded as pregnant, expectant women had a 50% higher chance of developing pneumonic complications. Once complications had developed, such women were 50% more likely to die. Studies of the two subsequent epidemics and of non-epidemic seasons have shown that pregnant women were at particularly high risk from influenza towards the end of their pregnancy.[11] During the 'Asian flu' outbreak in 1957, women were particularly vulnerable during the last trimester of their pregnancy.[12]

The mortality among pregnant women during both the 1918 and 1957 pandemics appeared to be abnormally high. In the US during 1918, among the 1,350 reported influenza cases among pregnant women, the proportion of deaths was said to be 27%. In Chicago in 1918, 45% of the 86 pregnant women hospitalised with influenza died.[13] In 1920, Dr Joseph, Medical Officer of Health (MOH) for Warrington, confirmed the danger that pregnant women were under. He reported that 'influenza was especially deleterious to pregnant women and women in child-birth'. It was his belief that 'the pregnant woman was more liable to the disease than the average woman at the same age'.[14] He stated that 'There is no doubt that an attack of influenza occurring towards the end of pregnancy was a very serious matter, both for mother and child'.[15]

As there was no supplementary study of the pandemic for Ireland, the subject of pregnancy-related mortality due to influenza was not investigated at the time or subsequently. The Registrar-General for Ireland's (RGI) report for 1918 stated that of the 509 deaths definitely returned as either caused or associated with pregnancy or childbearing, 26 were due to influenza and 15 to pneumonia, equating to 8.1% of pregnancy-related deaths.[16] In 1919, 524 deaths were returned as either caused or associated with pregnancy or childbearing, 53 of these were due to influenza and six to pneumonia, equating to 11.3% of pregnancy related deaths.[17] Although these figures might not seem overly high, the RGI reported in 1919 that:

> There is not much difference in the mortality from septic puerperal conditions and accidents of childbirth as compared with 1918, but the deaths from causes associated with pregnancy have increased since the year 1917, when they numbered 51, to 90 in 1918 and to 106 in 1919,: the 106 deaths include those of 53 women, who suffered from influenza.[18]

The annual report of the Rotunda Maternity hospital in Dublin for the year ending 31 October 1918 stated that three of the 11 deaths that occurred in the extern department were from pneumonia during the influenza pandemic. It also reported there was a great increase in total morbidity which was due to influenza and if these cases were subtracted then the morbidity rate would have fallen to 4.52%.[19]

To contract influenza while pregnant would considerably increase the chances of a pregnancy-related death as evidenced by the deaths in Larne of Catherine Thompson (21), Mary Lindsay (31), and Ellen Connor (23) who all died during childbirth due to complications from the disease. In many cases, not only did the mother die, but also their premature babies, however, these infants were not counted in the influenza death toll. For example, in Churchill in Letterkenny poor law district, Baby Callaghan's cause of death was recorded on 14 November 1918 as premature birth. Her mother, Bridget, died two days later from influenza. In the same district Baby Buchannan death was recorded as premature birth on 5 December 1918 and his mother Marjory died four days later from influenza and cardiac failure. In Ballycastle, Agnes Hill (21) died on 19 November 1918 from influenza and lobar pneumonia combined with a premature confinement while her premature daughter died four hours after birth. The deaths of these children were not registered as influenza deaths but as a premature birth, however, there is no doubt that if their mothers had not contracted influenza, then their chances of survival would have been considerably better.

Professional Nurses and Influenza

Pregnancy was not the only area where females were more at risk from influenza, the traditionally female occupation of nursing the sick was also hazardous. Nursing and caring for the ill by washing, feeding and ensuring comfort was traditionally seen as a female responsibility.[20] According to Carol Byerly, the influenza pandemic rendered the male physicians in the US army medical corps helpless but empowered female nurses at a time of crisis. Doctors and nurses both knew that traditional nursing care provided the best and only effective treatment for influenza. Therefore, it was nurses not medicine that saved lives.[21] In fact, during the height of the pandemic in October 1918, General John Pershing, commander of the American Expeditionary Force in Europe, requested more medical personnel but wanted 1,500 nurses rather than the equivalent number of doctors to be sent to France.[22] Dr Donough Macnamara, newly qualified doctor at the Mater Hospital in Dublin remarked that during the pandemic 'before all and above all -really competent nursing, was the highest form of treatment that could be devised'.[23]

Nursing during the pandemic was an area where women were to the fore and consequently, more vulnerable to infection, as they acted not only as professional or volunteer nurses in the military and in local infirmaries, but were also the chief providers of nursing in the home for members of their families. The professional job could be arduous as evidenced by the testimony of a district nurse during this period, who stated 'we had to superintend the removal of the dead before we could start nursing the living'.[24] Esylt Jones argued that the conditions faced by both volunteer and trained nurses on emergency influenza wards in Winnipeg were far from ideal. She suggested that there was a great emotional toll placed on the nurses by caring for dying patients.[25] Certainly a nurse's description in the *Queen's Nurses' Magazine* of February 1919 of how 'in some cases the eyes swelled and burst and the patient died in acute suffering' would explain how certain nurses would find the situation harrowing.[26]

Jones stated that in Winnipeg, the highly contagious nature of influenza, as well as the demands placed on the nurses, resulted in many of them becoming ill themselves.[27] At the December meeting of the Committee of the Queen Victoria's Jubilee Institute for Nurses in Dublin, the committee was informed that during October 1918 six nurses visited 317 cases, of which 269 were influenza and pneumonia. Two of the nurses contracted influenza which placed a heavier burden on the remaining staff.[28] On 26 July 1919 the *British Journal of Nursing* stated:

> A testimony to the work of the Nurses is that during the influenza epidemic it became almost commonplace to hear that had it not been for the self-sacrificing care of the Nurses many more lives must have been lost, and it is a matter of the deepest regret that nine of the Queen's Nurses themselves succumbed to the disease.[29]

The same was true of nurses all over Ireland where there were numerous reports of professional nurses being infected with influenza while performing their duties. Dr Macnamara recollected that it was very busy at the Mater hospital and he had to visit the nurses' home 'where many of the girls were down with the disease and some had pneumonia'.[30] Many workhouse infirmaries reported the absence of their nursing staff due to influenza. During the first and second waves numerous nurses in the Belfast union infirmary contracted influenza, unfortunately during June 1918, one probationary nurse died and four more ladies died between 5 November and 3 December 1918.[31] In Londonderry union infirmary, again many nurses contracted influenza and two died during November 1918.[32] In the same month eight nurses in the Lurgan union infirmary contracted influenza, subsequently two nurses died from the disease.[33] These are just a few examples of the nurses' susceptibility to influenza. Not all nurses contracted influenza, nor did all those infected die, but there was still a high morbidity due to the disease. The annual report for year 1918 of the Society for Providing Nurses for the Sick Poor in Belfast advised that during the pandemic of influenza, three of their staff of ten nurses contracted influenza but that all had recovered.[34]

There was also a scarcity of professional nurses. Many trained nurses were attracted to both the army and naval medical corps, maybe because of the higher wages or perhaps to a sense of patriotism.[35] As a result, poor law infirmaries struggled during the pandemic to ensure that they were adequately staffed. This situation was exacerbated, especially once existing nurses contracted influenza themselves. Many union infirmaries had difficulty in recruiting nurses. In Naas the Medical Officer (MO), Dr Morrissey, praised the hard work of Nurse Mooney 'in the early part of the epidemic before she got assistance. Her attention and care saved many pneumonic cases'.[36] In Ballycastle the services of Mrs S. J. Lyle and Miss Boyd, who both had St John Ambulance Society certificates, saved the day. They volunteered to help in the infirmary when three permanent nurses were absent with influenza.[37] The clerk of the union was not only grateful for the services rendered by these volunteers, but also for the £6 saved by the guardians in salaries that would have had to be paid to professional nurses.[38]

Undoubtedly, army nurses were perceived as heroines. Carol Byerly cites US army nursing superintendent Dora Thompson, who told a nursing convention that the 'heroic self-sacrifice and fidelity to duty shown by nurses is without parallel'.[39] Irish war nurses also showed these traits. Elizabeth Harvey Watson of Dromore, County Down died of influenza in France on 5 November 1918. The month prior to her death was spent working in a ward of influenza and pneumonia cases.[40] Rachel Ferguson, from Moneymore, County Londonderry also succumbed to influenza in Italy after caring for soldier with the disease. On 26 June 1918 she was admitted to hospital and died later that day.[41] Lady Hermione Blackwood volunteered as a nurse during the war and in a series of letters to her mother, the Marchioness of Dufferin and Ava, she recorded how she and her comrades nursed soldiers with influenza in France. Her efforts were appreciated by the French authorities as she was awarded the 'French Medal of Honour for Epidemics' for her work in nursing those with the disease.[42]

Indeed, the contagious and virulent nature of influenza meant that nurses risked their lives daily in the pursuance of their profession as was evidenced by the death toll of nurses working in union infirmaries. Despite the risk of infection, women still volunteered to nurse the sick. Volunteer nurses such as Mrs Lyle and Miss Boyd in Ballycastle union showed great compassion and courage, but they were not the exception. In November 1918 there was an appeal in Cookstown 'for local young ladies who had a knowledge of nursing to voluntarily undertake the duties'.[43] The MO for Cookstown union reported that during November 1918, Nurse Milliken of the District Nursing Society organised the St John's Ambulance Association Nurses to take charge of different sections of the district, visiting the sick and distributing food. He stated that if it had not been for this organisation there would have been an appalling death rate and he expressed his appreciation of the devotion and self-sacrifice of these ladies as many contracted influenza in the discharge of their 'self-appointed duties'.[44] In Dunfanaghy union in County Donegal, local lady Mrs Short volunteered her services for 10 weeks in the fever hospital. The Dunfanaghy guardians were appreciative of Mrs Short's 'most unselfish action, and of the nobility of mind which prompted her to undertake so arduous and dangerous duties on behalf of the sick and suffering poor'.[45] Although these volunteers, unlike Lady Hermione Blackwood, did not receive any medals, it was evident that their efforts were very much appreciated during the crisis. Karen Robinson stated that since influenza had no known cure, that in America the practising nurse became a heroine in a fight against a killer.[46] In Ireland also the true heroines in the fight against influenza were the professional and volunteer nurses throughout the country.

Domestic Nurses

Svenn-Erik Mamelund stated that hospitalised patients in Norway who received care from professional health practitioners did not appear to have a lower mortality rate than those who were nursed by their families at home. He believed that quiet nursing at home may have been the key to survival.[47] Nursing of the sick at home was common and, for those who could afford it, was carried out by private nurses. Professor R. B. McDowell, formerly junior Dean of Trinity College Dublin, who lived in Belfast at the time of the pandemic, recollected that he contracted influenza when he was five years of age, which developed into double pneumonia. Everyone in his family and household fell ill except the maid and tragically his brother's elderly nanny died. Being from a fairly well-off middle-class family, however, they were able to afford two nurses to help care for them during their illness.[48] This would not have been possible for Irish working class families and the nursing of the sick at home would have been left to the female family members.

Although Mamelund argued that nursing at home was the key to the survival of influenza patients,[49] the women who nursed the sick were in a dangerous situation as they were susceptible to infection. In a survey for the 1920 Ministry of Health Report undertaken after the pandemic, Dr Joseph, the MOH for Warrington in Lancashire, found that of the people surveyed, the percentage of influenza cases was higher among those who worked in the home than those who worked away from home. However, he was not surprised by the result because he believed it was the 'housewife' in many instances that was in continuous contact for many days with severe cases of the disease'. He further established that one in five of those women nursing the sick at home contracted influenza themselves.[50] Dr Arnold, MOH for Leicester advised that 34% of women who went out to work, and 30.5% of those who stayed in the home, contracted influenza.[51] Dr Clegg, Deputy MOH for Newcastle-upon-Tyne, found that of the cases surveyed, 70% of the female influenza cases between the ages of 15 and 45 were engaged in 'home duties' and that the majority appeared to become infected from the nursing of other patients.[52] There were many newspaper reports of tragic deaths of females nursing their families. Margaret. McKee from Bessbrook contracted and died from influenza after nursing her husband and two children through it.[53] In Lurgan, Annie Turtledove, aged 28, died from influenza after visiting a local doctor about her three children who were also suffering from the disease.[54] These incidents would not have been unique during the pandemic as figures show that deaths among ladies described as housewives or housekeepers was high.

Influenza created a number of one-parent families as it not only took the mother from a family but in many cases the father may have died. In Dromore, County Down, factory worker Nathaniel Wilkinson died, leaving behind a widow and family of six children,[55] while John Johnston, a farmer from Drumlough, died from pneumonia leaving behind a widow and little son.[56] It is difficult to establish how these families would have been affected without the existence of oral testimony to that effect; however, the following examples illustrate that the death of a husband could leave his widow and children in greater financial need. At their meeting in December 1918, the Cavan guardians decided to grant 12 shillings per week outdoor relief to a widow in Cootehill whose husband had died from influenza and left her with six children.[57] However, other Ulster boards of guardians (BOG) were not so obliging. The Castledeg BOGs received a letter dated 7 June 1919 from a lady living in Christchurch, Castlederg requesting that they reconsider their decision to refuse to grant her outdoor relief. Her husband died from influenza in the previous winter and she and her four small children were left with 'absolutely no means of support'. After a vote, the guardians again refused her application.[58] It is not known what happened to this lady or her family but her options would have been few. Unless she had an extended family to give her financial help, she may have had to enter the workhouse in order for her and her family to survive. These cases were not unique. Virginia Crossman has argued that there was an aversion in the Ulster BOGs to providing outdoor relief, which she attributed to the effects of religious and financial austerity combined with a slower rate of board radicalisation.[59] Therefore, there may have been similar cases of widows seeking financial help and being refused in the aftermath of the pandemic right throughout Ulster.

It was also disastrous when a mother of a family died. Esylt Jones argued in Winnipeg that since men had potentially higher earning capacity than females that they were better able to provide for their children. Nevertheless, she stressed that the loss of a mother in the first year of life of a child had a more negative impact on the survival rates than the loss of a father, as in the early twentieth century an infant whose mother died could be four times more likely to die in the first year of life.[60] It is difficult to establish what happened to those men whose wives died, leaving them with children, but the following example might shed some light on how they coped. In Newry, Annie, the wife of Joseph Kavanagh, died on 5 November 1918, leaving her children and husband behind. Her daughters were sent to be raised by relatives and her sons remained in the family home with their father.[61] Elsyt Jones suggested widowers in Winnipeg were often forced to turn to institutionalisation of their children, either as a temporary or permanent solution to their domestic situation after the pandemic.[62] Therefore, it is possible that men, who neither had the income or extended family would have had to send their children to orphanages to be cared for in the aftermath of the pandemic.

However, when both parents died there was little choice for the children who would either be sent to an orphanage or an industrial school. At Ferns and Enniscorthy Petty Sessions, County Wexford, four children whose parents died during the influenza pandemic and eight children whose father died from the same cause were ordered to be sent to industrial schools.[63] It is telling that on 16 May 1919, the Presbyterian Orphan Society advised that not only the war but also influenza had left many orphans that had to be provided for.[64] Ida Milne, in her book *Stacking the Coffins*, gives voice to those families who suffered separation and hardship during the pandemic due to the death of a mother or father. The oral testimonies contained within tell of families torn apart. These testaments bring home more than any records or newspaper accounts could, the ongoing heartbreak, economic hardship and separation of families that still resonates today with many.[65]

Factory Working and Influenza

As discussed in Chapter 2, the influenza pandemic targeted young adults in particular. In Belfast, over 50% of people who died of influenza were between 15 and 45 years with the 25–35 age-groups suffering the highest mortality.[66] In 1918, 826 females and 688 males died from influenza in Belfast, which according to the RGI, was as a result of the extensive employment of females in factories and workshops in the city.[67] Andrea Tanner noted a similar situation in London, where she found a high mortality rate of 57% among young women. She attributed the spread of influenza in this particular age group to their widespread employment among artificially created communities during wartime such as factories and other large establishments.[68]

Ulster was in a unique position in Ireland as it was the industrial centre of the country and in many ways the north east of Ulster bore closer comparison to the more industrial regions in Britain than it did with other parts of Ireland.[69] Although Dublin was a major city, it was an administrative and communication centre rather than an industrial city in the same sense as Belfast.[70] Due to its industrial nature, Belfast bore more similarity to British cities such as Manchester than to the rest of Ireland. In fact, in 1891 Dr Henry Whitaker, Medical Superintendent Officer of Health (MSOH) for Belfast, advised in his annual report that no proper comparison of mortality rates could be made between a large manufacturing town like Belfast and any other districts in Ireland, which were more rural. Instead he thought it more appropriate to make comparisons with the death rates in some English manufacturing districts as well as Glasgow and Edinburgh.[71]

The 1920 Ministry of Health Report suggested that one of the reasons influenza may have spread among young adults in particular was because many young people had the opportunity to assemble together in military barracks, munitions factories and elsewhere due to circumstances of war. However, it also pointed out that this did not explain why the same age group suffered to the same extent in non-belligerent countries as in those countries involved directly in the war.[72] The Registrar-General for England and Wales in his Supplementary Report on influenza in those countries considered it too simplistic to suggest that the aggregation of young women in munitions factories in 1918 may have partly accounted for their specifically high mortality.[73] Nevertheless, even if this explanation was an oversimplification, the crowding of young people together in factories should not be totally rejected as a contributory factor to the high mortality of women in parts of Ulster. Female deaths from influenza outnumbered male deaths in the counties of Armagh, Donegal, Londonderry and Belfast County Borough and it was mainly in counties Armagh, Londonderry and Belfast that industrialisation proceeded furthest and fastest in Ireland.[74]

During the war years, certain employment opportunities opened up to women in the United Kingdom in munitions factories.[75] From 1914 to the end of the war, James Mackie & Sons, Limited—whose Albert Foundry was situated on the Springfield Road in Belfast—employed women to aid in the munitions contracts. During the war, the workforce in Mackie's doubled from their pre-war numbers of 650. The majority of the female workforce in Mackies were different to the women who worked in the linen mills and factories in Belfast. Many did not work in the factory from economic necessity like those women who had to work in the linen mills Moreover, Mackie's themselves believed their shift system of a 36 hour week appealed 'not merely to ordinary women of the mill type but to married women and girls of the middle classes whose pride was that, like their men folk, they were patriotic'.[76] The women who made shells in Mackie's produced a weekly workers magazine called *The Turret-Lathers Friend* for a limited period from November 1916 until March 1917. The style of prose from the magazine's contributors was quite advanced and hints that these women were probably better educated than those who worked in the linen mills.[77]

In June 1918, James Mackie & Sons, Limited was forced to close down a department mostly staffed by women because many of them were suffering from influenza.[78] Notices were placed in the Belfast newspapers by Mackie's and requested their lady workers to return to work on Monday 17 June 1918. This was one of the first mentions of influenza in the city.[79] Although the factory was forced to shut down in June 1918, there were no reports of either any fatalities from, or a loss of revenue to the factory, due to the influenza. The pandemic was not mentioned in Mackie's minutes of their Annual General Meetings or Directors' meeting for 1918 or 1919, which implies that influenza did not make a significant impact on their profits or production for those years.[80] Despite the lack of apparent fatalities from influenza at Mackie's, the fact that a department of a munitions factory, vital to the war effort, had to be closed due to the disease would indicate just how infectious influenza was during the first wave. This tallies with the Ministry of Health report, which stated that during the first influenza wave in June 1918 there were very many cases but the mortality was relatively low.[81]

Although munitions factories offered new wartime employment opportunities to females in Belfast, women already played a major part in the Ulster textile factory system, especially in the linen industry.[82] Mary Daly argued that younger women were much more likely to be employed in either Belfast or Londonderry not only because both cities had a higher proportion of working class families but also because many jobs were available in the textile and clothing factories in these towns. Women textile workers tended to work out of economic necessity and, because of this, many of them continued to work in the factory or mill after marriage. Many women worked until the eve of childbirth, returning to work after a short absence.[83] In 1892, Dr Whitaker, MSOH for Belfast linked this practice to the city's high infant mortality rate. According to Dr Whittaker, the main causes of infant mortality in Belfast were exposure to cold, improper food and neglect. The neglect was normally unintentional but was mainly due to mothers working away from home, who were therefore unable to attend to their infants and could not give them the care and attention necessary for their proper nutrition and health.[84] Mary Daly noted that the practice of returning to work so soon after the birth of a baby ruled out breast-feeding and left the infants vulnerable to disease.[85] It may have been this practice that contributed to the large numbers of both male and female children under five years of age who died during the pandemic in both Ulster and Belfast.

Although the Imperial Local Government Board (LGB) requested MOHs to include detailed accounts of the pandemic in their annual reports for 1918,[86] the Local Government Board for Ireland (LGBI) did not make a similar request in their jurisdiction. Consequently, there were no individual reports on influenza in Ulster towns. However, several studies were carried out in English industrial cities similar to Belfast and similarities would exist between the conditions in these cities and the industrial towns in Ulster. During the first wave of the pandemic, the MOH of Manchester, James Niven—as part of a Ministry of Health report—visited a textile factory in that city, where he interviewed the female employees who had contracted influenza. Although he described the first outbreak of influenza as mild and that generally the people attacked were not very severely affected, he noted that it spread rapidly through the factory. He thought that the use of common handtowels and wash basins as well as the women working in close proximity to infected people, and handling the same articles played, a part in its circulation.[87] Dr M. B. Arnold who surveyed factories in Leicester for the same report agreed with Niven. He highlighted the use of roller towels, sharing enamel drinking cups, the washing of teacups together and the passing of goods in various stages of manufacture from one worker to another as a possible means of spreading influenza.[88]

In Ulster, even without the influenza pandemic, the working conditions in the linen industry were already notoriously unhealthy for the women who undertook spinning and handloom weaving in factories. Spinning rooms were hot and damp in order to prevent the flax threads from breaking, which made them an ideal breeding ground for tuberculosis, while flax fibres covered spinners with a permanent layer of dust and caused serious lung damage.[89] The dangers to health caused by various processes in the linen industry should not be underestimated. One of the jobs in flax preparation that was predominantly carried out by women was carding. In 1892, Dr Whitaker, MSOH for Belfast, reported that the carder's average length of life was only 16.8 years of work. He stated that if a girl was employed at 18 as a carder it was likely that she would be dead by the age of 30.[90] Tuberculosis also was a major concern. E. H. Osborn conducted an enquiry into general mortality among linen textile workers in Belfast during years 1891–1892. He concluded that 53% of the female textile workers who died in that period died from phthisis (pulmonary tuberculosis) as opposed to 34.8% of male textile workers and 21% of male and females in other non-textile occupations.[91]

It is widely recognised that the main route for the spread of viruses such as influenza in humans is by exposure to droplet infection.[92] In

1920, Dr Arnold, MOH of Leicester, stated in his report for the Ministry of Health on the factories in the town that:

> The possibility of droplet infection through the air varies considerably in the various processes. Of those I saw, machining in the shoe factory seemed to offer the greatest opportunity. Workers sit on each side of a long bench and face one another. The distance across the bench is about 5 feet and the lateral distance between the workers about 3 feet.[93]

This implies that the close proximity of workers to one another was a factor in the spread of influenza within a factory workshop. According to Greta Jones, linen mills in Ulster tended to be larger and more crowded establishments than cotton mills. The Factory Inspectorate in 1914 considered that the floor and air space provided for cotton and linen operatives was roughly the same. However, a linen shed of 500 looms would contain around 250–300 workers whereas a cotton shed of similar size around 200.[94] It was also recognised that the most common method of spreading tuberculosis was by infected droplets in the air coughed out by a sufferer and taken into the lungs through the nose and mouth and that it was most frequently transmitted in enclosed environments.[95] It follows that the conditions that caused the spread of tuberculosis also played a part in the spread of influenza. Enclosed factory environments such as those of the spinning and weaving sheds were definitely a factor in the spread of the disease to the men and women who worked in them.

Another common practice that was carried out in both the cotton factories in England and linen weaving factories in Ulster was 'kissing the shuttle'. This was the practice of pulling the thread through the eye of the shuttle by sucking on it.[96] This practice meant that shuttles were 'kissed' hundreds of times a day and the same shuttle could have been used by a succession of weavers.[97] Cotton weavers in Blackburn believed that this practice was largely responsible for the spread of influenza in the town.[98] In 1902, this practice was deemed responsible for the spread of tuberculosis and was considered dangerous not only for the spread of infection but also because the weaver could suck up any dirt or dust that might be in the shuttle's eye.[99] In 1911 Dr John Brown of Bacup in Lancashire drew attention to this practice as a possible means of spreading infection, resulting in the Bacup Town Clerk recommending that the systematic disinfection of shuttles should be undertaken by the factory owners.[100] A further result of Dr Brown's recommendations was that an inquiry into 'shuttle-kissing' was undertaken in 1912. Although it found that the practice might have been a possible means of spreading infection, it did not recommend its cessation.[101] Even though the 'Shuttle-Kissing' Committee reported in October 1919 that 'shuttle-kissing' should be abolished in the cotton weaving industry,[102] and despite the continued dangers of 'kissing the shuttle' and its associations with the spread of tuberculosis, the practice was only officially abandoned In Belfast's linen mills in 1958.[103]

The working conditions in textile factories, the high employment of women in an already unhealthy environment, working in close proximity to one another and sharing utensils, towels and even shuttles was a contributory factor in the high mortality of women in Ulster, especially in the more industrial towns such as Belfast, Londonderry and Lurgan. However, in Ulster, smaller villages as well as major towns could be linen centres. Upperlands near Maghera, County Londonderry, home to William Clark & Sons weaving factory was forced to close during the last week of November 1918 as many workers were absent with influenza. Entire families in the district contracted the disease, which was reported to be responsible for about 16 deaths in the area.[104] Most of these deaths were of female workers, or wives, or children of male operatives who worked in the linen industry.

The linen industry—with its predominantly female workforce—was one of the main industries in the north east of Ulster and in 1911, over half of the female workforce in Belfast was employed in various aspects of the textile and finishing industry.[105] Apart from the core processes of spinning and weaving of linen, the industry was also linked to certain related low-paid industries, in particular dressmaking, shirtmaking and 'making-up'.[106] 'Making-up' was where the manufacturers provided the materials to the women to make up shirts in their own home. Home-working was a common practice in all the textile trades. The shirt industry was located in the north west of the province, mostly in Londonderry and was dominated by women.[107] This trade, like many textile trades in Ulster, involved a combination of both factory and homework. Home-work played a major role in the shirt-making industry and it was reported in 1899 by the Inspector of Factories that one Londonderry firm employed 1,200 inside and 3,000 outside workers while two other firms each employed 600 people within the factory with 1,500 and 2,000 as home-workers respectively.[108] During July 1918, over 350 employees in a Londonderry shirt and collar factory contracted influenza, resulting in the temporary closure of the business.[109]

This poses the question, was the practice of home-working instrumental in the spread of influenza from industrial town centres to the more rural areas of the country? Home-working involved materials being distributed either directly from a factory workshop or indirectly through an agent throughout the country districts. The shirt industry in Londonderry also used outstations, which were depots that were situated in different districts for the distribution of 'unmade goods' and collection of completed goods. Once goods were completed, they were returned to the factory and examined and then the home-worker would be paid.[110] Margaret Neill argued that the shirt-making industry was of great importance not only in Londonderry but also in Donegal. The 1901 census reported that shirt makers and seamstresses accounted for 40.2% of females in employment in Donegal and 34.6% of those in Londonderry. In Donegal the greatest concentration of shirt makers was along the Inishowen peninsula, where one quarter of those detailed in the census lived.[111]

Another important textile trade in Ulster was the making up of handkerchiefs: a trade centred around Lurgan and Portadown and again it combined both factory and home-work.[112] Outside Belfast, Lurgan was the most important industrial town in Ulster, providing employment for thousands of women in the districts of Lurgan, Portadown, Banbridge and Dromore.[113] As with the shirt-making industry, both the factory labour force and home workers were predominantly female.[114] Female members of Lurgan households often worked at home folding, packing, stitching and sewing linen fabrics and home-working became an essential feature of the local linen industry.[115] Making-up trades such as machine stitching, hemstitching, embroidery and thread-drawing of cambric handkerchiefs were all outsourced from factories in areas such as Lurgan, Dromore and Portadown.[116] Furthermore, it has been suggested that in 1911, 22% of the rural Lurgan population were involved in some way in the linen and textile trades.[117]

The method of distributing material to home-workers depended on where they lived. In the urban areas the materials were usually distributed directly from an office in the factory either to the home-workers themselves or to their children. These materials were carried to their homes and returned to the factory again when finished. In the rural areas the materials were distributed by agents, either from a shop, an office or from some spot where the agents arranged to meet the workers.[118] One lady from Derrytrasna, situated about seven miles from Lurgan, recollected that in the early part of the twentieth century she walked to Queen's Street in Lurgan to fetch yarn from a factory, brought it home where she and her mother worked alongside each other weaving the webs to be returned to the manufacturer for sale. She also was involved in thread-drawing of handkerchiefs and again collected the handkerchiefs from the factory and returned them there once the work was completed.[119] The practice of home-working facilitated the contact of people living in rural areas with those of more industrial and crowded towns. It should also be noted that many people who lived in rural parts of Lurgan were employed in the linen factories in the town and again this is a way that the disease could be spread from urban to rural areas.

Women and children from different parts of Ulster collected materials from industrial and infected areas and brought both the materials and maybe the virus back with them to rural communities to work on for long hours in close proximity to one another. It is possible that these actions could have been a factor in the spread of influenza to rural areas from industrial centres. In November 1918 influenza was described as abating in Lurgan town but that it had spread into the adjoining country districts of Moira, Maralin, Aghalee and Waringstown during the previous week resulting in a few deaths in these districts.[120] In Waringstown, 15 people died from influenza or pneumonia during November and December 1918. Seven of these were either people involved in the textile industry or wives and children of the same and five were female. In Lurgan poor law union 31% of the influenza and pneumonia deaths that occurred during 1918 and 1919 were of men and women who worked in the linen industry or wives and children of the same people, 75% of these were female.[121]

In conclusion, there was a high proportion of women workers in cities such as Belfast and Londonderry as well as towns such as Lurgan, Portadown and Lisburn, and interestingly the influenza mortality among females was marginally higher in counties Armagh, Donegal, Londonderry and Belfast Borough County than that of males. In Ulster, a substantial number of females were employed in the linen industry which was a notoriously unhealthy working environment even without the introduction of epidemic influenza. Overcrowded workshops, hot and damp conditions and unhygienic working practices such as 'shuttle-kissing' encouraged the spread of infection that could have played a significant part in the higher mortality of females in the industrial towns in Ulster.

There were many factors that should have made females more susceptible to infection. Pregnant women were in particular danger especially during the latter part of their pregnancy. Many courageous and selfless women acted as both professional and voluntary nurses putting themselves in daily danger to care for those suffering from influenza. Meanwhile on the domestic front many women looked after other sick family members and neighbours, often at the sacrifice of their own lives. Also in Ulster towns such as Belfast, Lurgan, Londonderry and Lisburn, there was high female employment in the linen and textile industry. This meant that women were more exposed to the risks of contracting the disease due to the already unhealthy and crowded factory conditions. Therefore, the real surprise is that taking all these factors into consideration that the female influenza mortality in Ulster was not even higher.

Notes

1. Johnson (2006), p. 91.
2. *Fifty-Fifth Detailed Annual Report of the Registrar-General (Ireland) 1918 (Births, Deaths and Marriages)* SP 1919 [Cmd.450], x, 849, xvi.
3. *Fifty-Sixth Detailed Annual Report of the Registrar-General (Ireland) 1919 (Births, Deaths and Marriages)*, SP 1920 [Cmd. 997], xi, 629, xvi.
4. Johnson (2006, p. 92).
5. *Report on the Mortality from Influenza in Scotland During the Epidemic of 1918–19: A Supplement to the Annual Reports of the Registrar-General for Scotland* [Cmd 282], H.C. 1919, x, 1223, pp. 9–10.
6. Figures calculated from *Fifty-Fifth Detailed Annual Report of the Registrar-General (Ireland) (1918)*, p. xvi and *Fifty-Sixth Detailed Annual Report of the Registrar-General (Ireland) (1919)*, p. xvii.
7. Sandra Tomkins, 'Britain and the Influenza Epidemic 1918–1919' (Ph.D. thesis, University of Cambridge, 1989), p. 28.
8. Johnson (2003, p. 141; 2004, pp. 221–222).
9. Johnson (2003, p. 141; 2004, p. 222).
10. Bourne (1922, p. 39).
11. Reid (2005, pp. 32–33).
12. Stuart-Harris and Schild (1976, p. 99).
13. Rasmussen et al. (2008, p. 96).
14. Joseph (1920, p. 549).
15. Joseph (1920, p. 552).

16. *Fifty-Fifth Detailed Annual Report of the Registrar-General (Ireland)*, p. xxv.
17. *Fifty-Sixth Detailed Annual Report of the Registrar-General (Ireland)*, p. xxvi.
18. Ibid., pp. xxv–xxvi.
19. 'Report of the Rotunda Hospital, 1917–1918', *Dublin Journal of Medical Science: 4th Series*, 1:9 (1920), p. 418.
20. Jones (2007, p. 65).
21. Byerly (2005, p. 144).
22. Byerly (2005, p. 145).
23. Macnamara (1954, p. 306).
24. Baly (1987, p. 87).
25. Jones, (2007, pp. 67–69).
26. Baly (1987, p. 87).
27. Jones (2007, p. 68).
28. *The British Journal of Nursing*, 14 December 1918, p. 369.
29. *The British Journal of Nursing*, 26 July 1919, p. 58.
30. Macnamara (1954, p. 306).
31. The Public Records Office of Northern Ireland [Hereafter PRONI], BG/7/A/99 Belfast Board of Guardians minutes, 25 June 1918, *Irish News*, 26 June 1918; PRONI, BG/7/A/100, Belfast Board of Guardians minutes, 2 July 1918, 5 November 1918; 26 November 1918 and 3 December 1918; *Irish New*, 2 July 1918.
32. PRONI, BG/2/A/33, Londonderry Board of Guardians minutes, 9 November 1918, *Derry Journal*, 11 November 1918.
33. PRONI, BG22/A/114, Lurgan Board of Guardians Minutes, 21 November 1918 and 5 December 1918.
34. PRONI, D1630/23; Society for Providing Nurses for the Sick Poor, Belfast (incorporated), Forty-Fifth annual meeting, 26 February 1919.
35. Barrington (1987, p. 73).
36. Milne (2018, p. 38) and *Kildare Observer and Eastern Counties Advertiser*, 30 November 1918.
37. PRONI, BG/3/A/49, Ballycastle Board of Guardians Minutes, 3 December. 1918.
38. *Northern Constitution*, 7 December 1918.
39. Byerly (2005, p. 145).
40. The National Archive, Kew [Hereafter TNA], WO/399/8761; Service record of Elizabeth H. Watson.
41. TNA, WO/399/2695, Service record of Rachel Ferguson.
42. PRONI, D1231/G/7/218, Lady Hermione Blackwood, First World War nursing letters; Letter to Harriet Marchioness of Dufferin and Ava, 8 March 1919.
43. *Irish News*, 16 November 1918.

44. *Irish News*, 23 December 1918.
45. *Fermanagh Herald*, 1 February 1919.
46. Robinson (1990, p. 25).
47. Mamelund (2006, p. 936).
48. *Irish Times*, 29 March 2008 and typescript of oral interview between Ida Milne And R. B. McDowell courtesy of Ida Milne (2009).
49. Mamelund (2006, p. 936).
50. Joseph (1920, p. 546).
51. Arnold (1920, p. 451).
52. Clegg (1920, pp. 556–557).
53. *Newry Reporter*, 12 November 1918.
54. *Lurgan Mail*, 32 November 1918.
55. *Dromore Leader*, 13 July 1918.
56. *Dromore Leader*, 14 December 1918.
57. *Anglo-Celt*, 7 December 1918.
58. PRONI, BG/8/A/50, Castlederg Board of Guardians minutes, 13 June 1919.
59. Crossman (2006, pp. 50–51).
60. Jones (2007, p. 54).
61. Coyle (2018, p. 19).
62. Jones (2007, p. 155).
63. *Irish Times*, 7 January 1919.
64. *Lisburn Standard*, 16 May 1919.
65. Milne (2018, pp. 164–196)—this chapter of Milne's book summarises the oral testimonies of influenza survivors and gives a fascinating insight into the human cost of the pandemic.
66. Mortality figures calculated from *Fifty-Fifth Detailed Annual Report of the Registrar-General (Ireland)*, p. xvi and *Fifty-Sixth Detailed Annual Report of the Registrar-General (Ireland)*, p. xvii.
67. Thompson (1920, pp. 7–8).
68. Tanner (2002, p. 56).
69. Ollernshaw (1985, p. 62).
70. Lynch (1998, p. 19).
71. Blaney (1988, p. 9).
72. Newman (1920, pp. xiv–xv).
73. *Supplement to the Eighty-First Annual Report of the Registrar-General of Births, Deaths, and Marriages in England and Wales: Report on the Mortality from Influenza in England and Wales During the Epidemic of 1918–19* [Cmd 700], H.C. 1920, 791, x., p. 8.
74. Ollernshaw (1985, p. 62).
75. Marwick (1977, pp. 57–60).
76. PRONI, D3964/T/40' Alfred S. Moore, 'History of Mackie's', pp. 54–56.

77. PRONI, D3964/T/38, *Mackie's Magazine* or *The Turret-Lathers Friend*.
78. *Belfast Evening Telegraph*, 11 June 1918; *Belfast News-Letter*, 12 June 1918.
79. *Belfast News-Letter*, 12 June 1918; *Northern Whig*, 12 June 1918.
80. PRONI, D3964/P/1, AGM Minutes of James Mackie and Son Ltd for 1918 and 1919; PRONI, D3964/P/2; Meeting of the Directors Minutes of James Mackie and Son Ltd., July 1918–Oct. 1919.
81. 'A General Account of Influenza in the United Kingdom', p. 66.
82. Daly (1997, p. 28 and Ollernshaw (1985, p. 62).
83. Daly (1997, p. 33).
84. Blaney (1988, p. 15).
85. Daly (1997, p. 33).
86. Tomkins, 'Britain and the Influenza Epidemic 1918–1919', p. 129.
87. Niven (1920, p. 472).
88. Arnold (1920, p. 450).
89. Daly (1997, pp. 29–30).
90. Annual Report of the Chief inspector, 1893, pp. 194–95, cited in Anderson (1922, p. 102).
91. Jones (2001, p. 70).
92. Smallman-Raynor et al. (2002, p. 454).
93. Arnold (1920, p. 450).
94. Jones (2001, p. 73 and Notes, 92).
95. Ibid., p. 15.
96. Ibid., p. 75.
97. *The British Journal of Nursing*, 18 February 1911, p. 130.
98. *The Times*, 14 September 1918; *The British Journal of Nursing*, 30 November 1918, p. 342.
99. *The British Journal of Nursing*, 29 November 1902, p. 433.
100. *The British Journal of Nursing*, 18 February 1911, p. 130.
101. *Report to the Home Office and Local Government Board upon an Inquiry into the Alleged Danger of the Transmission of Certain Diseases from Person to Person in Weaving Sheds by Means of 'Shuttle-Kissing'* [Cd. 6184], H.C. 1912–13, pp. 13–14.
102. *Annual Report of the Chief Inspector of Factories and Workshops for the Year 1919* [Cmd. 941], H.C. 1920, p. 4.
103. Messenger (1978, pp. 131–132) and Jones (2001, p. 108).
104. *Mid-Ulster Mail*, 30 November 1918.
105. Daly (1997, p. 28), Ollernshaw (1985, p. 62), and Hepburn (1996, p. 225).
106. Patterson (1985, p. 162).
107. Daly (1997, p. 28) and Ollernshaw, (1985, p. 62).
108. Neill (1994, pp. 5–6).

109. *Irish News*, 4 July 1918.
110. Neill (1994, p. 3).
111. Neill (1994, p. 8).
112. *Reports of the Chief Inspectors of Factories and Workshops to Her Majesty's Principal Secretary of State for the Home Department, for the Year Ending 31 Oct. 1887*, p. 23, H. C. 1888 [Cd. 5328], xxvi, p. 417.
113. Neill (1994, p. 9).
114. Patterson (1985, p. 163).
115. McBurney et al. (1994, p. 19).
116. *Committee of Inquiry into the Conditions of Employment in the Linen and Other Making-Up Trades of the North of Ireland* [Cd. 6509] H.C. 1912–1913, xxxiv, p. 152.
117. Patricia Marsh, 'The Impact of the Linen Industry on Lurgan' (M.A. thesis, Queen's University, Belfast, 2004), p. 74.
118. *Committee of Inquiry into the Conditions of employment in the Linen and Other Making-Up Trades of the North of Ireland*, p. vi.
119. Tallon (1987, p. 98).
120. *Irish News*, 23 November 1918.
121. Figures calculated from www.Irishgeneology.ie website for the indexes of the Civil Registration of Irish Deaths from influenza and pneumonia during 1918 and 1919 in Lurgan poor law union.

References

Anderson, Adelaide Mary. *Women in the Factory: An Administrative Adventure, 1893 to 1921*. London, 1922.

Arnold M.D., M. B. 'Report on an Inquiry into the Recent Epidemic of Influenza in the County Borough of Leicester', in *Ministry of Health, Report on the Pandemic of Influenza, 1918–19*, 445–470. London: HMSO, 1920.

Baly, Monica E. *A History of the Queen's Nursing Institute*. London: Croom Helm, 1987.

Barrington, Ruth. *Health, Medicine and Politics in Ireland 1900–1970*. Dublin: Institute of Public Administration, 1987.

Blaney, Roger. *Belfast: 100 Years of Public Health*. Belfast: Belfast City Council and Eastern Health and Social Services Board, 1988.

Bourne, Aleck W. 1922. 'Influenza: Pregnancy, labour, the puerperium and diseases of women', in Influenza: Essays by several authors, edited by Francis Graham Crookshank, 433–443. London: Heinemann.

Byerly, Carol R. *Fever of War: The Influenza Epidemic in the U. S. Army During World War I*. New York and London: New York University Press, 2005.

Clegg MD, S. J. 'Analysis of an Influenza Census at Newcastle-upon-Tyne', in *Ministry of Health, Report on the Pandemic of Influenza, 1918–19*, 556–563. London: HMSO, 1920.

Coyle, Claudine. *The 1918 Spanish Flu: Newry and Surrounding Areas*. Newry, 2018.

Crossman, Virginia. *The Poor Law in Ireland 1838–1948*. Dundalk: Dundalgan Press, 2006.

Daly, Mary. *Women and Work in Ireland*. Dundalk: Dundalgan Press, 1997.

Hepburn, A. C. *A Past Apart: Studies in the History of Catholic Belfast, 1850–1950*. Belfast: Ulster Historical Foundation, 1996.

Johnson, Niall P. A. S. 'The Overshadowed Killer: Influenza in Britain', in *Spanish Influenza Pandemic of 1918–1919: New Perspectives*, edited by Howard Phillips and David Killingray, 132–156. London: Routledge, 2003.

Johnson, Niall P. A. S. 'Scottish Flu': The Scottish Experience of "Spanish Flu"', *The Scottish Historical Review*, 83:2 (2004): 216–226.

Johnson, Niall P. A. S. *Britain and the 1918–19 Influenza Pandemic: A Dark Epilogue*. London: Routledge, 2006.

Jones, Esylt W. *Influenza 1918: Disease, Death and Structure in Winnipeg*. Toronto, Buffalo and London: University of Toronto, 2007.

Jones, Greta. *'Captain of All These Men of Death': The History of Tuberculosis in Nineteenth and Twentieth Century Ireland*. Amsterdam and New York: Editions Rodopi B.V., 2001.

Joseph MD, G. W. N. 'Report on an Investigation of the Incidence and Effects of Influenza Among the Population of Warrington (Lancs.)' in *Ministry of Health, Report on the Pandemic of Influenza, 1918–19*, 539–555. London: HMSO, 1920.

Lynch, John. *A Tale of Three Cities: Comparative Studies in Working-Class Life*. Basingstoke: Palgrave Macmillan, 1998.

Macnamara, Dr, D. W. 'Memories of 1918 and "The Flu"', *Journal of the Irish Medical Association*, 35:208 (1954): 304–309.

Mamelund, Svenn-Erik. 'A Socially Neutral Disease? Individual Social Class, Household Wealth and Mortality from Spanish Influenza in Two Socially Contrasting Parishes in Kristiania 1918–19', *Social Science & Medicine*, 62:4 (2006): 923–940.

Marwick, Arthur. *Women at War 1914–1918*. London: Fontana, 1977.

Messenger, Betty. *Picking up the Linen Threads: A Study in Industrial Folklore*. Austin and London: University of Texas Press, 1978.

McBurney, C., F. Grieg, K. Clendinning and J. Trimble. *Lurgan Town Trial*. Craigavon, 1994.

Milne, Ida. *Stacking the Coffins: Influenza, War and Revolution in Ireland, 1918–19*. Manchester: Manchester University Press, 2018.

Neill, Margaret. 'Homeworkers in Ulster, 1850–1911', in *Coming into the Light: The Work, Politics and Religion of Women in Ulster 1840–1940*, edited by Janice Holmes and Diane Urquhart, 2–32. Belfast: Queen's University: Institute of Irish Studies, 1994.

Newman, Sir George. 'Chief Medical Officer's Introduction', in *Ministry of Health, Report on the Pandemic of Influenza, 1918–19*, iv–xxiii. London: HMSO, 1920.

Niven, James. 'Report on the Epidemic of Influenza in Manchester 1918–19', in *Ministry of Health, Report on the Pandemic of Influenza, 1918–19*, 471–520. London: HMSO, 1920.

Ollernshaw, Philip. 'Industry, 1820-1914', in *An Economic History of Ulster 1820-1940*, edited by Liam Kennedy and Philip Ollernshaw, 62–108. Manchester: Manchester University Press, 1985.

Patterson, Henry. 'Industrial Labour and the Labour Movement, 1820–1914', in *An Economic History of Ulster 1820–1940*, edited by Liam Kennedy and Philip Ollernshaw, 160–174. Manchester: Manchester University Press, 1985.

Rasmussen, Sonja A., Denise J. Jamieson and Joseph S. Bresee. 'Pandemic Influenza and Pregnant Women', *Emerging Epidemic Disease*, 14:1 (2008): 95–100.

Reid, Alice. 'The Effects of the 1918–19 Influenza Pandemic on Infant and Child Health in Derbyshire', *Medical History*, 49:1 (2005): 29–54.

Robinson, Karen R. 'The Role of Nursing in the Influenza Epidemic of 1918–1919', *Nursing Forum*, 25:2 (1990): 19–26.

Smallman-Raynor, Matthew, et al. 'The Spatial Anatomy of an Epidemic: Influenza in London and the County Boroughs of England and Wales, 1918–1919', *Transactions of the Institute of British Geographers*, 27:4 (2002): 452–470.

Stuart-Harris, Charles H. and Geoffrey C. Schild. *Influenza: The Viruses and the Disease*. London: Edward Arnold, 1976.

Tallon, Alfie. *Memories of Old Lurgan*. Lurgan: Inglewood Press, 1987.

Tanner, Andrea. 'The Spanish Lady Comes to London: The Influenza Pandemic 1918-1919', *London Journal*, 27:2 (2002): 51–76.

Thompson, William. 'Mortality from Influenza in Ireland', *Journal of Statistical and Social Inquiry Society of Ireland*, 14:1 (1920): 1–14.

CHAPTER 4

'Mysterious Malady Spreading': Newspaper Coverage of the 1918–19 Influenza Pandemic

Introduction

In Ireland, as in Britain, the paucity of archival records concerning the influenza pandemic is problematic. Niall Johnson suggested that there was a lack of British archival records on influenza compared to other nations. He argued that influenza left its imprint throughout the fabric of government activities in other countries, but in Britain it is much more difficult to find traces of the pandemic.[1] The Irish situation was worse still as even the major contemporary Ministry of Health study of influenza in the United Kingdom, published in 1920, virtually ignored Ireland with only four pages of approximately 600 given over to discussion of the disease in the country.[2]

During 1918 it was common for Medical Officers of Health (MOH) reports to devote more attention to other diseases even though there was a much higher mortality from influenza.[3] Surprisingly, considering the extent of the disease, Irish records such as the minutes of local authorities and boards of guardians' (BOG) meetings do not always provide much information on influenza in towns and poor law districts. Therefore, contemporary newspapers were used to overcome this problem as they provided more information on the day-to-day progress of influenza in the country. A different set of problems arise when using both local and national newspapers, as the political bias of these publications influenced how the pandemic was reported in different parts of the country. This

P. Marsh, *The Spanish Flu in Ireland*, Palgrave Studies in Economic History, https://doi.org/10.1007/978-3-030-79500-9_4

chapter explores how different agendas at play within Ireland during this period impacted on the reportage of the pandemic in Irish newspapers.

A number of newspapers at both national and local levels were used. The *Irish Times*—a conservative, protestant and unionist newspaper which during this period was sympathetic to Britain—provided the national picture, along with the *Irish Independent*—an independent and constitutional nationalist newspaper. Both newspapers had a circulation throughout Ireland.[4] Belfast newspapers, the *Belfast News-Letter* and *Irish News* were also compared. The *Irish News* was a pro-catholic, conservative and nationalist newspaper that backed the Irish Parliamentary Party (IPP) but it did not support Sinn Féin.[5] The *Belfast News-Letter*, in contrast, advocated unionist, conservative and protestant principles.[6] The *Belfast News-Letter* circulated throughout Belfast; the rest of Ulster and had general circulation in the leading towns in the rest of Ireland and the *Irish News* circulated all over Ireland.[7] The other Belfast newspapers the *Belfast Evening Telegraph* and *Northern Whig* were also unionist.[8] Local Irish newspapers were also used, especially those in Ulster. Starting with the first wave, this chapter reflects on how the pandemic was reported in Ireland by exploring the different narratives and themes adopted by the Irish newspapers and poses the question: did the manner in which the pandemic was reported have any impact on how it has been remembered in history.

First Wave: May 1918–September 1918

Some themes contained in the narrative discourses of the reportage of the pandemic in the Irish newspapers were also present in publications in the rest of the United Kingdom (UK). One such theme was the way in which influenza was presented as being associated with belligerents of the Allies during the war. Debra Blakely argued that during the war the *New York Times* in June 1918 presented influenza as a German disease.[9] Similar rhetoric was used by President Donald Trump during his 2020 Presidential campaign when he referred to the Covid-19 pandemic as the 'Chinese Virus' or the 'Plague from China'.[10]

Sandra Tomkins has suggested that one way to keep wartime morale raised was to soften reporting on the death toll and the threat of influenza in Britain, while reporting the widespread and adverse effect of the disease on Germany and Austria.[11] Irish newspapers with unionist sympathies took a similar approach during the first wave, as they often associated influenza with Germany. Although the nationalist *Irish Independent* made one of the earliest references to influenza on 25 May 1918 under 'World News', suggesting that the delay of the German offensive on the western front was due to 'mutinies and influenza,'[12] it was the unionist-run newspapers that made most of German associations. On 17 June 1918 the *Belfast Evening Telegraph* ran a story with the headline 'Influenza in Germany, Berlin has Belfast's epidemic, and apparently rather worse'.[13] On 19 June 1918, the *Belfast News-Letter* mentioned 'influenza is exceedingly rife in Berlin', towards the end of an article that reported the spread of the disease in Belfast.[14] On 28 June 1918, the *Portadown Express* claimed that influenza was imported from the German lines of the western front, 'probably conveyed there by German soldiers back from leave, as it had previously been epidemic in Berlin,'[15] implying the disease originated in Germany.

The *County Down Spectator* reported on 29 June 1918 that influenza was causing havoc in the German trenches but that it had not appeared yet in the Allied camps or trenches.[16] However, a week later the same newspaper along with the *Armagh Guardian*, agreed that 'the German army has been suffering very severely for some time past from what the enemy describe as the "Flanders disease"—a very infectious form of influenza,' but it acknowledged that 'our own men have not been entirely immune'. It further stated that although influenza may have impacted on the delay in the resumption of the German offensive, the hold-up was mainly due to its heavy casualties. There may have been more than an element of truth to this as Howard Phillips has suggested that the first influenza outbreak in the late spring of 1918 contributed to the German defeat as one in five of the German soldiers were ill with influenza during this critical part of the offensive.[17]

Between 3 and 9 July 1918 the *Irish Times*, along with reports on influenza in Ireland, produced daily articles on how the disease was reaching epidemic proportions in both Germany and Austria.[18] In mid-July 1918 both the *Portadown Weekly News* and conservative *Lisburn Standard* still associated the 'new disease' with Germany and professed that influenza was raging in southern Belgium, brought there by recent convoys of German troops.[19] Debra Blakely argued that when newspapers framed the severity of the influenza epidemic in foreign countries they indirectly associated the blame for the disease with the said foreign country.[20] Therefore, as unionist newspapers placed emphasis on

Germany as a source and disseminator of influenza they thus associated the disease with the enemy, Germany.

Not surprisingly, influenza in Spain featured among the earliest mentions of influenza in Irish newspapers. On 28 May 1918, the *Belfast News-Letter* reported that King Alfonso XIII had contracted the 'Epidemic in Spain'[21] and on 31 May 1918 the *Irish Times* advised that 'the epidemic which has broken out in Spain is not of a serious character'.[22] On 1 June 1918 the *Westmeath Examiner*, *Ballymena Weekly Times*, *Frontier Sentinel* and *Ulster Herald* also mentioned influenza in Spain. Interestingly these articles describe the disease as 'mysterious'.[23] It was the use of words like mysterious which led to misconceptions about the disease posing the question, was it influenza or another disease entirely? The uncertainty created around this mysterious disease generated fear and apprehension and it was this aspect that some nationalist Irish newspapers concentrated on. During June 1918, influenza was described by some in Belfast as 'trench fever', a disease caused by lice to soldiers in the trenches during World War I. Although this theory was rejected by doctors at the time, it was seized upon by the *Irish News* because the appearance of influenza coincided with the return of discharged soldiers.[24] Also in June 1918, the *Derry Journal* referred to influenza as a 'mystery illness' and enquired 'is the malady directly due to the war?' In the same editorial it stated

> These questions have not been settled by any definite reply from those in a position to speak with authority, but by many the swiftly-gripping ailment is set down as a form of 'trench fever.' The fact that its appearance in some parts of Ireland followed soon upon the return of soldiers discharged from the seat of war lends an air of probability to that supposition.[25]

On 15 June 1918, under the headline 'Is it the Plague', the *Anglo-Celt* advised that a third of the Spanish people were suffering from a mysterious malady.[26] On 29 June 1918, nationalist newspapers the *Frontier Sentinel* and *Ulster Herald*, under the heading 'Mysterious Malady Spreading', advised that 'The mysterious influenza plague that made its appearance in Belfast over a week ago has spread to Dublin'.[27] The same newspapers, along with the *Fermanagh Herald* and *Derry People*, also referred to influenza as 'the plague'.[28] The word 'plague' was also used in several news items in the *Irish Independent* during June and July 1918.[29]

Although unionist-run newspapers also questioned what the disease might be, they attempted to play down its effects. The *County Down Spectator* on 29 June 1918, reported: 'How the complaint got its name is not quite clear for it is neither Spanish nor influenza'. However, unlike the nationalist newspapers, it criticised the public over-reaction to the disease with 'Needless to say, there has, as usual been no lack of scaremongers to magnify the outbreak into a very epidemic of chronic influenza. This it certainly is not, though from its contagious character cases are to be found generally in little groups'.[30] In early June 1918, the *Belfast News-Letter* declared that many exaggerated stories had been spread in the city, but there was no cause for alarm.[31] Similarly, the *Northern Whig* reported that people were becoming 'panicky' and believed they had contracted influenza if they sneezed or had a headache and 'undoubtedly this over-anxiety largely increases the roll of alleged victims'.[32]

However, nationalist newspapers such as the *Irish News* continued to promote the suggestion that influenza was something more sinister and was directly caused by war. In an editorial on 12 July 1918 it described influenza as a 'virulent infectious "poison,"' suggesting that it had originated in the trenches. It quoted a Dublin doctor, home on leave from the war, stating: 'he has found within the past week several cases of "influenza" in which the "symptoms" are very similar to those observed in soldiers who were "gassed" in the trenches'. The symptoms were 'far milder of course but startlingly alike in many respects'.[33] In June 1918, the *Donegal Vindicator, Derry Weekly News* and *Fermanagh News*, under the headline 'Mysterious Influenza', suggested that 'Doctors consider that it is a mild form of influenza occasioned and spread by war conditions'.[34] The *Connaught Tribune* asked 'Is it Influenza?' on 22 June 1918. It reported a severe outbreak in Ballinasloe, described again as 'a 'Mysterious Malady' and that 'the doctors are baffled as to the nature of the illness'.[35]

It is important to point out that the Irish newspapers were not alone in their scepticism about influenza. Tom Quinn noted that many of the world's top scientists were convinced that the disease was not in fact influenza as they were fooled by the ferocity of the disease and by the speed at which it incapacitated its victims and killed them.[36] Irish doctor, Donough Macnamara who treated patients and in the Mater hospital in Dublin during the pandemic stated in 1954:

> I was never satisfied in my own mind that the illness was influenza. To me it was something much more terrible, and although I have never seen a case, I always looked on it as pneumonic plague. For it was truly a plague, a Black Death or what you will, but not influenza as we know it today.[37]

During the second wave in October 1918, nationalist newspapers, the *Freeman's Journal* and *Irish Independent* seized upon the English *Daily News*'s article 'Influenza Theories -Soldiers Say it is Trench Fever,'[38] which reported that some soldiers believed the disease was either trench fever or a form of malaria.[39] There was speculation in the London *Times* during October 1918: 'that a high medical authority states that the disease is directly traceable to the German use of poison gas, the after effects of which have induced growth of a new type of streptococcus'.[40] In China, influenza was believed to be due to 'the contamination of the world's atmosphere by the use of gas and other explosives in Europe'[41] Most American newspapers printed the suspicions of Colonel Philip S. Doane that influenza had been started deliberately in theatres and cinemas by German agents put ashore from U-boats.[42] In Ireland, during December 1918, there were unlikely rumours in the *Irish Independent* that the disease was 'Swine fever caused by American bacon'.[43]

The focus of nationalist run newspapers on the mysteriousness of the disease was primarily to do with political concerns. During 1918–1919 a large increase in venereal disease was reported in Ireland,[44] and Sinn Féin, as part of their anti-conscription campaign, directly associated the dangers of venereal disease with soldiers returning to Ireland. Ben Novick has argued that Sinn Féin propagandists blamed the British for the presence of drink, immoral entertainment and the slaughter of war and thus presented themselves as the champions of decency and morality in Ireland.[45] Newspaper articles associating returning soldiers with venereal disease were censored by the authorities, but this did not appear to be the case with those on influenza.[46] Dr Kathleen Lynn, Director of Public Health for Sinn Féin and an active anti-conscription supporter, was particularly interested in the political impact of infectious diseases and blamed the British Army for the spread of venereal disease.[47]

Phillips and Killingray argued that the association of influenza with war—or as a weapon of war—was good propaganda for belligerents such as Sinn Féin.[48] Lynn used influenza to good effect. She attacked the victors of World War I by blaming the Allies for the spread of the disease.[49] Her report on influenza, which was adopted at the Sinn Féin Árd Fheis in April 1919, stated:

> The factory of fever is still in full working order in Flanders...the battle-field....The English and French have left millions of men and horses to rot unburied where they fell.....In France and Flanders the poisonous matter from millions of unburied bodies is constantly rising up into the air, which is blown all over the world by the winds.[50]

It was true that the war facilitated the spread of influenza. However, there has been some debate on whether the war played a part in its virulence. Jay Winter argued that the war was not a factor in the virulence of the disease.[51] However, the conditions on the western front were perfect to encourage the spread of the influenza virus.[52] Carol Byerly agreed that the war created an ecological environment in the trenches in which the influenza virus could thrive and mutate to unprecedented virulence.[53] Therefore, it would be unfair to totally dismiss the nationalist newspapers' scepticism and concern regarding influenza. The outbreaks of influenza in Ireland during the first wave were very sporadic and occurred in Belfast, Dublin, Drogheda, Ballinasloe, Tipperary, Athlone and Cork and it is notable that these towns were close to a military base. A contemporary report during the summer of 1918 stated that there were approximately 5,000 influenza cases among the Ulster Brigade and all the military hospitals in the province were proportionately affected. Elsewhere in Ireland, at the military medical hospital at Queenstown, there were 87 influenza admissions between 26 June and 27 July 1918.[54] Therefore, there was more than a grain of truth in the allegations of newspapers such as the *Irish News*, *Irish Independent* and *Derry Journal* that the war and returning soldiers were linked to influenza.[55]

The association of influenza with trench fever, poison gas and returning soldiers, provided Sinn Féin propagandists with the opportunity to increase fear and suspicion by questioning whether the disease was indeed influenza or another 'poison' brought back to Ireland from the western front. The anti-conscription campaign was one that united both Sinn Féin and the IPP during this period.[56] The insinuation that war and returning troops brought infections such as venereal disease and the 'mystery illness' of influenza to Ireland no doubt helped increase the suspicion of soldiers and fear of conscription, with the suggestion that healthy Irishmen would be sent to war only to return with infectious diseases.

Nevertheless, the apprehension felt by people during the pandemic should not be underestimated as was articulated by a newspaper article in 2003 which reported the recollections of a survivor of the 1918 pandemic, Molly Deery from Lifford, County Donegal. She recalled that influenza: 'hit very hard and the people were very fearful and frightened of it ... You see the people had no idea what caused it. I'm not sure of the exact numbers of victims as we didn't read newspapers in them times'. But she recalled that 'It was a terrible, terrible flu though, and people were told to keep to one side of the road if someone in a house had it'.[57] Similarly, Dr Macnamara, recollected 'the terrible fear that was everywhere, which gripped the people like a vice' which was hardly surprising as 'once one was smitten with the disease there was no reasonable certainty or recovery'.[58]

It is probable that referring to influenza as 'plague' and 'mysterious malady' in Irish nationalist newspapers would have helped increase the fear and suspicion of the disease among their readerships.[59] Philip Alcabes argued that when alarmist media use the word 'plague' they are clearly alluding to one of the greatest disease outbreaks in western history, the Black Death.[60] The constant use of this particular word held fearful connotations and the evidence shows that people did associate influenza with plague. During January 1919, thanksgiving prayers appeared in the *Irish Independent*, giving 'Thanks to the Sacred Heart and St Roch for preservation from influenza'.[61] St Roch was a saint associated with the plague and people prayed to him as a protector from the disease.[62] Thanksgiving notices to St Roch appeared in the *Irish Independent* during January, February and March 1919.[63] These, along with the following prayer to St Roch found in the *Westmeath Chronicle* in November 1918, would indicate that people did indeed associate influenza with the plague:-

> O God, who by the ministry of an angel didst give to glorious St Roch a promise engraven on a table, that whosoever shall invoke his name should be preserved from pestilence, grant that we, who revere his memory, may through his intercession be delivered in soul and body from all mortal contagion, through Jesus Christ, Our Lord. Amen[64]

Another consequence of referring to influenza by these terms is that it merges influenza in the public's consciousness with another disease. Echenberg suggested that references in Australian newspapers to influenza as a plague contributed to the fusion of the two diseases of influenza and bubonic plague in the public perception. Echenberg argued that this eventually led to the removal of the influenza pandemic from the collective memory in that country.[65]

During the first wave, some local newspapers did not mention the pandemic at all. Janice Hume found that many of the popular contemporary American magazines had no articles on influenza. She argued that the silences in certain publications around epidemics are equally enlightening as the coverage, suggesting it was easier for editors to report on war, where there were identifiable protagonists, than to focus on a serious domestic crisis.[66] Certainly, this would seem to be the case in Ulster, where local unionist-run newspapers such as the *Down Recorder*, *Mid-Ulster Mail*, *Northern Constitution*, *Ulster Gazette* and the *Ulster Guardian* made no mention of influenza during the first wave. This may be because influenza did not affect all Irish towns during this outbreak so there may have been nothing to report.

However, the lack of articles could also have been an attempt to minimise reporting of the disease to raise morale and help the war effort. Of course, it was important not to create panic especially during a time of conflict. Charles Graves' global history of the pandemic, *Invasion by virus*, was postponed for publication in 1958 due to the outbreak of Asiatic Flu in 1957. The book was only subsequently published in 1969 after the Hong Kong Influenza of 1968 was found not to be a major killer. Graves stated in his 'Foreword', 'No publisher in his right senses would have dared to face charges of frightening the public still further than it had already been by the newspaper reports'.[67]

Silence in newspapers could also be caused by staff shortages due to influenza itself. During the second wave, several newspapers were unable to produce issues due to influenza absences.[68] Other newspapers were unable to produce their normal issues due to depletion of their staff.[69] On 4 November 1918, the size of the *Kilkenny Journal* was reduced owing to illness of practically all of its staff.[70] Although most disturbances happened during the autumn 1918, during the first wave, the *Portadown Express* told its readers on 5 July 1918 that if the newspaper was not as interesting as usual 'they can blame the "flu"' which had caused the 'diminishing its otherwise smooth running business machinery'.[71] This implied that staff shortages in newspapers also occurred during the first wave which may also have led to the lack of influenza articles during this wave.

Second and Third Wave: October 1918–May 1919

During the second wave there were fewer references to influenza in Germany. Nevertheless, occasionally, columns of reports on influenza in various Irish towns would often be followed by an account of the seemingly large casualties in either Austrian or German cities.[72] Most of the German associations were made in unionist-run newspapers before the armistice on 11 November 1918, placing emphasis on the high mortality among the Germans. On 23 October 1918, the *Belfast News-Letter* referred to the reoccurrence of a large number of influenza cases in Berlin.[73] On 1 November 1918, the *Armagh Guardian* stated that 'the mortality in Germany and Austria is very much greater than in this country'[74] and the *Portadown Weekly News* on 2 November 1918 claimed there were 180,000 new cases of influenza in the German army.[75]

Reports on foreign casualties, however, were not only confined to European cities as, in October 1918, articles appeared in relation to severe influenza outbreaks in South Africa.[76] These articles were perhaps an attempt to downplay the effect of the pandemic in Great Britain and Ireland by reporting the huge influenza casualties elsewhere. Debra Blakely, argued that British coverage of the pandemic concentrated on attributing the origin of influenza elsewhere. Added to this emphasis was placed on the seriousness of the international form of the disease as opposed to the local effects of influenza.[77] Similarly, Niall Johnson argued that 'it may be the scale of the impact elsewhere that made the impact on Britain seem trivial'.[78]

During this wave, as in the first, nationalist newspapers continued to use words like 'plague' and 'mysterious' when referring to influenza. An editorial in the *Derry Journal* on 28 October 1918, suggested that the suddenness of the disease made some contend that the 'term influenza as applied is a misnomer' and went on to ask 'Is it influenza at all?'[79] On 6 November, an editorial in the same newspaper entitled 'Mysterious Malady' further stated 'it is supremely tragic to find that a colossal toll in human lives is being taken through a disease called influenza, doubtless for want of a name to specify it with more exactitude?' The editorial questioned what the disease was and described it as a 'mysteriousplague'.[80]

Again, the *Irish Independent* often used the word 'plague' or 'scourge' to describe influenza in Ireland especially during October and November 1918.[81] An editorial in the nationalist *Irish News* entitled 'A Public Peril' queried that '"Influenza" is not the name that should be applied to the deadly plague now ravaging towns and cities throughout the world'.[82] An editorial in the same newspaper on 29 October described influenza as a 'new plague' and on 30 October influenza was described as 'the Plague, which has already taken a terrible toll of victims in Ireland' in an article and editorial.[83] On 13 November 1918, the *Dungannon Democrat* reported that: 'It can be seen that this is no ordinary influenza but some form of disease which up to the present baffles the best skill of medical men'.[84] It is notable that most of these references occurred before the armistice on 11 November 1918 and were probably still part of the continuing Sinn Féin and IPP anti-conscription propaganda regarding war and influenza.

This was not the only way that Sinn Féin used influenza for propaganda purposes. Due to the global nature of influenza, Sinn Féin was unable to attribute blame for the disease on to the British administration. Nevertheless, their propagandists were adept at using any situation to their advantage, so it was no real surprise that influenza was exploited for propaganda purposes in Ireland. The main focus of Sinn Féin's propaganda regarding the pandemic concerned the prison conditions of the Irish internees who were held in both Irish and British jails.

Sinn Féin Propaganda and Influenza

During the second and third waves of the pandemic the plight of the Sinn Féin prisoners interned in the UK was highlighted by some newspapers. On the 17 May 1918, over 100 Sinn Féin and Irish Volunteer members were arrested and interned under the Defence of the Realm Act (DORA), in relation to the alleged 'German Plot' and the majority were sent to British prisons.[85] At the same time there were 200 Sinn Féin prisoners incarcerated in Belfast Jail on short-term sentences who were not among those arrested in May 1918.[86] Although all the prisoners escaped influenza in the summer of 1918, those in Belfast and Usk Prisons were not so fortunate during the more virulent second wave in the autumn of 1918.

In late October 1918 newspaper reports appeared stating that over 100 Sinn Féin prisoners in Belfast Jail were suffering from influenza.[87] Questions had already been asked in parliament regarding the treatment of prisoners in the jail. During June 1918, the prison governor had been forced to temporarily remove the ameliorated conditions of the DORA prisoners and, as a result, the prisoners retaliated violently and wrecked their cells. They resisted prison officials and had to be forcibly removed. The actions of the prison officials became the subject of an inquiry, as the prisoners made several allegations of ill treatment. Although some prisoners lost their privileges because of this incident, their ameliorated conditions were re-instated a short time afterwards and were in place during the influenza outbreak.[88]

Consequently, on news of influenza reaching Belfast Jail in October 1918, questions were again asked in parliament regarding the influenza patients and their treatment. The Attorney General for Ireland, Arthur Samuels, dismissed Sinn Féin's allegations that the prisoners had insufficient food and unsatisfactory medical or nursing arrangements. He reported that special treatment and diet were provided for each of the prisoners and two extra doctors had been engaged to assist in the prison.[89] Further questions were asked and on 7 November 1918, the Chief Secretary made a statement in parliament on the conditions in Belfast Jail. He reported there were 17 prisoners in outside hospitals, 21 minor cases in the prison hospital, and 96 cases were convalescing. All the prisoners were on a most satisfactory special, full and varied diet and that everything possible was being done to prevent the epidemic spreading.[90] An article in the *Irish Independent* on 30 October quoted a letter read out at the Sinn Féin Ard Fheis from Belfast prisoner Austin Stack in which he recounted that there were 112 men under the doctor's care, 17 were in the prison hospital which was full to capacity and the rest were in their cells. There was no nurse and two orderlies were dishing out quinine every day. He had written to the Board to request medical doctors and six to ten nurses. This article also advised that 'some 150 are stricken with the influenza plague. There was accommodation for only 15 in the hospital. Bread and margarine with tea was their food up to a day-or-two ago, while the plank bed rule was unaltered. The article went on to say that to keep men in prison under such conditions is murder pure and simple.[91]

Fionán Lynch, an inmate in Belfast Jail during this period, later concurred with the official account. He recounted that both prisoners and warders were ill with influenza and that cell doors were left open all day and night to permit the more able prisoners to nurse those who were incapacitated with the disease. Lynch attributed the prisoners' very good medical treatment to Sinn Féin's highly efficient propaganda machine. He believed that the British authorities wanted to avoid the negative publicity that would occur if any prisoners died during this outbreak. In consequence, he believed that all available Belfast doctors were asked to assist at the prison and that they were most attentive. He commented that 'they prescribed large doses of brandy for those who were ill'.[92] Eoin O'Duffy, another Belfast inmate, agreed that the governor was not only forced to leave cells open at night but also had to supply alcohol for medicinal purposes.[93] As a result of the influenza outbreak, a portion of the prison occupied by Sinn Féin prisoners was converted into a hospital, meaning that the already lax discipline which had applied to them was further relaxed, as they were now hospital patients.[94]

Eoin O'Duffy stated that before the pandemic 'a coach and fours was driven through the prison regulations and our men have practically received their own terms'. He boasted that the prison governor's authority almost entirely collapsed during the outbreak of influenza.[95] Therefore, it is no surprise that the prisoners did not allow the pre-pandemic conditions of discipline to be re-established and while they were convalescing from influenza; they mutinied and damaged prison property, forcing the governor to again suspend their ameliorated treatment. Belfast inmate, Austin Stack recounted that ameliorations were suspended from 21 January 1919 and the prisoners were kept in solitary confinement until the 29 April 1919 when they were removed to Manchester.[96]

The *Irish Independent*, in particular, reported on the 'callous treatment' in Belfast Jail, via articles and correspondence between 29 October and 8 November 1918. Quoting the Lord Mayor of Dublin who said: 'if they were not treated "as Christians instead of wild beasts," the disgrace and dishonour would be on the heads of the Government. Ireland demands that the men in prison suffering from this virulent disease shall be treated with humanity'.[97] It seems that these reports achieved their desired effect of keeping the plight of the prisoners in the public eye. The Belfast prisoners' situation was so expertly exploited that even Dr Kathleen Lynn, who was herself trying to evade capture by the authorities, as well as treat hundreds of influenza patients in Dublin, wrote in her diary of 30 October 1918 'Back to work, injected about 250 in all....Belfast prisoners bad. Epidemics (Pneumonia Plague) fearful'.[98]

Although there was no evidence that influenza visited Belfast Jail during the third wave, the Belfast prisoners' predicament was kept in the public consciousness. On 8 March 1919, the *Irish Independent* reported that as influenza was raging in Belfast if it 'should penetrate to the prison it is feared that the present condition of the Sinn Féin prisoners will find them an easy prey to the ravages of the disease'.[99] However, this negative propaganda appeared to have little effect on the authorities because, although the prisoners interned in British prisons were released to return home to Ireland in March 1919, those held in Belfast and other Irish jails were not set free.[100] In fact, as Austin Stack advised, the remaining 11 Sinn Féin prisoners held in Belfast were sent to Strangeways Prison in Manchester at the end of April 1919.[101]

During the three waves of the pandemic, the official mortality from influenza in Belfast could have been as high as 2,352.[102] Ironically, despite all of the publicity and anxiety about the Belfast prisoners, they, unlike the population of the city, suffered no fatalities.[103] Fionán Lynch agreed that 'whilst the 'flu was killing off people by the million all over the world, not a single prisoner died of it in Belfast Jail'.[104] Perhaps this was due to the superior medical treatment, diet and isolation provided for the Belfast internees, conditions that were not afforded to the normal Belfast citizen during this medical emergency. Therefore, it appeared that Belfast Jail was the safest place to be in the city during the pandemic. In fact, only one prisoner died of influenza in Irish prisons during 1918, Martha Moore aged 23, a female prisoner in Londonderry Jail, who entered the jail with the disease and subsequently died on 20 October 1918.[105]

The Irish internees held in Usk Prison in Wales also contracted influenza during the winter of 1918, but they were not as fortunate as those in Belfast. Usk prisoner, George Lyons, advised that influenza was prevalent in the district for some time before the prison was affected. In an interview for the *Irish Independent*, he advised that first the prison officers and then the prisoners contracted influenza. The official prison doctor was away at war and the local doctor only paid intermediate visits to the prison, as there were over 200 cases in the local town. A resident doctor was eventually arranged for the prison on 1 December 1918. However, by that time, Herbert Mellows, John Joseph Clancy, Eamon Moane, Joseph McGrath, Richard Coleman and W. J. Brennan Whitmore had contracted influenza. The patients were removed to a new prison hospital on 2 December, but were not provided with a male nurse until 6 December 1918 and then for only one hour per day. Prior to this, the prisoners nursed their sick comrades themselves, which meant that they too contracted influenza.[106] Usk prisoner, George Geraghty, stated in a letter to his wife that it was next to impossible for the influenza sufferers to get proper nourishment.[107] Geraghty escaped influenza and acted as a 'night nurse to his comrades'. He recounted that due to the lack of medication at the prison, the two bottles of Jameson's Whiskey, which he had brought back to Usk from his ten-day parole, were used as medicine for those who were ill.[108]

One tragic outcome at Usk was the death of Richard Coleman on 9 December 1918 from pneumonia following on from influenza. Coleman had been a Volunteer who fought during the Easter Rising at Ashbourne. Although sentenced to death for his part in the Rising, his sentence was commuted to penal servitude and he was released on amnesty. He was subsequently imprisoned twice and had been through two hunger strikes, and finally was interned in Usk prison as part of the alleged 'German Plot' arrests.[109] It was Coleman's death that was the focus of the Sinn Féin propaganda campaign leading up to and beyond the General Election of December 1918. Frank Gallagher, who was an assistant in the Sinn Féin Department of Propaganda,[110] stated that Coleman's inquest disclosed 'utter neglect of the sick in Usk Prison, where many Irish prisoners struck down by the epidemic had only one untrained male nurse to attend to them'.[111] The testimony of two of the prisoners who also suffered from influenza at Usk Jail and who spoke at the inquest—John O'Reilly and John Joseph Clancy—would confirm this.

Clancy stated that there was inadequate nursing in the isolation ward with only one inexperienced male nurse provided. On Tuesday morning 3 December 1918, between 5 am and 12 noon, the patients on the ward were only served soda water despite their requests for milk. The prisoners complained to the doctor regarding the lack of milk as well as excessive noise made by the warders in the isolation ward. John O'Reilly stated that Coleman 'was nursed by his compatriots'. The drinks he was supplied were provided by his compatriots for at least three nights'.[112] Their inquest testimony was reported at length in the *Irish Independent*[113] and the same newspaper also reported that Coleman's brother, Frederick, who had travelled from Ireland, was unable to see him before he died due to 'prison red-tapeism'.[114] At the inquest Frederick advised that his brother 'was dead when I got to the Prison Ward'.[115]

The newspapers' reports of the conditions at Usk prompted outrage in Ireland. Information was received from Sinn Féin headquarters that two trained nurses had volunteered their services to attend the Usk prisoners and that ten other nurses were available for similar worked if needed.[116] Sinn Féin sent a telegram to the Irish Office stating 'Irish trained nurses ready to leave for English Prisons to nurse Irish Prisoners stricken with influenza. Wire necessary permits'. On 14 December 1918, the Home

Office rejected this offer claiming that all necessary provision for prisoners had been made, and that nurses were not required since the worst of the epidemic at Usk was over.[117] The internees' correspondence reflected the strength of public feeling with regard to Coleman's death. George Lyons received a letter at Usk stating 'Richard Coleman's death has caused a profound feeling of anger and remorse among all classes of the Irish people ..... If you are not all released by Christmas from your unjust imprisonment it will look as if the authorities are courting trouble and taking a leaf out of the Kaiser's book'.[118]

Although feeling was high in Ireland with articles reporting Coleman's death and funeral to be found in Irish papers such as the *Irish Times*, *Freeman's Journal*, *Irish Independent*, *Donegal Vindicator*, *Dungannon Democrat* and *Fermanagh News*,[119] there was little reportage of the death or its cause in the English newspapers. The exception was a small article in *The Times* on 14 December 1918, tucked away on page 5 stating that the 'body of Richard Coleman, one of the Sinn Féin prisoners interned in Usk, arrived at Kingstown from Holyhead yesterday. Coleman died from pneumonia'.[120] Countess Markievicz, who was interned in Holloway, in a letter to her sister dated 12 December 1918 noted: 'Did you see that one of us died at Usk? It was not in the English papers.....We are so lucky here. Usk is evidently very hard'.[121] The lack of publicity in English newspapers upset both prisoners and their correspondents as noted by the censor, who commented in his December report that 'The death of Richard Coleman in Usk Prison gave rise to a certain amount of hostile criticism and letters both to and from Ireland showed that efforts were being made to exploit it as a further instance of British inhumanity. The silence of the English press on the subject was noted with resentment'.[122]

Although it appeared that the authorities ignored Coleman's death, the evidence shows they did not. Fear of further deaths in custody may have prompted the unconditional release from Usk of George Lyons on medical grounds, as well as W. J. Brennan Whitmore and Con O'Donovan, both suffering from complications following on from influenza.[123] Count Plunkett, who was interned in Birmingham prison, was released on medical grounds by the Secretary of State in December 1918 even though he was not actually ill. Concern about his health was raised by the following passage in a suppressed letter from Edward Waldron in Birmingham Prison stating that 'Health as good as can be expected under circumstances. Count Plunkett being the only one who seems about to break down rapidly'. This prompted the Home Office to request a medical report in which the Medical Inspector for Prisons stated Plunkett was a 'frail old man and that while there is nothing in particular the matter with him at present, his general condition is such that if he caught influenza or other disease he would probably die quite quickly'. Based on this, the Secretary of State released Plunkett on medical grounds.[124] Plunkett's son, Joseph Mary Plunkett was executed in 1916 for his part in the Easter Rising and this fact, along with the threat that, at the age of 67, Plunkett could possibly become ill and die in custody, so close to the death of Coleman, probably encouraged the decision for his early release.

Kathleen Clarke, held at Holloway, claimed that her heart trouble facilitated her early release from prison on medical grounds. Both her husband, Tom Clarke, and her younger brother, Edward Daly were executed for their parts in the Easter Rising and it is likely that this fact along with her constant illness during internment led to her early release, so that the authorities could avoid adverse publicity. Ironically, it was after Clarke's release from Holloway in February 1919 that she contracted influenza. She was very unwell and remained in a nursing home for seven weeks where she reported that 'during which time death and myself had a big tussle'.[125] However, she did make a full recovery and lived to the ripe old age of 94.

It has been argued that during the influenza pandemic the authorities were more favourably inclined towards internees' requests for compassionate parole.[126] Darrell Figgis, interned in Durham Prison, was refused compassionate parole in November 1918 to visit his wife who was ill with influenza. A letter dated 14 November 1918 to Mrs Figgis advised that 'if unfortunately you should become dangerously ill, the Chief Secretary will sanction the temporary release of your husband'.[127] It appeared that her health must have improved, as Figgis was not granted parole on this occasion. However, in late February 1919 he was granted parole due to the illness of his wife as well as a fire in his flat.[128] This suggests that there was a wariness of negative publicity by the prison authorities after Richard Coleman's death, prompting them to be more amenable to the internees' requests for compassionate paroles. In fact it was noticeable that the majority of paroles due to family illness were granted to Irish internees in British jails after Coleman's death, in January and February 1919,[129] which suggests the prison authorities were wary of further adverse publicity relating to these prisoners.

The plight of the Usk prisoners and especially the death of Dick Coleman provided one of the best propaganda opportunities for Sinn Féin, a fact that the Censor was well aware of. In his December report he noted 'The death of Richard Coleman in Usk Prison gave rise to a certain amount of hostile criticism and letters both to and from Ireland showed that efforts were being made to exploit it as a further instance of British inhumanity'. Newspaper articles were also critical. Irish newspapers reported on the adjourned Dublin Corporation meeting of 16 December 1918, where the Lord Mayor, Laurence O'Neill, expressed the council's sympathy with the Coleman family. His criticism of the treatment of Coleman by the British authorities was clear:

> Young Coleman's case is only a sample of the reign of Prussianism we are going through. This young man, taken from his bed in the middle of the night, torn from his mother's arms, arrested on the deposition of a country policeman, carried away in a military wagon, thrown into an English jail – away from home and friends. Even the little packages of necessaries sent him by loving hands pilfered by the authorities, his constitution undermined owing to constant imprisonment, and then the worn-out frame gives out, and all this barbarous treatment given to a man against whom no charge whatever had been made. What a victory for English legislation![130]

The Censor however suspended publication of Councillor Doyle's more vitriolic contribution to the meeting that 'He had reason to know the callousness and brutality which was shown by the authorities to Irishmen in English Prisons.......When a person became sick in prison he was left there like a dog'.[131]

Coleman's death occurred a few days before the general election, which was held on 14 December 1918, therefore newspaper coverage of the circumstances of his death, inquest and well organised funeral bought Sinn Féin valuable and timely publicity. Not surprisingly, Sinn Féin attempted to obtain political gain for the upcoming election and at a meeting in support of Alderman Thomas Kelly in Dublin, Mr M. J. O' Mullane referring to Coleman's death stated:

> The time for talking about policy had passed, [and the time had come to avenge the murder of Dick Coleman, for murdered he was by the British tyrants so sure as Tom Ashe was murdered in Mountjoy]. If they got hold of Lloyd George they would hang him on the nearest lamp post [for that

> murder], but since they could not get hold of him they would grip on him in another way on Saturday.[132]

A letter to Frank Fahy in Usk implied that Coleman's death would swing the election result: 'I see another one has been done to death in His Majesty's Hotel, Usk, which I am very sorry for but you can rest assured it did not do them any good in the Fall's election. Fr O'Flanagan spoke about it at the meeting last week. The people nearly went mad with rage over it'.[133] It was Frank Gallagher's opinion that Coleman's death turned the tide of public opinion by influencing undecided voters to vote Sinn Féin.[134]

Reports of the mistreatment of Usk prisoners appeared in newspapers directly after Coleman's death. As previously mentioned, details of his inquest were reported in the *Irish Independent* on 12 December 1918 and on 11 December 1918, Maude Gonne Mac Bride's letter about Coleman's death, printed in both the *Freeman's Journal* and the *Irish Independent* stated: 'influenza is in Usk prison, and in how many more of the prisons where Irish patriots are shut up we do not know. Why should these men and women, who are charged with no offence, be subjected to such hideous risk? Their continued imprisonment is a scandal'.[135] In an attempt to obtain release of the internees, Darrell Figgis sent a letter to the *Irish Independent* stating 'others are suffering from the influenza scourge, and unless something is immediately done we shall probably have further victims'.[136]

The early release of prisoners on medical grounds in late January and early February 1919 kept public awareness of prison conditions at Usk alive as once released, they gave newspaper interviews regarding the inadequate nursing at the prison.[137] The overall effect of these accounts should not be underestimated as the Press Censor noted 'the coloured accounts of men who have been released on grounds of ill health have worked up the country to a dangerous pitch.[138]

Reports concerning conditions at both Usk and Belfast prisons regarding influenza focused attention on the treatment of Irish prisoners, not only in the press, but also at political meetings and in parliamentary debates. The Censor was well aware of the propaganda benefits to Sinn Féin of using Coleman's death and warned that it would be used as further proof of British inhumanity to Irish internees. Insinuation in political speeches that Coleman was 'murdered' succeeded in giving him the status of national martyr. Meanwhile, Dublin Lord Mayor, Laurence

O'Neill's unfavourable comparison of the British authorities with 'Prussianism' and his suggestion that Coleman's death was due to 'barbarous treatment' portrayed an unfavourable image of British brutality and inhumanity to the Irish people.

In late January 1919, all remaining prisoners in Usk Jail were transferred to Gloucester Jail which George Lyons believed was due to the unsanitary conditions at Usk.[139] Inmate William Loughran, complained in a letter to Miss Rooney that 'I cannot say the change is anything for the better. The only thing we have done is to leave behind the damp beds and cold cells of Usk for the cold cells of Gloucester. There is no such thing as fire known here, and as for the food it is simply wretched and no-one with a human heart would offer it to a dog'.[140] These concerns about conditions at Gloucester may not just have been sour grapes, as towards the end of February 1919 the inmates of both Durham and Gloucester prisons were to fall victim to the third wave of influenza. On 4 March 1919, the *Irish Independent* reported that influenza was rampant in Gloucester Prison and Arthur Griffith 'is anything but well'.[141] Fortunately Griffith did recover from influenza but another Gloucester prisoner, Pierse McCan, was not so fortunate.

On 25 February 1919 five Gloucester prisoners were sent to a nursing home in the town with a mild form of influenza. On 6 March 1919 Pierse McCan,[142] the Sinn Féin TD for Tipperary East, died from broncho-pneumonia following on from influenza.[143] McCan's last letter home dated 22 February 1919 prophetically stated that Gloucester 'is full of influenza at present and nearly all the staff have got knocked up. None of us has got it yet, but the doctor says if it does break out we will be very bad subjects after our long confinement, and that the danger will be great'. Again, much was made of his death. Details of his public funeral were reported in the newspapers[144] and the *Irish Independent* described him as 'the third victim' to die while in British Custody.[145] William Murphy noted that Sinn Féin released a pamphlet claiming that McCan was 'slow murdered in Gloucester Jail'.[146] Colum claimed that the Irish public were so stirred by McCan's death that it initiated an inquiry into the conditions in prisons where the Sinn Féin leaders were interned with the result that a general release from prison was ordered.[147] This was an understandable assumption as the Press Censor advised that the released prisoners themselves 'commented unfavourably upon the treatment they had received and attributed their release to the death of Mr P McCann'.[148]

However, Sean McConville argued that a more likely reason for their release was because the British Government was faced with a breakdown of discipline among the Irish Internees, which had in turn led to a demoralisation of prison staff who feared confrontation with the prisoners.[149] Nevertheless, the fact that influenza was rife in both Gloucester and Durham Jails, and the subsequent illness of several of the inmates during late February/early March 1919, may have played a significant part in the release of the prisoners. On 4 March 1919, the War Cabinet advised the Home Office that 'Sinn Féin prisoners interned in England are to be released gradually, priority being given to those who have suffered in health by their confinement'.[150] This letter, dated 4 March 1919, pre-dated McCan's death on 6 March 1919 by two days, however, the majority of prisoners were not actually released until after his demise, making it look as if McCan's death precipitated their release. The fact that priority was to be given to those prisoners who had suffered from ill health suggests that the authorities were concerned that there would be further fatalities among the prisoners while in custody.

Although the British authorities appeared to be oblivious to the situation at Usk, it seems that they were concerned that there would be more deaths in custody. This would account for the early release on medical grounds of Count Plunkett, Kathleen Clarke and the three Usk prisoners in early January 1919. Also after Coleman's death the authorities were more generous in granting compassionate leave to internees to return home to visit sick relatives. Although the War Cabinet refused to release the internees in British jails in early February 1919, it is probable that the outbreak of influenza, and subsequent illness of several Durham and Gloucester Jail inmates in late February/early March 1919, was a deciding factor in their decision to free them in March 1919, not only to avoid further deaths in prison, but also to avoid further adverse publicity. However, their decision came too late as the death of Pierse McCan in custody created further propaganda opportunities for Sinn Féin and negative publicity for the British authorities.

Electioneering During the Pandemic

The fate of the political prisoners held in Irish and English prisons took precedence in nationalist newspapers during November and December 1918. However, the general election in December 1918 appeared to take priority in all newspapers during the height of the more virulent second wave of influenza. This was articulated in a letter from Mayo in the *Irish Independent* on 2 December 1918. The correspondent complained that while influenza raged along the western seaboard, 'the metropolitan papers, and indeed, some of our provincial papers are so busy with electioneering propaganda that this pestilential epidemic is now relegated to the status of stale unimportant news'.[151]

Election coverage seemed to dominate the newspapers during late November 1918 and December 1918. In the north of England the influenza pandemic affected campaigning for the 1918 election, where the fear of infection, along with war weariness, accounted for much of the apathy surrounding the election.[152] There were many articles in Irish newspapers that advised of large gatherings of people at election meetings. This was even though assembly in crowded meetings was discouraged by MOHs throughout Ireland. It appeared that election campaigners ignored this advice. The election committee for the East-Down constituency seriously discussed whether meetings should be held at all due to influenza in the district, but nevertheless decided to hold them. The *Down Recorder* noted that attendances everywhere were affected by influenza as people were warned to avoid the risk of infection associated with public assemblies. However, the question was posed 'can a contested election be conceived of without meetings? Or without canvassing? Hardly'.[153] The suggestion at the Dungannon rural council December meeting that they should not hold election meetings was met with laughter.[154]

Influenza impacted on certain election campaigns. The *Down Recorder* advised that there was a relatively small attendance at the pre-election meeting in Castlewellan for the candidature of East-Down unionist, David Reid.[155] In Saintfield no band accompanied Mid-Down unionist candidate Colonel James Craig's election meeting out of respect for those people suffering from influenza.[156] The Nationalist Convention for North Kilkenny to select a Parliamentary candidate for the constituency was postponed until 23 November 1918 owing to the prevalence of influenza.[157] Conversely, South Tyrone unionist candidate, William Coote's election campaign was unaffected as there was a 'large meeting' assembled at the Castlecaulfield Orange Hall and 'a well-attended meeting' in the courthouse in Moy in support of his campaign.[158] The *County Down Spectator* reported that large crowds assembled in the 'large Dufferin Hall' in support of the North Down unionist candidate.[159] On 3 December 1918 notices appeared in the *Irish Independent* in relation to election meetings for IPP candidate Tom Clarke at Dalkey Town Hall and for Sinn Féin Candidate P J Little at Rathmines.[160] Reports in the *Dungannon Democrat* of a 'largely attended Nationalist Convention' in Pomeroy on 24 November 1918 to propose Thomas Harbinson as the IPP candidate for North-east Tyrone,[161] and of 'A great meeting at Moy' as part of the South Tyrone campaign for John Skeffington, Nationalist and Labour candidate,[162] implied that not all meetings were restricted due to influenza.

Similarly, Sinn Féin's campaign continued despite the pandemic. Frank Gallagher recounted how he and other Sinn Féin workers travelled the country campaigning, saw for themselves the devastation of influenza and stated that they 'saw from the train windows funerals everywhere'.[163] Nevertheless, influenza did not seem to restrict their activities as he described how on one day he attended four outdoor meetings; Ballycastle in the morning, West Belfast in the afternoon, Balbriggan in the evening and Swords at midnight.[164] Newspaper reports confirmed that Sinn Féin candidates also brought out the crowds. The *Ulster Herald* reported there was 'a large gathering in Omagh town' to hear Fr O'Flanagan'. It also reported that there was 'a largely attended meeting' at Loughmacrory, as well as 'an enthusiastic meeting' near Donaghmore in support of Sinn Féin candidate Sean Milroy.[165] Although influenza may have caused attendances at meetings to have been reduced in places such as Castlewellan, the majority of meetings were not cancelled and in some cases had substantial attendances. As the numerous articles on the election campaign would adhere to, despite the risks, influenza did not curtail the election campaigns of any of the parties to any great extent, nor did it stop the arrangement of, or the attendance at, political meetings during this period.

During the third wave, news coverage of the pandemic in Irish newspapers declined considerably from that of the second in some of the local newspapers. Some provincial newspapers barely mentioned influenza even though it was prevalent again throughout Ireland. In some cases, it was only the presence of advertisements for treatments in the newspapers that would give any indication of the presence of the disease at all. These will be discussed in Chapter 5 in more detail.

An analysis of articles in Ulster newspaper shows that most influenza-related articles appeared during the second and most virulent wave of the pandemic and the fewest during the first. It is notable that the majority of influenza-related articles in each wave coincided with the peaks of that particular wave. That is, during the first, second and third waves the majority of influenza-related articles appeared in July 1918, November 1918 and March 1919, respectively. During this period newspapers were relatively thin by modern standards with even national newspapers comprising around eight to twelve pages.[166] There were paper restrictions due to the war and it was mentioned in the *Armagh Guardian* that the paper supply for 1918 was one-sixth of that for 1914.[167] Therefore, space was at a premium and perhaps, because of this, influenza paled into insignificance against other contemporary news stories such as the progress of the war and in December 1918 the upcoming election.

It is evident from researching the newspapers that influenza was not considered a particularly newsworthy subject in Ulster. Although there were articles on influenza in the newspapers, they were infrequent, especially in the local newspapers. Ida Milne argued that in Leinster, news of the pandemic took precedence in the local and national press and pushed war and other news items into the background. She also found that there was much criticism of the Government's handling of the pandemic from all sections of the press regardless of their political affiliation. This criticism was not apparent in Ulster newspapers. Milne concluded that questions needed to be asked as to why this disease, which dominated so many newspapers columns, had been left out of Irish historiography for so many years.[168]

The 1918–19 influenza pandemic was described by Alfred Crosby as the 'forgotten pandemic'.[169] There are many reasons why this health catastrophe was forgotten in Ireland and the rest of the world. Undoubtedly, World War I, contributed to worldwide amnesia on the pandemic and theories regarding the absorption of the event into the collective memory of the war have validity.[170] Phillips and Killingray have suggested that because the pandemic occurred at the climax of World War 1 with its massive death toll, that influenza has been overshadowed by these events.[171] Closer to home, the political upheaval in Ireland during this period—and subsequently—may also be a factor in why influenza has been forgotten specifically in Irish historiography. Added to this, influenza was an infrequent disease which struck suddenly, caused mayhem and then just as mysteriously disappeared.[172] There was also no known cure for influenza and doctors seemed to be powerless against it, so the medical profession would have no desire to remember their failures in that respect. Other contemporary diseases, such as tuberculosis were a much more prevalent and a frequent public health problem during this period. Between the '1890s and the first decades of the twentieth-century tuberculosis became a major, possibly *the* major, public health issue' in Ireland.[173] Moreover, in 1917 the mortality from all forms of tuberculosis in Ireland was 9,680 and in 1918 it was 9,576 as compared to the official influenza mortality of 10,651 for 1918.[174] Therefore, tuberculosis was a constant threat during this period and perhaps influenza paled in comparison to this disease.

There is little art or literature devoted to the pandemic; Edvard Munch's 'self-portrait after influenza' which shows the artist convalescing after an attack is one of the few artworks on the disease. Katherine Anne Porter's autobiographical novella *Pale Horse, Pale Rider* was published in 1939 tells the story of Miranda, a journalist who almost dies of the flu and the narrative closely follows an account of Porter's own illness from influenza and her recovery in 1918.[175] This was one of the few early works of literature on the disease. The Wellcome Library for the History and understanding of Medicine in London, which holds a wide-ranging collection of prints, illustrated books, pamphlets, posters and drawings relating to medicine and disease, has very little material on the 1918 pandemic.[176] Probably the most famous piece it holds is the pen and ink drawing by E. Noble, which is described in the catalogue as 'A monster representing an influenza virus hitting a man over the head as he sits in his armchair'. This paucity of literary and artistic material meant that the pandemic lacked a cultural dimension through which it can be evoked and may be a further reason as to why it has been forgotten.

As can be seen from Ida Milne's oral history chapter in *Stacking the Coffins*, the pandemic was remembered in Irish families who were affected by the death from influenza of a parent or sibling. The disease is remembered and spoken of within these families.[177] However Guy Beiner believes that although these memories are retained in families that without the official recognition of the pandemic with a commemoration or memorial that they are forgotten within the wider public in what he calls Social Forgetting. Certainly, there have been very few official memorials or commemorations in relation to the pandemic and these only appeared in recent years. In December 2017 in Canada, a memorial was installed in the Regina Cemetery and in November 2019 a memorial was unveiled at Pukeahu National War Memorial Park, remembering those in New Zealand who died from influenza.[178]

Janice Hume argued that mass media claim an important role in building public consciousness of an event, and that the lack of publicity regarding the pandemic in the American press was an important factor as to why influenza was forgotten in that country.[179] The evidence shows that contemporary media coverage of the pandemic especially in Ulster was sparse. Compared to other issues, such as the war and the general election in 1918, the pandemic received relatively little coverage in the press. The lack of publicity about influenza in the contemporary newspapers meant that the disease did not infiltrate the public consciousness to any great extent as news of the war, general election and political prisoners was given more column inches and thus importance. Therefore, it is reasonable to assume that along with the other reasons mentioned, the paucity of press coverage played a part in why the pandemic has been forgotten in Ireland.

Notes

1. Johnson (2003, p. 154).
2. French (1920, pp. 51–54).
3. Sandra Tomkins 'Britain and the Influenza Epidemic 1918–1919' (Ph.D. thesis, University of Cambridge, 1989), p. 24.
4. North (1986, p. 97) and *Seventy-Second Annual Issue of the Newspaper Press Directory and Advertisers Guide* (London, 1917), p. 211.
5. Rolston (1991, p. 158).
6. Legg (1998, p. 182).
7. Ibid., p. 208.
8. Ibid., p. 201.
9. Blakely (2006, p. 23).
10. *The Independent*, 11 June 2020.
11. Tomkins, 'Britain and the Influenza Epidemic 1918–1919', p. 32.
12. *Irish Independent*, 25 May 1918.
13. *Belfast Evening Telegraph*, 17 June 1918.
14. *Belfast News-Letter*, 19 June 1918.
15. *Portadown Express*, 28 June 1918.
16. *County Down Spectator*, 29 June 1918.
17. Phillips, Howard, 'No Great War, No Great Flu; No Great Flu, No German Defeat?', Paper presented at 'Pandemic: Ireland and the Great Flu 1918–19', Glasnevin Cemetery Museum, Dublin on 23 October 2018.
18. *Irish Times*, 3–6 July 1918, 8–9 July 1918.
19. *Portadown Weekly News*, 13 July 1918; *Lisburn Standard*, 12 July 1918.
20. Blakely (2006, p. 56).
21. *Belfast News-Letter*, 28 May 1918.

22. *Irish Times*, 31 May 1918.
23. *Ballymena Weekly Telegraph*, 1 June 1918; *Ulster Herald*, 1 June 1918; *Frontier Sentinel*, 1 June 1918.
24. *Belfast Evening Telegraph*, 11 June 1918; *Irish News*, 21 June 1918.
25. *Derry Journal*, 26 June 1918.
26. *Anglo-Celt*, 15 June 1918, p. 7.
27. *Ulster Herald*, 29 June 1918, *Frontier Sentinel*, 29 June 1918; *Fermanagh Herald*, 29 June 1918.
28. *Fermanagh Herald*, 6 July 1918, 13 July 1918; *Derry People*, 6 July 1918, 13 July 1918; *Ulster Herald*, 6 July 1918, 13 July 1918; *Frontier Sentinel*, 6 July 1918, 13 July 1918.
29. Articles in the *Irish Independent*, 25–26 June 1918, 9–10 July 1918, 12 July 1918 referred to the disease as 'influenza plague' or just plague or plague resembling influenza.
30. *County Down Spectator*, 29 June 1918.
31. *Belfast News-Letter*, 11 June 1918.
32. *Northern Whig*, 21 June 1918.
33. *Irish News*, 12 July 1918.
34. *Donegal Vindicator*, 28 June1918.
35. *Connaught Tribune*, 22 Jun 1918.
36. Quinn (2008, p. 45).
37. Macnamara (1954, p. 305).
38. *Freeman's Journal*, 29 October 1918; *Irish Independent*, 30 October 1918, *Anglo Celt*, 2 November 1918.
39. *Daily News*, 29 October 1918.
40. *The Times*, 10 October 1918.
41. *Derry Journal*, 4 November 1918.
42. Crosby (2003, p. 47).
43. *Irish Independent*, 16 December 1918.
44. Barrington (1987, p. 81).
45. Novick (2002, p. 47).
46. QUB, CO 904/ 167, The British in Ireland (Microfilm) Series 1—Dublin Castle Records: 1918–1919,) Censorship—Press Censorship Report, Censor's general report, 1 July 1918–31 July 1918, 14, 15, 21.
47. Smyth (1977, p. 53) and Ó hÓgartaigh (2006, p. 38).
48. Phillips and Killingray (2003, p. 6).
49. Ó hÓgartaigh (2006, p. 45).
50. Taken from Sinn Féin Papers. *Árd-Fheis* (Extraordinary Sinn Féin), 8 April 1919 as quoted in Ó hÓgartaigh (2006, pp. 44–45).
51. Winter (1977, p. 488).
52. Crawford (2000, p. 97).
53. Byerly (2005, p. 8).

54. The National Archive [Hereafter TNA], WO 35/179/4, Returns: historical review of medical and sanitary work in the Irish Command during the war, Report of the medical and sanitary work of the Ulster Brigade, p. 4 and Historical review of the medical and sanitary work of the Cork District during the war period.
55. *Irish News*, 12 July 1918; *Irish Independent*, 24 June 1918; *Derry Journal*, 26 June 1918.
56. McCoole (2003, pp. 66–67).
57. *Sunday People*, 11 May 2003.
58. Macnamara (1954, pp. 308–309).
59. *Ulster Herald*, 6 July 1918, 13 July 1918; *Derry People*, 6 July 1918; *Derry Journal*, 26 June 1918; *Frontier Sentinel*, 29 June 1918; *Ulster Herald*, 29 June 1918.
60. Alcabes (2009, pp. 21–22).
61. *Irish Independent*, 8 January 1919.
62. Crawfurd (1914, p. 108).
63. Thanksgiving prayer to a combination of the Sacred Heart, St Roch and the 'Little Flower' appeared in *Irish Independent*, on 8, 11 and 31 January 1919, 26 February 1919 and 21 March 1919.
64. *Westmeath Examiner*, 9 November 1918.
65. Echenberg (2003, pp. 237–238).
66. Hume (2000, p. 907).
67. Graves, (1969, p. 7).
68. *Donegal Vindicator*, 8 November 1918; *Dromore Leader*, 16 November 1918 were unable to produce weekly issues in November due to staff illness.
69. *Donegal Independent*, 9 November 1918; *Derry Weekly News*, 9 November 1918; *Newry Examiner*, 26 October 1918; *Banbridge Chronicle*, 30 November 1918.
70. *Irish Independent*, 4 November 1918.
71. *Portadown Express*, 5 July 1918.
72. *Northern Whig*, 24 October 1918; *Northern Whig*, 28 October 1918; *Belfast News-Letter*, 30 October 1918; *Ulster Guardian*, 2 November 1918.
73. *Belfast News-Letter*, 23 October 1918.
74. *Armagh Guardian*, 1 November 1918.
75. *Portadown News*, 2 November 1918.
76. *Northern Whig*, 21 October 1918, 23 October 1918, 12 November 1918; *Belfast Evening Telegraph*, 4 November 1918; *Belfast News-Letter*, 8 October 1918, 14 October 1918; *Irish News*, 8 October 1918; *Irish Independent*, 8 October 1918.
77. Blakely (2006, p. 36).
78. Johnson (2006, p. 164).

79. *Derry Journal*, 28 October 1918.
80. *Derry Journal*, 6 November 1918.
81. The word plague or scourge used in *Irish Independent*, on 9–10 October 1918, 15–16 October 1918, 28 October 1918, 13 November 1918, 21 November 1918, 2 December 1918, 9–10 December 1918.
82. *Irish News*, 25 October 1918.
83. *Irish News*, 29 October 1918; *Irish News*, 30 October 1918, p. 2.
84. *Dungannon Democrat*, 13 November 1918.
85. Laffan (1999, p. 143).
86. McGarry (2005, p. 38).
87. *Belfast News-Letter*, 30 October 1918; *Irish News*, 30 October 1918; *Irish Independent*, 30 October 1918.
88. *Forty-First Report of the General Prisons Board (Ireland) for 1918–19, with an Appendix of Statistics* [Cmd 687], H. C. 1920, xxiii, 53, v.
89. *Hansard 5 (Commons)*, cx [etc.], 30 October 1918, cols. 1460-1 and 1584; *Belfast News-Letter*, 31 October 1918; *The Times*, 31 October 1918; *Irish Times*, October 1918; *Irish Independent*, 31 October 1918; *Lancet*; 9 November 1918, 652.
90. *Hansard 5 (Commons)*, cx [etc.], 7 November 1918, cols. 2276-7; *Belfast News-Letter*, 8 November 1918; *Irish Independent*, 8 November 1918.
91. *Irish Independent*, 30 October 1918.
92. Lynch (1973, p. 69).
93. McGarry (2005, p. 38).
94. *Forty-First Report of the General Prisons Board (Ireland)*, vi.
95. McGarry (2005, p. 38).
96. Stack (1973, p. 81).
97. *Irish Independent*, 31 October 1918; *Irish Independent*, 29–31 October 1918, 1–2 November 1918, 8 November 1918.
98. Ó hÓgartaigh (2006, p. 41).
99. *Irish Independent*, 8 March 1919.
100. *Irish Independent*, 7 March 1919.
101. Lynch (1973, p. 74).
102. Patricia Marsh, 'The Effect of the 1918–19 Influenza Pandemic on Belfast' (Unpublished MA, Queens University Belfast, 2006), 49.
103. *Forty-First Report of the General Prisons Board (Ireland), for 1918–19*, vi.
104. Lynch (1973, p. 69).
105. *Londonderry Sentinel*, 24 October 1918.
106. *Irish Independent*, 24 January 1919.
107. *Freeman's Journal*, 11 December 1918.
108. Shouldice and Geraghty (1973, p. 31).
109. Hogan (1953, p. 53).

110. Novick (2002, p.27).
111. Hogan (1953, p. 53).
112. QUB, CO 904/196/60, The British in Ireland (Microfilm) Series 1—Dublin Castle Records: 1918–1919, Censorship—Press Censorship Report,) F. J. Coleman File—Evidence at Inquest of Richard Coleman, 34; *Irish Independent*, 12 December 1918.
113. *Irish Independent*, 12 December 1918.
114. *Irish Independent*, 11 December 1918.
115. QUB, CO 904/196/60, The British in Ireland (Microfilm) Series 1—Dublin Castle Records: 1918–1919, Censorship—Press Censorship Report, F. J. Coleman File—Evidence at Inquest of Richard Coleman, 35.
116. *Freeman's Journal*, 13 December 1918.
117. QUB, CO 904/186, The British in Ireland (Microfilm) Series 1—Dublin Castle Records: 1918–1919, Miscellaneous, Censorship of the correspondence of the Irish Internees 1918, 191.
118. TNA, HO 144/1496/362269/135, Ireland (Insurrection): Sinn Féin internees, 5th Report on Correspondence of the Irish Internees—16th December 1918–31st December 1918, Letter from P. O'Bevine to George Lyons, 21 December 1918, 43–44.
119. *Freeman's Journal*, 11 December 1918, 12 December and 16 December 1918; *Irish Independent*, 11 December 1918, 12 December 1918 and 13 December 1918; *Irish Times*, 16 December 1918 and 17 December 1918.
120. *The Times*, 14 December 1918.
121. Roper (1934, p. 198).
122. TNA, HO 144/1496/362269/135, Ireland (Insurrection): Sinn Féin internees, Censor's General report, 4th Report on Correspondence of the Irish Internees, 1 December–16 December 1918.
123. *Irish Independent*, 24 January 1919; *Freeman's Journal*, 3 February 1919.
124. TNA, HO 144/1458/315663/30, Ireland (Insurrection): File on Count Plunkett, Count Plunkett, internment in the United Kingdom, Letter from Edward Waldron to Michael Clair, 11 December 1918; Letter to Home Office, 24 December 1918 and Letter from Irish Office to Home Office, 28 December1918.
125. Clarke (1997, pp. 165–166).
126. McConville (2003, p. 646) and William Murphy, 'The Tower of Hunger: Political Imprisonment and the Irish, 1910–21' (Ph.D. thesis, University College, Dublin, 2006), 258.
127. Queen's University, Belfast, [Hereafter QUB] CO 904/ 201/141, The British in Ireland, File on Darrell Figgis, 51 ((Microfilm) Series 1—Dublin Castle Records: 1918–1919, Personalities, File on Darrell Figgis, Letter to Mrs Figgis, 14 November 1918.

128. McConville (2003, p.646).
129. TNA, HO 144/1496/362269/174, Ireland (Insurrection): Sinn Féin internees, List of releases of Irish internees (temporary).
130. *Irish Times*, 17 December 1918; *Meath Chronicle*, 21 December 1918; *Dungannon Democrat*, 18 December 1918.
131. QUB, CO 904/167, The British in Ireland (Microfilm) Series 1—Dublin Castle Records: 1918–1919, Censorship, Press Censorship Report, Treatment of Prisoners (Suspended by censor), 16 December 1918, Press Censorship, 1 December–31 December 1918, 391.
132. *Freeman's Journal*, Sinn Féin Meeting (Portions in brackets deleted by censor) 12 December 1918, QUB, CO 904/167, The British in Ireland (Microfilm) Series 1—Dublin Castle Records: 1918–1919, Censorship, Press Censorship Report, Press Censorship, 1 December–31 December 1918, 388.
133. TNA, HO 144/1496/362269/135, Ireland (Insurrection): Sinn Féin internees, 5th Report on Correspondence of the Irish Internees, 16 December–31 December 1918, Letter from George Rafferty to Frank Fahy, 21 December 1918, p. 42.
134. Hogan (1953, p. 54).
135. *Irish Independent*, 11 December 1918; *Freeman's Journal*, 11 December 1918.
136. *Irish Independent*, 11 December 1918.
137. *Irish Independent*, 24 January 1919.
138. QUB, CO 904/167, The British in Ireland (Microfilm) Series 1—Dublin Castle Records: 1918–1919, Censorship, Press Censorship Report, Censor's General Report, Press Censorship, 1 January–31 January1919, 41.
139. *Irish Independent*, 24 January 1919.
140. TNA, HO 144/1496/362269/135, Ireland (Insurrection): Sinn Féin internees, 8th Report on the Correspondence of the Irish Internees—1 February–15 February 1919, 24, Letter from W. Loughran to Miss Rooney, 4 February 1919.
141. *Irish Independent*, 4 March 1919.
142. Also known as Pierce McCann, Pierse McCann or Pierce McCan.
143. Medical report on Pierse McCann, 12 March 1919.
144. *Irish Independent*, 8 March 1919; *Freeman's Journal*, 8 March 1919.
145. *Irish Independent*, 7 March 1919.
146. Murphy, 'The Tower of Hunger', p. 269.
147. Colum (1959, p. 191).
148. QUB, CO 904/167).The British in Ireland (Microfilm) Series 1—Dublin Castle Records: Press Censorship, Censor's General report for March 1919, Press Censorship, 1 March–31 March 1919, 519.
149. McConville (2003, p. 650).

150. TNA, HO 144/1496/362269/179, Ireland (Insurrection): Sinn Féin internees; Letter to M. Waller, 4 Mar. 1919.
151. *Irish Independent*, 2 December 1918.
152. Tomkins, 'Britain and the Influenza Epidemic 1918', pp. 249–250.
153. *Down Recorder*, 7 December 1918.
154. *Tyrone Courier*, 5 December 1918.
155. *Down Recorder*, 7 December 1918.
156. *Down Recorder*, 14 December 1918.
157. *Weekly Freeman's Journal*, 16 November 1918.
158. *Tyrone Courier*, 5 December 1918.
159. *County Down Spectator*, 7 December 1918.
160. *Irish Independent*, 3 December 1918.
161. *Dungannon Democrat*, 27 November 1918.
162. *Dungannon Democrat*, 4 December 1918.
163. Hogan (1953, p. 47).
164. Hogan (1953, p. 52).
165. *Ulster Herald*, 30 November 1918.
166. Kenneally (2008, p. 2).
167. *Armagh Guardian*, 5 July 1918.
168. Milne (2018, pp. 50–52).
169. Crosby (2003).
170. Phillips and Killingray (2003, pp. 13–14) and Johnson (2003, p180).
171. Phillips and Killingray (2003, p. 11).
172. Killingray (1994, pp. 66–67).
173. Jones (2001, p. 19).
174. *Fifty-Fifth Detailed Annual Report of the Registrar-General (Ireland) (1918) (Births, Deaths and Marriages)*, SP 1919 [Cmd.450], xvii.
175. Porter (1939).
176. Johnson (2006, p. 178).
177. Milne (2018, pp. 164–196).
178. Guy Beiner referred to Social forgetting in his talk *Lost and Found: Memory of the Spanish flu* given on 6 February 2021 for Trasna na Tire.
179. Hume (2000, p. 910).

References

Alcabes, Philip. *Dread: How Fear and Fantasy Have Fuelled Epidemics from the Black Death to Avian Flu*. New York: Public Affairs, 2009.

Barrington, Ruth. *Health, Medicine and Politics in Ireland 1900–1970*. Dublin: Institute of Public Administration, 1987.

Blakely, Debra. *Mass Mediated Disease: A Case Study Analysis of Three Flu Pandemics and Public Health Policy*. Lanham: Lexington Books, 2006.

Byerly, Carol R. *Fever of War: The Influenza Epidemic in the U. S. Army During World War I*. New York and London: New York University Press, 2005.

Clarke, Kathleen. *Revolutionary Woman: My Fight for Ireland's Freedom*. Dublin: The O'Brien Press, 1997.

Colum, Padraic. *Arthur Griffith*. Dublin: Browne and Nolan, 1959.

Crawford, Dorothy H. *The Invisible Enemy: A Natural History of Viruses*. Oxford: Oxford University Press, 2000.

Crawfurd, R. *Plague and Pestilence in Literature and Art*. Oxford: Clarendon Press, 1914.

Crosby, Alfred W. *America's Forgotten Pandemic: The Influenza of 1918*. Cambridge: Cambridge University Press, 2003.

Echenberg, Myron. '"The Dog That Did Not Bark" Memory and the 1918 Influenza Epidemic in Sengal', in *Spanish Influenza Pandemic of 1918–1919: New Perspectives*, edited by Howard Phillips and David Killingray, 230–238. London: Routledge, 2003.

French, Herbert C. B. E. 'The Clinical Features of the Influenza Epidemic of 1918–19' in *Ministry of Health, Report on the Pandemic of Influenza, 1918–19*, 66–109. London: HMSO, 1920.

Graves, Charles. *Invasion by Virus: Can It Happen Again?* London: Icon Books Limited, 1969.

Hogan, David. [Frank Gallagher] *The Four Glorious Years*. Dublin: Irish Press, 1953.

Hume, Janice. 'The "Forgotten" 1918 Influenza Epidemic and Press Portrayal of Public Anxiety', *Journalism and Mass Communication Quarterly*, 77:4 (Winter 2000): 898–915.

Johnson, N. P. A. S. 'The Overshadowed Killer: Influenza in Britain', in *Spanish Influenza Pandemic of 1918–1919: New Perspectives*, edited by Howard Phillips and David Killingray, 132–156. London: Routledge, 2003.

Johnson, Niall P. A. S. *Britain and the 1918–19 Influenza Pandemic: A Dark Epilogue*. London: Routledge, 2006.

Jones, Greta. *'Captain of All These Men of Death': The History of Tuberculosis in Nineteenth and Twentieth Century Ireland*. Amsterdam and New York: University of Toronto, 2001.

Kenneally, Ian. *The Paper Wall: Newspapers and Propaganda in Ireland 1919–1921*. Cork: Collins, 2008.

Killingray, David. 'The Influenza Pandemic of 1918–1919 in the British Caribbean', in *Social History of Medicine*, 7:1 (1994): 59–87.

Laffan, Michael. *The Resurrection of Ireland: The Sinn Féin Party 1916–1923*. Cambridge: Cambridge University Press, 1999.

Legg, Marie-Louise. *Newspapers and Nationalism: The Irish Provincial Press, 1850–1892*. Dublin: Four Courts, 1998.

Lynch, Fionán. 'Recollections of Jail Riots and Hunger Strikes: Grim Times in Mountjoy, Dundalk and Belfast Jails', in *Sworn to Be Free: The Complete Book of IRA Jailbreaks 1918–1921*, edited by Florence O'Donoghue, 63–76. Tralee: Anvil Books Ltd, 1973.

Macnamara, Dr, D.W. 'Memories of 1918 and "The Flu"', *Journal of the Irish Medical Association*, 35:208 (1954): 304–309.

McCoole, Sinead. *No Ordinary Women: Irish Female Activists in the Revolutionary Years 1900–1923.* Dublin: The O' Brien Press, 2003.

McConville, Sean, *Irish Political Prisoners, 1848–1922: Theatres of War.* London: Routledge, 2003.

McGarry, Fearghal. *Eoin O'Duffy: a self-Made Hero.* Oxford: Oxford University Press, 2005.

Milne, Ida. *Stacking the Coffins: Influenza, War and Revolution in Ireland, 1918–19.* Manchester: Manchester University Press, 2018.

North John S. (ed.). *The Waterloo Directory of Irish Newspapers and Periodicals, 1800–1900.* Waterloo, ON: North Waterloo Academic Press, 1986.

Novick, Ben. 'Propaganda 1: Advanced Nationalist Propaganda and Moralistic Revolution, 1914–18', in *The Irish Revolution 1913–1923*, edited by Joost Augusteijn, 34–53. Basingstoke: Palgrave, 2002.

Ó hÓgartaigh, Margaret. *Kathleen Lynn: Irishwoman, Patriot, Doctor.* Dublin: Irish Academic Press, 2006.

Phillips, Howard and David Killingray. 'Introduction', in *Spanish Influenza Pandemic of 1918–1919: New Perspectives*, edited by Howard Phillips and David Killingray, 1–26. London: Routledge, 2003.

Porter, Katherine Anne. *Pale Horse Pale Rider.* 1939.

Quinn, Tom. *Flu: A Social History of Influenza.* London: New Holland, 2008.

Rolston, Bill. 'News Fit to Print: Belfast's Daily Newspapers', in *The Media and Northern Ireland*, edited by Bill Rolston, 152–187. Basingstoke: Macmillan, 1991.

Roper, Esther (ed.). *Prison Letters of Constance Markievicz.* London: 1934.

Shouldice, Frank and George Geraghty. 'The Break-Out from Usk Jail in Wales by Four "German Plot" Prisoners', in *Sworn to Be Free: The Complete Book of IRA Jailbreaks 1918–1921*, edited by Florence O'Donoghue, 25–34. Tralee: Anvil Books Ltd, 1973.

Smyth, Hazel P. 'Kathleen Lynn, MD, F.R.C.S.I. (1874–1955)', *Dublin Historical Record*, 30:2 (1977): 51–57.

Stack, Austin. 'Journal of the Big Belfast Jail Riot', in *Sworn to Be Free: The Complete Book of IRA Jailbreaks 1918–1921*, edited by Florence O'Donoghue, 114–122. Tralee: Anvil Books Ltd, 1973.

Winter, Jay. 'The Impact of the First World War on Health in Britain', *The Economic History Review, New Series*, 30:3 (1977): 898–915.

CHAPTER 5

'The Doctors Are Being Run off Their Feet': Medical Response to Influenza in Ireland

Introduction

As stated in the previous chapter, there was scepticism about influenza with some newspapers asking 'Is it influenza at all?[1] Tom Quinn argued that many of the world's top scientists were convinced that the disease was not influenza due to both its ferocity as well as the speed at which it incapacitated its victims and killed them.[2] This meant that the medical profession was at a loss to deal with the disease. In this chapter the medical response to influenza in Ireland is discussed. Starting with causes and symptoms of the 1918–1919 pandemic. It moves on to a brief description of public health in Ireland. Issues around the lack of medical personnel to treat the disease are discussed. The absence of sound medical knowledge on how to cure influenza is illustrated through the examination of suggested cures and advertisements—promising alleviation of the disease—published in the newspapers during this period.

What Caused the 1918–19 Pandemic

The influenza 'A' virus, which causes almost every type of influenza pandemic, was not isolated until 1933.[3] It was discovered by Wilson Smith, Christopher Andrews and Patrick Laidlow at the National Institute for Medical Research facilities in north London.[4] Consequently, before that discovery, there were many inaccurate theories as to what caused

P. Marsh, *The Spanish Flu in Ireland*, Palgrave Studies in Economic History, https://doi.org/10.1007/978-3-030-79500-9_5

influenza and how it was spread. Medieval Italians believed influenza was caused by a malevolent supernatural force. Beveridge suggested that there was a vague idea that influenza was spread by a mysterious malign agent—called a miasma—a condition of the air, something like a bad smell. Even as late as 1894, Charles Creighton, the British epidemiologist, believed that influenza was transmitted by a miasma spread over the land rather than by contagion.[5]

Despite Creighton's views at the time of the 1889–1890 influenza pandemic, most doctors had accepted the germ theory of infectious diseases. F. B. Smith noted that during the 1889–1890 pandemic, students of influenza epidemics merged the new bacteriology with the centuries-old contexts of airs, waters and places. They believed that some great elemental force had to be activated to move the miasmas or fomites in the atmosphere. Some doctors cited earthquakes and volcanic eruptions as agents that activated and spread the disease in mechanistic terms rather than as a sign of 'displeasure of the gods'.[6] Despite these beliefs, in Germany Dr Richard Friedrich Johann Pfeiffer—head of the research department of the Berlin Institute for Infectious Diseases—isolated a particular bacterium that was present in great numbers in the throats of influenza patients in 1890. It was named after him as *Pfeiffer's bacillus*. Most of the world was convinced that this bacillus caused influenza and was responsible for the 1918–1919 pandemic. This theory was hardly surprising as during the second wave in the autumn of 1918, bacteriologists found large numbers of *Pfeiffer's bacillus* in patients' throats. Nevertheless, suspicions were aroused as to whether *Pfeiffer's bacillus* was to blame for influenza. Drops of cultures were placed in the noses of volunteers. However, these inoculations usually had little effect as influenza was produced in only a few instances.[7]

Despite numerous attempts to isolate the 1918–1919 virus it was not in fact achieved until the 1990s, when Jeffery K. Taubenberger and his associates isolated it from the lung tissue sample of a United States serviceman who was a victim of the 1918 pandemic. In their study published in 1997 they argued that the 1918 strain was an H1N1 virus, different from all subsequently characterised strains and that the 1918 influenza appeared to be most closely related to early swine influenza strains. They suggested that the 1918–1919 strain may have been a common avian ancestor for both human and swine H1N1 virus lineages.[8] Moreover, research work carried out by Taubenberger and his collaborators suggested the 1918 virus had several of the same mutations that can be found in the bird flu, H5N1. They reported striking similarities between the 1918–1919 pandemic genes and those of flu viruses found only in birds. They also suggested that the 1918 influenza had possibly developed from a bird virus and did not need to combine with a flu strain already adapted to humans to become so deadly.[9]

Symptoms of Influenza

In the Ministry of Health Report into influenza published in 1920, Dr Herbert French stated that there were two sharply distinguished parts to the 1918–1919 pandemic. French noted that although there were very many cases of influenza during the first wave, in June 1918, the mortality from the disease was relatively low. Patients were severely stricken, but they recovered quickly after a short attack and it was widely described as 'influenza of the three-day fever type'. However, the second and third waves in October 1918 and February 1919 differed from the first as there was high mortality from pulmonary and general septicaemic complications and during this wave, heliotrope cyanosis was a prominent feature of the fatal cases.[10]

Charles Graves argued that the symptoms of the virulent second wave of influenza were initially indistinguishable from ordinary influenza, but then acute complications set in and the patients died so rapidly that it was clear that it was not pneumonia but septicaemia that killed them. He stated that patients complained initially about chest pains, had a short dry hacking cough, their skin became hot, dry and pungent and occasionally a temperature rash like scarlet fever was noted, breathing became rapid and the pulse rate rose. The face was at first flushed and red, but then in severe cases it became more and more lavender, heliotrope or violet in colour—this was the symptom known as heliotrope cyanosis. Indeed, of all the symptoms, the most noticeable was the colour of the patient. Army doctors were content while the patient's face remained red, regardless of the lung signs, temperature, pulse rate or respiration rate. However, when the heliotrope cyanosis set in then 'the prospect was grave indeed'.[11]

Undoubtedly, it was this symptom that caused the most anxiety, as was confirmed in Sir Herbert French's description of heliotrope cyanosis in patients in the 1920 Ministry of Health Report:

> The faces, at first flushed and red, with a peculiar drooping of the eyelids giving a weary look, might remain purely red throughout, but in

> nearly half the cases affected by the pulmonary complications the red tint rapidly changed to one of progressive cyanosis. It was when this dreaded heliotrope cyanosis appeared that one knew that the prognosis had now altered so completely that the patient was almost certain to die; a small percentage of cases managed to recover, even after the cyanosis had developed, but the great majority succumbed, and it was amongst cases of this type that the great mortality of the epidemic occurred.[12]

French confirmed that heliotrope cyanosis 'developed in less than half of the pulmonary cases, but once it became definite the prognosis was so bad that I should say out of every 100 "blue" cases 95 died'.[13] There was no doubt that heliotrope cyanosis was a profoundly serious and noticeable symptom, but it did not appear in all cases. This was confirmed by Dr Donough Macnamara who recollected only one influenza case at the Mater Hospital in Dublin in which 'the patient's body turned a dusky blue'.[14] The Assistant Director of Medical Services at the Curragh Military Camp in County Kildare, also reported that there were very few cases of heliotrope cyanosis among their military patients suffering from influenza during the pandemic.[15]

Although heliotrope cyanosis was one of the more alarming symptoms, others experienced during this wave were severe headaches, body pains and fever. Patients also coughed blood and bled from the nose. Bacteria invaded the lungs and turned these vital organs into sacks of fluid, which caused death by effectively drowning the sufferer in their own body fluids.[16] Post-mortems of victims showed that their lungs as well as other major organs were often filled with a solid red jelly.[17]

Public Health in Ireland

Prior to 1918, Ireland was no stranger to epidemic disease that was common throughout the eighteenth and nineteenth centuries. The main infectious diseases during these centuries were bacillary dysentery, Asiatic cholera, smallpox, tuberculosis and fever, a generic term, which embraced the diseases of typhus, relapsing fever, and typhoid.[18] However, one of the biggest killers in Ireland during the nineteenth and early twentieth centuries was tuberculosis in all its forms. Official sources state that the death rate from tuberculosis in Ireland rose slightly from the 1860s until about 1900, declining only after 1905.[19] Greta Jones advised that tuberculosis deaths were recorded in Ireland dating back to the seventeenth century.[20] Ruth Barrington noted that in the early 1900s, tuberculosis claimed more than 11,500 lives per year and that it was by far the most common cause of death among Irish people, accounting for nearly twice as many deaths as all other forms of infectious disease combined. Jones noted that Irish mortality rates from tuberculosis only began to decline in the decade 1901–11 and even then the rates remained higher than those of other parts of the British Isles throughout most of the twentieth century.[21]

Tuberculosis was associated with poverty, poor diet and bad housing. The absence of accommodation for isolation of those in the advanced stage of the disease, concealment of the disease by family members and the widespread habit of spitting, all greatly increased the opportunity of spreading the infection. Jones noted that nineteenth-century Irish public health manuals instructed Medical Officers of Health (MOH) to encourage cleanliness, ventilation and reduction of overcrowding in public institutions to combat tuberculosis. It is notable that these recommendations were also used to stop the spread of influenza during 1918 and 1919. It is apparent that the poor were more susceptible to infectious diseases due to their living conditions and Barrington argued that a major reason for low standards of health among the Irish was due to the material poverty in which so many people lived. Added to this was the apathy with which public health issues were treated in Ireland. She noted that the elected representatives in Ireland did not seem to adhere to the opinion that the whole community benefited from fresh water, clean streets and good housing.[22] Again, as will be seen in later chapters, these factors impacted on the Irish people during the influenza pandemic.

Medical relief in Ireland was provided by the dispensary system, which was established by the Medical Charities Act of 1851. By May 1852, the division of Ireland into 723 dispensary districts was completed and the new medical service was operational. An intrinsic part of the medical services provided by the dispensary system was the provision of free drugs and medical appliances to the holders of the black and red tickets. These tickets enabled a poor person to get medical relief. Black tickets entitled the applicant to medical care at the dispensary and red tickets to care in their own home. It was the responsibility of the board of guardians (BOG) to supply all drugs and other requirements to the dispensary and they were answerable to the Poor Law Commissioners (later the Local Government Board for Ireland) for the expenditure of the dispensaries in their area. Doctors were free to prescribe whatever medicine they felt the patient required. Some dispensaries had a resident apothecary but often it was the doctor himself who dispensed drugs for the sick.[23] In 1918, the Local Government Board for Ireland (LGBI) was the principal health authority in Ireland. It controlled the activities of the BOGs in relation to the administration of the dispensary medical system, union infirmaries and fever hospitals, as well as rural and urban sanitary authorities in the administration of the Public Health Acts and county councils in relation to county infirmaries and sanatoria.[24]

The Public Health Act in 1848 was the first major piece of legislation in which Government positively intervened to prevent disease and promote health.[25] However, the first piece of public health legislation, which had any real impact, was the Public Health Act of 1878. This consolidated and amended the earlier legislation.[26] It gave local authorities the power to destroy unsound food, supervise slaughterhouses and isolate those people who were suffering from certain notifiable diseases, trace the disease to the source and stop the spread.[27] By 1918 the list of notifiable diseases included scarlet fever, measles, typhus, cholera and tuberculosis. However, influenza was not one of these diseases.

Dispensaries in Ireland provided an out-patient service, while the inpatient service for the sick poor who required hospital treatment were the workhouse infirmaries and fever hospitals. Individuals suffering from dangerous infectious diseases were segregated from general patients, either in separate wards or in detached buildings.[28] There was a stigma attached to using the workhouse and fever hospital for treatment because of the association of the workhouse and pauperism.[29] This was illustrated in Newtownards when, in September 1918, a committee was formed to reconsider the question of re-naming the hospitals so that the word union might be deleted from future records. The committee recommended that they should be known as "The Newtownards Hospital" and "The Newtownards Fever Hospital."[30] It is uncertain if this was as a direct result of the pandemic or because any deaths that occurred in these hospitals would be recorded as having taken place in the workhouse infirmary. The implication being that the deceased was an inmate, indicating that there was a shame associated with medical care in the infirmary.

Barrington believed that Irish public health officials were aware of the problems with sanitary affairs in Ireland and of the responsibility on public authorities to improve the situation. However, she thought that the poverty and squalor of much of Irish life, combined with the relaxed attitude of the Irish administration, as well as the reluctance of local bodies to undertake improvements that would increase local taxation, were more than a match for the public health official's best efforts.[31] Later chapters illustrate that these financial concerns were a major issue when the influenza pandemic hit Ireland in 1918.

Physicians and Influenza

The rapidity of deaths from the alarming symptoms as described meant that the medical fraternity were found wanting in relation to influenza. As discussed in Chapter 4, there was confusion as to whether the disease was influenza at all? Sir Arthur Newsholme, head of the Imperial Local Government Board (LGB) remarked that influenza was an enigma to the medical profession who were both ignorant of the causes and powerless to prevent the disease.[32] The number of influenza patients was overwhelming, which meant doctors found their task to cure the sick an impossible one. Dr Macnamara recounted that for six months as a resident doctor in the Mater, all he saw was "flu".[33] The Mater was not alone, as elsewhere in Ireland, influenza patients flocked to the dispensary doctor in the poor law unions for treatment and to chemists to alleviate the symptoms. Dispensary doctors worked long hours to treat their patients, paying over 100,000 more home visits during this period than in the previous year, not including the number of patients that were treated at the dispensary itself, indicating the work pressure that dispensary doctors were under during this period.[34] In Lisburn, during November, it was reported that 'the doctors are being run off their feet'[35] and this was the same throughout Ireland. Dr Macnamarra recounted that doctors were scarce and there was great difficulty getting a replacement if one was ill. He thought this was due to both the number of seriously ill people and because many doctors themselves had the disease.[36] The same was true at the poor law unions where reports that workhouse infirmaries were full to capacity were common and one of the widespread problems was a lack of temporary doctors to cover for illness of Medical Officers (MO), or to help them in dispensaries that were particularly under pressure.

Medical Shortages during the Pandemic

Medical practitioners were scarce as many, like the nurses, were serving on the Western Front, which led to dispensary doctors throughout Ireland being under severe pressure. In the Banbridge poor law district,

Dr James Taylor, MO at Tandragee dispensary issued 230 dispensary tickets between 23 October and 22 November 1918, 200 of these were for influenza. As the disease was widespread in the district, Dr Taylor required assistance at the dispensary. He had difficulty recruiting a temporary nurse, so he appointed a pharmaceutical chemist to compound medicines. Much of a dispensary doctor's time would have been taken up compounding medicines, so a chemist was more useful to him than an extra doctor during the outbreak. Dr Taylor eventually recruited a nurse, but refused to dispense with the services of the chemist as requested by the Banbridge BOG. Although the nurse was essential, she was unable to compound medicines and this service was still needed due to the number of influenza patients. The guardians agreed that the chemist could remain for another two weeks. Dispensary doctors also treated private patients and depended on the payment they received from these patients to supplement their income. However, the pressure from dispensary work meant that they were losing this important form of income. Dr Taylor reported a loss of £50 of private work during the week ending 25 November 1918 due to his increased workload in the dispensary.[37]

In the Newtownards dispensary, MO, Dr Jamison advised that between 13 June and 13 July 1918, he attended 197 dispensary cases and made 770 home visits. Although, his son, who was also a doctor, assisted him through this period, he had been unable to attend many of his private patients because of the 'enormous increase in the amount of visiting and dispensing' due to influenza.[38] During the second wave, the Downpatrick and Portaferry dispensaries were also under great pressure. Although Dr McComiskey agreed to assist Dr Murray in Downpatrick, he withdrew his services after a few days because he was unable to treat patients, compound the prescriptions and visit his private patients. Similarly, Dr McDonald agreed to assist Dr Smyth in Portaferry. He also withdrew his support after three days as he 'found it impossible owing to the numerous calls in connection with his private practice to continue to assist'.[39]

In the Downpatrick poor law union there was a dispute over Dr Moore's remuneration. He had covered dispensary duties in both Strangford and Killough single-handedly for six weeks. As a result, he requested the help of another doctor in Killough and additional remuneration to compensate for his financial loss during the period, as the salary did not cover his transport expenses.[40] Dr Moore resigned on 25 January after the guardians did not comply with his ultimatum to increase his salary to five guineas per week. He was replaced by Dr Comiskey, who requested

10 guineas per week. The guardians baulked at this salary and reinstated Dr Moore on six guineas per week until a permanent replacement could be found. The upshot was that the guardians advised the LGBI that it was a necessity to recruit a resident MO in the Killough dispensary district for the sake of the poor in the area.[41]

The issue of MOs' salaries and conditions in the dispensary districts was a continuous source of complaint over the years and was under constant debate during this period.[42] In Monaghan, during June 1918, the MOs at the Carrickmacross poor law union threatened strike action unless their salary was increased to six guineas per week, a decision that the County Monaghan Medical Committee fully supported.[43] Similarly the MOs from Omagh dispensary were also unhappy with their remuneration. They went on a modified strike on 24 August 1918, where they attended all urgent cases but threatened to cease all dispensary work after 21 September 1918 if their grievances were not addressed. The guardians agreed on 12 October 1918 to allocate each MO an annual salary increase of £40 effective from 1 July 1918. The MOs were not satisfied with the offer and in November 1918 they advised that, as they were in middle of an influenza outbreak, they were reluctant to adopt extreme measures, but would be forced to do so if they were a denied a fair settlement. Nevertheless, the guardians decided that a reasonable offer had been made to the MOs as the cost of living was likely to decrease because the war was over.[44] The dispensary MOs from the Limavady union also threatened strike action unless their salaries were reconsidered. The guardians proposed a sum of £135 per annum which would rise incrementally to a maximum of £175 after five years. Again, the doctors rejected this proposal and threatened to strike on 30 December 1918 if their offer was not reconsidered.[45]

The Influenza pandemic highlighted a growing concern regarding the salaries of the dispensary doctors in Ireland. In May 1919, the *British Medical Journal* quoted an editorial printed in the *Irish Independent* stating that young doctors were not eager to fill dispensary vacancies due to the inadequate salaries offered by many unions. It is to be hoped that guardians, when soliciting applications in future, will offer salaries worthy of the acceptance of the members of a noble profession.[46] Dr Macnamara recollected that a doctor friend of his refused a locum position in Wexford of £15 5 shillings per week as well as private fees, because he could get more money elsewhere due to the scarcity of doctors.[47]

It was apparent that the war impacted on the availability of doctors, which meant that those available could in many cases exact whatever salary they wanted. This put a financial strain on the poor law system. The LGBI noted that during the influenza outbreaks, fees claimed by the temporary doctors employed were generally reasonable. Nevertheless, they complained that in certain cases the fees demanded were so excessive that they had refused to sanction the payments, even though it was a step that they were loath to take.[48] Therefore, it appeared that medical aid for the poor, even during a time of epidemic, was constrained by financial concerns, that is, the salaries that doctors were willing to work for, the amount that individual BOGs were prepared to pay for temporary medical personnel, and whether the LGBI was prepared to sanction the amount.

Cures and Remedies

Unsurprisingly, as the real cause of influenza was not determined at the time and as there is still no known cure for the disease, there was little consensus among the Irish medical profession on the best treatment for, or prevention against the disease, which resulted in many cures and treatments being suggested. Dr Macnamara recollected that a multitude of drugs were recommended at the Mater hospital in Dublin for influenza. He recounted that ‘a purge if required, some drug of the aspirin family, an expectorant mixture if cough was present, stimulants and as the help to rest at night, trional’. In addition, ‘poulticing was carried out as a routine in the pneumonic cases’. Oxygen and injections of camphor in olive oil were also popular, as was oil of eucalyptus as a prophylactic. Cinnamon was popular for a while and some people recommended tincture of iodine in a drop or slightly larger doses, while others favoured quinine or cinchona.[49] Larne and Cookstown MOH’s among others, recommended gargling with a weak solution of permanganate of potash.[50] The Dungannon MOH advocated the use of turpentine capsules, which he claimed to have marvellous effects. He had tried the capsule with a patient in the infirmary one evening and had found that in the morning the patient was much better’.[51] It is debatable that the capsule aided their recovery.

Not surprisingly, quinine was widely prescribed by Irish doctors, as during the ‘Russian influenza’ pandemic in the 1890s it was popular as both as a treatment and a prophylactic.[52] Belfast Medical Superintendent

Officer of Health (MSOH), Dr Hugh Bailie and Dr Graves the MOH for Cookstown recommended taking quinine tablets of between 2 and 5 grains twice daily as a tonic and preventative.[53] Arthur Griffith, Sinn Féin leader contracted influenza at Gloucester Jail in 1919. Padraic Colum's biography stated that Griffith: 'put a bottle of quinine beside him when he went to bed'... 'All one night, whenever he awoke in fever, he took a pull at his bottle. And in the morning he found the bottle was empty and that the epidemic had fled before the attack'.[54] Whether quinine cured him is debatable as when fellow prisoner, Denis McCullough saw Griffith the next day, he was alarmed at his appearance as 'his eyes were protuberant' and 'the veins on his forehead were as large as my little finger'. McCullough was worried that Griffith would 'collapse as much from the remedy as from the disease'.[55]

Lori Loeb has argued that successive influenza epidemics in Britain had provoked public panic, as doctors were unable to identify its cause or how the infection was transmitted.[56] Therefore, 'quack' remedies were plentiful during this period. A self-professed 'quack professor', Professor J. Canarie, attributed influenza to the presence of lice. He published a pamphlet which recommended 'a bath at least once a week' as well as a potion made up from ten packets of Epsom Salts, four packets of Cream of Tartar and hot water mixed with a jelly made from eucalyptus leaves, which was to be taken each morning.[57] Tom Quinn noted that some people painted the inside of their noses with zinc, while in Africa people drank whale oil or inhaled eucalyptus steam, and the consumption of onions and garlic soared.[58] Apart from 'quack remedies', people in many countries also turned to a wide range of alternative medicines, including traditional folk medicine, herbal remedies as well as patent medicines.[59]

Many outlandish remedies were published in Irish newspapers that had no basis in science. The *Armagh Guardian* reported that one lady recovered from influenza by only drinking large quantities of water with a little lemon juice and abstaining from food for 48 hours, after which her first meal was a raw egg and the juice of two oranges.[60] The *Belfast Evening Telegraph* reported an influenza cure from Vienna of an injection of mercury per-chloride to destroy the 'streptococcus bacillus' that caused the disease.[61] A correspondent to the same newspaper suggested as a cure, both for inflammation and fever in influenza, the use of one handful of dried mint and one handful of dried elder covered with boiling water and left for thirty minutes, strained and sweetened with black treacle. The patient should drink this mixture while hot.[62] These remedies showed people's desperation to obtain a cure for influenza. So much so that they were willing to try anything, however, if they did recover by using these cures it would be down to good luck or coincidence more than anything else.

As in 2020 with the Covid-19 pandemic, the use of masks was widely debated. In Japan, it was compulsory for policemen and members of the armed forces to wear gauze masks, and in some towns it was also obligatory for people travelling on public transport or attending cinemas or theatres.[63] In January 1919, the New South Wales Cabinet ordered everyone to wear masks and that all maskless persons would be liable to arrest.[64] The MOH for Manchester, Dr James Niven, advised the public to use muslin masks but few of the population did so.[65] In Edinburgh the MOH advocated the use of masks when visiting places of public entertainment and advised that they would be provided free by the Health authorities to people in the poorer parts of the city for the purpose of prevention.[66] Nearer home, a correspondent in the *Derry Journal* thought that wearing masks should be made compulsory in Derry in the interests of public health.[67] In February 1919, the *Belfast Evening Telegraph* reported that, although the value of masks had been advocated in many quarters, it was unlikely that the practice would be taken up in Belfast by the general public.[68] That was a correct assumption as the wearing of masks by the general public did not occur in Ireland or indeed mainland Britain, although the Local Government Board (LGB) in London did advise 'the wearing of a mask and glasses when nursing or in attendance on a person suffering from influenza'.[69]

Alcohol as a Treatment

Another controversial cure was the use of alcohol.[70] Some doctors widely endorsed the use of alcohol in cases of influenza to relieve pain and bolster strength.[71] In 1890, during the Russian influenza outbreak, French doctors were said to prescribe warm alcoholic drinks based on the theory that 'alcoholics did not catch influenza'.[72] In Myron Echenberg's study of influenza in Senegal, he advised that the MO for the French colony, Dr Thoulon, recommended alcohol in all its forms—champagne for Europeans and wine and rum for the indigenous population—was to be administered.[73] However, others stated that the use of wine and spirits were the worst possible antidote to the disease.[74] Dr Macnamara advised that 'older men favoured whiskey or brandy in heroic doses' which he described as 'no less Best worthless than any of the other nostrums, and at least its customers had a merry spin to paradise'.[75]

The lack of alcohol prompted the Ministry of Food to consult with the Liquor Control Board to arrange for the release of spirits for medicinal purposes. During December 1918 the Ministry of Food arranged to direct special supplies of spirits for influenza patients to districts where there was a shortage, and where medical opinion showed the need existed. Bottles of spirits supplied for this purpose would only be sold against a doctor's certificate.[76] On 18 February 1919, due to a lack of stimulants in Athlone: 'Representations have been made to the Liquor Control Board with a view to the release of supplies'.[77] On 19 February 1919, the *Irish Times* feared that supplies of whiskey would run out before April 1919 due to the reappearance of influenza throughout the country.[78] In February 1919, a request was made by the Dublin Public Health Committee to the War Cabinet to call for the immediate release of supplies of whiskey in the interests of public health.[79] The release of alcohol supplies was not just an Irish concern, as, Lori Loeb argued that by 1918, the Ministry of Food regarded the shortage of spirits in some districts as a health problem.[80] On 22 February 1919, a letter to the editor of the *Irish Times* suggested that 'chemists be allowed to sell whiskey at sixpence per glass on the production of a doctor's certificate' so that the working classes could afford it.[81] On the same date, it was reported that the *Evening News* had called attention to the whiskey hold-up by the Government, and quoted the opinions of medical men 'who contend that whiskey is an excellent preventative for influenza'.[82]

The use of alcohol as an influenza cure was not advocated by all. Sir Malcolm Morris, consultant surgeon at St Mary's Hospital, London, presiding at a conference on influenza, stated that 'alcohol was not essential' and queried the request to increase the supply of spirits. At the same conference, the MO for Tottenham said that 'alcohol stimulated the vital activities and he would continue to use it'.[83] Meanwhile in Ireland, the Assistant Director of Medical Services for the Curragh army camp advised that they did not stint on the use of alcohol as he was convinced of its stimulating properties and that it was also a food. He stated that 'good whiskey is better than bad brandy. Port wine and hot soda water is perhaps preferred by ladies'.[84]

The use of alcohol was criticised by the guardians in some Ulster unions. A lively debate took place at the Lisburn BOG on 28 February 1919. Mr Scott, a member of the Finance Committee, with strong temperance beliefs, came under great criticism not only from the MO, Dr Murphy, but also his pro-temperance guardian colleagues for not signing a requisition for alcohol. Mr Scott defended his position at the guardians' meeting on 11 March 1919. He claimed that he had been previously misrepresented as he had refused to sign an account for whiskey, which had already been supplied rather than a requisition to provide whiskey. Nevertheless, Dr Murphy did not retract his accusation. He believed that as a result of Mr Scott's action there was an absence of whiskey in the workhouse at the time because the supplier was reluctant to supply more alcohol to the institution due to the non-payment of his previous account.[85] It appeared that it was not Mr Scott's first objection to the use of alcohol for medical purposes. In June 1918 he complained about the quantity of whisky that was used in the workhouse hospital, despite Dr Murphy vouching to its success in curing a case of pneumonia and typhoid.[86] A correspondent to the *Belfast News-Letter*, S. W. Boyd thought that the attitude of Mr Scott showed 'a complete exposure of the lengths to which teetotal fanaticism can be carried in endangering human life'.[87]

The Lisnaskea BOG also debated the use of alcohol in the workhouse at a meeting on 22 March 1919. The chairman queried the use of 24 glasses of whiskey and 10 of brandy for the workhouse during the week, remarking that 'You would not get more outside a public house'.[88] At the guardians' meeting on 11 April 1919, it was noted that over £80 was spent annually on alcohol in the institution. The question was asked could it be guaranteed that it was only supplied to the patients and not to others in the institution.[89] These discussions were not minuted by the Lisburn and Lisnaskea BOG but were reported in the newspapers. They show that, although it was the consensus among medical professionals that alcohol was needed for medicinal purposes, in certain Ulster unions, where individual guardians held strong temperance beliefs, the medical advice could be over-ruled because of these beliefs.

Alcohol as a cure for influenza was a contentious issue during the prohibition debate in America. During the early 1920s in America there were persistent claims that alcohol had saved many lives during the 1918–1919 influenza pandemic. The replies to a questionnaire sent out by the *Journal of the American Medical Association* indicated that 75 percent of the doctors who favoured the use of whisky prescribed it for influenza and pneumonia. Charles Taber Stout, a chemotherapist, testified during the 1921 Congressional hearings on medicinal malt liquor that the American Medical Association (AMA) had refused to act upon the knowledge that spirituous liquor was valuable in treating influenza. He argued that proper digestion was essential in fighting an acute infectious disease and that alcohol was an antidote to the effects of toxins on the digestive organs. In 1920, a resolution to condemn the use of alcohol in the treatment of influenza was tabled at a meeting of the AMA. A Harvard professor of medicine snubbed the Scientific Temperance Federation of Boston when it requested an opinion concerning the value of alcohol in treating influenza. The professor stated that alcohol was useful in treating influenza and insisted that its prescription was a matter best left to the discretion of the individual doctor. Another un-named doctor, who had served aboard a troop ship, reported that brandy had not improved the condition of any of his influenza patients who would have gotten better anyway. Dr Bernard Fantus, who went on to open the world's first blood bank, argued that spirits had made some afflicted persons feel better during the influenza epidemic. Consequently, they did not retire to bed to aid recovery and some contracted fatal pneumonia as a result.[90]

It is hardly surprising that the use of alcohol as a cure for influenza was contentious in Ulster as temperance had always been an important issue in the province. In 1833 there were over 150 temperance societies with 15,000 members in Ulster[91] and Elizabeth Malcolm noted that during the nineteenth and early twentieth centuries, both Roman Catholic and Protestant Irish people subscribed to teetotalism in remarkably large numbers[92] After the Armistice, and up to the general election, the Ulster Temperance Council ran a series of advertisements in newspapers throughout Ireland in support of their agenda. For the first time the Representation of the People Act extended the vote to women aged over 30, who were either householders or married to householders.[93] These advertisements were directed at women and encouraged them to refuse to support candidates who would not work actively for prohibition in the next Parliament.[94] The Ulster Temperance Council's main worry was that demobilised soldiers would drink excessively once home and demanded 'prohibition during demobilisation' and thus encouraged women to vote for candidates who advocated temperance during demobilisation.[95] The dangers of drink were also an issue for advanced nationalists as they associated drink and drunkenness with the British. They believed that patriotic Irishmen did not drink.[96] It was also a concern in the rest of the United Kingdom as, during 1914, David Lloyd George felt that excessive alcohol consumption was diminishing the quality and output of munitions factory workers. Therefore, during the war, measures were put in place to curb alcohol consumption such as the reduction of opening hours in public houses and restrictions were made on the output of alcohol.[97] Nevertheless, this did not curtail the use of alcohol in treating influenza throughout Ireland.

As alcohol was widely endorsed by Irish doctors in influenza cases, it was hardly surprising that medicated wines and tonics were not only advertised as influenza remedies but also as post influenza 'pick-me-ups'.[98] Larne wine merchant, John Crawford advocated 'Port Wine' for 'Fighting the Flu'.[99] The makers of Snaed (influenza wine) claimed that 'positively no influenza can exist where Snaed is used'.[100] Also a tonic wine 'Anti-Laria' advertised itself as 'an influenza anti-dote'.[101] Throughout the pandemic, medicated wines such as Hall's Wines claimed to act as a restorative for whatever ailed you but during the first wave and third waves the product claimed to act specifically as a restorative after influenza.[102]

The Use of Vaccines

The issue of vaccines for influenza was a controversial one. Niall Johnson stated that there were numerous attempts to create a vaccine in many countries, which was problematic as the organism that was causing the disease was unknown. Nevertheless, the streptococcus of *Pfeiffer's Bacillus* became the basis of many vaccines. The Imperial LGB made several alternative vaccines available but uptake of these was mixed due to lack of specificity.[103] The LGBI advised in their annual report for 1918 that they closely followed any available information regarding experiments on prophylactic vaccine treatment. However, they were not confident that such a treatment would confer immunity from influenza attack.[104] Therefore, they did not advocate the use of vaccination or supply vaccines to BOGs for use in the treatment of influenza.

Dr William Crofton, a lecturer in Special Pathology at University College, Dublin, believed that the best prevention for influenza was isolation and immunisation. Believing that influenza was a bacterial disease, he thought it was practical to immunise every individual against influenza and that vaccines should be available for every member of the community no matter how poor. He stated: 'it will be found that in the present epidemic that preventative inoculation will have proved effective in over

90 percent of cases'. [105] In a letter to the *Irish Independent*, Prof. Culverwell of Trinity College, Dublin, advocated the use of the vaccine 'made from a pure culture of the bacillus' as it was used in Howth for some time 'with complete success to all cases where it had been given early'.[106] Although Sir Charles Cameron, MSOH for Dublin, agreed that there had been favourable results after using the vaccine in the city, he did not think that any positive opinion could be formed on the subject.[107]

In Belfast, a letter in the *Belfast Evening Telegraph* signed 'Sanity' stated that instead of diminishing the disease, inoculation had caused a rapid increase of cases.[108] On 2 December 1918 a Dublin doctor returning from America stated that 'the microbe or organism responsible for the influenza is unknown'. He was not prepared to say that *Pfeiffer's bacillus* was responsible for the disease and stated that 'the prophylactic vaccine treatment is purely experimental' and was not effective in the United States.[109]

Nevertheless, Irish MOHs were happy to use vaccines even if the guardians thought it was expensive. Dr Dormin, MOH in the Keady dispensary district used a vaccine on his patients, but there is no information as to its success.[110] The MOH for Lisnaskea used an influenza vaccine supplied by Trinity College Dublin for the treatment of a patient in the dispensary, again it is not known if it was successful or not.[111] Dr Timmon, MOH for Navan, used vaccine for influenza patients with very good results.[112] In Dungannon the MO for Caledon dispensary district, Dr Patterson had little success when he used a vaccine on his patients.

Even though the LGBI did not approve of vaccines, most doctors that used them were reimbursed by the guardians. Nevertheless Dr McMullin, MOH for Ballyshannon workhouse was criticised by the board over his use of vaccines in January 1919. The guardians initially declined to reimburse him for the vaccines he had purchased to treat influenza patients. He explained that he had been unable to wait for the next guardians' meeting to request the vaccine as it was to be used as a preventative rather than a cure. After being questioned as to the experimental nature of the vaccine, he advised that it had been made specially and used in the hospital rather than for private patients. The board was happy with the explanation and passed the account for payment. The editor of the *Donegal Vindicator* was not happy at the 'excessive cost of a fancy vaccine' and implied that Dr McMullin was ill informed. It quoted an official memorandum issued by the Royal College of Physicians, London that 'the virus of influenza is a living organism.. Yet the nature of the virus is still uncertain. It is possibly beyond the present range of microscopic vision', 'No drug has yet been proved to have any specific curative effect on influenza. In the uncertainty of our present knowledge considerable hesitation must be felt in advising Vaccine treatment'.[113] This editorial highlights the main objection to the use of vaccines the financial cost of the treatment to the guardians. Probably it was the expense of vaccines as well as the medical evidence that was behind the LGBI lack of support of them.

The military in Ireland used vaccines with varying degrees of success. The military hospitals in Cork found that vaccines were of value as a prophylactic and for treatment in the early stage of the disease. However, the results at the Curragh military camp, Co. Kildare found that the treatment of patients with either a stock-vaccine or an antogenous vaccine was discouraging, as all patients so treated appeared to become worse and the treatment was discontinued. An anti-influenzal vaccine was administered to all the troops in Finner Camp, County Donegal,[114] but the report does not say how successful this treatment was. Elsewhere, Kathleen Lynn vaccinated her patients in Charlemont Street, Dublin with a vaccine prepared by Dr William Crofton and was confident that it was successful both as a preventative and a curative.[115]

As one Belfast doctor, who was not very hopeful of the success of the vaccine treatment, correctly stated: 'If you don't know the cause of the disease what vaccine can you use?'[116] The organism that caused influenza was unknown and most of the vaccines were based upon the assumption that it was caused by a bacteria and in particular *Pfeiffer's bacillus*, as Johnson rightly stated, the success of any of these vaccines was more down to good luck than anything else.[117]

Advertisements

As there was no cure for influenza, people in Ireland, resorted to other methods to help with the treatment of the disease.[118] Throughout the pandemic, advertisements for a multitude of products appeared in both national and local Irish newspapers. There were a variety of products that claimed to have curative or preventative powers against influenza and some such as Formamint tablets were happy to exploit public fears. During June 1918, the advertisement for Formamint was presented as a 'Public Notice' on the 'Spanish Influenza Epidemic', which claimed that Formamint had preventative powers against influenza, using official statements supplied by the chief medical officer of the LGB, to add extra authority to the claims.[119] The official style of this advertisement gave credence to the product's claims.

Pharmacists took the opportunity to promote their businesses through influenza products. J. A. Woodside, a Ballymena chemist, advertised in the local newspapers under the banner 'Influenza Epidemic', about both its stocks of disinfectants and preventative drugs to combat the disease.[120] Pharmacists advertised patent influenza remedies, such as G. Holmes and Sons, with outlets in Lurgan, Portadown and Belfast who described their patent medicine, 'Anti-Flu' as a 'Sure Cure for Influenza'.[121] Lyon's Medical Hall, Omagh were the agents for influenza remedy 'nonflu'—the great preventative,[122] while 'KureKold' was made only by W. S. Taylor in Enniskillen.[123] 'Nostroline' claimed to be a preventative nasal cream for influenza and chemists throughout Ireland used advertisements for this product to promote their businesses.[124]

As influenza was believed to be a bacterial infection, disinfection was considered a good preventative. A nationally established disinfectant declared 'Guard against Influenza by the daily use of Jeyes' Fluid'[125] and disinfection with Jeyes' Fluid was one of Dr Cameron's, MSOH for Dublin, recommendations in combatting influenza.[126] Lifebuoy soap claimed to be a 'reputable germicide and sure disinfectant'.[127] Local firms also advertised disinfectants as footnotes to articles on influenza in the Belfast newspapers.[128]

Oxo and Bovril were popular beef teas of the day and there was an assortment of advertisements for Oxo during the second and third waves which declared that it 'fortifies the system against influenza infection'.[129] Bovril was so popular that a series of advertisements appeared, especially in December 1918, which apologised for the shortage of Bovril during the influenza outbreak.[130] Bovril was considered a very important form of nourishment. During November 1918, the Belfast BOG augmented the nurses' rations of Bovril by one quarter of an ounce per day to boost their nourishment in order to help them cope with their increased workload in the infirmary.[131] However, it was not very successful in this regard as many nurses in the Belfast union infirmary contracted the disease and four died during November 1918.

People were advised to 'Gargle with Condy's Remedial Fluid' as a 'prevention and cure of influenza' and advertisements for this product appeared in newspapers throughout the country.[132] Condy's Fluid was a popular remedy and, it was reported in December 1918 that there was not a single case of influenza among the 800 boarders at Christ's Hospital school, Horsham in Sussex, because compulsory measures were taken for every boy to use a nasal douche of weak Condy's Fluid.[133] Snuff was advertised as a preventative and, during the first and second waves, Belfast tobacco firm Gallaher's recommended their High Toast Snuff 'To prevent influenza or colds in the head'.[134] 'Dr. J.C. Murray's ozonized snuff' recommended the 'potency of snuff' for influenza.[135] Again these claims may not be as implausible as they seem, as one of the popular recommendations to avoid influenza at the time was 'Make yourself sneeze night and morning'.

Tenuous links were made between products and influenza. A Belfast butcher declared 'defy the 'Flu—Finlay's Meat Costs less than the doctor',[136] as well as 'Feed him up—that's what the doctor orders after influenza'.[137] Maybe the most extraordinary claim came from the Dunlop Rubber Company, who extolled the virtues of cycling with 'Very few of the people who've had influenza are regular cyclists. Those who bicycle regularly have been less liable to attack'.[138] Ironically, as Ida Milne recounts, in County Louth the champion cyclist and county GAA footballer, Joe Ross died from influenza during the second wave.[139] So unfortunately cycling was of little or no benefit to him. Hair preparation, 'Ashmore's Pilocarpine Lotion', claimed that 'one of the most noticeable features of the influenza epidemic is the tendency of the hair to fall out during convalescence'.[140] Towards the end of the third wave products claimed to aid convalescence after influenza, such as, Fort-Reviver, a non-alcoholic tonic that proclaimed to fortify and revive. Sanatogen claimed to nourish the blood cells after influenza.[141] During April 1919, 'Ker-nak' professed to 'tone and repair your run-down system after influenza', although it normally claimed to 'get rid of painful stomach and bowel trouble'.[142]

The proliferation of advertisements for different products to cure or prevent influenza occurred because of the lack of one effective cure or vaccine against the disease. Mark Honigsbaum argued that the message from Sir Arthur Newsholme, head of the Imperial LGB concluded that 'the active cooperation of each member of the community' was needed to prevent influenza.[143] This shifted the responsibility for influenza prevention from local authorities and the medical profession onto the individual. Therefore, individuals sought their own cure for the disease through quack cures and patent medicines. Consequently, astute businessmen seized upon their opportunity to cash in on the crisis by providing an unlikely assortment of so-called cures, preventatives and restoratives for influenza.

Newspapers also printed articles containing advice for individuals to follow. The *Daily Chronicle's* recommendations on how to avoid influenza were popular in Irish newspapers during the autumn of 1918. These included: breathe through your nose, never through your mouth; wash the inside of your nose with soap and water night and morning; gargle with clean water; make yourself sneeze night and morning; having sneezed take deep inspirations and respire forcefully through nostrils; do not wear anything tight around your neck such as a muffler; walk home from work; sleep with the windows open and your bed warm; do not "dope" and concluded do not drug yourself overheat or overclothe and take as much moderate outdoor exercise as is possible.[144]

Several newspapers listed the preventative recommendations of Sir Charles Cameron MSOH for Dublin and Dr Hugh Bailie, MSOH for Belfast, as well as the recommendations of the Imperial LGB. Again, these recommendations reiterated avoiding crowds, as well as thorough cleanliness, free ventilation and the burning of all vegetable and organic waste.[145] Many of these recommendations such as avoiding crowds, free ventilation, go to bed if sick and isolation of the sick were all good advice during a viral pandemic.

However, when all else failed, the Irish public increasingly turned to the power of prayer. During October 1918, in Dublin, Archbishop Walsh issued a letter to the clergy in his diocese directing that special prayers should be said during Masses 'appealing to the Almighty that He in His infinite goodness may be pleased to deliver us from the dangers that threaten us'[146] A correspondent to the *Belfast News-Letter*, who signed themselves, 'A Firm Believer in Prayer' advocated 'that in all our churches, as well as in every home, prayer be offered up to Almighty God asking Him to remove from our midst this awful affliction'.[147] During November 1918 in Carrick-on-Shannon, along with a national novena on behalf of the martyred saints in Ireland, prayers were offered for the 'spiritual and temporal welfare of Ireland that God might save the people from influenza epidemic'.[148] In Roscommon in October 1918, at the Sacred Heart Church, a special novena was held and prayers were offered up for 'peace among the people of the warring nations and for the protection of the people against the influenza epidemic'.[149] Ironically, the gathering of people at church services or prayer meetings to pray for deliverance from the disease would have helped to spread the virus among the wider community. Nevertheless, the appearance of thanksgiving prayers in the *Irish Independent* during January, February and March 1919 was proof that people in Ireland increasingly resorted to prayer during this pandemic.[150]

The lack of an effective cure meant that many different treatments were suggested by the medical profession. The large number of advertisements that appeared in newspapers for many varied products that claimed to cure or prevent influenza or act as post influenza 'pick-me-ups' show the lack of a robust medical response to the disease. There was a scarcity of doctors in Ireland to treat the numerous patients due to the combined factors of war, illness and the financial constraints of the dispensary system. The medical profession in Ireland was found wanting during the pandemic—not their physical efforts of visiting and treating their patients—but in relation to the cures and treatments that they had at their disposal. It meant that the public resorted to folk remedies, over the counter medicines and as the last resort, prayer to combat the disease. The following chapters will examine the local responses to influenza in towns and cities in the province of Ulster building a picture of how influenza impacted on Irish towns and what official steps were taken to combat the disease.

Notes

1. *Derry Journal*, 28 October 1918.
2. Quinn (2008, p. 45).
3. Tognotti (2003, p. 108).
4. Johnson (2006, p. 21).
5. Beveridge (1977, pp. 1–2).
6. Smith (1995, p. 62).
7. Beveridge (1977, pp. 2–3); Kolata (1999, pp. 64–5).
8. Taubenberger et al. (1997, pp. 1793–1796).
9. Kaiser (2005, p. 28); *Irish Times*, 6 October 2005.
10. French (1920, p. 66).
11. Graves (1969, p. 31).
12. French (1920, p. 73).
13. Ibid., p. 69.
14. Macnamara (1954, p. 305).
15. The National Archive [hereafter TNA], WO 35/ 179/4, Returns: historical review of medical and sanitary work in the Irish Command during the war, Report of the medical and sanitary work of the Dublin and Curragh Brigade, sanitary work during the war, 1.

16. Phillips and Killingray (2003, p. 5).
17. Rivaz Hunt (1918, pp. 419–421).
18. Geary (2004, pp. 70–73).
19. Guinnane (1997, p. 113).
20. Jones (2001, p. 1).
21. Jones (2001, p. 35).
22. Barrington (1987, p. 13); Jones (2001, p. 47).
23. Burke (1987, pp. 244–248).
24. *Report of the Irish Public Health Council on the public health and medical services in Ireland* [Cmd 761], H. C. 1920, xvii 2, 1075, 4.
25. Campbell (2003, pp. 4–5).
26. Burke (1987, p. 273).
27. Barrington (1987, p. 12).
28. Geary (2011, p. 203).
29. Geary (2011, p. 198).
30. *North Down Herald and County Down Independent*, 5 October 1918.
31. Barrington (1987), p.14.
32. Honigsbuam (2009, p. 90).
33. Macnamara (1954, p. 304).
34. *Annual Report of the Local Government Board for Ireland for the year ended 31st March 1919*, p. xxvi.
35. *Lisburn Standard*, 1 November 1918.
36. Macnamara (1954, p. 308).
37. Public Record Office Northern Ireland [Hereafter PRONI], BG/6/A/146, Banbridge Board of Guardians [Hereafter BOG] Minutes, 18 November; 25 November 1918.
38. PRONI, BG/25/A/166, Newtownards BOG Minutes, 22 June 1918, *The Newtownards Chronicle*, 20 July 1918; PRONI, LA60/2CA/5, Newtownards Urban District Council Minutes, 1 July 1918; *The Newtownards Chronicle*, 12 October 1918.
39. PRONI, BG/12/A/83, Downpatrick BOG Minutes, 7 December 1918.
40. PRONI, BG/12/A/83, Downpatrick BOG, 21 December 1918.
41. PRONI, BG/12/A/84, Downpatrick BOG Minutes, 11 January 1919; 1 February 1919).
42. Barrington (1987, p. 10).
43. *Northern Standard*, 15 June 1918.
44. PRONI, BG/26/A/85, Omagh BOG Minutes, 14 September 1918; 12 October 1918 and 30 November 1918.
45. *Belfast News-Letter*, 25 December 1918.
46. *British Medical Journal*, 24 May 1919, 665.
47. Macnamara (1954, p. 308).
48. *Annual Report of the Local Government Board for Ireland for the year ended 31st March 1919*, xxvii.

49. Macnamara (1954, pp. 305–306).
50. PRONI, LA/43/27/A/4, Proceedings of Larne Urban District Council, Public Health Committee Minutes, 30 October 1918.
51. *Tyrone Courier*, 5 December 1918.
52. Loeb (2005, p. 210).
53. *Irish News*, 31 October 1918; *Belfast News-Letter*, 31 October 1918.
54. Colum (1959, pp. 187–188).
55. Colum (1959, p. 191).
56. Loeb (2005, p. 220).
57. Johnson (2006, p. 168).
58. Quinn (2008, pp. 141–142).
59. Johnson (2006, p. 166).
60. *Armagh Guardian*, 21 June 1918.
61. *Belfast Evening Telegraph*, 1 November 1918.
62. *Belfast Evening Telegraph*, 29 November 1919.
63. Rice (2003, p. 81); Rice and Palmer (1993, pp. 401–405).
64. *Belfast News-Letter*, 6 February 1919.
65. Van Hartesveldt (1992, p. 99).
66. *The Scotsman*, 22 February 1919.
67. *Derry Journal*, 5 March 1919.
68. *Belfast Evening Telegraph*, 24 February 1919.
69. *Armagh Guardian*, 28 February 1919.
70. Graves (1969, p. 27).
71. Loeb (2005, p. 220).
72. McGinnis (1988, p. 124).
73. Echenberg (2003, p. 234).
74. Graves (1969, p. 27).
75. Macnamara (1954, p. 306).
76. *Northern Whig*, 10 December 1918; *Irish Times*, 17 December 1918.
77. *Irish Times*, 18 February 1919.
78. *Irish Times*, 19 February 1919.
79. *Irish Independent*, 22 February 1919.
80. Loeb (2005, p. 209).
81. *Irish Times*, 22 February 1919.
82. *Irish News*, 22 February 1919.
83. *Newtownards Chronicle*, 8 March 1918; *County Down Spectator*, 8 March 1918.
84. TNA, WO 35/179/4, Returns: historical review of medical and sanitary work in the Irish Command during the war Report of the Dublin and Curragh Brigade, 3.
85. *Lisburn Standard*, 14 March 1919; *Belfast News-Letter*, 14 March 1919.
86. *Lisburn Standard*, 28 June 1918.
87. *Belfast News-Letter*, 7 March 1919.

88. *Fermanagh Times*, 27 March 1919; *Fermanagh Herald*, 29 March 1919.
89. *Dungannon Democrat*, 16 April. 1919; Fermanagh *Herald*, 26 April 1919.
90. Jones (1963, pp. 62–63).
91. Holmes (2006, p. 99).
92. Malcolm, (1986, p. 331).
93. Laffan, (1999, p. 151).
94. These advertisements appeared in *Irish Independent* and *Irish Times*, from 19 November 1918 to 7 December 1918.
95. *Northern Whig*, 30 November 1918.
96. Novick (2002, pp. 40–41).
97. Puirséil (2008, pp. 185).
98. Loeb, (2005, p. 220).
99. *Larne Times*, advertisements appeared weekly from 8 to 29 March 1919.
100. *Belfast Evening Telegraph*,—Advertisements appeared on 8 November; 20 November and 28 November 1918.
101. *Belfast Evening Telegraph*, during November.1918, December.1918 and January 1919.
102. *Irish Independent*, 3 July 1918, *Irish Independent*, 10 March 1919, 19 March 1919.
103. Johnson (2006, p. 145). *Irish Independent*, 3 July 1918, *Irish Independent*, 10 March 1919, 19 March 1919.
104. *Annual Report of the Local Government Board for Ireland for the year ended 31st March 1919*, xxviii.
105. Crofton (1918, pp. 662–664).
106. *Irish Independent*, 24 October 1918.
107. *Irish Independent*, 25 October 1918.
108. *Belfast Evening Telegraph*, 30 October 1918.
109. *Irish Independent*, 2 December 1918.
110. *Armagh Guardian*, 29 November. 1918.
111. PRONI, BG/20/A/75, Lisnaskea BOG Minutes, 2 November 1918.
112. *Drogheda Independent*, 2 November 1918.
113. The Donegal County Archives Collection, Lifford, BG 38/1/84, Ballyshannon BOG Minutes, 4 January 1919, *Donegal Vindicator*, 24 January 1919.
114. TNA WO 35/179/4, Returns: historical review of medical and sanitary work in the Irish Command during the war, Historical review of the medical and sanitary work of the Cork district during the war period, p. 4; Historical review of the Dublin and Curragh Brigades, p. 2 and Report of the medical and sanitary work of the Ulster Brigade.
115. Milne, (2018, p 127).
116. *Belfast Evening Telegraph*, 24 February 1919.
117. Johnson (2006, p.145).

118. Loeb (2005 p. 203).
119. *The Times*, 28 June 1918; *Irish Times*, 3 July 1918. *Irish Independent*, 3 July 1918.
120. Both adverts appeared weekly in both the *Ballymena Observer* from 28 June-12 July 1918 and *Ballymena Weekly Telegraph*, 29 June–13 July 1918.
121. Appeared weekly in the *Lurgan Mail* from 21 December 1918–8 February 1919; *Portadown Express* from 6 December 1918–7 February 1919.
122. Appeared weekly in *Ulster Herald* from 9 November to 28 December 1918.
123. *Ulster Herald*, 28 December 1918; 11 January 1919.
124. These adverts appeared in a variety of Irish Newspaper throughout the second and third waves including *Larne Times*, *Ulster Gazette*, *Tyrone Courier*; *Newry Reporter; Mid-Ulster Mail, Leinster Reporter, Irish Independent; Belfast Telegraph; Freemans Journal; Sligo Champion* and *Ballymena Observer.*
125. Appeared in *Belfast News-Letter*, on 5 March, 12 March 1919 and 19 March 1919.
126. *Lurgan Mail*, 2 November 1918; *Larne Times*, 2 November 1918; *Ballymena Weekly Telegraph*, 2 November 1918; *County Down Spectator*, 2 November 1918.
127. *Northern Whig*, 28 November 1918; *Ulster Herald*, 15 February 1919; *Belfast News-Letter*, 12 March 1919; *Irish News*, 18 March 1919, 25 March 1919.
128. *Belfast News-Letter*, 30, 31 October 1918; 7, 12 November 1918; *Belfast Evening Telegraph*, 29, 30 October 1918, 1 November 1918.
129. Appeared in *Belfast News-Letter* and *Irish Independent* during November 1918 and F February 1919.
130. Appeared in *Irish Independent*, and *Irish Times* during November and December 1918.
131. PRONI, BG/7/A/100, Belfast BOG Minutes, 19 November 1918.
132. These adverts appeared in a variety of Irish Newspaper throughout the second and third waves including *Wicklow People, Belfast Telegraph; Irish Independent; Belfast Telegraph Belfast News-Letter*, *Larne Times; Mid-Ulster Mail, Londonderry Sentinel,* and *Kilkenny Moderator.*
133. *Belfast Evening Telegraph*, 24 December 1918.
134. Appeared in *Belfast News-Letter* during June; July and November 1918 and in *Belfast Evening Telegraph*, in November 1918.
135. Appeared in *Belfast News-Letter* during February 1919.
136. *Irish News*, 8 November 1918.
137. *Belfast News-Letter*, 21 November 1918; *Irish News*, 22 November 1918.

138. *Irish News*, 14 December 1918.
139. Milne (2018, p. 38).
140. *Irish Independent*, *Irish Times*, throughout April 1919.
141. *Belfast News-Letter*, 14 April 1919; *Irish Independent*, 2 April 1919.
142. *Ulster Gazette*, 5 April 1919, *Larne Times*, 12 April 1919; *Ballymena Weekly Telegraph*, 12 April 1919; *Irish Independent*, 13 November 1919.
143. Honigsbuam (2009, p. 90).
144. *Belfast News-Letter*, 29 October 1918; *Tyrone Courier*, 31 October 1918; *Ballymena Weekly Telegraph*, 2 November 1918; *Banbridge Chronicle*, 2 November 1918; *County Down Spectator*, 2 November 1918; *Larne Times*, 2 November 1918; *Newry Reporter*, 2 November.1918; *Ulster Guardian*, 2 November 1918.
145. *Belfast News-Letter*, 29 October 1918; *Lurgan Mail*, 2 November 1918; *Belfast News-Letter*, 31 October 1918; *Irish News*, 31 October 1918; *Ballymena Observer*, 1 November 1918.
146. *Irish Times*, 28 October 1918.
147. *Belfast News-Letter*, 23 November 1918.
148. *Leitrim Observer*, 9 November 1918.
149. *Roscommon Messenger*, 2 November 1918.
150. Thanksgiving prayers appeared in the notices pages of *Irish Independent*, in January, February and March 1919.

References

Barrington, Ruth. *Health, Medicine and Politics in Ireland 1900–1970*. Dublin: Institute of Public Administration, 1987.

Beveridge, W. I. B. *Influenza: The Last Great Plague: An Unfinished Story of Discovery*. London: Heineman, 1977.

Burke, Helen. *The People and the Poor Law in Nineteenth Century Ireland*. Dublin: Argus Press, 1987.

Campbell, Henrietta. 'Public Health: A Bond Between a Government and Its People', *The Ulster Medical Journal*, 72:1 (May 2003): 4–9.

Colum, Padraic. *Arthur Griffith*. Dublin: Browne and Nolan, 1959.

Echenberg, Myron. '"The Dog That Did Not Bark" Memory and the 1918 Influenza Epidemic in Sengal', in *Spanish Influenza Pandemic of 1918–1919: New Perspectives*, edited by Howard Phillips and David Killingray, 230–238. London: Routledge, 2003.

French, Herbert C. B. E. 'The Clinical Features of the Influenza Epidemic of 1918–19', in *Ministry of Health, Report on the Pandemic of Influenza, 1918–19*. 66–109. London: HMSO, 1920.

Geary, Laurence M. *Medicine and Charity in Ireland 1718–1851*. Dublin: University College Dublin Press, 2004.

Geary, Laurence, M. 'The Medical Profession, Healthcare and the Poor Law in Nineteenth Century Ireland', in *Poverty and Welfare in Ireland, 1838–1948*, edited by Virginia Crossman and Peter Gray, 189–206. Dublin: Irish Academic Press, 2011.

Graves, Charles. *Invasion by Virus: Can It Happen Again?* London: Icon Books Limited, 1969.

Guinnane, Timothy W. *The Vanishing Irish: Households, Migration, and the Rural Economy in Ireland, 1850–1914*. Princeton: Princeton University Press, 1997.

Holmes, Andrew R. *The Shaping of Ulster Presbyterian Belief and Practice, 1770–1840*. Oxford: Oxford University Press, 2006.

Honigsbaum, Mark. *Living with Enza: The Forgotten Story of Britain and the Great Flu Pandemic of 1918*. New York: Macmillan, 2008.

Hunt, E. Rivaz. 'Notes on the Symptomatology and Morbid Anatomy of So-Called "Spanish Influenza"', *Lancet* (28 September 1918): 419–421.

Johnson, Niall. *Britain and the 1918–19 Influenza Pandemic: A Dark Epilogue*. London Routledge, 2006.

Jones, Bartlett C. 'A Prohibition Problem: Liquor as Medicine 1920–1933', *Journal of the History of Medicine and Allied Sciences*, 18:4 (October 1963): 353–369.

Jones, Greta. *'Captain of All These Men of Death': The History of Tuberculosis in Nineteenth and Twentieth Century Ireland*. Amsterdam and New York: Editions Rodopi B.V., 2001.

Kaiser, Jocelyn. 'Resurrected Influenza Virus Yields Secrets of Deadly 1918 Pandemic', *Science*, 310 (October 2005): 28–29.

Kolata, Gina. *Flu: The Story of the Great Influenza Pandemic of 1918 and the Search for the Virus That Caused It*. New York: Simon & Schuster, 1999.

Laffan, Michael. *The Resurrection of Ireland*. Cambridge: Cambridge University Press, 1999.

Loeb, Lori. 'Beating the Flu: Orthodox and Commercial Responses to Influenza in Britain, 1889–1919', *Social History of Medicine*, 18:2 (2005): 203–224.

Macnamara, Dr, D. W. 'Memories of 1918 and "The Flu"', *Journal of the Irish Medical Association*, 35:208 (1954): 304–309.

Malcolm, Elizabeth. *'Ireland Sober, Ireland Free': Drink and Temperance in Nineteenth-Century Ireland*. Dublin: Gill and Macmillan, 1986.

McGinnis, Janice Dickin. 'Carlill v. Carbolic Smoke Ball Company: Influenza, Quackery, and the Unilateral Contract', *Canadian Bulletin of Medical History*, 5:2 (Winter 1988): 121–141.

Milne, Ida. *Stacking the Coffins: Influenza, War and Revolution in Ireland 1918–19*. Manchester: Manchester University Press, 2018.

Novick, Ben. 'Propaganda 1: Advanced Nationalist Propaganda and Moralistic Revolution, 1914–18', in *The Irish Revolution 1913–1923*, edited by Joost Augusteijn, 34–53. Basingstoke: Palgrave, 2002.

Phillips, Howard and David Killingray. 'Introduction', in *Spanish Influenza Pandemic of 1918–1919: New Perspectives*, edited by Howard Phillips and David Killingray, 1–26. London: Routledge, 2003.

Puirséil, Niamh. 'War Work and Labour,' in *Our War: Ireland and the Great War*, edited by John Horne, 181–208. Dublin: Royal Irish Academy, 2008.

Quinn, Tom. *Flu: A Social History of Influenza*. London: New Holland, 2008.

Rice, Geoffrey W. 'Japan and New Zealand in the 1918 Influenza Pandemic: Comparative Perspectives of Official Responses and Crisis Management', in *Spanish Influenza Pandemic of 1918–1919: New Perspectives*, edited by Howard Phillips and David Killingray, 73–85. London: Routledge, 2003.

Rice, Geoffrey W. and Edwina Palmer. 'Pandemic Influenza in Japan, 1918–1919: Mortality Patterns and Official Responses', *Journal of Japanese Studies*, 19:2 (1993): 389–420.

Smith, F. B. 'The Russian Influenza in the United Kingdom, 1889–1894', in *Social History of Medicine*, 8:1 (1995): 55–73.

Taubenberger, Jeffery K. et al. 'Initial Genetic Characterization of the 1918 "Spanish" Influenza Virus', *Science*, 275 (March 1997): 1793–1796.

Tognotti, Eugenia. 'Scientific Triumphalism and Learning from Facts: Bacteriology and the "Spanish Flu" Challenge of 1918', *Social History of Medicine*, 16:1 (2003): 97–110.

Van Hartesveldt, Fred, R. 'Manchester', in *The 1918–1919 Pandemic of Influenza: The Urban Impact in the Western World*, edited by Fred van Hartesveldt, 91–103. Lewiston, Queenstown, Lampeter: The Edward Mellon Press, 1992.

CHAPTER 6

'A Serious Menace to the Public Health of the City': Belfast and the Influenza Pandemic

Introduction

Belfast, situated in the north east coast of Ireland, was a port city and Ireland's major industrial city. At this time Belfast bore more similarities to those industrial cities in northern Britain than to other parts of Ireland. The economy in Belfast was dominated by three industrial concerns: linen and textile manufacture; shipbuilding, and engineering. The town was made up of terraced streets that housed the industrial workers. The tram network created a transport hub that provided access from the city centre to the outlying areas of the city.[1] The railway network provided access to other towns throughout the north of Ireland.

There were three separate waves of influenza in Belfast. Although the first outbreak took place in June 1918, it was the second, which occurred in autumn 1918, that was the most virulent, while the third outbreak in spring 1919 was the mildest. Even though Belfast had the third-highest influenza death rate per thousand of population of any county in Ireland in 1918,[2] the pandemic was largely ignored in contemporary reports on the city. It merited one paragraph in the Medical Superintendent Officer of Health for Belfast's (MSOH) report for 1918, while there was no mention of it at all in his 1919 report.[3] Belfast Corporation's records of the time such as the minutes of council and public health committee meetings barely mention the pandemic. However, the

P. Marsh, *The Spanish Flu in Ireland*, Palgrave Studies in Economic History, https://doi.org/10.1007/978-3-030-79500-9_6

contemporary newspapers reported the disease and it is from these articles as well as minutes from the Belfast board of guardians meetings that most of the information of how the pandemic affected the city can be gleaned.

First Wave in Belfast

The first newspaper reports of the disease in Belfast appeared as early 11 June 1918. A notice appeared in Belfast newspapers regarding the re-opening of a department, after influenza in local munitions factory, James Mackie & Sons, Limited.[4] Indicating that influenza was in the city from the beginning of June 1918. The closure of Mackies was not the only disruption to the working life in the city. It was reported that the shipyards had suffered 'in a marked degree' and up to four thousand workers in one of the city's largest industrial concerns were absent due to influenza.[5] The Belfast tramway system faced operational problems with 100 motormen and conductors absent by 1 July 1918 and tragically two tram conductors died from influenza on 24 June 1918, James Brown (33) and William Kyle (19).[6]

Education was disrupted as it was thought prudent to not only to close 120 schools, but also the Sunday schools in Belfast.[7] Boxing bouts at Celtic Park were cancelled because over 60 per-cent of the contestants were either suffering or recovering from influenza.[8] Unsurprisingly, pharmacists were kept busy with reports of huge queues forming at chemists' shops in Belfast city centre.[9] Staff from these establishments were not immune to the disease. Absenteeism, along with an increase of workload, meant that one Belfast chemist had to make up 450 prescriptions despite of 14 of his 18 assistants being absent with influenza.[10] Medical personnel were particularly vulnerable as indicated by widespread influenza among doctors and nurses at the Royal Victoria Hospital.[11] Medical officers from several dispensary districts within the Belfast Union were also absent with influenza as well as resident medical officer of the infirmary, along with several other officers. Eight nurses were ill and Catherine Fenton, a probationer nurse unfortunately died from the complication pneumonia.[12]

This first wave of the pandemic was considered mild in comparison with the autumn outbreak. Most people who contracted the virus recovered, nevertheless there were many tragic deaths. Among the casualties was Dr Joseph Leyden a young doctor who had graduated from Queen's

University, Belfast in the spring of 1918. He was the house surgeon at the Mater Infirmorum. He died on 3 July 1918 from pneumonia, a few days after contracting influenza.[13] Another death that struck a chord with the public was that of Robert Caines, a newsboy aged 11 who died from influenza on 19 June 1918. On Monday night his mother put him to bed after he complained of a headache. She slept with him through the night but on waking the next morning found that he was dead beside her. The case of Robert's mother, who had been abandoned by her husband, a discharged soldier, and left with eight children, aroused widespread public sympathy. Many donations were forwarded to give financial support to Mrs Caine and her family. A subscription list was printed in the *Belfast Telegraph*.[14] This was the only evidenced example in Belfast of direct philanthropy to help victims of the disease.

Belfast Union Hospital and the First Wave

In Belfast, as in the rest of Ireland, it was the poor law medical system that provided the medical relief and care for the poor suffering from influenza in the city. The number of influenza patients admitted to the Belfast union infirmary indicates how the disease escalated and declined in the city. By 15 June 1918 there were 40 influenza patients in the Belfast Union Hospital. At a guardians' meeting on 18 June 1918, an assistant doctor was requested for four-weeks to help with the extra workload in the Newtownards Road dispensary district of the city. The number of influenza cases in the infirmary had increased to 110 by 22 June 1918. Further proof of the escalation of the disease was that an additional 88 cases had been admitted during the subsequent four-day period. As later admissions were more severe than earlier cases, Dr Gardner Robb, Visiting Medical Officer for the Belfast union hospital, arranged for additional accommodation in the workhouse to accommodate convalescent cases from the infirmary. Additional nurses were transferred to the fever hospital from the infirmary; 15 new probationer nurses started their duties immediately and, due to the number of patients, any nurses who were on holiday were recalled to resume duty at the institution. Dr Robb urgently requested another house physician to assist with the increased admission of patients.[15]

Although influenza was said to be abating in the city by 2 July 1918,[16] the death toll from the disease was still high. In the seven-day period ending on 29 June 1918, 92 people died from pneumonia—many of which followed on from influenza.[17] By 9 July 1918, the disease appeared to be waning in the city as the number of cases in the union hospital decreased from 210 to 184 between 29 June and 6 July 1918. Despite this, there was a significant increase in the workload in the hospital. Dr Robb acknowledged the guardians' letter of appreciation of his efforts with 'Never in my recollection has the strain on the staff been so great as during the past few weeks'.[18] By the 13 July 1918 the number of influenza patients had decreased to 123, but eight nurses and several other officers were still absent from the workhouse with the disease.[19] On 23 July 1918, Dr Robb reported that influenza was declining and there were only 61 influenza patients left in hospital on 20 July.[20] The number of influenza patients in the institution steadily declined over the subsequent weeks, indicating that the first wave was coming to an end.

Belfast Corporation's Response During First Wave

If the poor law medical system provided medical relief in the city, it was Belfast Corporation that was responsible for public health through both the public health committee and public health department. The MSOH, Dr Hugh W. Bailie, was responsible for the city's response to the influenza crisis. His main response throughout the three waves of influenza was one of prevention. During the first wave there was no mention of influenza in the contemporary minutes of the Belfast City Corporation or Public Health Committee meetings, however, certain actions were put in place. According to the *Belfast News-Letter*, Dr Bailie recommended the closure of 'about a dozen schools accommodating several thousands of pupils' on 18 June in the East end of the city and that cinemas should be thoroughly disinfected once or twice a day. Many of the large business and industrial establishments in Belfast adopted a similar practice.[21] He also suggested that if a person contracted influenza that they should 'go to bed as soon as the symptoms are observed, and to get under treatment at once'.[22]

Nationalist Councillor O'Hare's suggested 'that the Public Health Committee should send out leaflets to the householders instructing them how to deal with influenza in its initial stages'. He believed that if it had been done at the outset then many lives may have been saved 'of those who through ignorance or neglect had taken no precautions'.[23] Councillor O'Hare's suggestion was ignored by the committee and, instead, Dr Bailie sent his department inspectors around their districts to advise people of measures to be taken if they contracted influenza. The editorial in the *Irish News* on 5 July 1918 criticised Dr Bailie's actions as unrealistic. It condemned the Public Health Committee for failing to take any practical steps to warn the public of the danger of infection, or the best methods of treating influenza cases.[24] The *Irish News'* concern was a valid one as it would have been a gargantuan task for the department inspectors to advise the Belfast public on a one-to-one basis on prevention measures for influenza.

Some newspapers played down the seriousness of influenza during this first wave.[25] This may have been an attempt to keep public morale boosted and thus help the war effort. Nevertheless, there was much disruption in the city due to absenteeism in the shipyards, factories and tramways, as well as school closures. Medical professionals were also under severe pressure due to the extent of the disease in the city. Although this first outbreak was milder than the second, it was still reasonably serious in Belfast since as many as 650 people died of influenza or pneumonia during this wave.[26] Taking this into account, the Belfast Corporation health officials appear to have taken a very rudimentary approach to prevention and treatment of influenza during this wave. This may be because this outbreak was treated as another seasonal influenza.

Second Wave in Belfast

Reports on 31 October 1918 that there were about 1,000 influenza cases in Belfast heralded the arrival of the second wave to the city.[27] However, the deaths from influenza of Louis Chalon and John Mullan on 21 October 1918 in the union infirmary, indicate that the disease may have taken hold in the city earlier in the month. Due to the serious nature of the second wave, various public institutions decided to close. On 8 November 1918, the Commissioners of National Education recommended the closure of national schools until Monday 18 November 1918. The authorities at Queen's University, Belfast suspended classes and lectures for a week from 8 November 1918 and did not open again until Monday 2 December 1918. On 9 November 1918, public notices in the newspapers advised that the Linenhall Library and Belfast public libraries would be closed from Monday 11 November 1918 until further notice. Other closures during November 1918 included the Belfast Ophthalmic Hospital, while both Purdysburn Asylum and Whiteabbey Sanatorium closed the institution to visitors during November 1918 until the 'risk of infection had died down'.[28] Pursdyburn Asylum was situated in the

Lisburn poor law district and during the second wave there were at least 14 influenza and pneumonia deaths in the institution.

Public notices continued to appear in newspapers advising of the continued closure of schools and as influenza continued unabated, this date was extended until after the Christmas holidays.[29] Although the managers of the national schools agreed to the recommendations to close their premises, not all schools in the city did so. Methodist College in Belfast remained open during this virulent wave with fatal consequences. Boarders at the school were mainly affected. Improvised wards were set up in the school and boys who had recovered from the disease helped in the kitchens, serving as orderlies when both the nurses and domestic staff contracted influenza. At its height only the medical officer, matron and headmaster avoided contracting the disease. Tragically, between 17 and 23 November 1918, two members of staff, George Manning (22) and the Rev Patrick O'Sullivan (44), as well as one of the boarders, Oliver Crawford (15), died from influenza.[30]

Businesses and places of employment were again under pressure and on 13 November 1918, the Post Office was reported to be 'performing the service with great difficulty'.[31] By late November 1918, as during the first wave, the tramway service was struggling to operate due to the absence of 120 employees with influenza.[32] The death toll was high and in the six weeks leading up to 18 December 1918, there were 929 interments in Corporation cemeteries, representing an increase of 404 as compared to the corresponding period in 1917. The increase in workload led the Belfast gravediggers to ask for an increase in pay.[33] Entire families in the city contracted influenza with tragic results. In November in the Harvey family from the Crumlin Road, husband Thomas, his wife Esther, two daughters and three sons all contracted influenza. Tragically Esther, (38) died on 27 November 1918 and her two sons, James (3) and Thomas (7) died of the complication pneumonia on 24 November and 28 November, respectively.[34] Others that tragically succumbed to influenza were the McQuillan family of Colinwell, Dunmurray. Mrs Mary McQuillan (58), her son John (32) and daughter Cissie, (29) all died within hours of each other from the disease. Tragically John died, leaving behind a young widow and infant child.[35] These were but a few examples among the high death toll in Belfast during this outbreak where at least 1,550 people from the city and surrounding area died from Influenza or pneumonia.[36]

Belfast Union Hospital and the Second Wave

Again, it was the increased activity at the union infirmary that indicated the seriousness of this outbreak. At the guardians' meeting on 29 October 1918 it was reported that 15 inmates and 21 nurses at the union hospital were suffering from influenza. The number of influenza patients increased from 75 to 140 between 2 and 9 November 1918.[37] Influenza again impacted on medical personnel in the institution. Absenteeism among medical staff and other workhouse officers was so high that one of the medical officers was appointed to solely treat employees suffering from influenza. Even though the number of influenza patents decreased slightly to 131 by 16 November 1918. The Visiting Medical Officers recommended that the 'nursing staff should have an increase in nourishment' and each nurse had their daily dietary rations of butter increased by one ounce and of Bovril by ¼ ounce. Despite this, the considerable absenteeism among the nursing staff placed the remaining nurses under a great strain and during November 1918 four nurses, Catherine Doocey, Mary Griffin, Josephine Neild and Rosanna Ellison, all in their twenties, died from pneumonia following on from influenza between 5 November 1918 and 3 December 1918.[38]

At the guardians' meeting on 26 November 1918 Mr McCormick, Chairman of the infirmary and the Child Welfare Committee, advised that 1,100 influenza cases had been treated at the workhouse up to 23 November 1918, of these cases 150 died from influenza or pneumonia.[39] Influenza began abating in Belfast by 30 November 1918 with a total of 399 influenza patients in the workhouse, but there were still 30 deaths during the week.[40] At the guardians' meeting on 31 December 1918 it was reported that 'the influenza epidemic in Belfast seems to be practically over' as admissions to the infirmary of patients suffering from this disease had almost ceased. Despite this there were still a large number of patients suffering from complications and after-effects of influenza. At this meeting, the Medical Officer advised that the true influenza figures treated in the institution may never been known.[41]

Belfast Corporation's Response During Second Wave

The Scavengers' Strike in Belfast

The labourers of the house cleansing and street cleansing departments (known as scavengers) began a strike on 2 October 1918 in Belfast that lasted until 12 November 1918 and coincided with the second outbreak of influenza in the city.[42] The strike started when the corporation rearranged the workers hours without their prior consultation. Questions were raised in Parliament about the health of Belfast due to the strike, as 'not a street had been swept or rubbish removed from a single house' since it started.[43] The *Belfast News-Letter* supported the Corporation's stance in its editorial on 14 October 1918 reporting that the new working arrangement was carefully thought out and that the workers had been treated generously.[44] On 18 October, an editorial in the *Irish News* suggested that the action of the Corporation's Improvement Committee, in rejecting the men's offer of arbitration, was an attempt to 'beat down the unions concerned by a prolonged strike'. It complained that if this uncompromising attitude persisted, it would result in 'a serious menace to the public health', and that it was vitally important when 'elaborate precautions' were considered necessary to prevent epidemic disease that the situation concerning municipal sanitation be resolved.[45]

On 25 October 1918, the *Irish News* again ran an editorial that criticised Belfast Corporation for not resolving the strike. It quoted a doctor who thought it was remarkable that during this period of grave peril to the entire community that Belfast Corporation had chosen to quarrel 'with the real guardians of the community's health'. The result was that the city's streets were becoming 'areas of infection' and the backyards 'fertile hot-beds of pollution'. It implied that if there was an influenza outbreak in Belfast, that there would be thousands of victims and that drastic steps should be taken to end 'the perilous and intolerable situation'.[46]

A letter in the *Northern Whig* on 22 October from a member of the Public Health Committee, Oswald Jamison urged the Improvement Committee to meet with the strikers to settle the dispute as he feared there might be an outbreak of typhoid or influenza under the present conditions.[47] An editorial in the *Irish News* on 29 October 1918 stated that the city streets were in a 'shocking and dangerous condition'. and on 31 October 1918, the same newspaper reported that 'matters are assuming a grave aspect, from the point of view of public health',[48] while the *Belfast Evening Telegraph* reported on 30 October 1918 that due to the strike 'the state of the streets could hardly be worse'. On the same date a letter to the newspaper stated that 'surely the dispute between the street cleansers and their employers is of a minor nature when compared with the health of the people and should have been brought to an end long ago'.[49]

On 2 November 1918, the *Irish News* condemned the Improvement Committee's decision to not enter into arbitration with the men on strike. It stated that the majority of the citizens were opposed to the corporation's decision as they wanted to see the 'filth removed from their streets, backyards, and "entries."' Dr Bailie was criticised again, as they did not understand why he had advised the public to maintain absolute cleanliness, while declaring that 'huge quantities of city filth are of no consequence while a deadly epidemic is raging'.[50] In early November the strikers refused to accept the terms offered by the Improvement Committee[51] and the strike continued. The *Irish News* commented on 5 November 1918 that if the committee had accepted arbitration three or four-weeks previously, the dispute would have been settled sooner. It stated that the strikers' decision to reject the committee's compromise was to be deeply regretted by all as 'the wretched and dangerous quarrel will go on, seriously to the detriment of the city and to the peril of the people's health'.[52]

In one of its final articles on the strike the *Irish News* reported the proceedings of the inquest of Alise Boswell, a child aged 3 from the Holywood Arches who died from bronchial pneumonia, following acute influenza on 9 November 1918. It quoted the jury's opinion that:

> The present unsanitary condition of Belfast is the cause of much suffering and sickness amongst the inhabitants, many lives being sacrificed, owing to a trivial dispute between employer and employed. We urge an immediate settlement of the dispute before the city is plague-ridden.[53]

The jury's statement was unusual, as most inquest reports only contained a verdict of the cause of death. It suggests that the sanitary situation in Belfast must have reached a profoundly serious level for the strike to be implicated in the cause of a death in an inquest in the city. The medical journal, *The Lancet* was also contemptuous of the corporation's lack of action and reported that owing to the strike and 'from a sanitary point of view there is not at the present moment a more actually filthy city than Belfast'.[54] The strike eventually ended on 12 November 1918 and an editorial in the *Belfast News-Letter* acknowledged for the first time that the accumulation of refuse, and the state of the streets, was serious due to the prevalence of influenza. It declared: 'the settlement of this strike is likely to have more effect in maintaining the health of the city than the adoption of the recommendation to close schools and places of public entertainment'.[55]

Under these circumstances the attitude of Belfast Corporation seemed somewhat cavalier in allowing the strike to continue. It was thought in 1918 that influenza was a bacterial disease and that cleanliness and disinfection were the main preventative measures against the infection. Therefore, by allowing the streets to remain in such a dirty state, the corporation was in opposition to the recommendations of the *Belfast Health Commission Report* published in 1908. These were, that rubbish should be removed at least twice a week from all small and confined backyards and that back-passages should be 'frequently and systematically cleansed'.[56] Furthermore, it was also contrary to Dr Bailie's own recommendations for prevention of influenza, which included cleanliness, free ventilation and the burning of all organic matter. The *Irish News* commented on 31 October 1918 that 'unfortunately these nuisances never existed to a greater degree in the city than at present'.[57] Therefore, the fact that the corporation let the streets get into such a filthy state and, more importantly, to remain so, was directly opposed to the Dr Baillie's recommendations for prevention of influenza and showed a disregard to contemporary medical advice. The state of the Belfast streets was not a new concern. At the July 1918 meeting of the corporation, Councillor Alexander stated 'They all knew the condition of the streets during the past few years was disgraceful and disgusting'. Although he was aware that it was difficult to procure labour, he felt that something should be done 'in order that the health of the people of the city might be protected'.[58]

Although the Corporation's attitude over the strike was worthy of criticism, the constant censure of the nationalist run *Irish News* probably had as much to do with the political makeup of the corporation, which was predominantly unionist, as with its actual performance. This too could account for the lack of criticism from unionist run *Belfast News-Letter*. Even after the strike was resolved, there was still reason to criticise the corporation. In its report on the Corporation meeting of 1 December

1918, the *Irish News* reported that Councillor Doran advocated that more attention should be paid to the health of the people in the city and stated that during the influenza outbreak.

> If they did not take proper steps to stem the disease, there was no telling where it would end. People were told to ventilate their houses but how could they do so when the yards and back passages were filled with decaying refuse? If the people opened their windows they would only be letting in germs.[59]

Dr Bailie's Recommendations

Even though the strike continued, on 5 November 1918, the public health committee recommended that all day and Sunday schools in Belfast should close for at least 10 days and that all places of public amusement should be closed for the duration of the disease.[60] Dr Bailie's list of precautions for the public, were published as a Public Notice in the press. They included avoid crowded gatherings as well as the disinfection of factories and workshops. He also discouraged spitting on the streets and advised that all sputum should be burned or put down gratings because it contained infection. He recommended Quinine tablets of from two to five grains to be taken twice daily as a preventative and that if attacked by influenza the patient should go to bed early and remain there until completely recovered.[61]

These public notices were also displayed in tramcar windows, a measure that also came in for criticism because it contradicted one of Dr Bailie's precautions—'avoid all crowded gatherings'—as the tramcars were invariably crowded.[62] The public health committee was aware that overcrowding in tramcars was a problem and instructed Dr Bailie to discuss the matter with the general manager of the tramways.[63] Not surprisingly, overcrowding on the trams was not resolved. The tramways service was unable to increase the number of tramcars on the system because of the shortage of men to run them due to absenteeism from influenza. Further to this, there was a lack of materials to make repairs to the cars.[64] Therefore, overcrowding continued and absenteeism among employees was high, resulting in the death of tram conductor James Lowry (32) on 5 December 1918.

Closure of Cinemas

Several Belfast councillors suggested that the cinemas should be closed during this outbreak. The *Lancet*'s correspondent seemed surprised that the public health committee lacked the authority to close cinemas, but this was indeed the case.[65] The committee requested authority for compulsory closure of places of entertainment from the Local Government Board in Ireland (LGBI), but were advised that compulsory closure of these institutions was not approved in any part of the United Kingdom. The LGBI did, however, sanction the following regulations for Belfast. It gave the corporation the power to exclude children from cinemas in districts where the elementary schools were temporarily closed because of influenza. It also sanctioned the following regulations regarding the length of performances in places of public entertainment: that such entertainments shall not be carried on for more than three consecutive hours, four hours in the case of cinemas, and that interval lengths between successive programmes should be thirty minutes, in order to thoroughly ventilate the buildings.[66]

The cinema owners refused to close their premises. They also declined to close intermittently for an hour at the end of each performance for ventilation and disinfection as requested by the Belfast Corporation's public health committee. The North of Ireland Cinematograph Exhibitors' Association were concerned that cinema closures would lead to over 600 job losses in Belfast as well as the loss of over £300,000 of invested capital. Consequently, they were not willing to close their premises and they forwarded their own proposals for the closure and ventilation of cinemas in Belfast. Although these differed from the public health committee's recommendations, it was these proposals that Dr Bailie subsequently adopted for the cinemas in the city rather than his own.[67] One Belfast cinema, 'The Picture House', in Royal Avenue, Belfast advertised that it was 'The healthiest place in town' due to its unique ventilation system.[68] Even though the corporation was unable to close cinemas, the military authorities in Belfast produced an order prohibiting the attendance of soldiers at theatres and cinemas. This was a precautionary measure and a similar step was taken in regard to sailors.[69]

Although the Cinematographic Act of 1909 gave local authorities responsibility to provide licences for cinema premises it did not give them the power to force cinemas to close during an epidemic. In Ulster, several councils singled out places of entertainment for closure and ventilation under the pretext that people gathered there. However, people congregated in many places, including churches, but it was not suggested that church services should be abandoned in the same way. According to Tomkins, one of the main actions that the Imperial Local Government Board (LGB) took was regarding cinemas. They published regulations that limited the duration of performances and recommended ventilation practices that had to be followed, but they did not force closure of the premises. Tomkins argued that these regulations reflected anti-vice concerns around the perceived immorality of cinemas rather than having anything to do with public health.[70]

This would seem to be the case in Newtownards where some councillors wanted to postpone the renewal of the licence for the 'Picture House' in the town until the influenza outbreak was over because the proprietor had reopened the premises against the council's wishes. The chairman stated that, although he was not personally in favour of cinemas that the proprietors had carried out the council's requests. Therefore, he thought it was only fair to renew their licence. The license was not renewed on that occasion due to the abstention of five of the ten councillors.[71] Portadown urban council also disapproved of cinemas. One councillor described the 'Picture House' in the town 'as one of the greatest blots on Portadown at the present time'.[72]

In Dublin Sir Charles Cameron, MSOH rather than close the cinemas had been persuading the cinema proprietors in the city not to admit any children under 12 years of age and also to close their premises for half an hour daily for the purposes of disinfection and ventilation.[73] On 2 November 1918 it was reported that a deputation representing over 50 cinema theatres had assured him, none of their employees had contracted influenza. However, they had promised him that no children would be admitted to their premises.[74] The attendance of children at the cinema performances was a concern, as the schools were closed in cities such as Belfast and Dublin. This meant that children would attend crowded cinemas instead of schools thus encouraging the spread of influenza.[75] The cinemas in Dublin did not close, a step that Dr Donough Macnamara appreciated. He was under severe work pressure in the Mater hospital and 'the only really convenient escape one had from all the work and worry was an occasional dash of an evening to the comparatively new Bohemian Picture House'.[76]

It is not clear if it was anti-vice concerns that prompted Belfast Corporation to recommend cinema closures during this influenza outbreak, but the closure of these premises would have helped stop the spread of the disease. Nevertheless, the public health committee lacked the authority or resolve to enforce their original recommendations for closure and ventilation of Belfast cinemas. Other local authorities in the United Kingdom were more successful, such as Manchester, where the Medical Officer of Health (MOH), James Niven, ensured that the regulations regarding closure and ventilation of theatres and for non-admission of children under 14, were strictly observed.[77] Also, several London boroughs fined cinemas for non-compliance with the regulations.[78]

People gathering in the cinemas, theatres and trams were not the only cause for concern and the *Irish News* feared that the congregation of huge masses of people on the streets during the armistice celebrations would further spread the disease.[79] According to Niall Johnson, an ironic impact of the war was the extra infections and deaths that occurred as a result of the armistice celebration. He argued that celebrations became the foci of new or recrudescent outbreaks of influenza.[80] It should be noted that the armistice occurred during the peak of the second wave of influenza in Belfast. John Baxter was about 14 years of age during 1918. He recalled that his sister contracted and recovered from influenza, but had no other recollections of the pandemic. Nevertheless, he vividly remembered the armistice celebrations in Belfast. As a member of the Boys Brigade and part of the bugle band, he and his friends got together during the two or three days of excitement around the armistice. He recalled that: 'it seems everybody was out on the main roads of the city and the city centre, following the war's end'. He further recalled: 'There were bands, flags and banners all around and people milling about, singing and dancing and, as we walked down the middle of the road, they were lined up four or five deep and covering the whole area including the city centre'.[81] This recollection illustrates the extent of the crowds of people on the street over a series of nights during the peak of the most virulent influenza wave of the pandemic in Belfast, ignoring Dr Bailie's advice 'to avoid all crowded gatherings'. Therefore, it was maybe no surprise that in Belfast the mortality from influenza and pneumonia peaked on 23 November 1918 not long after these celebrations.[82]

The LGBI decided that influenza should not be added to the list of notifiable diseases. They believed that its short incubation period and infectivity during the early stages of attack would be ineffective in checking the spread of the disease.[83] Although Belfast Corporation did not make influenza notifiable, one of its most proactive measures during

December 1918 was to make septic pneumonia notifiable for a period of six months under the Infectious Disease (Notification) Act 1889.[84] Although it was not the first local authority in Ulster to do so, it was still one of the few in Ireland that did. At the Corporation's January 1919 meeting, unionist Councillor Stirling criticised the health authorities for not making influenza notifiable sooner. He pointed out that there was an admitted lack of professional medical knowledge about the nature and the real cause of the disease. Councillor English, chairman of the public health committee, replied that Belfast had been much more fortunate than many other places with regard to influenza, and that it was outside the committee's jurisdiction to set up a research department to ascertain the cause of influenza, but it was their duty to administer the law. The *Irish News* agreed with Councillor Stirling that the public health department had an almost 'dilatory' and 'lackadaisical attitude' towards the pandemic.[85] The medical correspondent of the *Lancet* agreed with the *Irish News and* was contemptuous of the chairman's statement that the committee's duty was only to administer the law and not to research the cause of the disease in the city. It asked: 'is it any wonder that in Belfast for 1918 we have a high general mortality rate and high rates for tuberculosis and infantile mortality?'.[86]

Third Wave in Belfast

On 12 February 1919 the *Irish Independent* reported that there were several non-virulent influenza cases in Belfast indicating the arrival of the third wave in the city.[87] Despite the tramcars being disinfected, the tramway service was again under pressure. Ninety-one of their employees were absent with influenza at the end of February 1919 resulting in the death of tram inspector David Montgomery.[88] Many employees from the General Post office were ill with influenza and some local bakeries were finding it difficult to maintain their regular bread deliveries due to bread servers being sick.[89] On 3 March 1919, *the Belfast News-Letter* reported that the disease was not as widespread—or as dangerous—as during the second wave and that 'Extensive precautions have been taken in all directions with a view to preventing the spreading of infection and these, it is believed are meeting with a good deal of success'.[90]

Although this was the mildest outbreak in the city, there were still fatalities especially in the Belfast police force, where 90 Ninety members were reported to be suffering from influenza at the end of February 1919. [91]

Two police officers Constable John Fowler (34), and William Carter (35) from the College Square barracks died from influenza on 23 February and 27 February 1919, respectively.[92] In Mountpottinger, Constables Joseph Burnside (40) and Edward Woods (31) died on 18 February and 27 February 1919 from the disease.[93] These deaths were followed by that of Constable Felix McConnell (35) on 18 March 1919 and his wife Linda the next day, both from the complication pneumonia. They left behind three children who were described as 'dangerously ill'.[94] It is not known what happened to these children. There is no record of their deaths but if they survived, with both parents dead, and if no extended family could be found, there was little choice for these children who would either be sent to an orphanage or an industrial school.

Belfast Union Hospital During the Third Wave

At the guardians' meeting of 18 February 1919, it was reported that there were 26 influenza cases in the hospital. By 8 March 1919 the number of patients peaked at 130. An extra physician was appointed to assist in the Newtownards Road dispensary district due to the unusually large number of influenza cases that were described as 'serious requiring daily supervision'. Again, the workhouse staff were susceptible to the infection and the nursing staff and others in the institution including Visiting Medical Officer, Dr Robb contracted influenza but fortunately there were no fatalities on this occasion. By 5 April 1919, the number of influenza patients in the Union hospital had declined to 59.[95] There was a steady decline of patients in the Union hospital until June 1919 which signified the end of the third and final wave of influenza in Belfast.

Belfast Corporation's Response During Third Wave

During the third outbreak of influenza, Dr Bailie acted promptly. With effect from 21 February 1919, he circulated a public notice, similar to the one he issued during the second wave, listing precautions that should be taken regarding the influenza pandemic. These notices were again published in newspapers, displayed in tramcars and on public hoardings.[96] He organised the disinfection of tramcars twice daily[97] and ordered the closure of all national, Catholic maintained and Sunday schools in the city. As the schools were closed, the public health department issued an order prohibiting children under 14 years of age admission to amusement houses and the military authorities put all Belfast cinemas and theatres out of bounds to military personnel. The suggestion that the corporation should spray the principal streets at regular intervals with disinfectants, as had taken place in Dublin, was rejected in Belfast for the dual reasons of shortage of labour to do the job as well as the belief that disinfectants would be washed away in the first rain shower.[98]

At the March 1919 Corporation meeting, Councilor English, chairman of the Public Health Committee was confident that this influenza outbreak was not as serious as the previous one. He anticipated that if the precautionary recommendations were adhered to then the further spread of influenza would be prevented, stating: 'On the whole they had every right to congratulate themselves that they had escaped and he hoped in a few weeks to announce that the epidemic was gone'.[99] The *Belfast News-Letter* reported on 4 March 1919 that as the health committee had taken prompt action, Belfast would probably suffer much less than in the previous outbreaks.[100] During this wave Belfast suffered fewer fatalities and had the lowest influenza mortality rate in Ireland of 0.83 per thousand of population.[101] However, it was doubtful that the mild nature of the third wave in Belfast was due to the public health committee's actions but rather to immunity gained from the previous waves of influenza. Indeed, the 1920 Ministry of Health report inferred that this was the case with Belfast but provided no statistical evidence to support this claim.[102]

The Effectiveness of Belfast Corporation's Response

In Dr Bailie's annual report on the health of Belfast for 1918, he stated that the health department had done everything possible to prevent the spread of influenza. He listed that the measures taken were the display of posters throughout the city with instructions for the public to follow regarding influenza; the closure of all Belfast schools and making septic pneumonia notifiable.[103] Although Dr Bailie took some steps towards preventing the spread of influenza, he did not tackle the problem of how to assist sufferers if they contracted the disease. This is in contrast to several London borough councils who recognised the limitations of just having preventative measures to deal with influenza, so they also directed their efforts at dealing with the effects of the pandemic by provision of nursing, domestic help and hospital services to those afflicted.[104]

Dr Bailie never made any recommendations beyond the general preventative measures mentioned and he appeared to lack the authority to get some of these sanctioned. Questions had been previously posed as to whether Dr Bailie was competent to carry out the position of MSOH. In 1908 the *Belfast Health Commission Report* criticised his appointment in 1906 because although he was a qualified doctor and possessed the statuary qualification required for the post, a Diploma in Public Health, he lacked previous experience in public health administration.[105] In Belfast, it was customary to fill the post of MSOH by electing a former member of the corporation.[106] Dr Bailie, a former Conservative alderman in the council, resigned to be eligible for the post and was appointed in preference to several better-qualified candidates.[107] The LGBI voiced their disapproval of his appointment, believing he had inadequate experience to fill the post. In a letter to the corporation they said that Belfast required the services of 'a medical officer of wide experience and possessing a special training as a medical officer or assistant medical officer of health acquired in some larger towns where public health problems of a similar kind to those confronting Belfast have had to be dealt with'.[108] Perhaps because of this, Dr Bailie appeared to lack authority within the corporation, which was evidenced by his absence of influence during the strike of the labourers of the house cleansing and street cleansing department. This prompted the *Irish News* to ask in October 1918 'Has Dr Bailie any authority or influence with the heroic Corporators? If he has why is it not exerted?'.[109]

The *Belfast Health Commission Report* of 1908 also criticised the public health administration in the city. The MOH's were supposed to establish the origin of infectious diseases within their dispensary districts and to report these regularly to the Corporation. The MSOH was required to perform similar duties for the County Borough of Belfast and also supervise the duties of the MOHs. However, in Belfast as no information regarding mortality returns were given to the MSOH, the Commission reported that he was 'in complete ignorance of all the useful details of the vital statistics of the city'. They also criticised the MOHs who did not seem to learn or respond to anything they gleaned from the vital statistics of their districts.[110] This situation had not improved by 1918 and could not have helped Dr Bailie perform his duties concerning the pandemic in the city.

The public health administration of Belfast had been under criticism prior to 1908. In 1896, the Harrison committee described the public health administration of the city as 'being feeble and inefficient, not only because the Public Health Committee were themselves indifferent to their responsibilities, but also because they had not under their control 'a sufficient staff of efficient men under proper organisation and discipline'.[111] In 1918 the city's health was still a matter for concern regardless of the influenza pandemic and in October 1918, the *Lancet* reported that the health of Belfast was in a serious condition and approximately one-third of all deaths in the city between 20 December 1917 and 20 June 1918 were of children under five years. It should be noted that influenza did not a factor in these figures.[112] Infant mortality had always been relatively high in Belfast in comparison to England, Wales, Scotland and the rest of Ireland and according to Roger Blaney was still the subject of intense investigation as late as the 1960s.[113]

During the 1918–1919 pandemic, the main public health thinking in relation to infectious disease put the emphasis on disinfection, isolation and personal prevention.[114] The public health committee along with Dr Bailie attempted to endorse them. They also attempted to obtain powers from the LGBI for compulsory closure of schools and places of entertainment but were refused.[115] However, without this power they lacked the authority to enforce some of their recommendations in Belfast and as it will be seen in later chapters, other local authorities also had this problem.

Belfast's official response, especially during the second and third outbreaks, was one of prevention, with the closure of schools and disinfection of work premises and tramcars. Sir Arthur Newsholme, head of the Imperial LGB, concluded that 'the active cooperation of each member of the community' was needed to prevent influenza.[116] This shifted the responsibility for influenza prevention from the medical and local authorities and placed it instead on to the individual. This policy was one that Belfast and other Ulster towns followed, as one of their main responses was to produce public notices with recommendations for the individual on how to prevent the disease.

Apart from the subscription list set up for the family of newsboy, Robert Caines after his untimely death during the first outbreak in the city, there was no evidence that any organisation in Belfast, whether official or charitable, provided assistance to people who had suffered the effects of the disease. In Manchester, the public health committee also supplied additional help to those who were need in the city. They provided nurses and domestic assistance to those who needed it and, further to this, they supplied food and coal to those unable to provide the same for themselves during the pandemic.[117] In Ulster, as will be described in Chapter 10, the authorities in towns such as Newry, Clones and Cookstown encouraged their middle-class citizens to provide extra aid for the poor in those towns. However, there was no evidence that similar relief schemes were put in place in Belfast. In fact, Councillor English's statement that 'their duty was to administer the law as it was laid out'[118] illustrated their lack of commitment to do anything above and beyond the preventative recommendations of the LGBI.

Notes

1. Royle (2006, pp. 24–25).
2. *Fifty-fifth detailed annual report of the* ***Registrar-General*** *(Ireland) (Births, Deaths and Marriages) 1918*, [Cmd.450], H. C. 1919, x, 849, pp. xvi–xvii.
3. Bailie (1918), p. 5); Bailie (1919).
4. *Belfast Evening Telegraph*, 11 June 1918; *Northern Whig*, 12 June 1918; *Belfast News-Letter*, 12 June 1918.
5. *Belfast Evening Telegraph*, 22 June 1918.
6. *Irish News,* 2 July 1918.
7. *Irish News*, 24 June 1918; *Belfast News-Letter*, 24 June 1918.
8. *Irish News*, 29 June 1918.
9. *Irish News*, 25 June 1918.
10. *Belfast News-Letter*, 22 June 1918.
11. *Irish News*, 4 July 1918.
12. Public Record Office Northern Ireland [Hereafter PRONI], BG/7/A/99, Belfast Board of Guardians Minutes, 25 June 1918 and PRONI, BG/7/A/100, Belfast Board of Guardians Minutes, 2 July 1918; *Irish News*, 26 June 1918.
13. *Irish News*, 4 July 1918, *Belfast Evening Telegraph*, 3 July 1918.
14. *Irish News*, 20 June 1918; *Belfast Evening Telegraph*, 22 June 1918; *Northern Whig*, 21 June 1918; PRONI, BELF/6/1/2/13, Belfast Coroners record of Inquests of Robert Caines, 20 June 1918.
15. PRONI, BG/7/A/99, Belfast Board of Guardians Minutes, 18 June and 25 June 1918; *Irish News*, 26 June 1918.
16. *Irish News*, 2 July 1918.
17. *Belfast Evening Telegraph*, 4 July 1918.
18. PRONI, BG/7/A/100, Belfast Board of Guardians Minutes, 9 July 1918.

    Irish News, 10 July 1918; *Belfast News-Letter*, 10 July 1918.
19. PRONI, BG/7/A/100, Belfast Board of Guardians Minutes, 16 July 1918; *Belfast News-Letter*, 17 July 1918.

20. *Irish News*, 23 July 1918.
21. *Belfast News-Letter*, 19 June 1918; *Belfast News-Letter*, 24 June 1918.
22. *Belfast News-Letter*, 5 July 1918.
23. *Irish News*, 2 July 1918.
24. *Irish News*, 5 July 1918.
25. *Belfast News-Letter*, 11 June 1918, *Northern Whig*, 21 June 1918.
26. Figures from www.Irishgeneology.ie website for the indexes of the Civil Registration of Irish Deaths from influenza and pneumonia deaths during 1918 and 1919 in Belfast poor law union.
27. *Belfast Evening Telegraph*, 30 October 1918, *Irish News,* 31 October 1918, *Belfast News-Letter*, 31 October 1918.
28. *Irish News*, 8 November 1918; *Irish News*, 9 November 1918; *Irish News,* 30 November 1918; *Seventy-third annual report of the Belfast Ophthalmic Hospital 1918* (Belfast, 1919), 6; *Belfast Evening Telegraph*, 1 November 1918; *Belfast Evening Telegraph*, 8 November 1918.
29. *Irish News,* 29 November 1918.
30. Henderson (1939, p. 271).
31. *Belfast Evening Telegraph*, 13 November 1918.
32. *Belfast News-Letter*, 27 November 1918.
33. PRONI, LA/7/11/AB/8, Belfast Corporation—Minutes of Cemetery and Parks Committee, 4 December 1918; 18 December 1918 and 1 January 1919.
34. *Belfast Evening Telegraph*, 29 November 1918.
35. *Irish News*, 14 November 1918.
36. Figures from www.Irishgeneology.ie website for the indexes of the Civil Registration of Irish Deaths from influenza and pneumonia deaths during 1918 and 1919 in Belfast poor law union.
37. PRONI, BG/7/A/100, Belfast Board of Guardians Minutes, 29 October 1918; 5 November 1918 and 12 November 1918.
38. PRONI, BG/7/A/100, Belfast Board of Guardians Minutes, 5 November; 19 November; 26 November 1918 and 3 December 1918.
39. *Belfast News-Letter*, 27 November 1918; PRONI, BG/7/A/100, Belfast Board of Guardians Minutes, 26 November 1918.
40. PRONI, BG/7/A/100, Belfast Board of Guardians Minutes, 3 December 1918; *Irish News*, 4 December 1918.
41. PRONI, BG/7/A/100, Belfast iBoard of Guardians Minutes, 31 December 1918.
42. *Irish News*, 18 October 1918.
43. *Hansard 5 (Commons*), cx [etc.], 12 November 1918, col. 2509.
44. *Belfast News-Letter*, 14 October 1918.
45. *Irish News*, 18 October 1918.
46. *Irish News*, 25 October 1918.
47. *Northern Whig*, 22 October 1918.

48. *Irish News*, 29 October. 1918; *Irish News*, 31 October 1918.
49. *Belfast Evening Telegraph*, 30 October 1918.
50. *Irish News*, 2 November 1918.
51. *Belfast News-Letter*, 6 November 1918.
52. *Irish News*, 5 November 1918.
53. *Belfast Evening Telegraph*, 11 November 1918, *Irish News*, 12 November 1918.
54. *The Lancet*, 16 November 1918, 684.
55. *Belfast News-Letter*, 13 November 1918.
56. *Belfast Health Commission report to the Local Government Board for Ireland*, vii, 141, 11 [Cd 4128], H.C. 1908, xxxi, 699, p. 101.
57. *Irish News*, 31 October 1918. Belfast *News-Letter*, 31 October 1918.
58. *Belfast News-Letter*, 2 July 1918, *Irish News*, 2 July 1918.
59. *Irish News*, 3 December 1918.
60. PRONI, LA/7/9/AA/14, Belfast Corporation, Minutes of the Public Health Committee, 5 November 1918.
61. *Irish News*, 31 October 1918; *Belfast News-Letter*, 31 October 1918.
62. *Lancet*, 16 November 1918, p. 684.
63. PRONI, LA/7/9/AA/14, Belfast Corporation, Minutes of the Public Health Committee, 19 November 1918.
64. *Irish News*, 3 December 1918.
65. *Lancet*, 16 November 1918, p. 684.
66. PRONI, LA/7/9/AA/14, Belfast Corporation, Minutes of the Public Health Committee, 3 December 1918, *Annual report of the Local Government Board for Ireland for year ended 31 March 1919*, [Cmd 578], H. C. 1920, xxi, 1, xxxviii.
67. PRONI, LA/7/9/AA/14, Belfast Corporation, Minutes of the Public Health Committee, 17 December 1918.
68. *Northern Whig*, 28 November 1918.
69. *Belfast News-Letter*, 2 November 1918.
70. Tomkins (1992, p. 443).
71. *Newtownards Chronicle*, 7 December 1918.
72. *Portadown Express*, 6 December 1918.
73. *Belfast News-Letter*, 30 October 1918.
74. *Belfast News-Letter*, 2 November 1918.
75. *Irish News*, 3 December 1918.
76. Macnamara (1954, p. 307).
77. Van Hartesveldt (1992, p. 99).
78. Tomkins (1992, p. 450).
79. *Irish News*, 13 November 1918.
80. Johnson (2006, p. 193).
81. PRONI, T3582/1, Relationships and the Social Scene, John Baxter, The Baxter/Kyle Connection 1780/1980, 105–107.

82. Figures from www.Irishgeneology.ie website for the indexes of the Civil Registration of Irish Deaths from influenza and pneumonia deaths during 1918 and 1919 in Belfast poor law union.
83. *Annual report of the Local Government Board for Ireland for year ended 31 March 1919*, [Cmd 1432], H. C. 1920, pp. xxxvii–xxxviii.
84. PRONI, LA/7/2/EA/25, Belfast Corporation City Council Minutes Book, meeting, 14 December 1918.
85. *Irish News*, 2 January 1919; *Belfast News-Letter*, 2 January 1919.
86. *The Lancet*, 18 January 1919, 121.
87. *Irish Independent*, 12 February 1919.
88. *Northern Whig*, 27 February 1919; *Irish News*. 3 March 1918.
89. *Northern Whig*, 3 March. 1919.
90. *Belfast News-Letter*, 3 March 1919.
91. *The Times*, 26 February 1919.
92. *Northern Whig*, 26 February 1919, *Northern Whig*, 1 March 1919.
93. Supplied by Peter McGoldrick in association with his article 'Police Deaths in Ireland as a result of the Spanish Flu Epidemic, 1918' (January 2021).
94. *Belfast Evening Telegraph*, 20 March 1919.
95. PRONI, BG/7/A/101, Belfast Board of Guardians Meeting, 18 February 1919; 4 March 1919; 11 March 1919; 25 March1919, 31 March 1919 and 7 April 1919, *Irish News*, 19 February 1919. *Irish News*, 5 March 1919,
96. *Belfast News-Letter*, 4 March 1919.
97. *The Times*, 26 February 1919.
98. *Irish News*, 3 March 1919; *Irish News*, 4 March 1919; *Belfast News-Letter*, 1 March 1919; *Belfast News-Letter*, 4 March 1919.
99. *Irish News*, 4 March 1919; *Belfast News-Letter*, 4 March 1919, *Northern Whig*, 4 March 1919.
100. *Belfast News-Letter*, 4 March 1919.
101. *Fifty-sixth detailed annual report of the* ***Registrar-General*** *(Ireland) (Births Deaths and Marriages) 1919*, SP 1920 [Cmd.997], xi, 629, pp. v and xxv.
102. 'A General Account of Influenza in the United Kingdom During 1918–1919', in Ministry of Health, *Report on the Pandemic of Influenza, 1918–1919*, 54.
103. Bailie, (1918, p. 5).
104. Tomkins (1992, p. 450).
105. *Belfast Health Commission Report*, 70; Blaney (1988, p. 46).
106. *Belfast Health Commission Report*, 72.
107. Budge and O'Leary (1973, fn. on 131 and fn. on 133), 'Public Health in Belfast' *Lancet*, 16 October 1906, Vol 168, 1,002.

108. 'Belfast and its Medical Officer of Health', *Lancet*, 10 November 1906, Vol 168, 1312.
109. *Irish News*, 29 October 1918.
110. *Belfast Health Commission Report*, 70–71.
111. Ibid., 73.
112. *Lancet*, 5 October 1918, 467.
113. Blaney (1988, p. 14).
114. Tomkins (1992, p. 453).
115. PRONI, LA/7/9/AA/14, Belfast Corporation, Minutes of the Public Health Committee, 3 December 1918.
116. Honigsbuam (2009. p. 90).
117. Niven (1920, p. 483).
118. *Irish News*, 2 January 1919.

References

Bailie, H. W. *Report on the Health of the County Borough of Belfast for the year 1918* (Belfast, 1919).

Bailie, H. W. *Report on the Health of the County Borough of Belfast for the Year 1919* (Belfast, 1920).

Blaney, Roger. *Belfast: 100 Years of Public Health*. Belfast, Belfast City Council and Eastern Health and Social Services Board 1988.

Budge, Ian and Cornelius O'Leary. *Belfast: Approach to Crisis*. A Study of Belfast Politics 1613–1970. London: Palgrave Macmillan, 1973.

Henderson, John Watson. *Methodist College, Belfast, 1868–1938: A Survey and Retrospect Vol. 1*. Belfast, 1939.

Honigsbaum, Mark. *Living with enza: The Forgotten Story of Britain and the Great Flu Pandemic of 1918*. New York: Macmillan, 2008.

Johnson, Niall. *Britain and the 1918–1919 Influenza Pandemic: A Dark Epilogue*. London and New York: Routledge, 2006.

Macnamara, Dr, D. W. 'Memories of 1918 and "The Flu"', *Journal of the Irish Medical Association*, 35:208 (1954): 304–309.

Niven, James. 'Report on the Epidemic of Influenza in Manchester, 1918–1919' in *Ministry of Health, Report on the Pandemic of Influenza, 1918–1919*, 471–520. London: HMSO, 1920.

Royle, Stephen A. 'Belfast: Foundations of the Twentieth Century', in *Enduring City: Belfast in the Twentieth Century* edited by Frederick W. Boal and Stephen A. Royle. Belfast: Blackstaff Press, 2006.

Tomkins, Sandra M. 'The Failure of Expertise: Public Health Policy in Britain During the 1918–1919 Influenza Epidemic', *Social History of Medicine*, 5:3 (1992): 435–454.

Van Hartesveldt, Fred, R. 'Manchester', in *The 1918–1919 Pandemic of Influenza: The Urban Impact in the Western World* edited by Fred van Hartesveldt, 91–103. Lewiston, NY: Edward Mellon Press, 1992.

CHAPTER 7

'Derry Catches Infection': The Influenza Pandemic in Derry

Introduction

Londonderry situated in the north west of Ireland was a port and an industrial city, described during this period as the second city in Ulster. It specialised in the textile industry, especially the shirt-making industry.[1] There were three waves of influenza in Londonderry, in summer 1918, autumn 1918 and spring 1919. As in Belfast, the pandemic was largely ignored in official records for the city, such as the minutes of Londonderry City Corporation and board of guardians (BOG) for 1918 and 1919. Using these limited records and contemporary newspaper reports on the disease, this chapter recounts the problems faced by the province's second city during the pandemic.

First Wave in Londonderry

On 25 June 1918 the *Irish News* reported that many people in Londonderry were 'confined to bed' as a result of influenza. Numerous factory and shipyard workers had contracted the disease and there were many cases in Ebrington Military Barracks in the Waterside which resulted in the men being confined to camp. The schools, which had previously been closed because of measles, had reopened on Monday, 24 June 1918, only to close again on 25 June on the recommendation of the public health committee because of influenza.[2] On 1 July it was reported that Derry

P. Marsh, *The Spanish Flu in Ireland*, Palgrave Studies in Economic History, https://doi.org/10.1007/978-3-030-79500-9_7

was in the 'grip of influenza', entire families had contracted the disease, some shops had to close and practically the entire staff in numerous business establishments were ill.[3] Factory workers were particularly vulnerable and in early July 1918, one Londonderry shirt and collar factory had closed temporarily as over 350 of its employees had contracted influenza. Forty post office staff were absent resulting in the death of Postal Clerk, James Devine (43) on 18 July 1918, from the complication pneumonia.[4]

Although there were 100 influenza cases in the workhouse hospital and half the infirmary staff had contracted the disease,[5] there was little mention of it at the BOG meetings. The city chemists were under severe pressure. At the BOG meeting on 13 July 1918, the City dispensary compounder advised that his workload had significantly increased because of the severe influenza outbreak. He added that he would not make-up medicines during a similar epidemic period unless he had adequate assistance. Nevertheless, the BOG declined to provide him with an assistant on this occasion.[6] He was not the only pharmacist that was under pressure as at the August 1918 guardians' meeting it was reported that 1,653 items had been compounded and dispensed in the William Street dispensary in the city during one fortnight.[7]

The death rate was high and it was reported on 29 June 1918 that there had not been such a large number of burials within such a limited time period in 30 years.[8] As the death rate continued to increase, there were a record number of burials at the Londonderry City Cemetery with 50 taking place during the week ending 6 July 1918. Furthermore, there were nearly 20 burials solely on Monday 8 July 1918; these figures did not include those burials in the country districts just outside the city. Consequently extra gravediggers were employed.[9] Although the Public Health Department reported on 11 July 1918 that influenza was starting to decrease, but there were still a large number of people suffering from the disease.[10] Londonderry had a high mortality during this wave and by 12 July 1918, the death-rate from all causes was 53.4 per thousand of population,[11] reaching a record figure of 69.1 by 20 July 1918, of which 11.7% were influenza deaths.[12] However, by 27 July 1918 influenza was abating in the city.[13] Between 24 June, when the first influenza death was recorded, and the end of August 1918 there were 103 deaths from influenza and pneumonia recorded in the Derry poor law district.[14]

It was the individual tragedies that best illustrated the impact of this high mortality. Whole families contracted influenza and although many made a recovery, others succumbed to the disease. It was reported on 24

July 1918, that the Rankin family from Lower Nassau Street in the city were 'wiped out inside three weeks'. The father Alexander, a baker (34), died on 28 June 1918, followed by his son Andrew (six) on 30 June, his wife, Elizabeth (33) on 10 July 1918 and their four year old son William on 19 July. Two other relatives had already died from the disease.[15]

In the week ending 13 July 1918, mortality from influenza and pneumonia peaked in Londonderry and it had the highest mortality for pneumonia, of 0.80 per thousand of population, of all the principal towns in Ireland. Despite this, there seems to have been little reaction from Londonderry Corporation to the outbreak except for the closure of schools. Official council minutes make no reference to influenza at all during this wave. There was a measles epidemic in Londonderry prior to the influenza outbreak. This may account for the lack of official response as this first outbreak may have been regarded as another seasonal influenza.

Second Wave in Londonderry

Although the first report of influenza in Londonderry was on 21 October 1918,[16] there were deaths earlier in October among soldiers at Ebrington barracks. Nine soldiers from the 47th Dorsets were registered as dying from influenza between 12 and 25 October 1918 at the military barracks, where the disease was said to be rampant.[17] Not surprisingly, on 4 November 1918, the military were prohibited from attending places of amusement.[18] By 25 October 1918 it was reported that many factory workers and some bank officials had contracted influenza.[19]

On 4 November 1918, there were reports that over 100 people in two of the city's institutions were absent due to influenza and the First Derry Presbyterian Church Sabbath Schools and Young Men's Bible Classes decided to close.[20] On the same date, all the schools in the city were closed for a fortnight.[21] On 11 November 1918, the *Irish News* reported that the influenza death rate in Londonderry was 'alarmingly high' and that the latest returns showed that in one week the mortality in the city equalled the birth rate. It stated that three catholic priests in one parish were confined to bed with influenza, and one of the priests in St Columb's College was dangerously ill.[22]

Medical personnel were vulnerable and at the BOG meeting on 2 November 1918, the workhouse Medical Officer (MO) reported that Nurse Geddis and Probationer Nurse McDermott were ill with influenza.

Unfortunately, Nurse Margaret McDermott (23) died on 3 November 1918. She was not alone as later in the month Nurse, Rachel Crilly (37) died at home after contracting influenza at the infirmary. Consequently, the workhouse MO engaged two nurses for temporary duty in the infirmary. The workhouse schoolmaster and ambulance driver both contracted influenza and at the guardians' meeting on 16 November 1918 the MO voiced his concerns that all the staff were considerably overworked due to the absence of nurses and he was making every effort to recruit replacements. On his recommendation, the guardians ordered that the nurses' allowance in lieu of rations be temporarily increased by five shillings a week during the influenza outbreak.[23]

On 9 November 1918, due to the large number of patients in the hospital, the guardians agreed to appoint James Glendinning from Waterside dispensary as 'an apothecary'. He was to visit the hospital every day to make up the medicines needed for the sick and started compounding medicine at the workhouse hospital on 11 November 1918. However, due to the severe workload, he advised that he would be unable to continue working at the hospital unless the guardians increased his remuneration to 30 shillings a week. The guardians agreed to pay him this amount until the end of December 1918.[24]

Influenza was first mentioned at the Londonderry Corporation meeting on 12 November 1918. Unionist Alderman T. G. Bible suggested that public entertainments should be abandoned to stop the spread of the disease. However, this suggestion does not appear to have been acted upon by the corporation as the local cinemas not only remained open but the local newspapers encouraged attendance at the new films that were on release. The Mayor, Robert Newton Anderson, stated that the corporation had done everything possible to combat influenza; that the public health department were on top of the situation and everyone to whom they had made any requests had acceded to their wishes, including the schools' managers. Unfortunately, it was not noted who, other than the school managers, were spoken to or what they were requested to do. The meeting was advised that there was a great demand for disinfectants in the town.[25] At the Londonderry Corporation committee meeting held on 18 November 1918, unionist Alderman W. H. Elliott, who was also a physician, moved that necessary steps should be taken for the preparation of rooms and staffing of Gwynn's Institution for the reception and treatment of uncomplicated influenza cases. His personal experience was that influenza was not subsiding and there were still many cases. It was decided that the Medical Superintendent Officer of Health (MSOH), Dr F. W. Craig should report on the suitability of Gwynn's Institution for the purpose of adapting and altering the same for the reception of influenza patients, the staff required and probable cost.[26]

The nationalist *Derry People,* agreeing with Alderman Elliott, noted that the Corporation's health department should consider his suggestion of using Gwynn's Institution for typhus or similar infectious diseases. The editorial stated that the danger of an epidemic of contagious disease was very real as demobilisation was imminent, meaning there would be an influx of thousands of men from Europe. The editorial stated that preparations should be made in case their was an influx of patients because, Foyle Hill Hospital would not be sufficient for a city the size of Londonderry.[27] Despite these concerns, at the public health committee meeting on 10 December 1918, the MSOH advised the Corporation that although there were still fresh cases of influenza, the disease had almost run its course. He had surveyed the Gwynn's Institution for its suitability as a temporary hospital and was of the opinion that considerable repairs would need to be carried out to make it appropriate for use. The repairs along with the estimated staffing expenses would cost around £4,500. He thought a better alternative would be to erect a wood and iron hospital that would accommodate 20 beds at an estimated cost of £2,500 plus £400 for equipment and furnishing and an annual running cost of £1,700. The upshot was that neither option was approved by the Corporation.[28] The corporation's inaction could have been due to the expense of providing a temporary hospital, which may have been considered too high, or because it was deemed to no longer be necessary as influenza was abating in the town.

Putting off decisions until the next monthly committee meeting could make it seem like the authorities were being active without any action being taken. At the 18 November 1918 Corporation meeting' nationalist Councillor Con Doherty raised the question of housing in the city and he was told that it would not be debated at that meeting but could be discussed on a notice of motion. In reply he said 'that was always the way at that Corporation. Everything was deferred until it was too late'.[29] Doherty's complaints may have had more to do with the political make-up of the Corporation, which was predominantly unionist.[30] Nevertheless, it appears the Corporation deferred the decision concerning hospital accommodation for those suffering from influenza in Londonderry, until there was no perceived need to act on it.

Typhus in Londonderry

Although influenza was rife in Londonderry, both the BOG and Corporation were more concerned about the typhus outbreak that coincided with it. Although the typhus outbreak originated in Burt in County Donegal, this district came under the auspices of the Londonderry poor law union and as such any cases were transferred to the fever hospitals in Londonderry. At the BOG meeting on 16 November, the master reported seven typhus cases in the Londonderry fever hospital as well as 20 contact cases under observation. It was alleged that the sanitary inspectors had been negligent in their duty in the district of Donegal where the outbreak originated. Councillor Con Doherty stated that the epidemic had been allowed to develop since August, and that the houses were in such a bad condition that two of the typhus victims were lying on beds of straw. The guardians requested that the Local Government Board for Ireland (LGBI) send their Inspector to inquire into the origin of the typhus outbreak and report back.[31] At the BOG meeting on 30 November 1918, nine typhus cases were reported in the workhouse hospital and six in the Foyle Hill Hospital. The medical inspector's report on the typhus outbreak in Londonderry and the Burt District in Donegal stated that its spread was caused by a failure to recognise the disease in the earlier cases in the rural district; highlighting the necessity of keeping all contact cases under strict supervision for a period of at least four weeks. The Inspector also recommended that the Corporation and the Rural Sanitary Authority should arrange for the steam disinfectant at the Foyle Hill Hospital to be made available for the disinfecting of clothing from the rural district.[32]

Even though the MSOH reported on 12 December 1918 that influenza had almost run its course, typhus was still worryingly present with nine cases in the Foyle Hill Hospital. There had been a total of 23 cases since 16 October 1918 from eight different houses. The MSOH did not anticipate an epidemic of the disease and while there was sufficient hospital accommodation for typhus patients that there was not enough accommodation for the contact cases.[33] During this outbreak, there were 27 typhus cases in total in the Londonderry County Borough, 17 occurred in two houses and six people died of the disease between October and December 1918.[34]

Again, during the second influenza outbreak Londonderry Corporation made little attempt to combat influenza. Apart from the recommendation to close the schools, there was no evidence of any other steps taken. The only mention of influenza in the Corporation's official minutes was regarding the possible use of Gwynn's Institution as a hospital for influenza patients, a proposition that never came to pass. A factor that may have impeded the Corporation's reaction to influenza was the appearance of typhus in the district at the same time. From the official records, as well as newspaper reports, it appeared that there was more concern about typhus than influenza even though there were considerably more cases and higher mortality from influenza than typhus. Typhus unlike influenza was a notifiable disease and, as such, there were clear instructions on how to stop its spread and eradicate it. Consequently, unlike influenza, which was baffling the medical profession throughout the world, typhus was a disease that could be dealt with efficiently, and more to the point, be seen to be dealt with by the authorities.

Third Wave in Londonderry

By 1 March 1919, a third outbreak of influenza was in Londonderry. Again, the military authorities prohibited troops and members of the Queen Mary Army Auxiliary Corps entering local places of amusement.[35] At the Londonderry BOG meeting on 8 March 1919, the master reported that there were 137 patients in the infirmary, many of whom were suffering from influenza, adding that there were more patients than during the previous outbreak. There were 20 influenza cases in the fever hospital and the matron and land steward were both suffering from the disease.[36] At the March 1919 meeting of the Corporation, Dr Craig, MSOH, stated that although there were a considerable number of people ill in the city, that influenza was declining and it was not as serious as the previous outbreak.[37] At the Londonderry guardians' meeting on 22 March 1919, the master of the workhouse reported there were 140 patients in the infirmary because of the influenza outbreak. This led to overcrowding in the infirmary, prompting a committee to be specifically appointed to ascertain if the nursery could be converted into an auxiliary ward. Three nurses were absent with influenza and it was impossible to get replacements. The remaining nurses were overworked, so the BOG attempted to obtain the services of a number of probationers.[38] Thenurses' hard work during the influenza outbreaks did not go unnoticed and at the meeting on 17 May 1919 it was ordered that all nursing staff, including probationers, should 'be granted one week's extra leave this year because of their heavy workload during the recent outbreaks of influenza and typhus'.[39] Again there was no evidence that the Corporation took any action during this wave as the minutes do not mention influenza or any recommendations concerning prevention of the disease. Although the workhouse staff tried their best to accommodate and nurse the sick, they were beset by staff shortages and overcrowding in the institution. This was mainly due to the presence of inmates from Strabane union during the second and third waves of the pandemic.

Influenza in Strabane

Strabane is located in the north west of Ireland and is south of Londonderry. It was a market town with also a flax spinning centre linked to the town of Sion Mills, three miles south of Strabane. The first wave appeared in Strabane during late June and early July 1918. According to the *Strabane Weekly* the doctors were busy attending patients but that there had been no deaths yet. Many factory, post office and railway workers were absent with influenza.[40] Although this first wave caused disruption in the area, there were only eight deaths from influenza and pneumonia in the poor law union district.

By the end of October 1918 it was apparent that the second influenza outbreak was a serious problem in the town.[41] Difficulties arose in Strabane because, just prior to the outbreak of influenza in October 1918, the military had acquired the workhouse for the treatment of troops. Londonderry BOG unanimously agreed in September 1918 to receive 60 inmates from the Strabane workhouse and most of these people were sent to the Londonderry workhouse.[42] This action led to a heated discussion at the Strabane Urban district Council (UDC) on 4 November 1918.[43]

According to Mr Charles Browne, chairman of the Strabane UDC, the poor in the town were being treated scandalously by the guardians due to the absence of a suitable hospital for urgent medical cases. He blamed the recent deaths of three people from unspecified causes to neglect because they were not provided with proper medical attention in a suitable hospital. He highlighted the case of a recent influenza victim, a boy, who had 'lain on a bed of straw and bags'. He thought it was 'a shocking and terrible state of affairs'. He recognised that the workhouse was transferred to the military authorities before the influenza outbreak, but was adamant that something should be 'done at once for the suffering poor of the town' because the disease was in currently in Strabane'.[44]

The Strabane BOG advised the UDC that although a committee to examine certain details arising out of the military acquisition of the workhouse had been appointed, that it was not in their remit to provide a hospital for the poor of the town. The committee believed that the acquisition of a motor ambulance to transport patients to Londonderry would prove to be as quick as the old ambulance transporting patients to the Strabane workhouse. The UDC suggested that the guardians should immediately erect a temporary hospital. The BOG advised them that as the entire workhouse had been taken over by the military and the guardians had disbanded, that there was no-one to staff the fever hospital. However, Mr Browne disagreed, saying there was a nurse, master and matron. He also thought that it was unwise to convey patients 17 or 18 miles in the cold weather by motor ambulance. He was adamant that the poor with influenza should 'receive all possible attention'.[45]

After a prolonged discussion at an emergency meeting on 7 November 1918, the BOG resolved to temporarily re-open the fever hospital for the treatment of influenza, pneumonia and emergency cases other than fever. Three wards were to be fitted-up for reception of patients and by 12 November 1918, the fever hospital was again opened to the public. However, in the interim, sick cases from the different dispensary districts were re-allocated to Castlederg and Stranorlar workhouse. It was evident that there was a definite need for a local hospital in Strabane during this influenza outbreak as 26 patients were admitted to the hospital once it was reopened.[46] As in other towns, the guardians had difficulty procuring nurses. The workhouse MO reported that they needed three nurses, but only had one, Nurse Mayne, attending to nine patients—some of whom were dangerously ill. The BOG decided that as Nurse Mayne was performing the work of three that they would grant her 15 shillings per week for rations as she required extra nourishment due to her increased workload.[47]

The problems faced by the Londonderry union regarding overcrowding have already been alluded to. The transfer of patients from Strabane could only have added to their overcrowding problem. This was illustrated at the guardians meeting on 16 November 1918 when the death from diphtheria of child from Strabane was reported. The child died shortly after been admitted to the institution on the Sunday morning. The nurse had no place to put the child on arrival at the institution, consequently he remained for some time in a motorcar in the fever hospital yard. The nurse phoned for the doctor to treat the child, but there was none available. The death of this child was probably as a direct result of overcrowding in the infirmary as well as lack of medical professionals in the institution to treat the sick.[48]

Overcrowding of the Londonderry infirmary continued to be a problem during the third wave. In March 1919, the workhouse MO suggested that due to overcrowding in the infirmary that any patients from Strabane should be returned to Strabane union hospital. He was advised that these patients could not be removed until the military had evacuated the Strabane workhouse. The military promised the Strabane guardians that they would vacate the workhouse on or before 1 March 1919. However, they did not hand over the premises until May 1919. The upshot was that Londonderry infirmary continued to have overcrowding problems during both the second and third influenza outbreaks, due to the influx of local patients as well as those from Strabane.[49]

It was not only Strabane workhouse that was requisitioned by the military during this period. During the war many civil medical institutions acted as Auxiliary Military Hospitals and it was common for workhouses to be used by the military for the treatment of soldiers.[50] It was an action that was not universally approved of. Concerns were raised in Omagh during December 1918 regarding the treatment of the local poor. The military occupied part of the workhouse and the MO had to admit influenza patients into the fever hospital. This was not desirable for all concerned as patients with influenza shared the same wards as those with infectious diseases such as typhus. The MO stated that there would have been plenty of room for the influenza patients if the BOG had not transferred two wards to the military. He believed it was unfair to the nursing staff and the patients, to have to nurse patients with very infectious cerebo-spinal meningitis, while still attending to other patients. He thought it was outside the remit of the nurses and the MO to attend military patients without the proper remuneration from the military authorities. In January 1919, the military authorities rejected the Omagh BOG request to surrender the two wards they occupied in the workhouse for use for influenza cases. They stated that: 'after careful investigation it is regretted that as the portion of the workhouse taken over by the War Department is at present fully occupied by troops it cannot be evacuated unless it is absolutely essential'.[51]

The accommodation of the military could be contentious. During July 1918 in Sligo there was an objection from the Sinn Féin Alliance who strongly protested the admittance of military patients into the County

Sligo Fever Hospital, as 'this involves great risk of contagion from diseases always foreign to our people'. The committee advised that they had no power to refuse admittance to the military even though they were as 'desirous as any Sinn Féin club not to admit any military to the Hospital'. Nevertheless, the military were only allowed ten beds in the hospital.[52] On 1 June 1918, Dr Flood, who treated soldiers at the Finner camp, County Donegal, advised the Ballyshannon BOG that the Army Medical Services Corps in Belfast requested that they take in all military patients to Ballyshannon hospital. They would be paid for at a rate of 4*s* 9*d* per day, which would be of considerable benefit to the rates. The Ballyshannon guardians declined the request, even though they would have benefited financially and instead the military authorities hoped that the Enniskillen BOG would continue to admit military patients, which they did.[53]

However, in general it seems that treatment of military patients was considered by many BOG to be more important than that of the local poor. This may have been due to patriotic fervour on behalf of the unionist-run BOG, such as Newtownards who were happy to accommodate the military, providing 180 more beds in the military hospital during October 1918. However, in some cases the guaranteed fees they received from the military was a welcome source of income for the BOG.[54]

The war had a great impact on the poor law system in Ireland. Medical institutions such as the workhouse infirmaries were requisitioned for military patients. In many cases wards, or entire workhouse hospitals, were taken over by the military. In the case of Strabane this action had a direct impact on the local sick poor, as they had to transfer to Londonderry to be treated, and depending on the nature of their illness, this may have led to further complications or in the worst event death. An indirect impact of the war effort was the overcrowding of workhouse infirmaries such that of Londonderry. This institution was already overcrowded due to the influx of influenza and typhus patients, but it also had to cope with the inmates and patients from Strabane workhouse. The losers in this situation were the sick poor in these towns. As stated in Chapter 5, the LGBI noted that the scarcity of temporary doctors throughout Ireland during the pandemic was mainly due to large number of practitioners serving in the army overseas. As noted in Chapter 3, nurses were also in short supply as many volunteered their services to nurse during the war. Unfortunately, the result of these combined factors, as was experienced in Strabane and Londonderry, was that the sick poor suffered because the war effort was considered more important than the welfare of the poor.

Notes

1. Murphy (1981, p. 212).
2. *Irish News*, 25 June 1918; *Derry Journal*, 26 June 1918; *Dungannon Democrat*, 26 June 1918.
3. *Derry Journal*, 1 July 1918.
4. *Londonderry Sentinel*, 4 July 1918;*Derry People*, 27 July 1918; *Irish News*, 4 July 1918.
5. *Irish News*, 8 July 1918.
6. I would like to acknowledge the Deputy Keeper of the Records, Public Records Office of Northern Ireland [Hereafter PRONI], BG/2/A/33, Londonderry Board of Guardians [hereafter BOG] Minutes, 13 July 1918.
7. *Derry People*, 10 August 1918.
8. *Derry Journal*, 1 July 1918; *Fermanagh Herald*, 6 July 1918.
9. *Derry Journal*, 10 July 1918; *Irish News*, 9 July 1918.
10. *Derry Journal*, 12 July 1918.
11. *Irish News*, 12 July 1918.
12. *Derry Journal*, 20 July 1918.
13. *Derry People*, 27 July 1918.
14. Figures calculated from https://civilrecords.irishgenealogy.ie/: website for the indexes of the Civil Registration of Irish Deaths from influenza and pneumonia deaths during 1918 and 1919 in Londonderry poor law union.
15. *Irish News*, 24 July 1918; *Irish Independent*, 24 July 1918; *Northern Whig*, 25 July 1918.
16. *Irish Independent*, 21 October 1918.
17. *Derry People,* 9 November 1918.
18. *Belfast News-Letter*, 6 November 1918; *Irish News*, 6 November 1918.
19. *Irish News*, 25 October 1918; *Irish Independent*, 25 October 1918.
20. *Belfast News-Letter*, 4 November 1918.
21. *Belfast News-Letter*, 6 November 1918; *Irish News*, 6 November 1918.
22. *Irish News*, 11 November 1918.
23. PRONI, BG/2/A/33, Londonderry BOG Minutes, 2 November; 9 November and 16 November 1918, *Derry Journal*, 11 November 1918.
24. PRONI, BG/2/A/33, Londonderry BOG Minutes, 16 November 1918, *Derry Journal*, 11 November 1918; *Irish News*, 18 November 1918; *Belfast News-Letter*, 18 November 1918; *Derry People*, 23 November 1918.
25. *Derry Journal*, 13 November 1918; *Derry People*, 16 November 1918; *Belfast News-Letter*, 14 November 1918; *Irish News*, 15 November 1918; *Londonderry Sentinel*, 19 November 1918.

26. Londonderry Council Minutes and Reports January 1917 to December 192; Council meeting, 18 November 1918 (Derry City Council Archive, 40A), *Derry Journal*, 20 November 1918.
27. *Derry People*, 16 November 1918.
28. Derry City Council Archive, 40A, Council Minutes and Reports January 1917 to December 1921, Londonderry Council Minutes, 16 December 1918, *Belfast News-Letter*, 12 December 1918.
29. *Derry Journal*, 20 November 1918.
30. *Belfast News-Letter*, 16 January 1915.
31. PRONI, BG/2/A/33, Londonderry BOG Minutes, 16 November 1918, *Irish News*, 18 November 1918; *Belfast News-Letter*, 18 November 1918; *Derry People*, 23 November 1918.
32. PRONI, BG/2/A/33, Londonderry Union Minutes, BOG, 30 November 1918, *Derry People*, 7 December 1918.
33. Derry City Council Archive, 40A, Council Minutes and Reports January 1917 to December 1921, Londonderry Council meeting, 16 December 1918, *Belfast News-Letter*, 12 December 1918.
34. *Annual report of the Local Government Board for Ireland for the Year Ended 31st March 1919*, p. xxxv.
35. *Irish Times*, 1 March 1919; *Belfast News-Letter*, 1 March 1919; *Irish Independent*, 1 March 1919.
36. *Irish Times*, 3 March 1919; *Derry People*, 8 March 1918; *Londonderry Sentinel* 4th March 1919; *Northern Constitution*, 8 March 1919; *Irish Independent*, 10 March 1919; *Irish News*, 10 March 1919.
37. *Fermanagh Herald*, 15 March 1919; *Derry Journal*, 12 March 1919.
38. PRONI, BG/2/A/34, Londonderry BOG Minutes, 22 March 1919 *Belfast News-Letter*, 25 March 1919; *Irish News*, 24 March 1919; *Northern Constitution*, 29 March 1919.
39. PRONI, BG/2/A/34, Londonderry BOG Minutes, 17 May 1919).
40. *Strabane Weekly*, 13 July 1918.
41. *Derry People*, 26 October 1918; *Ulster Herald*, 26 October 1918.
42. PRONI, BG/2/A/33, Londonderry BOG Minutes, 28 September 1918; PRONI, BG/27/A/50, Strabane BOG Minutes, 27 September 1918 and 8 October 1918.
43. Newspaper reports have been used to follow this debate as unfortunately, the council meeting minutes were destroyed in a bomb in the 1970s.
44. *Belfast-Newsletter*, 6 November 1918; *Derry People*, 9 November 1918; *Ulster Herald*, 9 November 1918.
45. Marsh (2011, pp. 212–213).
46. Ibid.
47. *Ulster Herald*, 30 November 1918.
48. Marsh (2011, p. 214).
49. Ibid.

50. The National Archive, WO 35/179/4, Returns: historical review of medical and sanitary work in the Irish Command during the war, Report of the medical and sanitary work of the Ulster Brigade.
51. PRONI, BG/26/A/85, Omagh BOG Minutes, 7 December 1918, 14 December 1918; 11 January 1919.
52. *Sligo Independent*, 20 July 1918.
53. Marsh (2011, p. 215).
54. Ibid.

References

Marsh, Patricia. "'An enormous amount of distress amoung the poor" Aid for the Poor in Ulster during the Influenza Pandemic of 1918–19', in *Poverty and Welfare in Ireland, 1838–1948*, edited by Virginia Crossman and Peter Gray, 207–222. Dublin: Irish Academic Press, 2011.

Murphy, Desmond. *Derry, Donegal and Modern Ulster 1790–1921*. Londonderry: Aileach Press, 1981.

CHAPTER 8

'Many Lurgan Workers Down': Influenza in Lurgan and Portadown

Introduction

Lurgan and Portadown situated in County Armagh were industrial towns specialising in the linen and textile industry. Lurgan is located about 25 miles west of Belfast and south-east of Lough Neagh. Lying between Belfast, Dungannon and Newry, in an area that was known as the 'linen triangle' and Lurgan—along with other towns in this area such as Lisburn, Banbridge and Waringstown—was known to specialise in weaving fine linens.[1] After Belfast, Lurgan was reported to be the most industrial town in Ulster.[2] The 1921 *Irish Trade Directory* listed 43 linen factories in Lurgan involved in power-loom weaving, cambric manufacture and handkerchief manufacture and hemstitching in the town.[3] Portadown was in the same poor law union and is about six miles from Lurgan. Described in 1918 as a prosperous market town, Portadown also was known for the manufacture of linen. At this time there were nine large weaving factories, a spinning mill and several hemstitching factories in the town.

First Wave in Lurgan and Portadown

Lurgan Urban Council was responsible for public health in the town. The Medical Officer of Health (MOH) was Dr Samuel Agnew and for many years he had also been Medical Officer to Lurgan Number 1 dispensary district. Unlike other MOH's, Dr Agnew produced detailed monthly

P. Marsh, *The Spanish Flu in Ireland*, Palgrave Studies in Economic History, https://doi.org/10.1007/978-3-030-79500-9_8

reports for the Lurgan Urban Council which contained the number of births and deaths along with detailed reports on all three waves of the pandemic in the district. Dr Agnew reported that influenza started in Lurgan in mid-June 1918, and it had spread to both Lurgan and Portadown 'in epidemic form'. By the end of June 1918 many factory operatives had contracted the disease but at this juncture none of the schools were closed.[4] According the press, on 1 July 1918 hundreds of workers from 22 factories in Lurgan were absent from work. This led to an influx of influenza sufferers in the union infirmary, which reported that it had its greatest number of patients for 30 years.[5] On 7 July 1918, the Lurgan parish priest, Rev Peter McEvoy announced at Sunday Mass that more than 300 people in the town were suffering from influenza and that some of these cases were very serious. On 9 July 1918 there were reports that local doctor, Michael Deeny, JP, had been ill with influenza for the past week. This was hardly surprising as he had been extremely busy since the start of the outbreak making house calls all through the day and night.[6] Dr Michael Deeny was the father of James Deeny, who became Chief Medical Adviser to the Department of Local Government and Public Health in Dublin in 1944. At the time James was a pupil of Clongowes Wood College in County Kildare. An institution that suffered from a severe outbreak of influenza during the second wave.[7]

On 1 July 1918 Dr Agnew reported that: 'Within the past fortnight an acute outbreak of influenza occurred which prostrated in an alarming manner vast numbers of the working classes' and that there were a few fatalities from the disease.[8] According to Dr Agnew, influenza would disappear as quickly as it started and die out rapidly. He diagnosed that it seemed communicable and infectious, being conveyed from person to person in the same household but that it was not carried through the air.[9]

The disease was also rife in the neighbouring town of Portadown. It was reported on 5 July 1918 that over 100 workers in at least two of the town's factories were absent with influenza. The *Portadown Express* faced operational problems, reporting that influenza had 'been the cause of diminishing its otherwise smooth running business machinery'.[10] The strain that influenza was having on the poor law union district was apparent and at the Lurgan Board of Guardians' (BOG) meeting of 17 July 1918, serious complaints were made by the medical officers (MO) of the district. Dr Agnew from Lurgan, Dr Duff from Aghalee dispensary and Dr Rowlett from Portadown were concerned about the great delay in obtaining supplies of medicines for dispensary purposes from their usual

Union contractors. Dr Rowlett was forced to turn away 40 patients from the Portadown dispensary due to the lack of medicines. It was feared that the Portadown dispensary would have to close, because there was a great demand for medicines due to the large number of influenza patients. The Lurgan BOG gave Dr Rowlett permission to purchase any medicines that he required until they sorted out supplies with official contractors.[11]

On 5 August 1918, Dr Agnew reported there had been 63 deaths during July in the poor law district, 'mainly due to the very severe outbreak of localised influenza', and that since the middle of June there were 31 influenza deaths in the Lurgan town area.[12] The *Lurgan Mail* commented that the number of deaths in Lurgan was absolutely astounding, considering the very brief duration of the disease, and it highlighted 'the cumulative dangers in periods of epidemic to which populous industrial centres must always be liable'.[13] Dr Agnew declared on 31 August 1918 that 'the short but severe epidemic of influenza, which caused such disastrous results during the previous months subsided as quickly as it sprang up'.[14]

This first wave was much more serious in Lurgan town than in Portadown (see Fig. 8.1). There was no evidence from Dr Agnew's reports or the Council minutes for both Lurgan and Portadown that any specific steps were taken to prevent the spread of influenza in either town during the first wave. The reason for this inactivity may be because this was the third epidemic that had occurred in Lurgan that year. At the beginning of the year, there had been an epidemic of measles, followed in May 1918 by whooping cough which caused the deaths of 16 children.[15] It is obvious from Dr Agnew's comments at the beginning of the wave that he believed it to be another seasonal affliction, however it became more apparent as the death toll ramped up that this was a serious outbreak.

Second Wave in Lurgan and Portadown

The second wave was first reported in Lurgan on 26 October 1918 and was described as a more virulent type than before.[17] On 4 November 1918, the *Irish Independent* reported there were some 500 or 600 people suffering from influenza in Lurgan, with many deaths occurring during the previous week and children being as affected by the disease as adults.[18] The suggestion that this wave was more virulent than the previous outbreak was dismissed by Dr Agnew, probably rightly so as can be seen from Fig. 8.1. He agreed that many families had been

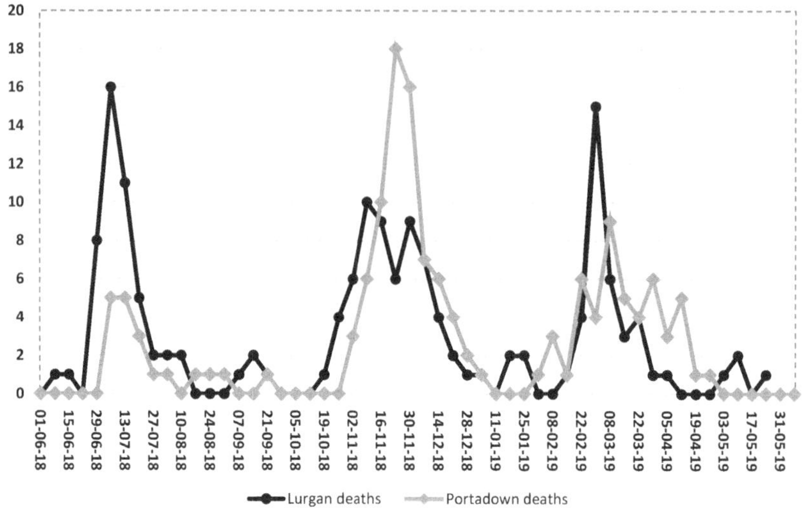

Fig. 8.1 Influenza and Pneumonia Deaths in Lurgan and Portadown (1918–1919)[16]

attacked by influenza, but that this outbreak was not as severe as the July outbreak. However, 'the occurrence of the three deaths in the one family gave rise to exaggerated rumours and reports'. He was referring to the Dynes family whose tragic deaths occurred within days of each other. Mrs Bridget Dynes from Brownlow Terrace died on Saturday 19 October 1918, her daughter Lizzie, (25) and who worked at Messrs Mathers and Bunting's wareroom, died on 21 October and her son Arthur (22) and was employed as a shop assistant in Messrs Donnelly and O'Neil's, died on 23 October.[19] Frank McCorry argued that these tragic deaths were because this family was known to be 'delicate' (prone to disease), before the outbreak of influenza.[20] However, the fact that both young people were working in locations that experienced large absences due to influenza during the most virulent wave of the pandemic would seem to be significant.

Dr Agnew continued his monthly report with a lengthy description of symptoms and causes of influenza before he made the following recommendations for prevention of the disease in the town. The patient should be isolated during the infective period; people should avoid contact with those with influenza; and that there should be free ventilation, not only of the sick room, but also throughout the house. He did not endorse the use of disinfectants, except to encourage cleanliness and ventilation, nor did he recommend the use of quinine pills or other advertised preventatives. He believed that the best preventative was to keep the body in good health and to avoid unnecessary exposure to the disease, such as crowded and sick places that did not permit free ventilation.[21] These were good recommendations for individuals to follow to avoid contracting influenza, but they did not involve the intervention of Lurgan Council. Although not mentioned in the Council minutes, the *Lurgan Mail* reported that the chairman, Mr Pedlow recommended that Dr Agnew's suggestions could be printed and circulated. He believed that this measure would help with the prevention of influenza and curtail its spread. He also thought it would be a wise precaution to disinfect the town hall both before and immediately after public meetings. However, there was no evidence that either of these measures were taken. Although Dr Agnew believed that cinemas were a source of danger, Mr Pedlow understood they were thoroughly disinfected regularly.[22]

All the schools in Lurgan were closed as a preventative measure against influenza during early November 1918.[23] Similarly, schools in Portadown were closed from 1 November 1918 until 6 January 1919 on the recommendation of Dr Rowlett, MOH for the town.[24] Unlike his counterpart in Lurgan Dr Rowlett did endorse the use of disinfectants and recommended that a plentiful supply of disinfectants should be used, especially in factories and places of amusement where many people congregated. The public were advised to observe strict cleanliness and ensure their dwellings were thoroughly ventilated. On 29 October 1918, Dr Rowlett recommended that the cinema manager be requested to close the children's Saturday matinee performance to stop the spread of influenza. It seems the cinema manager did not grant this request as at the 2 December 1918 council meeting the clerk was instructed to write to the Local Government Board for Ireland (LGBI) stating that the influenza epidemic was very bad in Portadown, that all schools are closed but that the "Picture House" still remained open and asking if the Council had any power in the matter or what steps should be taken'. In January 1919, the LGBI advised the council they were considering the question of the temporary closure of the cinema. The *Portadown News* reported under the headline 'LGB's Dilly-Dally Methods' councillor W J Johnston's remark that 'The influenza will be over before they act 'to which the clerk replied 'that's always the way with the LGB'. Mr Johnston was probably correct in his assumption as there was no confirmation of the LGBI's decision, however, it was likely—as in Belfast—that the cinema was not forced to close. On 2 December 1918, the application for use of the pork market for hobby horses and swing boats was rejected by the Council as 'it would not be advisable, owing to the present serious epidemic, when overcrowding is a danger, to allow this entertainment to remain in occupation in the pork market any longer'.[25]

The Lurgan workhouse nurses were particularly vulnerable. It was reported at the guardians meeting on 21 November 1918 that eight nurses had contracted influenza and Nurse Louisa Curran, aged 24 had tragically died from the disease on 8 November 1918. Illness among the nurses led to staff shortages so three young probationary nurses were employed to assist out in the infirmary. Unfortunately, one of these girls, Kathleen McStravick, (26) contracted influenza and subsequently died from pneumonia on 22 November 1918: she had only been working for five days in the infirmary.[26] At the January meeting of the Portadown Council, the town inspector advised that influenza was disappearing in the town and that it was 'nothing like what it was a month ago'.[27] However, this outbreak in Portadown was much more severe than the first wave, where about 20 people died from either influenza or pneumonia, whereas approximately 71 deaths occurred between 1 November 1918 and 31 January 1919, a higher death toll than that of Lurgan (see Fig. 8.1). In Lurgan, Dr Agnew's December report described how during November 1918, influenza was continuing 'with increased virulence, mainly attacking those who had escaped it in June and July'. His January report advised that there had been a very marked reduction in the number of influenza cases in the latter half of December 1918.[28] He advised that in Lurgan, 30 influenza deaths occurred in July, five in August, one in September, one in October, 16 in November and 12 in December 1918, a total of 65. However, he thought that many other provincial towns had suffered more severely than Lurgan during this outbreak.[29]

Again, there was little evidence of what steps Lurgan Council took during the wave, apart from closing schools and the proposed distribution of handbills. Although Dr Agnew produced detailed monthly reports, his recommendations were aimed at individual prevention rather than Council driven preventative measures or intervention to combat the effects of the disease. Dr Rowlett in Portadown also recommended school closures as well as disinfection of factories and workplaces. Under his recommendation, the council also attempted to close cinemas, but to no avail. Their main achievement was to ban the 'hobby-horses' in the town pork market. As with the closure of cinema, the council's disapproval of this form of entertainment may have provided the impetus for this move. However, unlike the cinemas, at least they had the authority to ban this activity in the town. In Portadown as in Belfast, even when local authorities endeavoured to put preventative measures in place, they were not given support from the LGBI to enforce these recommendations.

Third Wave in Lurgan and Portadown

On 1 March 1919, the *Lurgan Mail* reported the 'influenza epidemic has again visited Lurgan and district and during the past week' and that many residents were ill with the disease, which was causing 'much uneasiness in many households'. Local doctors were under pressure and doing their best to keep those infected isolated, however there had been four influenza deaths, three in Edward Street, and one in Kilmaine Street. Five police constables, District-Inspector Ryan and Head Constable Callaghan from the Church Place Police Barracks contracted influenza but fortunately they all recovered.[30] In his March 1919 report, Dr Agnew advised that there were a number of genuine influenza cases among those who escaped the previous two outbreaks and six deaths from pneumonia complications, but that the disease was not as infectious as in 1918. Four nurses in the workhouse infirmary contracted influenza and thankfully they all recovered.[31] Dr Agnew was incorrect that this outbreak in Lurgan was milder as, the deaths from influenza and pneumonia were higher during this wave than during the second wave in the autumn in 1918 (see Fig. 8.1). Influenza spread to the country districts outside Lurgan town with several cases reported in the Soldierstown and Aghalee districts, but it was the Montaighs district that was the most severely affected by the disease. The Derrymacash National School was closed due to influenza and on 25 February 1919 brother and sister, John and Jane McStravick from Derrytagh South died from the disease.[32]

On 28 February 1919, many influenza cases were reported in Portadown and a few deaths had occurred, one of which was that of Nellie Courtney, West Street, Portadown, aged 24. Only married for a few months, she contracted influenza while nursing her husband, who was a factory manager, and died on 20 February 1919.[33] On 14 March 1919, it was reported that there was still a number of influenza cases in Portadown but that they were milder than those during the previous waves. Nevertheless, schools in Portadown were closed until Monday 24 March 1919 as a precautionary measure against spread of the disease.[34] There was no mention of the third influenza outbreak in the Portadown Council reports. This wave was indeed milder than the second wave in Portadown as there were approximately 49 deaths in the town as compared to 71 during the second. This may account for the lack of any precautionary or preventative measures put in place by the Portadown Council.

In his report dated 3 May 1919, Dr Agnew heralded the end of the third wave in the Lurgan poor law union district with

> I am glad to say that the influenza epidemic is now completely over in this district and I hope that it will be long before there is any return of influenza or other serious infectious disease in an epidemic form.

It is not clear what steps, if any, Lurgan Council took during this third outbreak. In his April 1919 report, Dr Agnew advised that the LGBI—under the Public Health Act 1896—made acute primary pneumonia and acute influenzal pneumonia notifiable along with trench fever, malaria and dysentery. This was a decision he seemed to agree with—in the case of influenzal pneumonia.[35] However, there is no mention of other recommendations made by the Dr Agnew or Lurgan Council during this wave.

The public health strategy of an urban area such as Lurgan would be guided by the MOH for that town. Although Dr Agnew provided detailed reports that explained the extent of influenza in Lurgan and his own views on the disease as well as measures that individuals could take to avoid contracting it, they lacked any guidance or recommendations for the Council to take to fight the disease in the town. In his obituary in the *British Medical Journal*, it was noted that Dr Agnew brought about many sanitary reforms and was instrumental in establishing a baby club, as well as advancing both general and technical education in Lurgan,[36] which makes his apparent lack of action during the pandemic seem all the more surprising.

Notes

1. Crawford (1989, p. 139).

2. Neill (1994, p. 8).
3. Marsh, Patricia, 'The Impact of the Linen Industry on Lurgan'. M.A. thesis, Queen's University Belfast, 2004, p.71.
4. I would like to acknowledge the Deputy Keeper of the Records, Public Records Office of Northern Ireland [Hereafter PRONI], LA/51/9/D/6, Lurgan Medical Officer of Health [Hereafter MOH] Report, 1 July 1918, *Armagh Guardian*, 28 June 1918; *Lurgan Mail*, 29 June 1918.
5. *Irish News*, 1 July 1918; *Irish Times*, 1 July 1918; *Armagh Guardian*, 5 July 1918; *Belfast News-Letter*, 2 July 1918.
6. *Irish News*, 9 July 1918.
7. Milne (2018, pp. 168–160).
8. PRONI, LA/51/9/D/6, Lurgan MOH Report, 1 July 1918; *Irish News*, 5 July 1918.
9. *Lurgan Mail*, 6 July 1918.
10. *Portadown Express*, 5 July 1918.
11. *Belfast Evening Telegraph*, 19 July 1918; *Belfast News-Letter*, 20 July 1918; *Armagh Guardian*, 26 July 1918.
12. PRONI, LA/51/9/D/6, Lurgan MOH Report, 5 August 1918; *Lurgan Mail*, 10 August 1918.
13. *Lurgan Mail*, 10 August 1918.
14. PRONI, LA/51/9/D/6, Lurgan MOH Report, 31 August 1918.
15. *Lurgan Mail*, 11 January 1919.
16. Figures for graph from https://civilrecords.irishgenealogy.ie/: website for the indexes of the Civil Registration of Irish Deaths from influenza and pneumonia deaths during 1918 and 1919 in Lurgan Poor Law Union.
17. *Lurgan Mail*, 26 October 1918.
18. *Irish Independent*, 4 November 1918.
19. PRONI, LA/51/9D/6, Lurgan MOH Report, 1 November 1918, *Lurgan Mail*, 26 October 1918.
20. McCorry (1981–1982, p. 19).
21. PRONI, LA/51/9/D/6, Lurgan MOH Report, 1 November 1918.
22. *Irish News*, 8 November 1918; Lurgan MOH Report, 1 November 1918; *Lurgan Mail*, 9 November 1918; *Irish News*, 11 November 1918.
23. *Irish News*, 11 November 1918.
24. *Portadown Express*, 1 November 1918; *Portadown Express*, 6 December 1918.
25. PRONI, LA/64/2/CA/8, Portadown Borough Council minutes, 4 November 1918; 2 December 1918; 6 January 1919; *Portadown News*, 2 November 1918; *Portadown News*, 11 January 1919.
26. PRONI, BG/22/A/114, Lurgan Board of Guardians Minutes, 21 November 1918, *Belfast News-Letter*, 28 November 1918.
27. *Portadown News*, 11 January 1919.

28. PRONI, LA/51/9/D/6, Lurgan MOH Report, 2 December 1918; 4 January 1919.
29. *Lurgan Mail*, 11 January 1919.
30. *Lurgan Mail*, 1 March 1919.
31. PRONI, LA/51/9/D/6, Lurgan MOH Report, 1 March 1919, *Lurgan Mail*, 8 March 1919.
32. *Lurgan Mail*, 1 March 1919.
33. *Portadown Express*, 28 February 1919.
34. *Portadown News*, 15 March 1919; *Portadown Express*, 28 February 1919.
35. PRONI, LA/51/9/D/6, Lurgan MOH Report, 3 April 1919; 3 May 1919.
36. *British Medical Journal*, 9 February 1924, Vol. 1, 259.

References

Crawford, W. H. 'The Political Economy of Linen: Ulster in the eighteenth Century', in *Ulster: an Illustrated History*, edited by Ciaran Brady Mary O'Dowd and Brian Walker, 134–136. London: B. T. Batsford Ltd, 1989.

McCorry, Francis X. 'Demographic Crisis in Shankill Parish, Lurgan', *Review: Journal of the Craigavon Historical Society*, 4:3 (1981–1982): 17–20.

Milne, Ida. *Stacking the Coffins: Influenza, War and Revolution in Ireland, 1818–19*. Manchester: Manchester University Press, 2018.

Neill, Margaret. 'Homeworkers in Ulster, 1850–1911', in *Coming into the Light: The Work, Politics and Religion of Women in Ulster 1840–1940*, edited by Janice Holmes and Diane Urquhart, 2–32. Belfast: Queen's University: Institute of Irish Studies, 1994.

CHAPTER 9

'No Room in the Fever Hospital for a Great Number of Influenza Patients': Influenza in Larne and Ballyclare

Influenza in Larne and Ballyclare

Larne was a market town and seaport in County Antrim, situated in the north-east of Ireland about 17 miles from Belfast. At the start of the war in 1914, it became a naval port as its location made it a particularly good anti-submarine base. It was situated in the Larne poor law union. Ballyclare, located approximately 11 miles south-west inland from Larne was situated in the Antrim poor law union district. During this time it was a growing industrial town with a large paper mill in the south-west of the town and a large Linen Bleach Green. Influenza visited both of these towns and their local authorities responded in an organised and competent manner.

Influenza in Larne

Approximately 22 people died from either influenza or pneumonia in Larne during June and July 1918.[1] Nevertheless, there was no mention of the disease in the local press, the minutes of the board of guardians (BOG) or Larne Urban District Council (UDC). This suggests that no steps were taken by the same to combat the disease in town or poor law district. However, the authorities did act during the second wave in autumn 1918. At the guardians' meeting on 9 October 1918, the workhouse Medical Officer (MO) reported that, due to an influx of influenza

P. Marsh, *The Spanish Flu in Ireland*, Palgrave Studies in Economic History, https://doi.org/10.1007/978-3-030-79500-9_9

patients into the fever hospital, he was forced to request that the infirmary nurse return early from her holidays and hire a temporary nurse to assist in the hospital.[2] The first influenza deaths recorded during this wave were of sisters Martha Maguire and Mary Burke. They lived in the same lodging house in Mission Lane in Larne and died on 7 October and 10 October 1918, respectively.[3]

On 25 October 1918 the Larne Technical committee reported there had been a slight reduction of attendance over the previous few nights due to the influenza epidemic, but it was hoped that the absenteeism was not due to fear of infection. The classes had been sub-divided to avoid overcrowding, all rooms were airy and cleaned regularly with disinfectants. The Department's report stated that 'as in former sessions the building was a model of cleanliness and comfort'.[4] Nevertheless, on the Council's recommendation, the technical school closed on 2 November until the 18 November 1918.[5]

On 23 October 1918 influenza was really taking hold and the Larne MO reported there was no spare accommodation in the infirmary or fever hospital for many of the 40 influenza patients seeking admission. As a result, he prepared 15 beds in the disused girls' schoolroom for the patients and employed two temporary nurses to look after them.[6] At the BOG meeting on 13 November 1918, the Superintendent Nurse stated that, due to the influx of influenza patients a considerable quantity of additional clothing required laundering and disinfection. Consequently, the BOG agreed to employ an additional wards-maid for three days per week to relieve this situation. As elsewhere in Ireland, medical personnel in the poor law district were vulnerable and many of them contracted influenza including the midwife from Glenarm dispensary and Dr O'Kane, MO for Waterfoot dispensary district.[7] Unfortunately on 21 November 1918, Dr John B. Logan, MO Ballynure dispensary district, died from pneumonia following influenza.[8]

At the public health committee meeting of Larne UDC on 30 October 1918 the Medical Officer of Health (MOH), Mr J. M. Killen recommended that employers be advised to keep their premises well ventilated, and that the sanitary sub-officer would be available to disinfect houses if required. He warned that badly ventilated buildings like cinemas, concert halls and theatres were prone to spread infection. He also advised that people should go to bed immediately if they contracted influenza and remain there until the feverish stage had passed. Patients should be isolated and houses ventilated.[9] The Larne UDC had a clear plan of action on how to deal with influenza. On 31 October 1918, the UDC recommended that the Sunday school, the national day schools and the technical school close for 14 days. The sanitary sub-officer was to disinfect the national and private schools; obtain particulars of influenza cases from doctors; examine sanitary arrangements of any house in which influenza had occurred; carry out disinfection and undertake any other measures that might be required to prevent the disease from spreading.[10]

On 1 November 1918, a warning notice was issued as a handbill and placard, but it was not published in the local newspapers. It advised the following recommendations:

- That people refrain for the present from going to places where for hours large numbers of persons congregate. Over-crowding should be avoided. Children who are kept from School should be kept at home and not allowed to mix with other children, except friends known to be free from the disease.
- It is most important to avoid scattering infection in sneezing and coughing. A handkerchief should always be employed to intercept droplets of mucus, and the handkerchief should be boiled, or burnt if of paper. Expectoration should be received in a special receptacle, its contents being subsequently disinfected or burnt.
- After influenza a thorough washing and cleansing of rooms and their contents is desirable. The occurrence of Epidemic Catarrhs would be greatly decreased by continuous flushing with air of each occupied bedroom and living room.
- Relapse is less likely if the patient goes to bed on the first onset of the symptoms and remains there until all fever has gone; avoidance of chill or over exertion during convalescence is also of great importance as a means of avoiding relapse or complications.
- Patients should be isolated as much as possible.
- The taking of drugs internally as a preventative is of little use and may be injurious, but as infection occurs through the air passages the use of a mild antiseptic gargle is advisable. E.g. a weak solution of Permanganate of Potash.
- Dirtiness whether personal or in living or working rooms and dusty conditions favour infection. The wet cleansing of all invaded places is important.
- Indiscriminate spitting is always a source of risk of infection and is especially dangerous during the prevalence of Influenza.

- A safe rule is to regard all Catarrhal attacks and every illness associated with a rise of temperature during the prevalence of influenza as infectious and to adopt appropriate precautionary measures.[11]

As in Belfast, cinemas were regarded as problematic. On 1 November 1918, the manager of the 'Picture Palace' was requested to guarantee effective ventilation and disinfection of the premises. On 4 November, he was asked to close the premises as a precautionary measure. On the same date it was proposed that the management of the 'Electric Theatre' be asked to close for a fortnight and that should he refuse, they should take steps to exclude persons under 16 years of age from the premises.[12] Also on 4 November 1918 the naval surgeon supplied the MOH and sanitary sub-officer with a list of contact addresses of sailors who had recently contracted influenza. On 5 November 1918, a placard was issued concerning wakes and infection and the Local Government Board for Ireland (LGBI) was asked if any order had been made regarding prohibiting people from attending wakes. A notice was sent to the medical practitioners directing attention to the provisions of the Infectious Disease (Provision) Act 1890 as to speedy burial and the non-removal of bodies from hospital except for interment.

On 6 November 1918 the LGBI advised it was the UDC's responsibility to determine whether influenza came within the purview of Sect. 146 of the Public Health Act 1878 and not that of the LGBI. The LGBI advised that the Council had powers to add influenza and septic pneumonia to the schedule of notifiable diseases, but advised that influenza had not been made notifiable in other districts in Ireland. Although the MOH did not recommend making influenza notifiable because it would neither be useful in preventing or eradicating the disease, he did think it advisable to make septic pneumonia cases notifiable so that these cases were sent to hospital. Therefore, with effect from 14 November 1918, the UCD made septic pneumonia a notifiable disease under the Infectious Disease Notification Act 1889, making Larne, the first local authority in Ulster, if not Ireland, to take this step.[13] During November, the influenza outbreak was so severe in Larne that deaths outnumbered births in the town by 28 to 21, as compared to the corresponding month in 1917 when 22 births and nine deaths were registered.[14] At their meeting on 28 November 1918 the UDC ordered the Sanitary Sub-officer to inspect the 'Picture Palace' to ensure that it was properly cleansed. It was also reported that a few of the national schools had reopened contrary to the MOH's recommendations.[15]

Meanwhile at the Royal Naval Base, as nurses were in short supply, 14 members of the Larne Voluntary Aid Detachment (VAD) served in the emergency hospital during October, November and part of December 1918.[16] This action was much appreciated by the officers and men of the Larne Naval Base who sent a letter of gratitude to Miss McNeill, Commandant of Larne Harbour VAD as follows:

> The Officers and men of the Larne Naval Base desire to express their gratitude and appreciation of the work done by the V.A.D in nursing officers and men during the recent influenza epidemic. It has therefore been decided to purchase a small present from a suitable fund of the Naval Base, and your acceptance of the enclosed safety-pin is desired, with best wishes for 1919. Thank you so much for all you did for our men. I hope you will like this little pin.[17]

During this wave there were approximately 127 deaths from pneumonia and influenza in the Larne poor law union district. Fifty-seven of these were in Larne town.[18] There was little official documentary evidence that there was an outbreak of influenza in the Larne poor law district during the third wave, with no mention of the disease in either the council or the guardians' minutes. Nevertheless, influenza was present in the area and, although less serious than the second wave, there were at least 48 influenza and pneumonia deaths in the poor law union district, with 23 of these in Larne town.[19] It is not known what steps were taken during this wave regarding prevention or treatment as they are not recorded but Larne district did have the second lowest influenza death rate per thousand of population in Ulster during 1919. This may be explained by immunity gained from the previous wave along with more stringent precautionary recommendations put in place during the second wave. Both Larne and Belfast had a much lower death rate during 1919 and both made septic pneumonia a notifiable disease during the second wave. Perhaps this action may have helped to lower the infection and death rate in both districts.

Influenza in Ballyclare

Although Ballyclare is eleven miles from Larne it was situated in the Antrim poor law union district rather than that of Larne. Influenza was not very widespread in the Antrim district during the first wave but there were a few deaths from the disease and pneumonia. However, the second wave of influenza did visit the district. At the Antrim BOG meeting of 14 November 1918, the clerk reported that influenza was very serious in the district with the complication of pneumonia supervening causing several deaths in the infirmary. Dr David McKee, MO for Randalstown dispensary district was unfit to perform his duties for at least a week as he was suffering from pleurisy, a complication of influenza. The guardians could not find a temporary doctor to cover for Dr McKee at the dispensary despite being prepared to pay any salary for a replacement. As a result, the dispensary was closed for a week. It was reported that fortunately, there had been no serious cases and Dr McKee was hoping to return to work by the end of the week.[20]

Influenza also spread to Ballyclare and the Executive Sanitary Officer of the Ballyclare UDC, Edward Hill submitted a report dated 30 November 1918. It stated that during the first 10 days of the month, there were numerous influenza cases but because they were mild it had been difficult to convince the public of the dangers of the disease or persuade them to take necessary precautions to stop its spread. However, by the middle of the month, the number of influenza cases had risen rapidly and the complication of pneumonia had frequently developed with fatal results. By 30 November 1918 there were between 400 and 500 influenza cases in the urban district. The MOH reported that there were 19 deaths in the urban district between 10 and 30 November 1918, 11 of which were directly attributable to influenza.

The MOH made several interventions and recommendations to combat influenza. On 6 November 1918 he closed all the Sunday, day and technical schools for three weeks and on 29 November they were directed to remain closed until after Christmas. On 6 November 1918 circulars were sent to the controlling bodies of all public halls in the district requesting they refrain from letting their premises for three weeks. Notices were posted throughout the urban district, and published in the *Larne Times,* and leaflets were delivered to every house warning people of the dangers of visiting, attending public meetings or entertainments, sending children to school or going to 'wakes'. A similar warning was read in all of the churches on Sunday 1 December 1918. In Ballyclare, the use of disinfectants was considered an important preventative. On 18 November 1918 the MOH recommended the council procure a supply of 'Bacterol' disinfectant and to place the mist sprayers at the disposal of the public free of charge. The Executive Sanitary Officer requested four sprayers and a gallon of disinfectant from London and ordered a further supply of disinfectant from local suppliers. On 30 November 1918 all churches in the district were disinfected and the clergy were asked to ensure that ventilation during services was 'as perfect as possible'. Notices were sent to all factories, shops and offices in the district as well as places where the public frequented, requesting that they be disinfected regularly. Full advantage was taken of the sprayers, as over 50 houses were disinfected during one week. It was proposed that the Council give permission to continue disinfecting churches, halls, public places and to lend out sprayers and supply disinfectant to the public for the next few weeks.[21]

Disinfectants were not only advocated in Ballyclare and Larne, the Banbridge UDC also encouraged disinfection of premises. Banbridge UDC's Sanitary Sub-officer was told to procure a quantity of 'Jeyes' Fluid', for distribution to schools and to request that the teachers disinfect the buildings morning and evening. It was also agreed that all the low lying drains in the district be flushed with disinfectant.[22] The Newtownards UDC as well as recommending the closure of schools and cinemas, also gave instructions for public sewers to be disinfected, and suggested that people in the town use disinfectants liberally, especially in ashpits and gullies connected with house drains. They also requested that the BOG disinfect the workhouse sewers regularly especially during the influenza outbreak, since these sewers discharged into the town's main sewers.[23] The disinfection of factory premises by their proprietors was also one of the Lisburn UDC's recommendations during the second wave.[24] Similarly, in Upperlands, Maghera the owners of Messrs Clarke & Sons Weaving factory took every precaution to stop the spread of influenza by disinfecting the interior of the buildings every morning after the factory had been closed for a week due to influenza.[25] In Dublin, the Medical Superintendent Officer of Health, Sir Charles Cameron had the streets of the city treated with a solution of 'Jeyes Fluid' and carbolic acid.[26]

On 2 December 1918 the Executive Sanitary Officer Edward Hill advised that, in general the recommendations of Ballyclare's MOH were complied with, but in one or two cases private interests were put before the public health. He did not name the culprits because the council had no power to interfere with their decisions not to comply with the recommendations. However, on Mr Hill's suggestion, the council resolved that the LGBI should be made aware of the very limited powers which public health authorities had to close schools, churches, cinemas and public meetings in times of epidemic and suggested that these powers should be greatly increased.[27] The lack of powers to close buildings and locations where large public gatherings took place was a severe disadvantage to the public health of the larger community during a pandemic.

During the second wave 57 influenza and pneumonia deaths were recorded in the Antrim poor law district, 16 of those occurring in Doagh dispensary district in which Ballyclare was situated. Sixteen influenza and pneumonia deaths also occurred in Randalstown dispensary district, which was without a dispensary doctor and had to close for a week at the height of the outbreak. This would have had a detrimental effect on the sick poor in the area. Although the third wave was again in all parts of the Antrim poor law district, there was little documentary evidence to confirm this. However, 29 deaths from influenza or pneumonia occurred during the third wave in the union district. In Randalstown the dispensary doctor, David McKee, who during the second wave suffered from influenza and pleurisy, died from pneumonia on 27 March 1919.[28] In Ballyclare there were few casualties during the third wave, maybe because of the extensive preventative measures put in place during the second wave.

Although no preventative steps were taken during the first wave in Larne, the UDC and sanitary authority reacted quickly to the second, virulent outbreak of influenza in the town. They recommended the closure and disinfection of schools, produced handbills and placards with warnings about influenza and made septic pneumonia a notifiable disease as early as 14 November 1918, one month earlier than the Belfast Corporation. Ballyclare also reacted quickly, with similar measures. However, the Ballyclare MOH was restricted in implementing his recommendations because local authorities were powerless to enforce the closure of schools, cinemas or places of public entertainment. The reliance on sanctions from the LGBI before actions could take place put limitations on many local authorities on enforcing preventative measures regarding public health of the local people. So, although both Larne and Ballyclare UDCs endeavoured to put preventative measures in place, they like Belfast, Portadown and other local authorities, throughout Ireland, did not receive sufficient support or endorsement from the LGBI to enforce these recommendations.

Ida Milne argued that the LGBI came in for criticism from a number of different quarters such as Sinn Fein's advanced nationalists and their propagandists, as well as journalists and BOGs that were predominately nationalist in make-up, for their 'lack of handling' of the pandemic in Ireland.[29] This lack of support from the LGBI to both local authorities and BOGs happened throughout the country, but there was less criticism from BOGs located in Ulster. It is apparent from the records kept by BOG and local authorities in Ulster that the main contribution by the LGBI during the pandemic was to sanction payments for temporary doctors and nurses and the supplies of medicines or vaccines. By their own admission, the main LGBI contribution to combating influenza was that they 'afforded local authorities all possible facilities for the employment of additional medical and nursing assistance, and recommended County Councils that they might set free their Tuberculosis Officers to undertake the functions of District Medical Officers, where the need existed'. The LGBI also issued advice and suggestions for the general guidance of the public, 'founded on experience of epidemics of disease, for avoiding infection, and for dealing with attacks, when developed'.[30] This guidance placed the responsibility of preventing the disease on to the individual. The LGBI did not sanction enforcement of recommendations from local authorities or sanitary departments that may have stopped the spread of influenza, such as closure of schools, cinemas or other places of entertainment. Although the local authorities in Larne and Ballyclare attempted to close cinemas, schools, churches or places of entertainment to stop the spread of infection, the LGBI did not endorse their decisions. This left them powerless to act in the best interests of the public health of their citizens in a time of pandemic.

Notes

1. Figures calculated from https://civilrecords.irishgenealogy.ie/: website for the indexes of the Civil Registration of Irish Deaths from influenza and pneumonia deaths during 1918 and 1919 in Larne poor law union.
2. I would like to acknowledge the Deputy Keeper of the Records, Public Records Office of Northern Ireland [Hereafter PRONI], BG/17/A/132, Larne Board of Guardians [hereafter BOG] Minutes, 9 October 1918.
3. Figures calculated from https://civilrecords.irishgenealogy.ie/: website for the indexes of the Civil Registration of Irish Deaths from influenza and pneumonia deaths during 1918 and 1919 in Larne poor law union.
4. *Larne Times*, 2 November 1918.

5. *Larne Times*, 16 November 1918.
6. PRONI, BG/17/A/132, Larne BOG Minutes, 23 October 1918.
7. PRONI, BG/17/A/132, Larne BOG Minutes, 13 November 1918.
8. PRONI, BG/17/A/132, Larne BOG Minutes, 27 November 1918.
9. PRONI, LA/43/27/A/4, Larne Urban District Council, [hereafter UDC] Public Health Committee Minutes, 30 October 1918.
10. PRONI, LA/43/2/CA/10, Larne UDC, Public Health Committee Minutes 11 November 1918.
11. PRONI, LA/43/27/A/4, Larne Urban Sanitary Authority and UDC Minutes, 11 November 1918.
12. PRONI, LA/43/2/CA/10, Larne Urban Sanitary Authority and UDC Minutes, 4 November 1918, *Larne Times*, 9 November 1918.
13. PRONI, LA/43/27/A/4, Larne Urban Sanitary Authority and UDC Minutes, 11 November 1918.
14. *Larne Times*, 21 December 1918.
15. PRONI, LA/43/27/A/4, Larne Urban Sanitary Authority and UDC Minutes, 28 November 1918.
16. PRONI, T2031/8, Annual report of Saint John's Association for 1918.
17. PRONI, T2031/3, Letter from Commodore W. Carfendale, Naval Base, Larne Harbour to Miss Lucy McNeill, 8 February 1919.
18. Figures calculated from https://civilrecords.irishgenealogy.ie/: website for the indexes of the Civil Registration of Irish Deaths from influenza and pneumonia deaths during 1918 and 1919 in Larne poor law union.
19. Ibid.
20. *Irish News*, 14 November 1918; *Larne Times*, 23 November 1918.
21. PRONI, LA/13/9/AB/1, Ballyclare UDC (Sanitary) Minutes, 2 December. 1918; *Larne Times*, 30 November 1918.
22. PRONI, LA/19/2/CA/10, Banbridge UDC Minutes, 4 November 1918.
23. PRONI, LA/60/2/CA/5, Newtownards UDC Minutes 4 November 1918.
24. *Lisburn Standard*, 8 November 1918.
25. *Mid-Ulster Mail*, 30 November 1918.
26. *Larne Times*, 2 November. 1918.
27. PRONI, LA/13/9/AB/1, Ballyclare UDC (Sanitary) Minutes, 2 December. 1918.
28. Figures calculated from https://civilrecords.irishgenealogy.ie/: website for the indexes of the Civil Registration of Irish Deaths from influenza and pneumonia deaths during 1918 and 1919 in Antrim poor law union.
29. Milne (2018, p. 105).
30. *Annual Report of the Local Government Board for Ireland for the year ended 31st March 1919*, p. xxxvi.

Reference

Milne, Ida. *Stacking the Coffins: Influenza, War and Revolution in Ireland, 1918–19*. Manchester: Manchester University Press, 2018.

CHAPTER 10

'An Enormous Amount of Distress Among the Poor': Influenza in Newry, Cookstown and Clones

Introduction

It is apparent from the case studies that although the local authorities in Belfast, Londonderry, Lurgan, Portadown, Larne and Ballyclare all approached the pandemic with varying degrees of competence, none of them encouraged a charitable response to helping the poor in their districts. The public health committee in Manchester was aware of those in need in the city who required additional nursing, food or fuel to help and supplied the same as part of their response.[1] In this chapter the public health and medical response of Newry, Cookstown and Clones are discussed but what sets these towns apart from those already examined is that their citizens responded to their neighbour's plight in a philanthropic way.

Influenza in Newry

Newry is in the south-east of the province of Ulster. The west of the city lies in County Armagh and the east in County Down. The Clanrye River runs through the centre of the town and is parallel to the Newry Canal. The poor law union infirmary was situated in the Newry workhouse and is now the site of the Daisy Hill Hospital. Even though there was no major outbreak of influenza in Newry during the first wave, the Urban District Council (UDC) still discussed what precautions could be taken

P. Marsh, *The Spanish Flu in Ireland*, Palgrave Studies in Economic History, https://doi.org/10.1007/978-3-030-79500-9_10

if it visited the town. At the July 1918 meeting of the Newry UDC, it was rumoured that there might be several cases of influenza in Newry and the clerk thought that if the epidemic visited Newry to the same extent as it was in Belfast and Dublin it would not be possible to make arrangements to have the cases isolated. The chairman said they would have to be treated in their homes.[2] This did not bode well for the very severe second wave, which visited Newry poor law union district in the autumn of 1918.

Second Wave in Newry

Although first reports of influenza appeared in the newspapers on 19 October 1918,[3] the first fatality was of Rachel Mitchell (17), who died on 10 October from the complication of pneumonia. On 26 October 1918, the *Frontier Sentinel* reported that Newry had never experienced a disease so widespread in its attacks. Its victims were from all sections of the community especially textile operatives from the local mills. Even though it was reported that 'the fatal cases were few and far between, three members of the McArdle family died within days of each other'.[4] By the end of October 1918, fresh cases were reported daily and there were several deaths from the disease.[5] Between 26 and 30 October 1918 there had been an average of a dozen funerals a day to the Old Chapel burying ground.[6] This is hardly surprising as in the period 20 October to 31 October 1918 there were 77 deaths from influenza and pneumonia in the Newry poor law district and 50 of these were people from Newry town.[7]

The Newry UDC minutes only give influenza a cursory mention, but the newspapers provide a more detailed account of their proceedings. At the UDC meeting on 4 November 1918, the sanitary sub-officer reported that all the churches had been disinfected on Saturday evening and the cinemas were disinfected three times a day. The town surveyor had arranged for all the street gullies and surface water gratings to be cleaned out and filled with a solution of carbolic acid and, if the weather improved, he was going to use a similar solution to spray the streets.[8] All the schools in Newry and district were closed on 21 October 1918 and remained so until December 1918[9] as the situation in the town worsened. On 15 November 1918, the UDC produced a public notice under the heading 'Influenza Epidemic - Warning'. It recommended that the public should not relax any precautionary measures; should avoid large gatherings, as crowded assemblies were an easy means of spreading the disease; and as patients at the convalescent stage may be capable of spreading infection, they should abstain as far as possible from meeting other people.[10]

Interestingly, thearmistice celebrations took place in Newry town a few days before this advice, to avoid crowded gatherings, was published. An article from the *Newry Reporter* on 12 November 1918: reported the joyous scenes in the town where lively demonstrators paraded the streets. The men in the military barracks were given a holiday and spent the day merrily.[11] The employees of the local mills and factories as well as a number of other business in the town were given a half-holiday and the young people paraded with flags. At night there was a torch-light demonstration through the main street. The Newry citizens turned out practically *en masse*, and there was a large influx of people from the districts immediately surrounding the town. Shortly after 8 pm 'a procession of monster dimensions formed' and 'headed by several Belgian refugees, a large number of torchbearers, and all the local Unionist and Nationalist bands, marched triumphantly through Hill Street to Kildare Street, where the victorious termination of the war was fittingly celebrated'.[12] Most deaths in Newry poor law union district occurred in November 1918, with approximately 151 deaths from influenza and pneumonia recorded, and over 100 of these deaths occurred before 11 November 1918. This meant that influenza was rife in the town by the time the celebrations took place. The gathering of many people from within and outside the town would only have added to the infection rate throughout the poor law union.

At the 18 November 1918 UDC meeting, the clerk advised that he had temporarily discontinued renting out the town hall and minor town hall for meetings or entertainments, until both Dr R Flood and Dr H J Grant, the Medical Officers of Health (MOH) for Newry assured him that it was safe to congregate without risk of spreading infection. The public library and the circulating libraries in Newry agreed to the UDC's suggestion to remain closed. The clerk advised that people who had not already contracted influenza could do so if they came into contact with persons in the convalescent stage of the disease, especially in confined areas such as the cinema or other places of amusement. As mentioned in Chapter 6, the closure of cinemas was encouraged by local authorities and in Newry both its cinemas closed at the MOH's request for one week. However, the 'Imperial', reopened without consulting the public health authority, while, the 'Frontier', remained closed. As in Belfast, the clerk confirmed that the UDC had no power to close the 'Imperial' as influenza was not a notifiable disease.[13]

At the 2 December 1918 UDC meeting, the sanitary sub-officer stated that all the schools in town had been disinfected prior to re-opening. Dr Flood, MOH, Newry Number 1 district, reported that although influenza had now abated in the Newry Urban District, it had been a very severe outbreak and there had been between 90 and 100 deaths in the urban district to date.[14] In Newry many people died of the complication pneumonia and the UDC, as well as closing of schools, recommended the disinfection of drains and streets. During the 4 November 1918 UDC meeting, Dr Flood also recommended the stoppage of all wakes and the earliest possible burial of the dead. The UDC unanimously resolved that the executive sanitary officer be empowered to take whatever steps he deemed necessary regarding wakes and burial in fatal cases of influenza.[15] Following this, the clerk issued a public notice in the *Frontier Sentinel* which stated the

> THE URBAN DISTRICT COUNCIL Acting as the Public Health Authority have been advised To PREVENT THE HOLDING OF WAKES in the case of persons who have died from influenza or from any complication arising out of same, and to insist on the EARLY BURIAL of such persons. As these precautions are solely intended to prevent the risk of communicating disease and the spreading of infection, the Council earnestly trust that the Public will carry same into effect, and thereby obviate any unpleasant or drastic measure which otherwise might become necessary.[16]

It should be noted that this was only a strong recommendation as the public health authority had no powers to stop wakes.[17]

Again, it was both the workhouse hospital and dispensary system that were responsible for the medical wellbeing of the people in Newry. It was reported at the Board of Guardians (BOG) meeting on 26 October 1918, that a number of influenza cases had been admitted to the workhouse and it was suggested that nurses should be employed to look after the poor in the town who were suffering from the disease.[18] By the BOG meeting on 9 November 1918, there were 44 more patients in the infirmary than in the corresponding period of the previous year. It was reported that there had been 20 deaths during the previous fortnight, but influenza was now thought to be abating in Newry.[19] The Medical Officer's (MO) return of 9 November 1918 showed that there were 145 persons in the infirmary and six in the fever hospital during the week. As three members of the infirmary nursing staff contracted influenza, the MO needed extra staff to help with the large number of influenza patients. He requested four temporary nurses for the infirmary and fever hospital as well as four attendants to assist at night.[20]

At the BOG meeting on 12 December 1918, the workhouse MO acknowledged the hard work of the staff as the influenza outbreak was coming to an end. He advised 'they had a very trying, depressing, and anxious time, but did their duty, and indeed more than their duty, steadily and well without a murmur'.[21] Although the workhouse staff worked hard to help the sufferers from the disease, there were still many influenza deaths. The numerous obituaries and death notices of local businessmen and merchants that appeared in local newspapers were evidence of how the disease was dangerous to the middle-class residents of Newry, but it was the poorer people who were very much at risk from influenza. At the Newry UDC meeting on 4 November 1918, Dr R Flood reported that 'the mortality was very high, being equally divided between the well to do and the poor'.[22] The *Frontier Sentinel* reported on 2 November that the poor suffered great hardships, but that their cases were being specially considered by the St Vincent de Paul Society and indeed it was this charitable organisation that did the most for the poor in Newry.[23]

At the UDC meeting on 4 November 1918, Councillor, Mr Grant remarked that there was an 'enormous amount of distress among the poor', and it was the Council's duty to assist all they could and to supplement the valuable work of the different charitable organisations.[24] At the same meeting, Dr Flood reported: 'I regret to report that a serious outbreak of influenza arose in Newry Number 1 district 10 days ago and is still going on. The epidemic is of a serious nature, septic pneumonia being the chief complication'. Dr H J Grant, reported that during the last two weeks of October 1918 that a virulent form of influenza has swept over the Newry Number 2 district, scarcely leaving a house untouched. Most of the cases had either bronchopneumonia or lobar pneumonia as a complication, the latter form being very fatal, but that the number of fresh cases of influenza was rapidly diminishing. The UDC discussed the efforts of St Vincent de Paul Society and how they had spent considerably more money than was at their disposal to help with the distress of the poor of all religious denominations in the town during the influenza outbreak. The UDC agreed to seek public subscriptions for the St Vincent de Paul Society as well as the Nursing Society to assist these organisations with their charitable work. The UDC also requested that the health visitor advise of any cases of 'special distress' that she felt would benefit from this help.[25]

It is evident that members of Newry UDC were aware that the poor needed substantial charitable help. There was a serious milk shortage in Newry which was impacting on influenza patients and the council contractors were unable to cope with the demand. This was one way in which the UDC could help the poor and on 4 November 1918, the clerk of the UDC made arrangements with two Newry creameries; the White-cross Co-operative Creamery Ltd; and the Derrycughan Co-operative Creamery Ltd to supply sufficient quantities of pasteurised milk to the depots to meet the increased needs for free milk distribution that the influenza outbreak had caused. This was a welcome service as the clerk advised that free milk distribution had increased significantly owing to influenza.[26] As well as free milk, the provision of nourishing food was particularly important. During the closure of the Newry technical school, the staff of the domestic department worked day and night to make nourishing foodstuff such as beef tea and mutton broth for the sick, but this service was discontinued on 25 November 1918 when the school reopened.[27]

Despite this aid, the situation in Newry was so serious that a Relief of Distress Fund Committee was formed to 'consider the best means of meeting the exceptional expenditure that has been and is being incurred by the various charitable organisations in the relief of distress arising out of the influenza epidemic'. The first meeting was attended by clergy and laity of all religious persuasions. The local St Vincent de Paul Society (Roman Catholic) had already helped the poor in the town, spending several hundred pounds providing clothes, coal, groceries, butter, milk and other necessities. The Church of Ireland minister, Rev H. A. Swanzy of St Mary's reported that there had been little distress among his parishioners, but that any cases brought to his notice had been helped. Nevertheless, he thought that it was quite possible that a great many Protestants, who were not his parishioners, had suffered considerably. A circular was sent out inviting subscriptions to the fund and it was hoped to raise at least £1,000.

The fund was closed at the committee meeting held on 31 December 1918 and lists of subscribers and their contributions appeared in the *Newry Reporter* on 21 November and 28 November 1918.[28] Maria Luddy argued that Irish charitable societies were scrupulous about listing the names of subscribers and the amount subscribed as this provided the incentive for them to maintain their support.[29] The fund raised £734 4*s.* 2*d* and was allocated as follows: three-quarters (£550 13*s.* 2*d.*), to the Catholic Charitable Organisations such as the St Vincent de Paul Society, and one quarter (£183 11*s.*), to the local Protestant clergymen for distribution.[30] It is interesting to note the way the fund was distributed. The remarks of Rev Swanzy inferred that the Protestant community in Newry were not in as great as need as their Roman Catholic counterparts. This may well have been true, but the distribution of the fund echoed the religious breakdown of Newry urban district, which was—according to the 1911 census—75% Roman Catholic in denomination.[31] The St Vincent de Paul Society was reimbursed for the expenditure it had already incurred in Newry providing help to the poor. It was evident that this charitable society in Newry saw the hardship of the poor in the area and was proactive in its response to their plight during this medical emergency.

Third Wave in Newry

Several cases of influenza were reported in Newry on 10 February 1919.[33] However, at the 15 February 1919 meeting of Newry UDC, the town clerk disputed the rumours in the newspapers that there was another influenza outbreak in the town, because the last outbreak had never really died out in Newry. The figures show that there was a steady trickle of influenza deaths throughout January and into February 1919 in the Newry district (see Fig. 10.1). The third wave was less serious than the second, as confirmed at the Newry UDC meeting on 4 March 1919 when both MOHs stated that the health of the district during February had been satisfactory. The clerk reported that, although there were several cases of influenza, they were nothing to be alarmed about as the attack was a great deal milder than the last one.[34]

Although this wave was not as serious as the second wave, at least 59 people in the union district died from influenza or pneumonia. The disease was still considered serious enough for the Roman Catholic Bishop of Dromore, Edward Mulhern, to make changes to the Lenten abstinence for 1919. In a public notice in the *Frontier Sentinel* he stated: 'owing

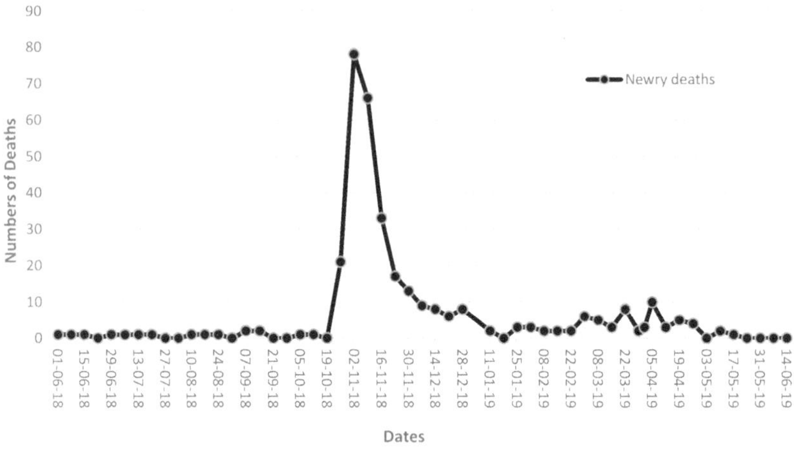

Fig. 10.1 Newry Poor Law Union Influenza and Pneumonia Deaths (1918–1919)[32]

to the low state of public health and the reappearance of the influenza epidemic, I hereby dispense the people of the diocese from the law of the fast for all the days of the coming Lent except Ash Wednesday, Spy Wednesday and Good Friday and transfer the abstinence from Saturdays to Wednesdays'.[35] Other Irish Bishops made similar amendments to the Lenten abstinence rules. In March 1919, the Bishop of Tuam, the Most Rev Dr Gilmartin, dispensed with fast and abstinence, except on Fridays, for the remainder of Lent.[36] Similarly the Bishop of Killaloe, the Most Rev Dr Fogarty, advised that owing to the prevalence of influenza and the scarcity of suitable food, he dispensed those in the diocese from the law of fast and abstinence during Lent with the exception of abstinence from meat on Fridays.'[37] The Archbishop of Dublin, the Most Rev Dr William Walsh, announced that fast and abstinence observed during Holy Week was to be reduced to that of an ordinary week during Lent, which had also been considerably reduced due to the influenza outbreak.[38]

It is apparent that the Newry UDC was aware that the hardship suffered by the poor because of influenza needed to be addressed, as well as its prevention in the district, and thus encouraged the relief effort in Newry. Despite the combined efforts by the UDC, the BOG and local charities to combat influenza and its effect on the population, the town had the second highest death rate from the disease in Ulster for 1918. During the second wave in one week ending 2 November there were at least 260 deaths from either influenza or pneumonia in the Newry poor law union district. Forty-three per cent of these deaths were in the Newry urban area.[39] The high death rate in the poor law union might be because no immunity was gained from the first wave as was the case in other towns. Nevertheless, this death rate could have been even higher if the UDC and local charities had not taken action to help the poor in the district.

Influenza in Cookstown

Cookstown in County Tyrone was described as a flourishing market and manufacturing town. It was the termini of the Midland Railway (Northern Counties Committee) and Great Northern Railway. There were numerous factories in the town and surrounding area, including linen factories, spinning mills, tape factories and many flax scutching mills as well as several cooperative creameries. There is also an extensive farming community in the district.[40] Like Newry, Cookstown also avoided the first wave of influenza, but unfortunately not the second. Influenza was first reported in Cookstown on 26 October 1918 by Dr Graves, MOH, who advised that he could not guarantee to do the midwife's work owing to the severe influenza outbreak.[41] The first death from the disease, however, took place on 21 October 1918. By 31 October 1918, there were reports that influenza in Cookstown had become more serious during the week and many families had contracted the disease. At the special meeting of Cookstown UDC on 30 October 1918, recommendations were made for closure of all the schools and the cinema in the town for 14 days. A leaflet was to be drawn up and approved by Dr Graves, MOH, setting out precautions to be adopted to prevent the spread of influenza. This leaflet was to be distributed to every house in the union district.[42]

Not all schools in Cookstown responded to the Council's recommendations to close, such as the Ladies' School and Cookstown Academy but the UDC took steps on 4 November 1918 to ensure closure of these schools. The technical school also refused to close so the Department of Agriculture and Technical Instruction was contacted to request its closure for one week.[43] Eventually all the Cookstown schools closed and remained so until after Christmas.[44] The UDC minutes for Cookstown make no further mention of the influenza outbreak or any of their recommendations during this virulent wave.

National and Technical School Closures in Ireland

One of the widespread recommendations of local authorities throughout Ireland was the closure of national day schools, Sunday schools and technical schools to stop the spread of influenza infection. School closures were widespread throughout mainland Britain except for London.[45] The question of whether schools should be closed or not during the pandemic was a decision that the central government in Britain left to the local authorities. The same was true in Ireland. The closure of educational establishments during outbreaks of infectious disease were common especially during epidemics of infectious childhood conditions such as measles. In Londonderry the schools reopened on 24 June 1918 after being closed due to an outbreak of measles only to be closed again the next day because of influenza.[46]

School closures were not universally approved of and the *Belfast Evening Telegraph* reported that the general medical opinion in Belfast was that little was gained by closing the schools, because the disease spread so quickly and so widely that these general measures had very little effect.[47] Lurgan MOH, Dr Agnew was not totally in favour of school closures, but he believed that children with the initial stages of influenza or suffering from head colds should be kept at home.[48] On 7 December 1918, the *County Down Spectator* commented that the closure of schools while churches and other places of assembly were left open was 'downright silly'. It stated that 'education was of no consequence in Ireland, so far as advancement is concerned, and that a year lost counts for nothing in the life of a boy or girl'. It further queried why only national schools had been ordered to close as the Bangor Grammar and Ladies School were open with average attendances and 'no mention of the epidemic'.[49]

Niall Johnson argued that in Britain, the decision to close schools was a controversial one as the question arose as to where children would congregate if not at school.[50] This too was a matter for discussion in Belfast as illustrated by a letter in the *Belfast News-Letter* from a school teacher concerned that, during the second wave, children were allowed to frequent cinemas in large numbers and 'often in the poorer districts in an unwashed and negligent condition' as well as 'congregating at the houses and funerals of influenza victims to their own grave danger'.[51] The LGBI allowed Belfast Corporation to exclude children from cinemas in districts where schools were temporarily closed due to influenza.[52] The implication was that children who were not attending schools were spreading influenza in the city at other venues.

Nevertheless, in general, the managers of the national schools throughout Ireland abided by the local authorities' recommendations, but not all schools did often with tragic results. As mentioned in Chapter 6, Methodist College in Belfast remained open with fatal consequences. The Friends School in Lisburn may have also regretted its decision to remain open during the second wave, as by 31 October 1918 only 17 of the pupils who boarded, as well as two members of staff had not contracted influenza. Three pupils Helen Clarke, Anna Magowan and Sadie Walsh died on 31 October, 3 November and 8 November 1918, respectively. It was only on the death of Anna Magowan on 3 November 1918, that the decision was made to close the school and the remaining 16 pupils were sent home. The school then acted as a hospital for the remaining students who were ill. The housekeeper, Miss Emma McCullough, (35) and the headmaster's daughter, Frances Ridges, (21), a student from Queen's University nursed the students suffering from influenza. Unfortunately, both ladies lost their lives to the disease on 10 November and 15 November 1918, respectively. The school eventually opened again in early January 1919.[53]

Despite these deaths Ulster schools fared much better than those elsewhere in Ireland. Ida Milne recounts the overwhelming impact that the flu had on the Jesuit run school in County Kildare, Clongowes Wood. During October and November 1918, there were 198 influenza cases, out of a college population of 300, in October 1918. The gymnasium and several of the dormitories were turned into infirmary wards. Willie Carroll, (14) from Listowel, County Kerry died at Clongowes on 2 November 1918 and Donal Gorman, died at home in Dublin in January 1919.[54] In Saint Colman's College, a boarding school in Fermoy, County Cork, two young students died within a day of each other, from influenza. William Caplice (16) died on 3 November 1918 and Daniel Canty (15) died the day before, on 2 November 1918. Daniel was the uncle of Michael D. Higgins, President of Ireland. He had returned to his home in Liscarroll to help organise a local Sinn Féin anti-conscription campaign but was sent back to school by his parents. Unfortunately, on his return to school, he contracted influenza and subsequently died.[55]

The non-closure of these schools seemed foolhardy especially as there were boarders sleeping in close quarters in dormitories and once influenza entered the institution it would spread very quickly. One reason for the non-closure of these schools maybe because they were attended by children of the middle-classes who were thought to be less at risk. The belief that only the poor were susceptible to infectious disease because of their 'unwashed and negligent condition' may have persuaded the school authorities that there was no necessity for these schools to close during the pandemic.

School closure not only disrupted children's education but also caused financial problems for teachers, whose salaries were dependent upon attendance that in many cases was reduced due to the pandemic. This prompted the Commissioners of the National Education in Ireland to request the Treasury 'to allow the substitution of an average attendance in the quarters ending September and December 1917 for the averages of the corresponding quarters in 1918 because of the abnormally low attendance in 1918 due to the influenza epidemic'. The Treasury agreed to the request, which was designed to prevent a reduction in teachers' salaries because of reduced attendance due to the influenza outbreaks.[56] This measure was extended for the quarter ending 31 March 1919 due to the third outbreak of influenza.[57] However, treatment of Irish teachers was superior in this respect than to English teachers as the Board of Education had invariably refused such applications in England.[58]

Technical education and grants were also a matter of concern throughout Ireland. At the January meeting of the Lurgan Technical Instruction Committee, the principal highlighted the serious reduction of the school's income because of reduced attendance owing to influenza. He estimated that the shortfall would be over £200. The committee adopted the resolution forwarded by the King's County Joint Committee of Technical Instruction. This called upon the Department of Agricultural and Technical Instruction for Ireland to apply the regulations governing science and art grants to cover the influenza pandemic, so that they would be reimbursed for the losses incurred during the time schools were compulsorily closed.[59] In April 1919, the Galway Joint Technical Committee were concerned about the reduction of their technical education grants because of poor attendance, so they requested that the department take the necessary steps to make up the shortfall as the Commissioners had done with the National Schools.[60]

At the December 1918 meeting of the Portadown Technical Committee, it was reported that attendances at the day and evening classes were considerably below the average during the previous five weeks, which was due to the prevalence of influenza in the district. The committee decided to temporarily close the college until 28 December 1918. As with Lurgan, the principal highlighted the serious loss in attendance grants due to the influenza outbreak, which he estimated as being between £200 and £300 for the session and consequently the committee would be faced with this deficit in the next session. The committee passed a resolution to request that the government act promptly to remedy the financial difficulties under which technical education in Ireland was labouring.[61] In February 1919, the County Antrim Joint Technical Instruction Committee applied to the Finance Committee of Antrim County Council for an increased grant of £250, as their grant would be very small due to attendance. It was pointed out that the Down County Council already provided £1425 for technical instruction. The Finance Committee refused the request as any extra money paid to the Technical Instruction Committee would be to the detriment of the Agriculture Committee.[62]

As a consequence of the low attendance and forced closures of many technical institutions throughout the country, the Department of Agriculture and Technical Instruction for Ireland approached the Treasury to ensure that the grants to Irish technical schools were not reduced due to non-attendance or closure because of influenza. After some debate, the Treasury agreed that 'as in England, the requirements as to the minimum number of hours of attendance required to qualify for grant may be waived at the discretion of the department where failure to complete the required number is due to epidemic'.[63]

The Cookstown Response to Influenza

On 9 November 1918, Dr Graves, MOH for Cookstown, contracted influenza so Dr Elliott was employed as his temporary replacement.[64] On 23 November 1918, there were 21 patients in the fever hospital, most were suffering from influenza. There was also a shortage of nurses and other staff at the infirmary so a temporary wards-maid, Mary Brennan was engaged to help. Two fully qualified nurses Mrs Shortt, who was visiting her brother, and Miss Curtain, volunteered their services to nurse in the fever hospital. Mrs James Forrest volunteered her services to cover for the resident infirmary nurse, who was ill with influenza. As the fever hospital nurse was also ill, Miss May Ramsay, who was at home recuperating after nursing during the war, was employed on a temporary basis at £2 per week with rations. Several other ladies in the town also volunteered in the infirmary.

Both Miss Rowan, the principal of the Ladies' School, and Mrs Shortt accompanied the ambulance on different occasions when no nurses were available. The master reported on 9 November 1918 that he had been unable to recruit additional nurses from Belfast and Omagh, but he had been greatly helped by the voluntary work of the above named ladies. The volunteer nurses who assisted at the workhouse were part of the initiative of the Cookstown Influenza Committee. As mentioned in Chapter 3 the guardians appreciated 'their most valuable and self-sacrificing actions in aid of the sufferers in the recent epidemic of influenza. Had it not been for their assistance it would have been impossible to carry on work in the hospital and infirmary'.[65]

The middle-class population of Cookstown rose to the challenge of helping the sick poor suffering from influenza in the town. An article in the *Mid-Ulster Mail* suggested that the tragic case of a mother, who died leaving a husband and four small children had occurred due to inadequate nursing and the lack of sufficient nourishing food. It claimed that there were several instances where whole families were ill and that there were no trained nurses available to help them. Action needed to be taken. On Thursday 14 November 1918, a public meeting was held under the auspices of the Child Welfare Committee and Sick Nursing Society, attended by many representatives from Cookstown, to consider a strategy to cope with nursing and other difficulties caused by the outbreak of influenza in the town. It was recognised that there was a need to provide sufficient nourishment, as well as nursing and other assistance, especially in the cases where an entire family had contracted influenza. Consequently, a committee was appointed to look after the sick in Cookstown and its dispensary district. The committee appealed for local ladies with knowledge of nursing to volunteer, as well as soliciting subscriptions, to provide the sick poor with proper nourishment and clothing. As in Newry, a subscription list was opened, and collectors appointed. Over £50 was subscribed at the meeting and the names of the initial subscribers were printed in the newspaper. The committee also requested that the UDC place the sum of £36, which was raised at the beginning of the war for the relief of distress in the town, at their disposal.[66]

The relief system in Cookstown was comprehensive. On 23 November 1918, the *Mid-Ulster Mail* reported that influenza in Cookstown and district appeared to be 'held'. It advised that, among the 'artisan population', there were incidents where people were suffering not because they did not have any food but because there was no-one physically able to prepare it. Therefore, following on from their initial meeting on Friday 15 November 1918, the Sick Nursing Society began to use the kitchen in the technical school to provide nourishing food for the 'working class population'. The MOH, Dr Graves, stated that without this provision of food aid, that 'the death rate would have been appalling'. The ladies under the direction of Miss Clerkin, the technical college domestic teacher, produced huge quantities of beef tea, milk foods, gruel, Bengers food (this was a food powder that was mixed with milk) and cooling drinks every day. There was a great demand for this service and, by 19 November 1918, over 150 houses in Cookstown, with up to eight patients in each, availed of it. Volunteers came to the Food Depot with tickets issued by the doctors or nurses requesting food and they then distributed it to those who needed it. As a result, a large percentage of the ladies who delivered the food also contracted influenza. While on their rounds, the ladies made investigations to see who needed the service and administered nourishment when there was no one else to do it. As milk was scarce, the Cookstown Academy schoolboys searched the country areas and brought it in every morning from farmers who were willing to give or sell it. The kitchen cost £5 per day and by 20 November 1918 over £100 had been subscribed. Again, a full list of the subscriptions appeared after these articles.[67]

On 30 November 1918, the deaths from influenza and pneumonia in the poor law district were at their peak and the *Mid-Ulster Mail* reported in detail how the committee had rallied to aid the poor and sick in Cookstown. The district nurse, Miss Milliken undertook most of the nursing in the town. As well as covering the duties of the midwife, who was on holiday, she also visited patients in their homes. She was assisted by Nurse McCullough, who was released temporarily by the Tuberculosis Committee. The article stated that the unique feature of this committee's work was the depot for preparing and supplying invalid food, established in the technical school kitchen. It listed the ladies who volunteered their services. Mrs Forrest particularly came in for much praise because as well as volunteering to help in the infirmary, when she was released from her duties, she worked in the kitchen and also helped to deliver the food.

Members of the Salvation Army also assisted with food delivery. While food was given to all those in need, if people could afford to pay the cost of the materials, then they were encouraged to do so. In some cases, everyone in the household contracted influenza, leaving no-one able to prepare invalid food and in that instance, they would purchase prepared food from the depot.[68] On 6 December 1918, Dr Graves recommended that the Food Depot close down as influenza was abating in the area. The committee agreed to this and to give gratuities to Nurses Milliken, McCullough and Ramsay of ten, five and two guineas respectively to show their appreciation of their services during the pandemic. Again, this article was followed by a list of subscriptions.[69]

The influenza outbreak in Cookstown during the autumn of 1918 was severe, but the Council's main recommendation was the closure of schools in the district. Dr Graves recommended the swift interment of the dead and thought that wakes should be abolished, but there is no evidence that these recommendations were acted upon. Although the union infirmary provided medical treatment to influenza patients, it depended on the charity of local ladies who volunteered to help nurse the sick when professional nurses were scarce. Moreover, the local ladies took charge of the situation by forming an influenza committee to take practical action. Subscriptions were raised and used to ensure that food and nursing was allocated to those who needed it, when they needed it. There was awareness in the town that not only the poor and destitute needed aid but, because of the way influenza incapacitated many in a household, there was the need for food to be prepared and delivered to save, even those that could afford it, from starvation. Interestingly, the volunteers were mainly local middle-class women who provided the physical help by providing the food, delivering it, and nursing the sick. The main subscribers to the fund were middle-class men who provided their aid in a monetary fashion and the reward for participation was to have one's contribution, whether as a volunteer or in a financial capacity, recognised by others in the town and district. Maria Luddy noted that the roles played by men and women in philanthropic organisation was similar to those played in the home, that is, while women dispensed the charity, the men oversaw the financial details and supported the women by their presence on a committee.[70]

Third Wave in Cookstown

The deaths of the Master of the workhouse William McCutcheon and his wife Isabella from septic pneumonia, a common complication of influenza, occurred on 30 January and 2 February 1919, respectively. They may have been among the final victims of the second wave or the first casualties of the third wave that took hold properly in Cookstown in March 1919. During this outbreak, the UDC's approach was more proactive and on 1 March 1919, the Cookstown MOH, Dr Graves, issued a public notice which appeared in the *Mid-Ulster Mail* listing precautions that should be taken to avoid influenza such as:

- Avoid all crowded gatherings.
- Secure good ventilation and cleanliness in the home and bedroom.
- Delicate people should take good plain nourishing food and avoid cold and fatigue as far as possible. Warm clothing should be worn as a precaution against pneumonia.
- If a tonic is required, take quinine in doses from 2 to 5 grains night and morning.
- All rooms used as Workshops, Factories etc., should be sprayed morning and afternoon with a dilution of Jeyes Fluid, or other disinfectant, in the strength of a small cupful to 3 gallons of water and thorough ventilation secured.
- A small pellet of permanganate of potash, about the size of a pickle or rice, dissolved in a wine glassful of warm water should be used for gargling the throat or sniffing up the nose twice daily.
- When a person has actually sickened, he should be isolated at once. Special care should be taken to destroy the sputum by burning, as the spit is very infectious.
- When coughing or sneezing the mouth and nose should be covered with a handkerchief.
- If attacked go to bed at once and remain there until allowed up by the doctor.
- When the doctor is required send for him as early in the day as possible.
- If medical aid is called in immediately and the foregoing precautions followed, the disease need not necessarily be particularly dangerous.[72]

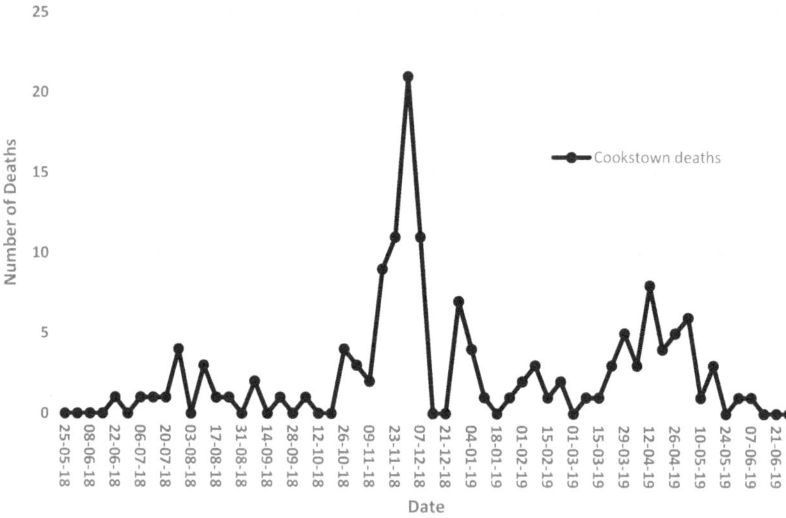

Fig. 10.2 Cookstown Poor Law Union Influenza and Pneumonia Deaths (1918–1919)[71]

At the meeting of Cookstown UDC on 7 April 1919, it was recommended that the leaflet drawn up by the MOH—giving advice for precautions to stop the spread of influenza—not only be published in the *Mid-Ulster Mail* but printed on handbills and delivered to each house in the Urban District.[73] This influenza outbreak was not as serious as the previous one, so there was no need for the Influenza Committee to be reconvened, but nevertheless approximately 41 people in the Cookstown poor law union district died of influenza and pneumonia during this wave, as opposed to 80 during the second wave (see Fig. 10.2).[74] There is no doubt, during the second wave, that it was the actions of the influenza committee that proved to be of most value to the people of Cookstown during this virulent outbreak, as without their diligence the death toll may have been much higher in the poor law union.

Influenza in Clones

Clones was a market town in County Monaghan, which was connected by railway with Cavan, Dundalk, Enniskillen and Belfast. Clones, like

Newry and Cookstown, avoided influenza during the first wave, but not the second. Although the first report of influenza in Clones district was on 2 November 1918,[75] the first death in the poor law district was on 18 October 1918 in Rosslea.[76] By 7 November influenza had spread very rapidly in the town and many cases, had developed into pneumonia. Seven members of the local police force contracted the disease and in Rockcorry, in the Clones poor law union district, Constable William Jameson died from influenza on 8 November 1918. On the recommendation of the MOH, Dr William Henry, the local schools were closed.[77] By 12 November 1918, hundreds of people in Clones had contracted influenza. The outbreak was said to have become more serious over the weekend when there were at least four deaths from the complication of pneumonia between 9 and 11 November 1918. Whole families had influenza and shops were closed due to a lack of staff. The two local doctors were unable to cope with the demands on their services due to the large number of influenza patients and added to this there was also a shortage of nurses.[78] Due to the prevalence of influenza and numerous deaths in the town there was no Armistice celebrations or public demonstration in Clones after the war ended.[79]

The situation in Clones did not improve and at the BOG meeting held on 14 November, it was obvious that influenza was wreaking havoc on the workhouse infirmary. Practically all the workhouse staff had the disease except for the night nurse and one of the wards-maids. The assistant clerk, Mr Travers, had just returned to duty after a bout of influenza. The workhouse MOH, Dr William Henry, contracted influenza and in addition to this he was also the MOH of the Fever Hospital and both Clones and Newbliss dispensary districts. Mr Knight, the Board's solicitor, urged that a temporary doctor be appointed immediately, both in the interests of the poor of the district and for the 30 or 40 pneumonia patients in the Clones fever hospital. This was easier said than done as Dr Tierney, who had formerly acted as a substitute for Dr Henry, was unable to help in this instance as he was already overwhelmed with influenza patients. After much discussion, and on the suggestion of Mr Knight, the BOG agreed to telegraph Dublin to procure a temporary doctor and to provide him with a motorcar so that he could attend the sick poor in the district. At Mr Knight's suggestion, a committee was appointed to deal with all urgent matters that occurred between the meetings of the board. It proved difficult to get a replacement doctor in Clones, but Mr Knight eventually employed Dr Stewart, who took up duty on the Saturday afternoon. In the intervening period, Dr W. More from Drum, visited the Clones hospital each day to help out, which was to the detriment of his own patients and at much inconvenience to himself.[80]

Temporary charge nurse Quigley, who assisted in the Clones workhouse infirmary, reported that it was crowded and, owing to staff shortages, that the patients were almost delirious. She begged that some help be sent to the infirmary, even voluntary assistance of any sort, and added that there was 'no use sending patients there to die'. The Clones BOG were alarmed about the situation at the workhouse and ordered that help should be found at once, regardless of expense. Fortunately, they were able to recruit a lady to help the nurses in the infirmary, where three or four deaths were being reported every day.[81] It was evident that the shortage of medical personnel was a severe problem in Clones and the BOG were thankful to Nurse B. Sherry for her 'services to the poor and others during the recent virulent outbreak of influenza in the Newbliss district'. It was stated that her assistance was invaluable during a period when there was a scarcity of doctors.[82] During this wave the death toll in Clones was high. In November 1918 at least 70 people died from influenza or pneumonia in the Clones poor law district with 31 deaths occurring on the week ending 23 November alone[83] (see Fig. 10.3). However, this did not stop the guardians counting the financial cost of the influenza outbreak. At the weekly meeting held in January 1919, the clerk reported that it cost £31 17*s.* to supply motor cars to the temporary doctors employed during the outbreak and in total the influenza pandemic had cost the Clones BOG £200.[84]

Nevertheless, extra medical assistance was needed and Mr Knight persuaded the men of the 343rd Field Ambulance of the Royal Army Medical Corps (RAMC) to both assist in the Clones union infirmary as well as visiting patients in their own homes.[85] Eight members of the RAMC volunteered to travel from Belfast to the Clones workhouse infirmary and they remained on duty night and day for the space of two or three weeks. The chairman of the BOG thanked those members of the RAMC who assisted in the male wards and he thought that their assistance and nursing saved the lives of many in the infirmary.[86] There is no doubt that the nursing assistance offered by the RAMC would have been vital in helping the sick poor in Clones.

The military could be inflexible in its approach, especially with relinquishing workhouse accommodation for the treatment of influenza

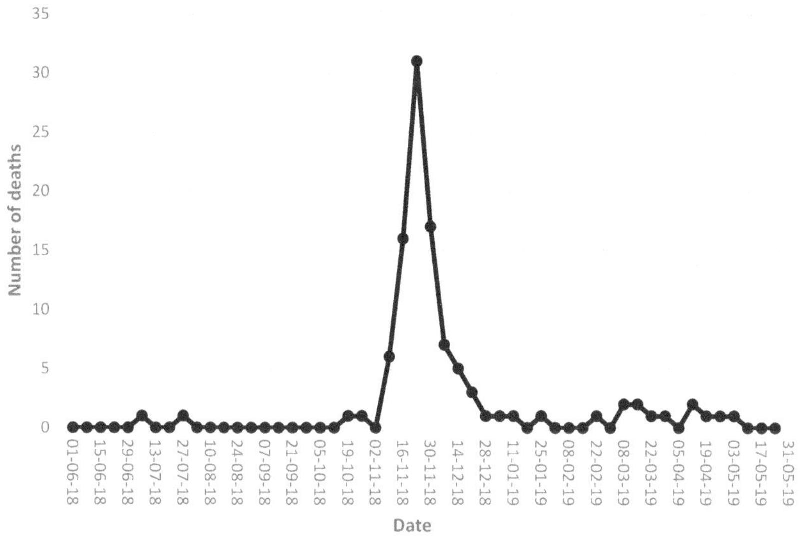

Fig. 10.3 Clones Poor Law Union Influenza and Pneumonia Deaths (1918–1919)

patients. However, the LGBI acknowledged in its annual report that: 'the Military Authorities, at our request, released for local services during the outbreak a number of practitioners that had just been granted temporary commissions'.[87] Therefore the RAMC not only helped with nursing but also with the provision of doctors. As there were fewer influenza cases among the military based at the Curragh military camp, County Kildare than among the civilian population in the town, the RAMC officers were allowed to treat local citizens when the doctors were unable to manage the increased number of patients.[88] After the war had ended, the military were more willing to help out in Ireland at a local level by releasing doctors to treat civilians during influenza outbreaks.

The Clones workhouse hospital was overcrowded; doctors were working to full capacity and added to this, there was a shortage of temporary medical professionals. Again, as in Newry and Cookstown, it was left to the charity of the middle-classes to help alleviate the situation of the poor in their town. The Clones Relief Committee was formed in November 1918, from ladies and gentlemen of all religious denominations in the town to provide both nourishment and nursing to families incapacitated by influenza. A kitchen was set-up in the Town Hall which prepared and distributed nourishing food such as porridge, soup and beef tea to patients who needed it, three times a day. The committee made use of funds from the St Vincent de Paul Society but they did not raise a public subscription list in Clones. Instead, the committee acted first, then sought reimbursement from the BOG afterwards.[89]

The Clones Relief Committee submitted a claim for £95 to the guardians for reimbursement for foodstuffs, medicine, fuel and clothing supplied to the poor of the town during the influenza outbreak. The BOG was not happy about this and there was a lengthy debate at their meeting on 29 January 1919. The chairman argued that if the BOG had been able to both accommodate and treat all the influenza patients in the local hospitals that it would have cost the BOG considerably more than the modest sum that the committee had claimed. Despite objections from some of the guardians, it was unanimously agreed to pay the committee for their outlay during the influenza outbreak.[90] Although, the middle-class of Clones volunteered both their time and services to help their less fortunate neighbours, they did not resort to public subscription believing it was the financial responsibility of BOG to pay for the aid given to the poor.

Clones was reported to have had one of the lowest death rates for 1918 of 1.79 per thousand of population. However, this figure is deceiving because many deaths that occurred in 1918 were not registered until 1919. According to figures calculated using the Irish genealogy i.e. website in the second wave 65 people in the Clones poor law union died of influenza and 26 from pneumonia, which equates to a death rate of 2.99 per thousand of population. This would indicate that the second wave in Clones was much more serious than the recorded figures would imply. The deaths from influenza and pneumonia for the third wave in the poor law union were 13. Clones union district influenza deaths peaked during November and gradually declined through December 1918[91] (see Fig. 10.3). Perhaps it was due to the combined efforts of the Clones Relief Committee, volunteer nurses and the RAMC that the death toll from the disease gradually declined and remained low right through until the end of April 1919.

In Clones, the local authority did not make any recommendations for the prevention of influenza, but the manner in which the town's people reacted brings to light two ways of dealing with the pandemic: the official approach of the BOG; and the charitable approach of the citizens, who were aware that action was needed to prevent further distress. The local authority did not instigate the Clones Relief Committee or its activities, but rather it was the philanthropy of the people that made it happen. This may be linked to the size of the town. A town with a relatively small population may have induced a more philanthropic approach from its residents as they would have closer ties with other members of the community and would have day-to-day dealings with these families after the pandemic was over. This was illustrated by the reply to the vote of thanks for the assistance that the board solicitor Mr Knight and his wife rendered during the pandemic. Mr Knight stated, 'It has been a very great pleasure to both my wife and myself to render any help in our power to relieve our unfortunate friends and neighbours who were laid low in this trying time'.[92] Whatever their reasons, the middle-classes in Clones took action, as did those in the towns of Newry and Cookstown, to provide help for those less fortunate in their respective towns.

Although their philanthropic pursuits may have differed in approach, these towns were among the few that did organise relief committees in Ulster. In Omagh local doctors, Langan and Thompson were very impressed by the response of the Cookstown ladies and suggested to the BOG that the ladies from Omagh should do the same. However, there is no evidence that the BOG encouraged a similar relief scheme in Omagh as that in Cookstown.[93]

In parts of Ireland, the locals were dependant on the philanthropy of the local landlords. In Rathvilly, Co Carlow, Nellie O'Toole recounted how when influenza hit her town: 'The only redemption came from 'the big house at Lisnavagh where the Rathdonnells lived. At midday, every day, they sent down a big phaeton with two men driving and two big churns of soup'. 'Only for that we were all gone'.[94] Again there is no evidence that local landlords provided a similar service in Ulster towns. At a meeting of Dungannon UDC in October 1918, one councillor complaining about the serious nature of influenza in the town thought that steps should be taken to provide the services of a nurse for poorer people. He suggested that Lord Ranfurly, the local landlord, be approached in the matter, to which the clerk replied that Lord Ranfurly could not possibly attend to such a thing.[95]

Elsewhere in Ireland a meeting was held in Dundalk in November to take measures for the relief of sickness and distress in the town. Kitchens, nursing, finance and distribution committees were set up and volunteer nurses were requested.[96] In Upperlands, Maghera, Co. Londonderry an outbreak of influenza forced the closure of Messrs Clark's & Sons linen factory and prompted the owners to help influenza sufferers. Mrs A.W Clark and Mrs H. J. Clark opened a relief fund, which raised a substantial sum of money. This was distributed among needy cases and they also secured the services of a trained nurse to help the influenza sufferers in the area.[97] Again the village of Upperlands would have been a close-knit community with the factory at the core and most families in the village would have worked there. Therefore, the proprietors would be aware of the hardship of their employees' family. Also, it would have been in the company's interest to have a healthy workforce to keep up production. There was no evidence that the middle-classes in the larger and more industrial towns such as Belfast, Londonderry, Lurgan and Portadown, took any similar action to help the poor in their towns. Perhaps this was due to a lack of connection between the middle-classes and their working-class neighbours in these towns.

The pandemic highlighted the flaws in the poor law system, which was overstretched due to a lack of suitable accommodation and medical personnel. In some cases, such as with Clones, there was not the capacity to accommodate influenza sufferers in the union infirmary. Needless to say, BOGs did not help the poor by providing food or other necessities. The middle-class population of Newry, Cookstown and Clones rose to the challenge to help their fellow residents especially during the more virulent second wave of the pandemic. They opened public subscription lists and the ladies of these towns volunteered their services to provide nourishing food and to nurse the local poor to alleviate the suffering of their sick neighbours often at risk to their own health. This meant that the guardians in some cases abdicated their responsibility for the poor in the union to the volunteers who were willing to help. However, as events in Clones show, even if the guardians were happy to leave the care of the poor and sick to the local volunteers, the Clones middle-class were not happy to let them off their financial obligations. Van Hartesveldt argued that public aid with food, fuel and nursing during the pandemic could be of much more value than treatment by local doctors.[98] Certainly in Newry, Cookstown Clones, Upperlands and elsewhere in Ireland the philanthropy of the middle-classes helped the poor in these towns by providing food, fuel and nursing. It is telling that in the bigger industrial towns like Belfast, Londonderry, Lurgan and Portadown there is no evidence of any philanthropic enterprise to help the needy in those districts which may account for their high death tolls during the pandemic.

Notes

1. Niven (1920, p. 483).
2. *Newry Reporter*, 2 July 1918; *Frontier Sentinel*, 6 July 1918.
3. *Newry Reporter*, 19 October 1918.
4. *Frontier Sentinel*, 26 October 1918.
5. *Newry Reporter*, 29 October 1918.
6. *Belfast News-Letter*, 30 October 1918.
7. Figures from https://civilrecords.irishgenealogy.ie/: website for the indexes of the Civil Registration of Irish Deaths from influenza and pneumonia deaths during 1918 and 1919 in Newry poor law union.
8. *Newry Examiner*, 9 November 1918. *Frontier Sentinel*, 9 November 1918.
9. *Belfast News-Letter*, 22 October 1918.
10. *Newry Reporter*, 16 November 1918.
11. *Newry Reporter*, 12 November 1918.
12. *Newry Reporter*, 14 November 1918.
13. *Newry Reporter*, 19 November 1918.
14. *Newry Reporter*, 3 December 1918.
15. I would like to acknowledge the Deputy Keeper of the Records, Public Records Office of Northern Ireland [Hereafter PRONI], LA/58/2/CA/6, Newry Urban District Council [hereafter UDC] Minutes, 4 November 1918, *Irish News*, 5 November 1918, *Frontier Sentinel*, 9 November 1918, *Irish Independent*, 5 November 1918.
16. *Frontier Sentinel*, 9 November 1918.
17. Wakes were discussed in more detail in Chapter 2.
18. *Newry Reporter*, 29 October 1918.
19. *Northern Whig*, 11 November 1918, *Newry Reporter*, 12 November 1918.
20. PRONI, BG/24/A/104, Newry Board of Guardians Minutes [hereafter BOG], 9 November 1918, *Newry Reporter*, 12 November 1918.
21. PRONI, BG/24/A/104, Newry BOG Minutes, 12 December 1918.
22. *Frontier Sentinel*, 9 November 1918.
23. *Frontier Sentinel*, 2 November 1918.
24. *Frontier Sentinel*, 9 November 1918, *Irish Independent*, 12 November 1918.
25. *Newry Examiner*, 9 November 1918.
26. PRONI, LA/58/2/CA/6, Newry UDC Minutes, 4 November 1918.
27. *Newry Reporter*, 29 October 1918; *Newry Reporter*, 28 November 1918.
28. *Newry Reporter*, 21 November 1918; *Newry Reporter*, 28 November 1918.

29. Luddy (1995, pp. 179–180).
30. *Newry Reporter*, 11 January 1919; *Belfast News-Letter*, 13 January 1919.
31. *Census of Ireland*, 1911. Province of Ulster, Newry UD (London, 1911), 130.
32. Graph produced from figures from https://civilrecords.irishgenealogy.ie/: website for the indexes of the Civil Registration of Irish Deaths from influenza and pneumonia deaths during 1918 and 1919 in Newry poor law union.
33. *Irish Independent*, 10 February 1919.
34. *Newry Reporter*, 4 March 1919.
35. *Frontier Sentinel*, 8 March 1919.
36. *Connaught Tribune*, 29 March 1919.
37. *Nenagh Guardian*, 8 March1918.
38. *Irish Independent*, 14 April 1919.
39. https://civilrecords.irishgenealogy.ie/ (Newry poor law union).
40. Belfast 1918 Street Directory found https://www.lennonwylie.co.uk/PT1918.htm.
41. PRONI, BG/11/A/62, Cookstown BOG Minutes, 26 October 1918.
42. PRONI, LA/28/2/CA/3, Cookstown UDC Minutes, 30 October 1918, *Mid-Ulster Mail*, 31 October 1918; *Belfast News-Letter*, 2 November 1918.
43. PRONI, LA/28/2/CA/3, Cookstown UDC Minutes, 7 November 1918, *Irish News*, 7 November 1918.
44. *Mid-Ulster Mail*, 30 November 1918.
45. Johnson (2006, p. 131).
46. *Irish News*, 25 June 1918; *Derry Journal*, 26 June 1918; *Dungannon Democrat*, 26 June 1918.
47. *Belfast Evening Telegraph*, 24 December 1918.
48. *Irish News*, 8 November 1918.
49. *County Down Spectator*, 7 December 1918.
50. Johnson (2003, p. 152).
51. *Belfast News-Letter*, 3 March1919.
52. *Annual Report of the Local Government Board for Ireland for Year Ended 31 March 1919*, xxxviii.
53. Newhouse (1974, pp. 90–91).
54. Milne, (2018, pp. 156–160).
55. Story of Daniel Canty recounted by President of Ireland, Michael D Higgins at Seminar 'Commemorating The Great Flu of 1918–1919', 31 May 2019.
56. *Irish News*, 19 February 1919.
57. The National Archive [Hereafter TNA], T1/12560/11288/19, Chief Secretary's Office, Ireland, payment of grants to national schools: special concession due to decreased attendance because of the influenza epidemic, Grants to National Schools, 28 March1919.

58. TNA, T1/12358/22021/19, Department of Agriculture and Technical Instruction, Ireland. Prevention of loss of grants to schools closed on account of epidemics of influenza, Letter to G. Fletcher, 23 May 1919.
59. *Lurgan Mail*, 11 January 1919; *Belfast News-Letter*, 6 January 1919.
60. *Connaught Tribune*, 12 April 1919.
61. *Portadown News*, 16 December 1918; *Lurgan Mail*, 21 December 1918.
62. *Northern Whig*, 5 February 1919.
63. TNA, T1/12358/22021/19, Department of Agriculture and Technical Instruction, Ireland. Prevention of loss of grants to schools closed on account of epidemics of influenza: Letter to Treasury from Department of Agriculture and Technical Instruction for Ireland, 15 May 1919 and Letter from Treasury to Department of Agriculture and Technical Instruction for Ireland, 2 July 1919.
64. PRONI, BG/11/A/62, Cookstown BOG Minutes, 9 November 1918.
65. PRONI, BG/11/A/62, Cookstown BOG Minutes, 23 November. 1918; 28 December 1918, *Mid-Ulster Mail*, 23 November 1918, *Mid-Ulster Mail*, 30 November 1918. *Belfast News-Letter*, 30 December 1918.
66. *Mid-Ulster Mail*, 16 November 1918; *Irish News*, 18 November 1918, *Belfast News-Letter*, 18 November 1918.
67. *Mid-Ulster Mail*, 23 November 1918.
68. *Mid-Ulster Mail*, 30 November 1918.
69. *Mid-Ulster Mail*, 7 December 1918.
70. Luddy (1995, p. 177).
71. Figures from https://civilrecords.irishgenealogy.ie/: website for the indexes of the Civil Registration of Irish Deaths from influenza and pneumonia deaths during 1918 and 1919 in Cookstown Poor Law Union.
72. *Mid-Ulster Mail*, 1 March 1919.
73. PRONI, LA/28/2/CA/3, Cookstown UDC Minutes, 7 April 1919.
74. Figures from https://civilrecords.irishgenealogy.ie/ (Cookstown poor law union).
75. *Anglo-Celt*, 2 November 1918.
76. Sourced from https://civilrecords.irishgenealogy.ie/ website for the indexes of the Civil Registration of Irish Deaths from influenza and pneumonia deaths during 1918 and 1919 in Clones poor law union.
77. *Belfast News-Letter*, 7 November 1918; *Irish News*, 7 November 1918.
78. *Belfast News-Letter*, 12 November 1918, *Irish News*, 12 November 1918.
79. *Belfast News-Letter*, 13 November 1918.
80. *Irish News*, 15 November 1918, *Belfast News-Letter*, 15 November 1918; *Anglo-Celt*, 16 November 1918; 23 November 1918; *Ulster Herald*, 23 November 1918.
81. *Anglo-Celt*, 23 November 1918; *Ulster Herald*, 23 November 1918.
82. *Fermanagh Herald*, 11 January 1919.
83. Figures calculated from https://civilrecords.irishgenealogy.ie/ (Clones poor law union).

84. *Anglo-Celt*, 18 January 1919.
85. *Anglo-Celt*, 30 November 1918; *Belfast News-Letter*, 14 December 1918.
86. *Anglo-Celt*, 14 December 1918.
87. *Annual Report of the Local Government Board for Ireland for the Year Ended 31st March 1919*, p. xxvii.
88. TNA, WO 35/179/4, Returns: historical review of medical and sanitary work in the Irish Command during the war; Report of the medical and sanitary work of the Dublin and Curragh Brigade, sanitary work during the war, Curragh,
89. *Belfast News-Letter*, 21 November 1918, *Anglo-Celt* 30 November 1918, 1 February 1919, 15 February 1919.
90. *Anglo-Celt*, 30 November 1918, 1 February 1919, 15 February 1919.
91. Figures calculated from https://civilrecords.irishgenealogy.ie/ (Clones poor law union).
92. *Anglo-Celt*, 14 December 1918.
93. PRONI, BG/26/A/85, Omagh BOG Minutes, 7 December 1918.
94. Fennell and Banbury (2006, p. 140).
95. *Tyrone Courier*, 24 October 1918.
96. *Irish Independent*, 5 November 1918.
97. *Mid-Ulster Mail*, 30 November 1918.
98. Van Hartesveldt (1992, p. 103).

References

Fennell, James, and Turtle Banbury. *Vanishing Ireland*. Dublin: Hodder Headline Ireland, 2006.

Johnson, Niall P. A. S. 'The Overshadowed Killer: Influenza in Britain', in *Spanish Influenza Pandemic of 1918–1919: New Perspectives*, edited by Howard Phillips and David Killingray, 132–156. London: Routledge, 2003.

Johnson, Niall P. A. S. *Britain and the 1918–19 Influenza Pandemic: A Dark Epilogue*. London Routledge, 2006.

Luddy, Maria. *Women and Philanthropy in Nineteenth-Century Ireland*. Cambridge: Cambridge University Press, 1995.

Milne, Ida. *Stacking the Coffins: Influenza, War and Revolution in Ireland, 1918–19*. Manchester: Manchester University Press, 2018.

Newhouse, Neville H. *A History of the Friends School, Lisburn*. Lurgan, 1974.

Niven, James. 'Report on the Epidemic of Influenza in Manchester, 1918–19', in *Ministry of Health, Report on the Pandemic of Influenza*, 1918–19, 471–520. London: HMSO, 1920.

Van Hartesveldt, Fred R. 'Manchester', in *The 1918–1919 Pandemic of Influenza: The Urban Impact in the Western World*, edited by Fred van Hartesveldt, 91–103. Lewiston, Queenstown, Lampeter: The Edward Mellon Press, 1992.

CHAPTER 11

Conclusion and Aftermath

One common theme that links the case studies of influenza in Ulster towns is the lack of a coherent policy or official guidance from central government, that is, the Local Government Board for Ireland (LGBI). Each town approached prevention of the disease in a different manner. It is notable that the first wave of influenza was mainly in Belfast, Londonderry, Lurgan and Portadown, and even though relatively mild, it caused havoc as businesses had to close or function on reduced staff with services disrupted. Nevertheless, the public health officials in these towns treated this outbreak like a seasonal influenza and, therefore, did not respond with preventative or indeed therapeutic recommendations for their citizens. During the second wave, the local authority response through their public health and sanitary officials was more apparent. It was also more consistent as many of the councils took similar preventative measures.

Closures of schools and technical colleges, although not universally approved of, was one action that most Local Authorities recommended and that, in general, school managers adhered to. However, this was only a recommendation and was not compulsory. The closure and ventilation of cinemas concerned several councils, but they did not have the authority to enforce these measures and, even when requested, the LGBI did not sanction this action. Public notices with lists of precautions to avoid influenza were produced by local authorities in Belfast, Ballyclare, Larne and Cookstown. This advice was culled from the memorandum sent out

P. Marsh, *The Spanish Flu in Ireland*, Palgrave Studies in Economic History, https://doi.org/10.1007/978-3-030-79500-9_11

to MOHs by the LGBI in late October 1918. The advice normally placed responsibility for prevention of influenza on the individual rather than preventative measures that the local authorities would take themselves. Although both Newry and Ballyclare councils produced public notices prohibiting wakes, as well as the prompt burial of influenza victims, again they did not have the authority to enforce these recommendations. The LGBI was not in favour of placing influenza on the list of notifiable diseases as they thought, probably correctly, that it would not curtail its spread. Nevertheless, Larne and Belfast councils made septic pneumonia notifiable during the second wave, mandating certain measures to be put into place in relation to notification, isolation and treatment of the disease.

The LGBI provided little guidance to local authorities on influenza, often shifting the onus back to the council when queried about a course of action. However, it is possible that local authorities wanted the sanction of the LGBI so that they could defer the responsibility for any unpopular measures they took, from themselves onto central government. This would allow them to placate ratepayers by avoiding the financial burden of some measures. Nevertheless, local authorities were ill equipped to respond to the public health catastrophe of the pandemic without adequate help and guidance from the LGBI. Despite this predicament, the LGBI seemed reluctant to provide that guidance, which meant that the response throughout Ireland lacked any cohesion and consistency. The main way in which the LGBI did seem to involve themselves was with sanctioning remuneration for temporary medical staff needed for the infirmaries and dispensary districts.

The 1918 influenza pandemic also illustrated the shortcomings of the poor law system especially during a time of war. War impacted on the Irish response to this pandemic in many ways especially during the first wave. The Imperial Local Government Board (LGB) came in for criticism for its lack of action. Sir Arthur Newsholme, head of the Imperial LGB, acknowledged at the Royal Society of Medicine that during the first wave more could have been done. Measures such as: the isolation of the sick from the healthy; prevention of mass migrations and overcrowding should have been taken, but he believed that due to the demands of war that this was not possible as 'it was necessary to carry on and the relentless needs of warfare justified incurring the risk of spreading infections'.[1] This lack of action in London, meant that there was also a lack of action in Ireland as the LGBI took its lead from London. In fact it was not until late October 1918 towards the end of the war that a memorandum was produced by the LGB with preventative measures for influenza and issued to the LGBI and it was from this memorandum that the public notices from local authorities derived.

Throughout the pandemic, people in Irish towns continued with everyday life and work unless sickness prevented them from doing so. Businesses only closed if forced to do so because of lack of staff and not as a preventative measure. The war impacted both directly and indirectly on the response to the disease. There was lack of hospital accommodation because the military requisitioned wards in the infirmaries or indeed the entire workhouse as was the case in Strabane. This led to overcrowding in wards as well as a lack of accommodation for the local sick. Care of military patients appeared to take precedent over local citizens. Whether this was due to patriotic fervor on behalf of the guardians or financial gain to the union is a matter for debate. BOG's had problems finding replacement nurses and doctors as many were away at war. Workhouse infirmaries had difficulties recruiting professional nurses and depended on local ladies volunteering to help. Replacement doctors were difficult to find as those physicians who remained in Ireland were under severe pressure due to the number of dispensary patients. They were also unhappy with the salaries offered as sometimes their expenses outweighed their remuneration. This meant that dispensaries were forced to close, leaving the local poor with no medical help at all. The poor law system was unable to cope with the number of influenza cases. Union infirmaries were filled to capacity and, as in the case of Clones, were unable to accommodate influenza sufferers, so helping families in need of food, fuel and nursing was not a consideration. In some towns, such as Cookstown, Newry and Clones it was the middle-class residents who volunteered to help these people, especially during the more virulent second wave of the pandemic.

The 1919–1920 Influenza Scare

Did the 1918–1919 pandemic make a significant impact on the LGBI, as Sandra Tomkins has argued it did in the context of the health authorities in the United Kingdom (UK), which were conscious of the threat of a further attack and prepared accordingly.[2] Tomkins argued that the newly formed Ministry of Health showed an awareness of the threat of new influenza outbreaks by their actions in the 1919–1920 influenza scare, ensuring a more prompt and complete level of readiness among the authorities. The response was practiced and focused on the implementation of therapeutic rather than preventative measures. She argued that the changes in influenza policy between 1918 and 1920 were quite remarkable, reflecting not only the greater post-war resources and attention to domestic affairs, but a shift in the type of action planned, indicating a more fundamental change in British public health organisation after the pandemic.[3] The 1919 Ministry of Health Bill proposed that most health functions be centralised in a ministry at central government, however, the Bill made no provision for Ireland. Therefore, when the next influenza scare occurred in 1920 the LGBI was still the principal health authority in the country.

During the 1920 influenza scare, the Ministry of Health emphasised the importance of sending memoranda to local authorities for the prevention of disease. A vaccine was issued to Medical Officers of Health (MOH) to be distributed free of charge with the recommendation to be used prior to the epidemic for the best results.[4] The LGBI acted promptly and on 6 February 1920 it was reported that they had issued a circular which advised about influenza epidemics in various parts of the world and urged sanitary authorities and the MOHs to take immediate measures to deal with the threatened outbreaks. Emphasis was placed on the importance of immediate notification of the disease.[5] The LGBI appeared to have changed their opinion on the usefulness of vaccines (see Chapter 5). They advised that although immunity was not guaranteed, the vaccine would greatly lesson the severity of the attack. By 14 February 1920, they arranged to supply influenza vaccine to doctors and dispensary MOHs free of charge.[6]

Some MOHs took up the offer of free vaccine, including Lurgan MOH, Dr Samuel Agnew who distributed it to the doctors in Lurgan, along with instruction leaflets which informed the public of the best way to prevent the disease and what they should do if attacked. In April 1920, he advised that all necessary precautions had been taken but, although there were many influenza case reported in the poor law district, 'the infectious nature of the disease was not very well marked or the virulence of the attack very distinct'.[7] The Holywood urban council also offered free vaccination. Vaccination commenced on 18 February 1920 and 1,037 persons were inoculated. As in Lurgan, there were many cases, but influenza was not as serious or widespread as in the 1918–1919 pandemic.[8] In Cavan, the MOH and executive sanitary officer of the urban district also recommended vaccination to avoid influenza and that employers should not penalise a worker for staying at home if they contracted the disease.[9] Belfast Borough County had the highest influenza mortality during this outbreak with 264 deaths.[10] This influenza attack was not anywhere as serious as the 1918–1919 pandemic and was in fact on a par with a seasonal influenza outbreak as it accounted for 1,256 deaths in Ireland, as compared to an annual average of 1,234 for the ten years preceding the 1918–1919 pandemic. Nevertheless 655 of these death occurred in the province of Ulster.[11] Again, the industrial nature of Ulster's major towns may have played a part in its virulence as the higher death tolls were in Belfast, Lurgan, Lisburn and Newry.[12]

What is evident during this milder influenza outbreak was that the central government response in Ireland was proactive. The LGBI followed the example of the Ministry of Health and sent out circulars to the sanitary authorities in Ireland, as well as leaflets informing the public of preventative measures to take and what they should do if attacked by influenza. Furthermore, they supplied prophylactic vaccine free of charge as a therapeutic measure to the different sanitary authorities. This is in stark contrast to what happened during 1918–1919 when the LGBI took no proactive steps against influenza, leaving prevention to individual local authorities, and did not advocate the use of vaccines for preventing an attack. In this instance, the LGBI ensured that the local authorities were aware of the risk of a recurrence of influenza and what measures should be taken to ensure it was not as serious as the 1918–1919 pandemic.

Encephalitis Lethargica in Ireland

Svenn-Erik Mamelund has suggested that Influenza survivors from the pandemic reported a number of post influenza conditions such as depression, sleep disturbances, mental distraction, dizziness and difficulties coping at work, and that in the United States several deaths occurred during the years 1918–1920 were 'significantly and positively related to suicide'.[13] One suicide case in Ireland that occurred as a result of influenza was of a soldier called Thomas Earnshaw who was based in Finner Camp in Donegal. He committed suicide after suffering from depression while recovering from influenza in August 1918.[14] Another phenomenon which was observed in the post pandemic period was the neurological condition *Encephalitis lethargica* (EL), which literally means, a swelling of the brain that makes one sleepy.[15] It is still a puzzle as to whether this condition resulted from the pandemic or it was simply that the vast numbers infected in 1918–1919 made it more noticeable. EL left thousands of ailing, disfigured and forgotten victims throughout the world in the decades following the epidemic.[16] EL was first identified prior to the 1918 influenza pandemic outbreak in 1916, during World War I, by Constantin von Economo, a military physician in the Vienna General Hospital. It was given his name 'von Economo disease', but became generally known as *encephalitis lethargica*. The disease has since been dubbed the 'sleepy' or 'sleeping' sickness.[17]

There has been some discussion on whether there is a direct link between influenza and EL. It has been suggested that the EL epidemic began earlier and lasted longer than the 1918–1919 pandemic, as evidence of this virus has not been found in archival post-mortem tissue.[18] Vilensky and McCall stated that it was impossible to prove a negative hypothesis between influenza and EL. They further added that if influenza was a cause for EL then it would provide a convenient explanation as to why the disease disappeared in the late 1920s, because the influenza strains that caused the 1918 epidemic had ceased circulation in humans before 1933.[19] However, this theory does not hold up as the influenza strain that caused the 1918 pandemic prevailed until 1957.[20] Unfortunately, the truth may never be known as the study of EL is hampered with a high ratio of contemporary observational evidence rather than objective data.[21]

In Belfast, it was noted that some authorities associated EL with the 1918–1919 influenza outbreaks.[22] Cecil Kidd in his MD thesis stated in 1933 that, although in some individual cases EL followed epidemic influenza as a sequel and were diagnosed as 'post influenzal encephalitis' that this did not create a relationship, as there were numerous cases of the disease that originated independently with no traceable connection to influenza.[23] Nevertheless, the worst influenza outbreak in Northern Ireland since the 1918–1919 pandemic occurred during the early part of 1924 prior to the most severe outbreak of EL in the province.[24]

There were occurrences of EL in Belfast as early as 1918. Dr Gardner Robb, Medical Superintendent of both the Belfast and Purdysburn Fever Hospital reported a widespread epidemic of EL in Belfast during 1920.[25] Between October 1918 and the end of 1923, Dr Robert Marshall reported 42 EL cases treated as in-patients in the Royal Victoria Hospital in Belfast. Dr Donough Macnamara believed he had treated the first Irish case of EL during either 1917 or 1918 in the Mater hospital, Dublin which he had misdiagnosed at the time as influenza.[26] However, the most severe outbreak of the disease took place in1924. Dr Robb reported there were a large number of EL cases in Belfast between the end of March 1924 and the end of June 1924, when 'the epidemic ceased even more suddenly than it began'.[27]

The symptoms were particularly worrying. Dr Craig from the Belfast Union Fever Hospital described those he observed:

> The onset of the disease bore similarities to an acute flu-like illness, which could either be severe, or so mild that it almost escaped detection. However, after this acute infection, the sequelae in the nervous system began to manifest. The common primary symptoms were double vision, extreme lethargy during the day, that occasionally led to coma, or wakefulness and activity during the night. The victim was sometimes gripped by very severe pain, usually in the head and neck region.[28]

> Other symptoms appeared either quite suddenly or over the course of weeks or months. The patient's face lost all expression, the body began to stoop and hunch over, the spine protruded awkwardly from the back, hands hung well below their knees and fingers were curled. Their gait was shifting, with tiny, zombie like, steps. There was often profuse salivation, and the speech became slurred and difficult to follow. Some patients were obviously mentally retarded; while intelligence had not been impaired in others.[29]

In Belfast, Dr Robb was not impressed by the suggested treatments of EL. The course of the disease was irregular, subject to wide fluctuations where sudden improvements in symptoms were followed by relapses making it very difficult to form a concrete opinion on the validity of results obtained by any particular treatment. Robb described many of the recommended treatments as 'weird in the extreme', but the number and severity of cases, led many desperate physicians to use some of these extraordinary treatments, only to quickly abandon them once they proved useless.[30] The 1928 Ministry of Health report on EL also noted there was little prospect of curing the disease at that time and that therapeutic treatments had no effect on the course of the disease or the fate of the patient.[31] The same report concluded that about 25% of EL sufferers recovered fully from their attack without any ill-effects. In Belfast, Dr Robb disagreed. His survey of EL patients two and a half years after the 1924 outbreak showed only nine per cent of the survivors of this attack had recovered and that few sufferers escaped without some vestige of their illness. He was not optimistic, claiming that if he examined these patients again in the future only five per cent would show no trace of the disease.[32]

One of the most marked vestiges of EL was the psychological change it caused in children. In 1928, 70% of children who survived the disease showed psychological changes and a third of the survivors showed severe or dangerous behavioural changes.[33] Dr A. F. Tredgold was a neurologist and psychiatrist associated with the Bethlem Royal Hospital in London. At a lecture on 'Mental Deficiency' in London in 1924, referring to the seriousness of the disease, advised that in 1918 there were only a few hundred cases of EL but that in 1924 there were over 6,000. At least 300 London school children had been seriously mentally affected because of the disease. One third had their whole mental and moral character altered and 'normal well-behaved children changed by this illness into perfect little fiends, capable of any act of cruelty and crime'.[34] There were similar reports throughout the United Kingdom, in Sheffield, Professor Arthur J. Hall, observed a change in moral character, especially in children and young people, whose moral make-up was not completely set. He found that 18 individuals under 20 displayed definite changes in moral behaviour after 18 months. Many of these children ended up in the asylum; the others could not regularly attend school due to their behaviour. Some even ended up in prisons or other penile institutions.[35]

Complete recovery was rare but not totally unheard of. Occasionally patients appeared to completely recover, only for their symptoms to recur a few months later, after which they steadily deteriorated but there was no way of knowing when this was going to happen.[36] During the 1960s, Dr Oliver Sacks found several seemingly comatose victims of the disease in Beth Abraham Hospital. In 1969, as depicted in the film *Awakenings*, after treatment with the experimental drug-L-dopa, some of these patients were able to describe exactly what it felt like to be trapped in their bodies by physical dysfunction while their minds were very much aware and live.[37] Sadly many survivors of the epidemic were condemned to a life in mental asylums, their minds lucid despite brain and body being damaged.[38] Around 60% of those who survived the 1924 attack in Belfast were unable to attend either work or school. Dr Thompson, Medical Superintendent Officer of Health for Belfast noted in his annual report that by 1931 there were still approximately 80 people, mostly young adults, suffering from the after-effects of the 1924 outbreak. A large proportion of these chronic cases were of the Parkinsonian type while there were also some cases of children with 'changed character'.[39]

The after-effects of this disease were devastating. Unfortunately, in Belfast and elsewhere in Ireland there was no specialist aftercare for either adults or children who suffered chronic effects from the 1924 outbreak and many were left to spend the rest of their days in the workhouse fever hospital or Purdysburn Asylum. In 1937, Dr Douglas B Lothian, reported in his annual report that a number of patients suffering the after-effects of EL were in Down Mental Hospital in Downpatrick. He said that 'the tragedy of their case is that while they are fully aware of their abnormality of their conduct they are quite unable to control it'.[40] What was most frightening about EL was: it is unknown what caused the disease; a cure was never discovered and many people continued to suffer the after-effects for the rest of their lives. According to Paul Foley, the most important question regarding EL was not whether it occurred before 1917 or after 1940 but what caused it to become epidemic during that period. He believed that influenza seemed to be the most logical explanation, leading to the question of whether EL will return in epidemic form with the next influenza pandemic.[41] It is not unreasonable to associate this viral, neurological disease with the pandemic of 1918 as there were influenza deaths associated with encephalitis in Clones, Newtownards and Lisburn during both 1918 and 1919. Annie Cox from Carrick-on-Shannon was a member of the Territorial Force Nursing Service and served in the 2nd Western Field Hospital, Manchester. She contracted *Encephalitis Lethargica* after Influenza and died on 06 February 1919.[42] EL like influenza in 1918 was an enigma to the medical profession as the cause or an appropriate treatment were never discovered; and the after-effects of the disease left many people without the appropriate long-term care they needed. If this disease was indeed associated with influenza, then the effects of the pandemic were not just confined to 1918 and 1919 but had more far-reaching consequences that were never fully addressed.

COVID-19 in Ireland and United Kingdom

At the time of writing the world is one year into arguably its most severe pandemic since 1918 with the Covid-19 or coronavirus pandemic, which first appeared in Wuhan province in China in December 2019. At the end of February 2021, the global death toll was as least 2,508,843 and rising.[43] Since it began there has been much discussion about this pandemic in newspapers, on television and social media. The public has been bombarded with information, facts, mortality figures, infection rates, scientific theories, as well as misinformation and conspiracy theories in relation to the disease. However, what is most surprising is that the world was so ill-prepared for this pandemic when it arrived. Since 1918, subsequent influenza outbreaks occurred: in 1957 'Asian Flu'; 1968 'Hong Kong Flu' and more recently in 2009 the 'Mexican swine flu' scare. Each one of these outbreaks prompted the question: was this the next big influenza pandemic? It has been a singular failure of politicians and others involved with pandemic preparedness plans that they have not read the extensive literature, especially in recent years, on the history of the 1918–1919 pandemic and other epidemics that have followed it. Scientists and others in the pandemics knowledge field have been warning that a new global pandemic was increasingly likely, given MERS and SARS and 2009 influenza scares. Most of these epidemics follow fairly predictable patterns and knowledge of these may have led to a different reaction to Covid-19. As information regarding the virus in the Wuhan region of China trickled out to the wider world, governments watched but did not take immediate action.

On 23 January 2020 Wuhan province locked down to curtail the spread of the virus and a week later on 29 January the first two Covid-19 cases in the UK were confirmed as Chinese nationals who were family members staying in a hotel in York. By 23 February, due to a surge in coronavirus cases in Italy, Italian officials locked down 10 towns in Lombardy in an attempt to control the virus, but by 28 February there were 800 people infected in Italy. On 4 March, COVID-19 cases surged in the UK, rising from 34 to 87. They then rose again to 373 by 10 March 2020. In March, although sporting events in the UK such as the London Marathon were postponed, the Cheltenham horse-racing festival still took place with at least 60,000 people in attendance from all over the UK and Ireland. On 16 March 2020, the UK Prime Minister, Boris Johnson urged the public to work from home and avoid pubs and restaurants to help the National Health Service (NHS) cope with the pandemic. The UK's death toll rose to 55. On 17 March, France had over 6,500 infections and more than 140 deaths and imposed a nationwide lockdown prohibiting all gatherings and only allowing people to go out for fresh air. On 23 March 2020, a UK lockdown was announced where the British Public were advised they should only go outside to buy food, to exercise once a day or to go to work if they absolutely could not work from home.[44]

In Ireland the first diagnosed case of Covid-19 was that of a middle-aged woman who had returned from Northern Italy on 17 February 2020.[45] On 12 March 2020, the Irish Government shut all schools and colleges in the country.[46] On 24 March, the Taoiseach, Leo Varadkar announced that all non-essential shops, restaurant and cafes were to close and there were restrictions on gatherings of more than four people. On 27 March he announced a lockdown where people would only be allowed to leave home to shop for food and for exercise briefly within 2 km of their homes.[47]

Comparison of Covid-19 and the Influenza Pandemic of 1918–19

There are both similarities and differences between the 1918 influenza pandemic and Covid-19. Both are contagious respiratory illnesses, however they are caused by different viruses. The H1N1 virus was responsible for the 1918 pandemic and a novel coronavirus has caused the ongoing COVID-19 pandemic. In 2020 as in 1918 there is no cure for the disease and a series of preventative public health measures such as quarantine, social distancing, hand hygiene and isolation are the main defences against the spreading of the infection. In 1918, influenza was renowned for targeting the age group 20 to 40, however Covid-19 targets those over 65 in particular. In both pandemics, diagnoses, treatments and vaccines were delayed. Although the 1918 virus did not disappear completely, people did gain immunity to it by 1920. Immunity to Covid-19 is more problematic and current studies show that immunity may only last up to eight months after infection.[48] However research in this area is ongoing.

Although both Ireland and the UK put lockdowns into place, they did so after some other major European countries, and these lockdowns were not as strict. It was only after the authorities in both UK and Ireland saw how the health services in Spain, Italy and France were struggling, that the Irish and British public were told to stay at home and only go out for essential purposes to protect their health services. The main fear in both countries was that the health services would be overwhelmed and thus unable to cope. This is reminiscent of 1918–1919 when the union infirmaries, poor law dispensaries and other Irish hospitals were overwhelmed with influenza patients and in some cases there was no accommodation available for them. Also medical personnel were extremely overworked and in 1918 many Irish nurses and doctors died. As of 2 February 2021, it is estimated that at least 230 frontline NHS workers and carers have died of Covid-19 to date.[49] Again as in 1918, medical personnel and other staff who work in frontline positions helping people who are infected with Covid-19 are at particular risk.

Factory workers in 1918 in Ulster and elsewhere in Ireland and Britain were particularly susceptible to influenza. Influenza spread quickly through factories incapacitating workers and causing closures and high mortality among the workforce and their families. In 2020 it was meat packing plants that were thought to have been a major risk for Covid-19 infection. There was a major outbreak in Gütersloh, North Rhine-Westphalia, when more than 1,500 of the 7,000 workers tested positive for Covid-19, causing major lockdowns in the local area. At least 129 of the 300 workers in one of Portugal's biggest poultry slaughterhouses, contracted Covid-19, causing closure of the company for a week. There were also outbreaks in Anglesey, Merthyr Tydfil, Wrexham and Kirklees associated with meat processing. There are several environmental factors that make these plants susceptible to spreading Covid-19. The virus thrives in lower temperatures and very high or very low relative humidity; there are metallic surfaces, which retain live viruses for longer than other environments; dense aerosols combining dust, feathers and faeces are produced in the plants, there is also intense water use, which carries materials extensively over surfaces. Added to this, due to the high level of noise, workers must speak loudly or shout, which releases more droplets and spreads them further. Finally the workplaces are crowded, meaning social distancing is difficult if not impossible to maintain.[50] In 1918 there was an awareness that influenza spread in these crowded environments due to the lack of social distancing and sharing of utensils. It seems that in 2020 the lesson was not learned that crowded factories or meat plants would still be a source of infection within a community.

How did measures to deal with Covid-19 compare to those of 1918 and could authorities in 2020 have learned from that pandemic? In both Ireland and the UK, the first lockdown occurred at the end of March 2020. During this lockdown, schools, universities and businesses were all closed. In the UK, those people that could work from home did so, and those that could not work from home were placed on furlough. While there was no formal lockdown or quarantine in Ireland in 1918–1919, factories and other businesses did close due to a lack of staff to run them rather than to stop the spread of infection. In the autumn of 1918, public libraries in Newry and Belfast closed as well as Queen's University Belfast for the month of November specifically to stop the spread of infection. Many local authorities recommended school closures in 1918 as it was recognised that they were a source of spread of infectious diseases. However other locations where the public gathered did not close, such as cinemas, theatres and public houses. Church services did not stop, while well attended funerals and wakes still took place. People gathered at election meetings and armistice celebrations throughout Ireland during November and December 1918. In 2020, all public gatherings were forbidden, church services were not allowed and funerals took place but with minimal attendance.

During 1918, as discussed in previous chapters, local authorities in Dublin, Belfast, Cookstown and Larne produced public notices with preventative measures against influenza, probably rewritten from the guidance in the LGBI's memorandum. Ida Milne argued that the Dublin Public Health Committee like Belfast, Cookstown and Larne produced their own list of recommendations that were less convoluted than the advice of the LGBI.[51] These public notices contained good advice, such as avoid crowded gatherings; thorough ventilation of workshops and factories; go to bed if you get influenza and remain there until well. However, they were normally presented as a list of precautions and often as was the case in Larne, written in complicated officious language, which may not have had the impact of public notices in 2020.

In 2020 in both the UK and Ireland, public notices along with television and radio campaigns have spread the public health message concerning Covid-19 to 'Stay Home and Save Lives'. In the UK the message was 'Stay Home - Protect the NHS - Save lives' and in Ireland, 'Stay Home - Stay Safe - Protect each other'. These campaigns use concise, punchy language and the posters are bright and noticeable. They advise: keeping a social distance of 2 metres, don't touch your face, cough or sneeze into your elbow, wash your hands well and often and use face coverings in enclosed spaces such as shops or public transport. As in 1918 these recommendations place the responsibility firmly on the individual to keep themselves and more importantly others safe. In 2020 the public are aware how the virus spreads and what precautions they should take to avoid catching or spreading it.

At the time of writing at the end of February 2021, the death toll in the UK was 122,070 and 2,047 of these were in Northern Ireland[52] and in Ireland the death toll was 4,271.[53] The UK has one of the highest death rates in the world and Ireland had the highest rate of coronavirus infection on week ending 10 January 2021.[54] So why, with lockdowns in place and clear public information campaigns, is this the case? Perhaps this is due to a number of factors. The unwillingness of central government in Ireland and the UK to—lockdown sooner initially and to have a stricter lockdown; the easing of restrictions too soon; and encouraging children back to school in September 2020—may have permitted the infection rate in both countries to continue to rise more that it would have otherwise.

The UK government in August 2020 encouraged people to go back to work and to 'Eat out to Help Out' to get the economy back on an even keel. However, this has had the opposite effect, in the longer term, as in order to keep the infection rate down, two more lockdowns have had to take place and many businesses have suffered. Also in 1918 it was apparent that the virus spread to different countries with the military returning home from the Western Front. Initial cases of Covid-19 in both Ireland and the UK were due to foreign travel. Despite this, both countries did not impose (early) restrictions on foreign travel or quarantine of foreign nationals which may have helped to curtail the spread of infection.

The UK and Ireland, like USA and many other European countries have decided to *suppress* the virus. Countries like New Zealand and Australia, Taiwan and China have chosen to *eliminate* it. These countries have had distinctly lower Covid-19 mortality than those that have pursued mitigation and suppression. They appear to have fared economically better as a preliminary paper in the *British Medical Journal* suggests that, the effect on gross domestic product (GDP), based on International Monetary Fund projections for all of 2020, was more favourable for countries with elimination goals than for those with suppression goals.[55] Covid-19 has taken the world, the UK and Ireland by surprise. The response in the UK and Ireland is similar in many ways to that of 1918 and unfortunately has not been successful so far in suppressing the disease in these countries.

Vaccines are currently being rolled out globally. In 1918, vaccines were also produced but they were based upon the disease being caused by *Pfeiffer's Bacillus*. In Ireland the LGBI did not advocate their use as they believed they would be of little or no therapeutic value. The LGBI were probably correct as these vaccines would have been useless in preventing the disease. However in 2020–2021, several vaccines have been developed. *Pfizer/BioNTech, AstraZeneca* and *Moderna* vaccines have been approved by the Medicines and Healthcare products Regulatory Agency for use in the UK. Two doses of these vaccines are required to give a high level of efficacy of between 90% and 95%. An extensive vaccination programme is currently underway using these vaccines in both Ireland and the UK. We will have to wait and see how this plays out.

Post-COVID syndrome known as Long-Covid has also raised serious concerns. According to the NHS website, many people feel better in a few days or weeks from Covid-19 and most will make full recovery within 12 weeks, but for some people the symptoms can last longer. The long-term effects of the illness can be debilitating, even for young, fit people. The exact number of people experiencing Long-Covid symptoms is unclear and perhaps as the pandemic is not yet over, while it is impossible, in the middle of the event to quantify. Research into the prevalence of the illness is ongoing, but there are currently an estimated 60,000 people in the UK thought to be experiencing Long-Covid, although this is likely to be higher as coronavirus infection rates rise. At the time of writing, across the NHS, 69 initial assessment services throughout England are supporting people with Long-Covid.[56] Long-Covid is an unknown consequence of Covid-19 and the long-term repercussions of this disease have yet to manifest. However it is probable that long-term, Covid-19 will put added demand on health services for years to come. Hopefully sufferers of any long-term effects will receive better treatment than those people who suffered the after-effects of EL. Again the world will have to wait and see what the long-term repercussion of Covid-19 will be.

Notes

1. Elyer (1997, pp. 268–269).
2. Sandra Tomkins 'Britain and the Influenza Epidemic 1918–1919' (Ph.D. thesis, University of Cambridge, 1989), p. 155.
3. Ibid.
4. *Irish Independent*, 29 January 1920.
5. *Irish Independent*, 6 February 1920.
6. *Irish Independent*, 14 February 1920.

7. I would like to acknowledge the Deputy Keeper of the Records, Public Records Office of Northern Ireland [Hereafter PRONI], LA/51/9/D/6, Lurgan Medical Officer of Health Report, 1 March 1920 and 2 April 1920.
8. PRONI, LA/38/9/AA/3, Holywood Public Health Committee Minutes, 4 March 1920; 8 April 1920.
9. *Anglo-Celt*, 28 February 1920.
10. *Fifty-Seventh Detailed Annual Report of the Registrar-General (Ireland) (1920) (Births, Deaths and Marriages)*, SP 1921 [Cmd.1532], ix, pp. 47, 30.
11. Ibid.
12. Ibid.
13. Mamelund, S. E. The Impact of Influenza on Mental Health in Norway, 1872–1929, p. 5. Workshop. May 2010. Carlsberg Academy, Copenhagen, Denmark. Assessed on 26 February 2021.
14. *Belfast Telegraph*, 19 August 1918.
15. Crosby (2010, p. 18).
16. Crosby (2010, pp. 203–204).
17. Triarhou (2006, p. 244) and Vilensky et al. (2007, p. 79).
18. Vincent (2004, p. 2).
19. Vilensky and McCall (2011, pp. 226–227).
20. Honigsbaum (2019, p. 31).
21. Mortimer (2009, p. 454).
22. Cecil W. Kidd, 'Epidemic Influenza: An Historical and Clinical Survey' (M.D. thesis, Queen's University of Belfast, 1933), p. 43.
23. Ibid., 51.
24. The Registrar-General's Third Annual Report containing general abstracts of Marriages, Births and Deaths registered in Northern Ireland during the year 1924, Belfast (1925), p. 14.
25. Robb (1925, p. 644).
26. Macnamara (1954, p. 308).
27. Robb (1925, p. 644).
28. Craig (1985, p. 57).
29. Ibid.
30. Robb (1925, p. 646).
31. Parsons (Parsons, p. 118).
32. Robb (1927, p. 616).
33. Hill (1928).
34. *The Times*, 9 December 1924.
35. Hall and Yates (1924, pp. 52–54).
36. Craig (1985, p. 58).
37. Crosby (2010, pp. 203–204).

38. Crosby (2010, p. 205).
39. *Report on the Health of the County Borough of Belfast for the Year 1929* (Belfast, 1930), p. 109; *Report on the Health of the County Borough of Belfast for the Year 1930* (Belfast, 1931), pp. 72–73; *Report on the Health of the County Borough of Belfast for the Year 1931* (Belfast, 1932), p. 76.
40. *Belfast Telegraph*, 21 August 1937.
41. Foley (2011, p. 77).
42. TNA, WO/399/10591, Service record of Ann Cox.
43. Coronavirus resource centre John Hopkins University—https://coronavirus.jhu.edu/map.html. Accessed on 26 February 2021.
44. COVID-19 Timeline—British Foreign Policy Group (bfpg.co.uk)—https://bfpg.co.uk/2020/04/covid-19-timeline/. Accessed on 6 February 2021.
45. Perumal et al. (2020, p. 128).
46. *Irish Times*, 12 March 2020.
47. *The Guardian*, 27 March 2020.
48. Dan et al. (2021, p. 1).
49. ITV News, https://www.itv.com/news/2021-02-02/covid-at-least-230-nhs-workers-have-died-during-the-pandemic-here-is-a-list-of-all-of-them. Accessed 9 March 2021.
50. Middleton et al. (2020, July).
51. Milne (2018, p. 97).
52. The official UK Government website for data and insights on Coronavirus (COVID-19)—https://coronavirus.data.gov.uk/details/deaths. Accessed on 26 February 2021.
53. Latest updates on COVID-19 (Coronavirus) gov.ie—Latest updates on COVID-19 (Coronavirus) (www.gov.ie)—Accessed on 26 February 2021.
54. *Irish Times*, 11 January 2021.
55. Baker, et al. (2020, p. 371).
56. Post-COVID syndrome (Long COVID). https://www.england.nhs.uk/coronavirus/post-covid-syndrome-long-covid/. Accessed 6 February 2021.

References

Baker, Michael et al. 'Elimination Could be the Optimal Response Strategy for Covid-19 and Other Emerging Pandemic Diseases', *BMJ* (2020): 371.

Craig, D. H. *Belfast and Its Infirmary: The Growth of a Hospital*. Belfast: Brough, Cox & Dunn 1985.

Crosby, Molly C. *Asleep: The Forgotten Epidemic That Remains One of Medicine's Great Mysteries*. New York: The Berkley Publishing Group, 2010.

Dan, Jennifer M. et al. 'Immunological Memory to SARS-CoV-2 Assessed for up to 8 Months After Infection', *Science* 371 (5 February 2021): 1–15.

Elyer, John M. *Sir Arthur Newsholme and State Medicine, 1885–1935*, 268–269. Cambridge: Cambridge University Press, 1997.

Foley, Paul. 'Encephalitis Lethargica-Like Disorders Prior to von Economo', in *Encephalitis Lethargica: During and After the Epidemic*, edited by Joel Vilensky, 55–82. Oxford: Oxford University Press, 2011.

Hall, Prof Arthur J. and A. Gurney Yates. 'Clinical Report', in *The Sheffield Outbreak of Epidemic Encephalitis in 1924*. London: HMSO, 1926.

Hill, T. R. 'Problem of Juvenile Behaviour Disorder in Chronic Epidemic Encephalitis', *Journal of Neurology and Psychology* 9 (1928): 1–10.

Honigsbaum, Mark. *The Pandemic Century: A History of Global Contagion from the Spanish Flu to Covid-19*. London: Penguin Random House, 2019.

Macnamara, Dr, D. W. 'Memories of 1918 and "The Flu"', *Journal of the Irish Medical Association*, 35:208 (1954): 304–309.

Mamelund, Svenn-Erik. 'Profiling a Pandemic: "Who Were the Victims of Spanish Flu?"' *Natural History* (September 2017): 6–10.

Middleton, John, et al. 'Meat Plants—A New Front Line in the Covid-19 Pandemic', *BMJ* (2020): 370.

Mortimer, P. P. 'Was *Encephalitis Lethargicia* a Post-influenzal or Some Other Phenomenon? Time to Re-examine the Problem', *Epidemiology and Infection* 137 (2009): 449–455.

Parsons, A. C. *Report of an enquiry into the after-histories of persons attacked by encephalitis lethargica. Reports on Public Health and Medical Subjects No. 49*. London: Ministry of Health: HMSO, 1928.

Perumal, Dr Vi, et al. 'First Case of Covid-19 in Ireland'. *Ulster Medical Journal*, 89:2 (September 2020): 128.

Ravenholt, R. T. and William H. Foeje. '1918 Influenza, Encephalitis Lethargica, Parkinsonism', *The Lancet*, 2 (1982): 860–864.

Robb, Dr Alexander Gardner. 'Epidemic Encephalitis: The Proportion of Permanent Recoveries.' *British Medical Journal*, (April 1927): 615–616.

Robb, Dr Alexander Gardner. 'Some Notes on Epidemic Encephalitis', *British Medical Journal*, (10 Octber 1925): 644–646.

Triarhou, Lazaros C. 'The Percipient Observations of Constantin von Economo on Encephalitis Lethargica and Sleep Disruption and Their Lasting Impact on Contemporary Sleep Research', *Brain Research Bulletin* 69 (2006): 244–258.

Vilensky, Joel A. and Sherman McCall. 'Etiology', in *Encephalitis Lethargica: During and After the Epidemic*, edited by Joel Vilensky, 206–234. Oxford: Oxford University Press, 2011.

Vilensky, Joel A., Paul Foley and Sid Gilman. 'Children and Encephalitis Lethargica: A Historical Review', *Pediatric Neurology* 37:2 (2007): 79–84.

Vincent, Angela. 'Encephalitis *Lethargica*: Part of a Spectrum of Post-streptococcal Autoimmune Diseases?', *Brain* 127 (2004): 2–3.

Bibliography

Archives

Public Record Office of Northern Ireland
Board of Guardian Minute Books

BG/3/A/49—BG/3/A/50 Ballycastle, June 1918–July 1919.
BG/4/A/69—BG/4/A/70 Ballymena, May 1918–June 1919.
BG/6/A/145—BG/6/A/146 Banbridge, June 1918–1919.
BG/7/A/99—BG/7/A/101 Belfast, December 1917–1919.
BG/11/A/61—BG/11/A/62 Cookstown, May 1918–June 1919.
BG/12/A/82—BG/12/A/84 Downpatrick, April 1918–June 1919.
BG/13/A/26—BG/13/A/28 Dungannon, May 1918–June 1919.
BG/17/A/132—BG/17/A/133 Larne, June 1918–1919.
BG/21/A/33—BG/21/A/34 Londonderry, June 1918–1919.
BG/22/A/113—BG/22/A/115 Lurgan, June 1918–1919.
BG/24/A/103—BG/24/A/104, Newry, June 1918–1919.
BG/25/A/66 Newtownards, June 1918–1919.
BG/26/A/84—BG/26/A/86 Omagh, June 1918–1919.
BG/27/A/49—BG/27/A/50 Strabane, June 1918–1919.

Local Authority Minute Books

LA/13/9/AB/1 Minutes (Sanitary) of Proceedings of the Ballyclare Urban District—February 1906–March 1925.
LA/19/2/CA/10 Banbridge Urban District Council Minutes, 1918.
LA/20/9/AA/5 Bangor Urban District Council Minutes, 1918.
LA/7/2/EA/25 Belfast Corporation City Council Minutes Books, 1918–1919.

P. Marsh, *The Spanish Flu in Ireland*, Palgrave Studies in Economic History, https://doi.org/10.1007/978-3-030-79500-9

LA/7/9/AA/14 Belfast Corporation—Minutes of the Public Health Committee, 1918–1919.
LA/28/2/CA/3 Cookstown Urban Council Minutes, 1918.
LA/38/9/AA/3A Holywood Urban Sanitary Authority and Urban District.
LA/43/2/CA/10 Proceedings of the Larne Urban Sanitary Authority and Urban District Council, 1918.
LA/48/9/AB/6 Lisburn Urban District Council Monthly Report, 1918.
LA/51/9/D/6 Lurgan Medical Officer of Health Monthly Report for 1918–1920.
LA/58/2/CA/6 Newry Urban District Council Minutes, 1918.
LA/60/2/CA/5 Newtownards Urban District Council Minutes, 1918.
LA/64/2/CA/8 Portadown Borough Council—Council in Committee Minutes, 1918–1920.

Other Records
BELF/6/1/2/13 Belfast Coroner Records of Inquests July 1914–August 1918.
BELF/6/1/2/14 Belfast Coroner Records of Inquests September 1918–June 1922.
T2031/8 Copy of an Annual Report of Larne Saint John's Association for 1918.
T2031/3 Copy of a Letter from Commodore W. Carfendale, Naval Base, Larne Harbour to Miss Lucy McNeill, The Corran, Larne Harbour.
D1630/23 Forty-Fifth Annual Meeting, Society for Providing Nurses for the Sick Poor, Belfast, February 26, 1919.
D1231/G/7/218 Lady Hermione Blackwood, First World War nursing letters.
D3964/T/40 Alfred S. Moore, History of Mackie's.
D3964/T/38 *Mackie's Magazine* or *The Turret-Lathers Friend.*
D3964/P/1 AGM Minutes of James Mackie and Son Ltd for 1918 and 1919.
D3964/P/2 Meeting of the Directors Minutes of James Mackie and Son Ltd, July 1918–October 1919.
T3582/1 The Baxter/Kyle Connection 1780/1980.

The National Archives, Kew, London
HO 144/1496/362269/135 Home Office: Registered Papers, Supplementary—IRELAND (INSURRECTION): Sinn Fein internees: Directorate of Military Intelligence Postal Censorship—2nd Report on Correspondence of the Irish Internees—9th and Final Report on the Correspondence of the Irish Internees, July 14, 1918–March 1919.
HO 144/1496/ 362269/179 Home Office: Registered Papers, Supplementary—IRELAND (INSURRECTION): Sinn Fein Internees—Communications on Decision to Release Sinn Fein Prisoners.
MH 10/83/171/18 Local Government Board Memo Book July 1, 1918–December 31, 1918.

WO 35/179/4 Returns: Historical Review of Medical and Sanitary Work in the Irish Command During the War.

WO 399/8761 Service Record of Elizabeth H. Watson.

WO 399/2695 Service Record of Rachel Ferguson.

WO 399/10591 Service Record of Ann Cox.

T1/12560/11288/19 Treasury Papers—Chief Secretary's Office Ireland—Grants to National Schools affected by epidemic of Influenza to cover quarter ending March 31, 1919. T1/12358/22021/19 Treasury Papers—Department of Agriculture and Technical Instruction, Ireland Proposals to Prevent Loss of Grants on Account of Influenza Epidemic.

Queen's University, Belfast

Colonial Office Files

CO 904/209/262 The British in Ireland (Microfilm) Series 1—Dublin Castle Records: 1918–1919 Personalities—File on Pierce McCann.

CO 904/186 The British in Ireland (Microfilm) Series 1—Dublin Castle Records: 1918–1919 Miscellaneous—Chief Secretary's Office, Ireland—Censorship of the Correspondence of the Irish Internees 1918.

CO 904/167 The British in Ireland (Microfilm) Series 1—Dublin Castle Records: 1918–1919 Censorship—Press Censorship Reports covering—July 1, 1918–March 31, 1919.

Derry City Council Archives, Londonderry

40A Londonderry Council Minutes and Reports January 1917 to December 1921.

Donegal County Archives Collection Lifford

BG 38/1/83–84 Ballyshannon Union Board of Guardians Minutes Books, 1918–1919.

BG 97/1/59 Inishowen Union Board of Guardians Minutes Books, 1918–1919.

Newspapers

Armagh Guardian, 1918.

Anglo-Celt, 1918–1919.

Ballymena Observer, 1918–1919.

Ballymena Weekly Telegraph, 1918–1919.

Banbridge Chronicle, 1918–1919.

Belfast Evening Telegraph, 1918–1919.

Belfast News-Letter, 1918–1919.

County Down Spectator, 1918–1919.

Connaught Tribune, 1918–1919.

The Daily News, 1918.

Derry Journal, 1918–1919.

Derry People, 1918–1919.
Derry Weekly News, 1918–1919.
Donegal Vindicator, 1918–1919.
Down Recorder, 1918–1919.
Dromore Leader, 1918–1919.
Dromore Weekly Timers and West Down Herald, 1918–1919.
Dungannon Democrat, 1918–1919.
Fermanagh Herald, 1918–1919.
Fermanagh News, 1918–1919.
Fermanagh Times, 1918–1919.
Freeman's Journal, 1918–1919.
Frontier Sentinel, 1918–1919.
Larne Times, 1918–1919.
Lisburn Standard, 1918–1919.
Leitrim Observer, 1918–1919.
Londonderry Sentinel, 1918–1919.
Lurgan Mail, 1918–1919.
Irish Independent, 1918–1919.
Irish News, 1918–1919.
Irish Times, 1918–1919.
Mid-Ulster Mail, 1918–1919.
Nenagh Guardian, 1918–1919.
Newry Examiner, 1918–1919.
Newry Reporter, 1918–1919.
Newtownards Chronicle, 1918–1919.
Northern Constitution, 1918–1919.
Northern Standard, 1918–1919.
Northern Whig, 1918–1919.
Portadown Weekly News, 1918–1919.
Portadown Express, 1918–1919.
The Times, 1918–1919.
Tyrone Courier, 1918–1919.
Ulster Guardian, 1918–1919.
Ulster Gazette, 1918–1919.
Ulster Herald, 1918–1919.
Weekly Irish Times, 1918–1919.
Westmeath Chronicle, 1918–1919.

Journals
Lancet,1918–1919.
The British Journal of Nursing, 1918–1919.
British Medical Journal, 1918–1919.

Transactions of the Royal Academy of Medicine in Ireland, 1918–1919.
The Dublin Journal of Medical Science, 4th Series, 1918–1919.

Official Publications

British Parliamentary Papers

Report of the Chief Inspectors of Factories and Workshops to Her Majesty's Principal Secretary of State for the Home Department, for the Year Ending October 31, 1887, [Cd. 5328], H. C. 1888, xxvi, 23.

Belfast Health Commission Report to the Local Government Board for Ireland, vii, 141, 11 [Cd 4128], H. C. 1908, xxxi, 699.

Committee of Inquiry into the Conditions of Employment in the Linen and Other Making-Up Trades of the North of Ireland [Cd. 6509] H. C. 1912–1913, xxxiv.

Report to the Home Office and Local Government Board upon an Inquiry into the Alleged Danger of the Transmission of Certain Diseases from Person to Person in Weaving Sheds by Means of 'Shuttle-Kissing' [Cd. 6184], H. C. 1912–1913.

Fifty-Fifth Detailed Annual Report of the Registrar—General (Ireland) (Births Deaths and Marriages) 1918, xxxv, 59 [Cmd 450], H. C. 1919, x, 849.

Annual Report of the Chief Inspector of Factories and Workshops for the Year 1919 [Cmd. 941], H. C. 1920.

Annual Report of the Local Government Board for Ireland for year ended 31 March 1919 [Cmd 578], H. C. 1920, xxi, 1.

Fifty-Sixth Detailed Annual Report of the Registrar - General (Ireland) (Births, Deaths and Marriages) 1919, xxxvi, 59 [Cmd 997], H. C. 1920, xi, 629.

Forty-First Report of the General Prisons Board (Ireland), for 1918–1919, with an Appendix of Statistics, [Cmd 687], H. C. 1920, xxiii.

Report on the Mortality from Influenza in Scotland During the Epidemic of 1918–1919: A Supplement to the Annual Reports of the Registrar-General for Scotland, [Cmd 282], H. C. 1919, x, 1223.

Fifty-Seventh Detailed Annual Report of the Registrar - General (Ireland) (Births, Deaths and Marriages) 1920, ix, 47 [Cmd.1532], H. C. 1921, ix.

Report of the Irish Public Health Council on the Public Health and Medical Services in Ireland [Cmd 761], H. C. 1920, xvii 2, p. 4, 1075.

Supplement to the Eighty-First Annual Report of the Registrar-General of Births, Deaths, and Marriages in England and Wales: Report on the Mortality from Influenza in England and Wales During the Epidemic of 1918–1919, [Cmd 700], H. C. 1920, x, 791.

Parliamentary Debates

Hansard 5 (Commons)

Other Official Reports

Bailie, H. W. *Report on the Health of the County Borough of Belfast for the Year 1918.* Belfast: Adams, 1919.

Bailie, H. W. *Report on the Health of the County Borough of Belfast for the Year 1919.* Belfast: Adams, 1920.

Biggar, E. Coey. *Report on the Physical Welfare of Mothers and Children.* The Carnegie United Kingdom Trust Vol. 4 (Ireland). Dublin: J. Falconer, 1917.

Ministry of Health, Report on the Pandemic of Influenza, 1918–19. London: HMSO, 1920.

Hall, Prof. Arthur J. and A. Gurney Yates. 'Clinical Report', in *The Sheffield Outbreak of Epidemic Encephalitis in 1924.* London: HMSO, 1926.

Health Protection, Scotland, the Scottish Government, *'Pandemic Flu': Guidance for Infection Control and Childminding.* Scotland, 2008.

Parsons, A. C. *Report of an Enquiry into the After-Histories of Persons Attacked by Encephalitis lethargica: Reports on Public Health and Medical Subjects No. 49.* London: HMSO, 1928.

Report on the Health of the County Borough of Belfast for the Year 1929. Belfast, 1930.

Report on the Health of the County Borough of Belfast for the Year 1930. Belfast, 1931.

Report on the Health of the County Borough of Belfast for the Year 1931. Belfast, 1932.

Seventy-Second Annual Issue of the Newspaper Press Directory and Advertisers Guide. London, 1917.

United States Navy Department, *Annual Report of the Secretary of the Navy, Miscellaneous Reports*, 2414–2506. Washington: Government Printing Office, 1919.

Weekly Returns of Births and Deaths in the Dublin Registration Area and in Eighteen of the Principal Towns in Ireland 1918. Dublin: HMSO, 1919.

Weekly Returns of Births and Deaths in the Dublin Registration Area and in Eighteen of the Principal Towns in Ireland 1919. Dublin: HMSO 1920.

Printed Primary Sources

Crofton, William, M. 'The Influenza Epidemic', *Studies: An Irish Quarterly Review*, 7:28 (1918, December): 659–665.

Hunt, E. Rivaz. 'Notes on the Symptomatology and Morbid Anatomy of So-Called "Spanish influenza"', *Lancet* (1918, September 2): 419–421.

Pearl, Raymond. 'Preliminary Note on the Incidence of Epidemic Influenza Among the Actively Tuberculosis', *Publication of the American Statistical Association*, 16:128 (1919): 536–540.

Thompson, William J. 'Mortality from Influenza in Ireland', *Journal of the Statistical and Social Inquiry Society of Ireland*, 14:1 (1920): 1–14.

Secondary Sources

Articles in Journals

Baker, Michael et al. 'Elimination Could be the Optimal Response Strategy for Covid-19 and Other Emerging Pandemic Diseases', *BMJ* (2020): 371.

Bakhshi, S. S. 'Code of Practice for Funeral Workers: Managing Infection Risk and Body Bagging', *Communicable Disease and Public Health*, 4:4 (December 2001): 283–287.

Beveridge, W. I. B. 'The Chronicle of Influenza Epidemics', *History and Philosophy of the Life Sciences*, 13:2 (1991): 223–224.

Campbell, Henrietta. 'Public Health: A Bond Between a Government and Its People', *The Ulster Medical Journal*, 72:1 (2003, May): 4–9.

Dan, Jennifer M., Jose Mateus, Yu Koto, Kathryn M. Hastie, Asther Dawen Yu and Caterina E. Faliti, 'Immunological Memory to SARS-CoV-2 Assessed for Up to 8 Months After Infection' *Science* 371 (5 February 2021) 1–15.

Freeman, T. W. 'The Changing Distribution of Population in Donegal, with Special Reference to the Congested Areas', *Journal of the Statistical and Social Inquiry Society of Ireland*, 16 (1940–1941): 31–46.

Freeman, T. W. 'The Congested Sistricts of Western Ireland,' *The Geographical Review*, 33:1 (1943, January): 1–14.

Geary, Laurence. 'Epidemic Diseases of the Great Famine', *History Ireland*, 4:1 (Spring 1996): 27–32.

Hill, T. R. 'Problem of Juvenile Behaviour Disorder in Chronic Epidemic Encephalitis', *Journal of Nuerology and Psychology*, 9 (1928): 1–10.

Hume, Janice. 'The "Forgotten" 1918 Influenza Epidemic and Press Portrayal of Public Anxiety', *Journalism and Mass Communication Quarterly*, 77:4 (Winter 2000): 898–915.

Johnson, Niall P. A. S. and Juergan Mueller. 'Updating the Accounts: Global Mortality of the 1918–1920 "Spanish" Influenza Pandemic', *Bulletin of the History of Medicine*, 76:1 (2002): 105–115.

Johnson, Niall P. A. S. 'Scottish Flu—The Scottish Experience of "Spanish Flu"', *The Scottish Historical Review*, 83:2 (2004): 216–226.

Jones, Bartlett C. 'A Prohibition Problem: Liquor as Medicine 1920–1933', *Journal of the History of Medicine and Allied Sciences*, 18:4 (1963, October): 353–369.

Kaiser, Jocelyn. 'Resurrected Influenza Virus Yields Secrets of Deadly 1918 Pandemic', *Science*, 310:5745 (2005, October): 28–29.

Killingray, David. 'The Influenza Pandemic of 1918–1919 in the British Caribbean', *Social History of Medicine*, 7:1 (1994): 59–87.

Langford, Christopher. 'The Age Pattern of Mortality in the 1918–1919 Influenza Pandemic: An Attempted Explanation Based on Data for England and Wales', *Medical History*, 46:1 (2002): 1–20.

Langford, Christopher. 'Did the 1918–1919 Influenza Pandemic Originate in China?' *Population and Development Review*, 31:3 (2005): 473–505.

Loeb, Lori. 'Beating the Flu: Orthodox and Commercial Responses to Influenza in Britain, 1889–1919', *Social History of Medicine*, 18:2 (2005): 203–224.

Mamelund, Svenn-Erik. 'A Socially Neutral Disease? Individual Social Class, Household Wealth and Mortality from Spanish Influenza in Two Socially Contrasting Parishes in Kristiania 1918–1919', *Social Science & Medicine*, 62:4 (2006): 923–940.

Macnamara, Dr. D. W. 'Memories of 1918 and "The Flu"', *Journal of the Irish Medical* Association, 35:208 (1954): 304–309.

McCorry, Francis X. 'Demographic Crisis in Shankill Parish, Lurgan', *Review: Journal of the Craigavon Historical Society*, 4:3 (1981–1982): 17–20.

McGinnis, Janice Dickin, 'Carlill v. Carbolic Smoke Ball Company: Influenza, Quackery, and the Unilateral Contract', *Canadian Bulletin of Medical History*, 5:2 (Winter 1988): 121–41.

Mortimer, P. P. 'Was *Encephalitis Lethargicia* a Post-Influenzal or Some Other Phenomenon? Time to Re-examine the Problem', *Epidemiology and Infection*, 137 (2009): 449–455.

Noymer, Andrew and Michel Garenne. 'The 1918 Influenza Epidemic's Effects on Sex Differentials in Mortality in the United States', *Population and Development Review*, 26:3 (2000): 565–581.

Oxford, J. S. 'The So-Called Spanish Influenza Pandemic of 1918 May Have Originated in France in 1916', *Phil. Trans. Royal Society London*, 356 (2001): 1857–1859.

Oxford, J. S. A. Sefton, R. Jackson, W. Innes, R. S. Daniels and N. P. A. S. Johnson. 'World War I May Have Allowed the Emergence of "Spanish influenza"', *The Lancet Infectious Diseases*, 2:2 (2002): 111–114.

Oxford, J. S., R. Lambkin, A. Sefton, R. Daniels, A. Elliot, R. Brown and D. Gill. 'A Hypothesis: The Conjunction of Soldiers, Gas, Pigs, Ducks, Geese and Horses in Northern France During the Great War Provided the Conditions for the Emergence of the "Spanish" Influenza Pandemic of 1918–1919', *Vaccine*, 23 (2005): 940–945.

Oxford, John S. and Robert Lambkin. 'Mother Nature and the Great Influenza Pandemic', *Biologist*, 52:4 (2005, August): 211–212.

Patterson, K. David and Gerald F. Pyle. 'The Geography and Mortality of the 1918 Influenza Pandemic', *Bulletin of the History of Medicine*, 76:1 (1991): 4–21.

Perumal, Dr. Vi, Dr. T. Curran and Dr. M. Hunter. 'First Case of Covid-19 in Ireland', *Ulster Medical Journal*, 89:2 (2020, September): 128.

Rasmussen, Sonja A., Denise J. Jamieson and Joseph S. Bresee. 'Pandemic Influenza and Pregnant Women', *Emerging Epidemic Disease*, 14:1 (2008): 95–100.

Ravenholt R. T. and William H. Foeje. '1918 Influenza, Encephalitis Lethargica, Parkinsonism', *The Lancet* 2 (1982): 860–864.

Reid, Alice. 'The Effects of the 1918–19 Influenza Pandemic on Infant and Child Health in Derbyshire', *Medical History*, 49 (2005): 29–54.

Reid, Ann H., Jeffery K. Taubenberger, Thomas G. Fanning. 'The 1918 Spanish Influenza: Integrating History and Biology', *Microbes and Infection*, 3 (2001): 81–87.

Rice, Geoffrey W. and Edwina Palmer. 'Pandemic Influenza in Japan, 1918–1919: Mortality Patterns and Official Responses', *Journal of Japanese Studies*, 19:2 (1993): 389–420.

Rice, Geoffrey, W. 'How Reminders of the 1918–19 Pandemic Helped Australia and New Zealand Respond to COVID-19', *Journal of Global History*, 15:5 (2020), 421–433.

Robb, Dr. Alexander Gardner. 'Some Notes on Epidemic Encephalitis', *British Medical Journal*, (1925, October 10): 644–646.

Robb, Dr. Alexander Gardner. 'Epidemic Encephalitis: The Proportion of Permanent Recoveries', *British Medical Journal*, (1927, April): 615–616.

Robinson, Karen R. 'The Role of Nursing in the Influenza Epidemic of 1918–1919', *Nursing Forum*, 25:2 (1990): 19–26.

Smallman-Raynor, Matthew, Niall P. A. S. Johnson and Andrew D. Cliff. 'The Spatial Anatomy of an Epidemic: Influenza in London and the County Boroughs of England and Wales, 1918–1919', *Transactions of the Institute of British Geographers*, 27:4 (2002): 452–470.

Smith, F. B. 'The Russian Influenza in the United Kingdom, 1889–1894', *Social History of Medicine*, 8:1 (1995): 55–73.

Smith, Kerri. 'Concern as Revived 1918 Flu Virus Kills Monkeys', *Nature*, 445 (2007, January 18): 237.

Smyth, Hazel. 'Kathleen Lynn, M. D., F.R.C.S.I. (1874–1955)', *Dublin Historical Record*, 30 (1977): 51–56.

Tanner, Andrea. 'The Spanish Lady Comes to London: The Influenza Pandemic 1918–1919', *London Journal*, 27:2 (2002): 51–76.

Taubenberger, Jeffery K., Ann H. Reid, Amy E. Krafft, Karen E. Bijwaard and Thomas G. Fanning. 'Initial Genetic Characterization of the 1918 "Spanish" Influenza Virus', *Science*, 275 (1997, March): 1793–1796.

Taubenberger, Jeffery, K. and David M. Morens. '1918 Influenza: Mother of All Pandemics', *Emerging Infectious Diseases*, 12:1 (2006, January): 15–22.

Tognotti, Eugenia. 'Scientific Triumphalism and Learning from Facts: Bacteriology and the "Spanish Flu" Challenge of 1918', *Social History of Medicine*, 16:1 (2003): 97–110.

Tomkins, Sandra M. 'The Failure of Expertise: Public Health Policy in Britain During the 1918–1919 Influenza Epidemic', *Social History of Medicine*, 5:1 (1992): 435–454.

Tomkins, Sandra M. 'Colonial Administration in British Africa During the Influenza Epidemic of 1918–1919', *Canadian Journal of African Studies*, 28:1 (1994): 60–83.

Triarhou, Lazaros C. 'The Percipient Observations of Constantin Von Economo on Encephalitis Lethargica and Sleep Disruption and their Lasting Impact on Contemporary Sleep Research', *Brain Research Bulletin*, 69 (2006): 244–258.

Vilensky, Joel A., Paul Foley, and Sid Gilman. 'Children and Encephalitis Lethargica: A Historical Review', *Pediatric Neurology*, 37:2 (2007): 79–84.

Vincent, Angela, '*Encephalitis Lethargica*: Part of a Spectrum of Post-streptococcal Autoimmune Diseases?', *Brain*, 127 (2004): 2–3.

Winter, Jay. 'The Impact of the First World War on Health in Britain', *The Economic History Review, New Series*, 30:3 (1977): 487–507.

Chapters in Edited Volumes

Bourne, Aleck W. 'Influenza: Pregnancy, Labour, the Puerperium and Diseases of Women', in *Influenza: Essays by Several Authors*, edited by Francis Graham Crookshank, 433–443. London: Heinemann, 1922.

Clear, Caitriona. 'Fewer Ladies, More Women', in *Our War: Ireland and the Great War*, edited by John Horne, 157–170. Dublin: Royal Irish Academy, 2008.

Crawford, W. H. 'The Political Economy of Linen: Ulster in the Eighteenth Century', in *Ulster an Illustrated History*, edited by Ciaran Brady Mary O'Dowd and Brian Walker. London: B. T. Batsford Ltd, 1989.

Echenberg, Myron. '"The Dog That Did Not Bark" Memory and the 1918 Influenza Epidemic in Sengal', in *Spanish Influenza Pandemic of 1918–1919: New Perspectives*, edited by Howard Phillips and David Killingray, 230–238. London: Routledge, 2003.

Echeverri, Beatriz. 'Spanish Influenza Seen from Spain', in *Spanish Influenza Pandemic of 1918–1919: New Perspectives*, edited by Howard Phillips and David Killingray, 173–189. London: Routledge, 2003.

Fitzpatrick, David. 'Militarism in Ireland 1900–1922', in *A Military History of Ireland*, edited by Thomas Bartlett and Keith Jeffery, 379–406. Cambridge: Cambridge University Press, 1996.

Foley, Paul. 'Encephalitis Lethargica-Like Disorders Prior to Von Economo', in *Encephalitis Lethargica: During and After the Epidemic*, edited by Joel Vilensky, 55–82. Oxford: Oxford University Press, 2011.

Geary Laurence, M., 'The Medical Profession, Healthcare and the Poor Law in Nineteenth Century Ireland' in *Poverty and Welfare in Ireland, 1838–1948*, edited by Virginia Crossman and Peter Gray, 189–206. Dublin: Irish Academic Press, 2011.

Johnson, Niall P. A. S. 'The Overshadowed Killer: Influenza in Britain', in *Spanish Influenza Pandemic of 1918–1919: New Perspectives*, edited by Howard Phillips and David Killingray, 132–156. London: Routledge, 2003.

Kilbourne, Edwin D., 'A Virologist's Perspective on the 1918–1919 Pandemic', in *Spanish Influenza Pandemic of 1918–1919: New Perspectives*, edited by Howard Phillips and David Killingray, 29–38. London: Routledge, 2003.

Lynch, Fionán. 'Recollections of Jail Riots and Hunger Strikes: Grim Times in Mountjoy, Dundalk and Belfast Jails', in *Sworn to Be Free: The Complete Book of IRA Jailbreaks 1918–1921*, edited by Florence O'Donoghue, 63–76. Tralee: Anvil Books Ltd, 1973.

Lynch, John. *A Tale of Three Cities: Comparative Studies in Working-Class Life*. Basingstoke: Palgrave Macmillan, 1998.

Marsh, Patricia. '"An Enormous Amount of Distress Among the Poor": Aid for the Poor in Ulster During the Influenza Pandemic of 1918–1919', in *Poverty and Welfare in Ireland, 1838–1948*, edited by Virginia Crossman and Peter Gray, 207–222. Dublin: Irish Academic Press, 2011.

McCracken, Kevin and Peter Curson. 'Flu Downunder: A Demographic and Geographic Analysis of the 1919 Epidemic in Sydney, Australia', in *Spanish Influenza Pandemic of 1918–1919: New Perspectives*, edited by Howard Phillips and David Killingray, 110–131. London: Routledge, 2003.

Neill, Margaret. 'Homeworkers in Ulster, 1850–1911', in *Coming into the Light: The Work, Politics and Religion of Women in Ulster 1840–1940*, edited by Janice Holmes and Diane Urquhart, 2–32. Belfast: Queen's University: Institute of Irish Studies, 1994.

Novick, Ben. 'Propaganda 1: Advanced Nationalist Propaganda and Moralistic Revolution, 1914–1918', in *The Irish Revolution 1913–1923*, edited by Joost Augusteijn, 34–53. Basingstoke: Palgrave, 2002.

Ollernshaw, Philip. 'Industry, 1820–1914', in *An economic History of Ulster 1820–1940*, edited by Liam Kennedy and Philip Ollernshaw, 62–108. Manchester: Manchester University Press, 1985.

Patterson, Henry. 'Industrial Labour and the Labour Movement, 1820–1914', in *An Economic History of Ulster 1820–1940*, edited by Liam Kennedy and Philip Ollernshaw, 160–174. Manchester: Manchester University Press, 1985.

Phillips, Howard and David Killingray. 'Introduction', in *Spanish Influenza Pandemic of 1918–1919: New Perspectives*, edited by Howard Phillips and David Killingray, 1–26. London: Routledge, 2003.

Puirséil, Niamh. 'War Work and Labour,' in *Our War: Ireland and the Great War*, edited by John Horne, 181–208. Dublin: Royal Irish Academy, 2008.

Rice, Geoffrey W. 'Japan and New Zealand in the 1918 Influenza Pandemic: Comparative Perspectives of Official Responses and Crisis Management', in *Spanish Influenza Pandemic of 1918–1919: New Perspectives*, edited by Howard Phillips and David Killingray, 73–85. London: Routledge, 2003.

Rolston, Bill. 'News Fit to Print: Belfast's Daily Newspapers', in *The Media and Northern Ireland*, edited by Bill Rolston, 152–187. Basingstoke: Macmillan, 1991.

Royle, Stephen A. 'Belfast: Foundations of the Twentieth Century', in *Enduring City: Belfast in the Twentieth Century*, edited by Frederick W. Boal and Stephen A. Royle. Belfast: Blackstaff Press, 2006.

Shouldice, Frank and George Geraghty. 'The Break-Out from Usk Jail in Wales by four 'German Plot' Prisoners', in *Sworn to Be Free: The Complete Book of IRA Jailbreaks 1918–1921*, edited by Florence O'Donoghue, 25–34. Tralee: Anvil Books Ltd, 1973.

Stack, Austin. 'Journal of the Big Belfast Jail Riot', in *Sworn to Be Free: The Complete Book of IRA Jailbreaks 1918–1921*, edited by Florence O'Donoghue, 114–122. Tralee: Anvil Books Ltd, 1973.

Taubenberger, Jeffery K. 'Genetic Characterisation of the 1918 "Spanish" Influenza Virus', in *Spanish Influenza Pandemic of 1918–1919: New Perspectives*, edited by Howard Phillips and David Killingray, 39–46. London: Routledge, 2003.

Van Hartesveldt, Fred, R. 'Manchester', in *The 1918–1919 Pandemic of Influenza: The Urban Impact in the Western World*, edited by Fred Van Hartesveldt, 91–103. Lewiston, Queenstown, Lampeter: The Edward Mellon Press, 1992.

Vilensky Joel A. and Sherman McCall. 'Etiology', in *Encephalitis Lethargica: During and After the Epidemic*, edited by Joel Vilensky, 206–234. Oxford: Oxford University Press, 2011.

Books

Alcabes, Philip. *Dread: How Fear and Fantasy have Fuelled Epidemics from the Black Death to Avian Flu*. New York: Public Affairs, 2009.

Anderson, Adelaide Mary. *Women in the Factory: An Administrative Adventure, 1893 to 1921*. London: J. Murray, 1922.

Baly, Monica E. *A History of the Queen's Nursing Institute*. London: Croom Helm, 1987.

Barrington, Ruth. *Health, Medicine and Politics in Ireland 1900–1970*. Dublin: Institute of Public Administration, 1987.

Barry, John M. *The Great Influenza: The Epic Story of the Deadliest Plague in History*. New York: Viking Books, 2004.

Beveridge, William. *Influenza: The Last Great Plague: An Unfinished Story of Discovery*. London: Heineman, 1977.

Blakely, Debra. *Mass Mediated Disease: A Case Study Analysis of Three Flu Pandemics and Public Health Policy*. Lanham, Oxford: Lexington Books, 2006.

Blaney, Roger. *Belfast: 100 Years of public health*. Belfast: Belfast City Council and Eastern Health and Social Services Board, 1988.

Budge, Ian and Cornelius O'Leary. *Belfast: Approach to Crisis*. London/Basingstoke: The Macmillan Press Ltd., 1973.

Burke, Helen. *The People and the Poor Law in Nineteenth Century Ireland*. Dublin: Argus Press, 1987.
Byerly, Carol R. *Fever of War: The Influenza Epidemic in the U.S. Army During World War I*. New York: New York University Press, 2005.
Clarke, Kathleen. *Revolutionary Woman: My Fight for Ireland's Freedom*. Dublin: The O'Brien Press, 1997.
Clarke, Richard S. J. *The Royal Victoria Hospital, Belfast: A History, 1797–1997*. Belfast: Blakstaff, 1997.
Collier, Richard. *The Plague of the Spanish Lady: The Influenza Pandemic of 1918–1919*. London: Macmillan, 1974.
Colum, Padraic. *Arthur Griffith*. Dublin: Browne and Nolan, 1959.
Coogan, Tim Pat. *Michael Collins: A Biography*. London: Hutchinson, 1990.
Coogan, Tim Pat. *De Valera: Long Fellow, Long Shadow*. London: Hutchinson, 1993.
Coyle, Claudine. *The 1918 Spanish Flu: Newry and Surrounding Areas*. Newry, 2018.
Craig, D. H. *Belfast and Its Infirmary: The Growth of a Hospital*. Belfast: Brough, Cox & Dunn, 1985.
Crawford, Dorothy H. *The Invisible Enemy: A Natural History of Viruses*. Oxford: Oxford University Press, 2000.
Crawfurd, R. *Plague and Pestilence in Literature and Art*. Oxford: Clarendon Press, 1914.
Creighton, Charles. *A History of Epidemics in Britain Vol 2: From the Extinction of the Plague to the Present Time*. Cambridge: Cambridge University Press, 1894.
Crosby, Alfred W. *America's Forgotten Pandemic: The Influenza of 1918*. Cambridge: Cambridge University Press, 2003.
Crosby, Molly C. *Asleep: The Forgotten Epidemic That Remains One on Medicine's Great Mysteries*. New York: The Berkley Publishing Group, 2010.
Crossman, Virginia. *The Poor Law in Ireland 1838–1948*. Dundalk: Dundalgan Press, 2006.
Daly, Mary E. *Women and Work in Ireland*. Dundalk: Dundalgan Press, 1997.
Davies, Pete. *Catching Cold: 1918's Forgotten Tragedy and the Scientific Hunt for the Virus That Caused It*. London: Michael Joseph, 1999.
Elliott, Martin and Gilbert Elliott. *The Public Health Acts and Other Sanitary Laws and Regulations*. London, 1907.
Elyer, John M. *Sir Arthur Newsholme and State Medicine, 1885–1935*. Cambridge: Cambridge University Press, 1997.
Fennell, James and Turtle Banbury. *Vanishing Ireland*. Dublin: Hodder Headline Ireland, 2006.
Ferriter, Diarmaid. *The Transformation of Ireland 1900–2000*. London: Profile Books Limited, 2004.

Figgis, Darrell. *Recollections of the Irish War*. London: Ernest Benn Ltd., 1927.
Foley, Catriona. *The Last Irish Plague: The Great 'Flu Epidemic in Ireland*. Dublin: Irish Academic Press, 2011.
Geary, Laurence M. *Medicine and Charity in Ireland 1718–1851*. Dublin: University College Dublin Press, 2004.
Graves, Charles. *Invasion by Virus: Can It Happen Again*. London: Icon Books Limited, 1969.
Guinnane, Timothy W. *The Vanishing Irish: Households, Migration, and the Rural Economy in Ireland, 1850–1914*. Princeton: Princeton University Press, 1997.
Haverty, Anne. *Constance Markievicz: An Independent Life*. London: Pandora Press, 1988.
Henderson, John Watson. *Methodist College, Belfast, 1868–1938: A Survey and Retrospect*, Vol. 1. Belfast, 1939.
Hepburn, Anthony C. *A Past Apart: Studies in the History of Catholic Belfast, 1850–1950*. Belfast: Ulster Historical Foundation, 1996.
Hogan, David [Frank Gallagher].*The Four Glorious Years*. Dublin: Irish Press, 1953.
Holmes, Andrew R. *The Shaping of Ulster Presbyterian Belief and Practice, 1770–1840*. Oxford: Oxford University Press, 2006.
Honigsbaum, Mark. *Living with Enza: The Forgotten Story of Britain and the Great Flu Pandemic of 1918*. New York: Palgrave Macmillan, 2009.
Honigsbaum, Mark. *The Pandemic Century:A History of Global Contagion from the Spanish Flu to Covid-19*. London: Penguin Random House, 2019.
Johnson, Niall. *Britain and the 1918–1919 Influenza Pandemic: A Dark Epilogue*. London: Routledge, 2006.
Jones, Esylt W. *Influenza 1918: Disease, Death and Structure in Winnipeg*. Toronto/Buffalo/London: University of Toronto, 2007.
Jones, Greta *'Captain of All These Men of Death': The History of Tuberculosis in Nineteenth and Twentieth Century Ireland*. Amsterdam-New York: Editions Rodopi B.V., 2001.
Kenneally, Ian. *The Paper Wall: Newspapers and Propaganda in Ireland 1919–1921*. Cork: Collins, 2008.
Kolata, Gina. *Flu: The Story of the Great Influenza Pandemic of 1918 and the Search for the Virus That Caused It*. New York: Simon & Schuster, 1999.
Laffan, Michael. *The Resurrection of Ireland: The Sinn Fein Party 1916–1923*. Cambridge: Cambridge University Press, 1999.
Legg, Marie-Louise. *Newspapers and Nationalism: The Irish Provincial Press, 1850–1892*. Dublin: Four Courts, 1998.
Luddy, Maria. *Women and Philanthropy in Nineteenth-Century Ireland*. Cambridge: Cambridge University Press, 1995.
MacFhionnghaile, Niall. *Donegal, Ireland and the First World War*. Donegal: An Crann, 1987.

Malcolm, Elizabeth. '"*Ireland Sober, Ireland Free*": *Drink and Temperance in Nineteenth-Century Ireland*'. Dublin: Gill and Macmillan, 1986.

Marwick, Arthur. *Women at War, 1914–1918*. London: Fontana, 1977.

Messenger, Betty. *Picking Up the Linen Threads: A Study in Industrial Folklore*. Austin/London: University of Texas Press, 1978.

McBurney, C., F. Grieg, K. Clendinning and J. Trimble. *Lurgan Town Trail*. Craigavon: Craigavon Historical Society, 1994.

McConville, Sean. *Irish Political Prisoners, 1848–1922: Theatres of War*. London: Routledge, 2003.

McCoole, Sinead. *No Ordinary Women: Irish Female Activists in the Revolutionary Years 1900–1923*. Dublin: The O' Brien Press, 2003.

McGarry, Fearghal. *Eoin O'Duffy: A Self-Made Hero*. Oxford: Oxford University Press, 2005.

Milne, Ida. *Stacking the Coffins: Influenza, War and Revolution in Ireland, 1918–1919*. Manchester: Manchester University Press, 2018.

Murphy, Desmond. *Derry, Donegal, and Modern Ulster 1790–1921*. Londonderry: Aileach Press, 1981.

Newhouse, Neville H. *A History of the Friends School, Lisburn*. Lisburn: Friends' School, 1974.

North, John S. (Ed.). *The Waterloo Directory of Irish Newspapers and Periodicals, 1800–1900*. Waterloo, ON: North Waterloo Academic Press, 1986.

Novick, Ben. *Conceiving Revolution: Irish Nationalist Propaganda During the First World War*. Dublin: Four Courts Press, 2001.

O'Donoghue, Florence (Ed.). *Sworn to Be Free: The Complete Book of IRA Jailbreaks 1918–1921*. Tralee: Anvil Books, 1973.

Ó hÓgartaigh, Margaret. *Kathleen Lynn: Irishwoman, Patriot, Doctor*. Dublin: Irish Academic Press, 2006.

Ó Suilleabhain, Sean. *Irish Wake Amusements*. Cork: Mercier Press, 1967.

O'Sullivan, John F. *Belfast City Hospital: A Photographic History*. Donaghadee: Ballyhay Books, 2003.

Phillips, Howard and David Killingray (Eds.). *The Spanish Influenza Pandemic of 1918–1919: New Perspectives*. London: Routledge, 2003.

Porter, Katherine Anne. *Pale Horse Pale Rider*. 1939.

Quinn, Tom. *Flu: A Social History of Influenza*. London: New Holland, 2008.

Roper Esther (Ed.). *Prison Letters of Constance Markievicz*. London: 1934.

Strange, Julie-Marie. *Death, Grief and Poverty in Britain, 1870–1914*. Cambridge, Cambridge University Press. 2005.

Stuart-Harris, Charles H. and Geoffrey C. Schild. *Influenza: The Viruses and the Disease*. London: Edward Arnold, 1976.

Tallon, Alfie. *Memories of Old Lurgan*. Lurgan: Inglewood Press, 1987.

Van Hartesveldt, Fred R. (Ed.). *The 1918–1919 Pandemic of Influenza: The Urban Impact in the Western World*. Lewiston, Queenstown, Lampeter: The Edward Mellon Press, 1992.

Van Voris, Jacqueline. *Constance de Markievicz: In the Cause of Ireland*. Amherst: University of Massachusetts Press, 1967.

Unpublished Theses

Foley, Catriona. *"The Last Irish Plague": The Great Flu in Ireland, 1918–1919*. Ph.D. thesis, University College, Dublin, 2009.

Kidd, Cecil W. *Epidemic Influenza: An Historical and Clinical Survey*. M.D. thesis, Queen's University of Belfast, 1933.

Marsh, Patricia. *The Impact of the Linen Industry on Lurgan*. M.A. thesis, Queen's University Belfast, 2004.

Marsh, Patricia. *The Effect of the 1918–1919 Influenza Pandemic on Belfast*. M.A. thesis, Queen's University Belfast, 2006.

Milne, Ida Mary. *Epidemic or Myth—The 1918 Flu in Ireland*. M.A. thesis, National University of Ireland, Maynooth, 2005.

Murphy, William. *The Tower of Hunger: Political Imprisonment and the Irish, 1910–1921*. Ph.D. thesis, University College, Dublin, 2006.

Norrington, Amy C. *"The Greatest Disease Holocaust in History": The British Medical Response to the Influenza Pandemic of 1918–1919*. B.Sc. thesis, Wellcome Institute for the History of Medicine, 2000.

Tomkins, Sandra. *Britain and the Influenza Epidemic 1918–1919*. Ph.D. thesis, University of Cambridge, 1989.

Websites

COVID-19 Timeline—British Foreign Policy Group (bfpg.co.uk)—https://bfpg.co.uk/2020/04/covid-19-timeline/. Accessed on February 6, 2021.

https://civilrecords.irishgenealogy.ie/. Accessed between January 2017 and February 2021.

Latest updates on COVID-19 (Coronavirus) gov.ie—Latest Updates on COVID-19 (Coronavirus) (www.gov.ie). Accessed on February 26, 2021.

Mamelund, S. E. *The Impact of Influenza on Mental Health in Norway, 1872–1929*. Workshop. May 2010. Carlsberg Academy, Copenhagen, Denmark. Assessed on 26 February 2021.

Middleton, John, Ralf Reintjes and Henrique Lopes. 'Meat Plants—A New Front Line in the COVID-19 Pandemic' *BMJ* 2020; 370: m2716. https://doi.org/10.1136/bmj.m2716. Published July 9, 2020. Accessed March 11, 2021.

The Official UK Government Website for Data and Insights on Coronavirus (COVID-19). https://coronavirus.data.gov.uk/details/deaths. Accessed on February 26, 2021.

Index

P. Marsh, *The Spanish Flu in Ireland*, Palgrave Studies in Economic History, https://doi.org/10.1007/978-3-030-79500-9

The manufacturer's authorised representative in the EU is Springer Nature Customer Service Centre GmbH, Europaplatz 3, 69115 Heidelberg, Germany. If you have any concerns regarding our products, please contact ProductSafety@springernature.com

Printed and bound by CPI Group (UK) Ltd, Croydon, CR0 4YY
30/09/2026
02225698-0015